"This excellent book gives a quantitative and pragmatic approach to measuring, analyzing, and understanding web servers. It presents a good tutorial on the performance issues of web servers, and presents the analytic tools needed to model them. Web servers have bursty and highly-skewed load characteristics. This book presents a new way to model, analyze, and plan for these new performance problems. The book is a valuable resource for students and for web administrators."

Jim Gray
Senior Researcher, Microsoft Research
1998 ACM Turing Award Recipient

"This is a welcome approach to the performance analysis of today's web-based Internet. It is a useful and practical treatment that is eminently accessible to the non-mathematical professional. An impressive feature the authors provide is to deal directly with the fractal nature of web-based traffic; no simple and practical treatment has been offered before, and theirs is a timely contribution."

Leonard Kleinrock
Professor of Computer Science, UCLA
Chairman and Founder, Nomadix, Inc.

Capacity Planning for Web Services

Metrics, Models, and Methods

Daniel A. Menascé

Virgilio A. F. Almeida

ISBN 0-13-065903-7

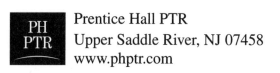

Prentice Hall PTR
Upper Saddle River, NJ 07458
www.phptr.com

90000

9 780130 659033

Library of Congress Cataloging-in-Publication Data

Menascé, Daniel A.
   Capacity planning for Web services: metrics, models, and methods/Daniel Menascé,
   Virgilio Almeida.
      p.   cm.
   Includes bibliographical references and index.
   ISBN 0-13-065903-7
      1. Computer capacity--Planning. 2. World Wide Web. I. Almeida, Virgilio A. F. II.
   Menascé, Daniel A. Capacity Planning for Web performance. III. Title.

   QA76.9.C63 M463 2001
   004.2--dc21

                                                            2001036953

Editorial/Production Supervision: Nick Radhuber
Acquisitions Editor: Tim Moore
Marketing Manager: Debby VanDijk
Manufacturing Buyer: Maura Zaldivar
Cover Design: Anthony Gemmellaro
Cover Design Direction: Jerry Votta
Interior Series Design: Gail Cocker-Bogusz

© 2002 by Prentice Hall PTR
Prentice-Hall, Inc.
Upper Saddle River, NJ 07458

Prentice Hall books are widely used by corporations and government agencies for training,
marketing, and resale.

The publisher offers discounts on this book when ordered in bulk quantities. For more information,
contact Corporate Sales Department, phone: 800-382-3419; fax: 201-236-7141; email: corpsales@prenhall.com
Or write: Corporate Sales Department, Prentice Hall PTR, One Lake Street, Upper Saddle River, NJ 07458.

Product and company names mentioned herein are the trademarks or registered trademarks
of their respective owners.

Printed in the United States of America

10 9 8 7 6 5 4 3 2 1

ISBN 0-13-065903-7

Pearson Education LTD.
Pearson Education Australia PTY, Limited
Pearson Education Singapore, Pte. Ltd
Pearson Education North Asia Ltd
Pearson Education Canada, Ltd.
Pearson Educación de Mexico, S.A. de C.V.
Pearson Education—Japan
Pearson Education Malaysia, Pte. Ltd
Pearson Education, Upper Saddle River, New Jersey

To my wife, Gilda, and my children, Flavio and Juliana.
                                                    –D.M.

To my wife, Rejane, and my children, Pedro and André.
                                                    –V.A.

Contents

6 Understanding and Characterizing the Workload   205

Preface

This is what makes this book unique and worth reading: Businesses, government agencies, and individuals are increasingly dependent on Web services for their day-to-day operation. As a consequence, quality of service, in particular performance and availability considerations, are becoming extremely important. Performance analysis of Web services is unique in many ways. First, Web services rely on large-scale systems that consist of thousands of computers, networks, software components, and users. Large-scale systems are inherently complex. The randomness associated with the way users request Web services compounds the problem of managing and planning the capacity of those services.

This book uses a quantitative approach to analyzing Web services. It provides a framework to understand the Web's complex relationships and how these relationships impact performance and availability of Web services. This approach lends itself to the development of performance and availability predictive models for managing and planning the capacity of Web services. Instead of relying on intuition, ad hoc procedures, and rules of thumb, we provide a uniform and sound way for dealing with performance problems. The models discussed here are based on probability fundamentals and on the theory of queuing networks. The techniques and models presented in this book provide a simple and practical approach to dealing with Web-based systems. Models are essential tools to simplifying the representation of complex systems and, at the same time, to capturing the most relevant characteristics of those systems.

There are several books on computer system performance evaluation, but they do not focus on Web-based systems. The Web has special features that make its performance problems unique and demand novel approaches to dealing with them. This book presents a sound and practical approach to addressing these challenges. Also, this book is not tied to any specific technology or product; it is general enough to be valuable in any Web-based environment.

This is an example-driven book. Many real-world examples with solutions are used to illustrate the use of models and analytic techniques. The models are available as Microsoft Excel worksheets, which makes it easy for readers to understand detailed situations of capacity planning of real-world Web services. The case studies presented are inspired in problems that come up very often in the course of planning, designing, implementing, operating, and managing Web services. The examples, case studies, and spreadsheets allow the reader to immediately put into practice the methods and models discussed here.

Who Should Read This Book

Information technology professionals must ensure that the Web services under their management provide an acceptable quality of service to their users. Managers must avoid the pitfalls of inadequate capacity and meet users' performance expectations in a cost-effective manner. System administrators, Web masters, network administrators, capacity planners and analysts, managers, consultants, and other IT professionals will benefit from reading parts or the entire book. Its practical, yet sound and formal, approach provides the basis for understanding modern and complex networked environments.

This book can be used as a textbook for senior undergraduate and graduate courses in Computer Science and Computer Engineering. At the undergraduate level, the book is a good starting point to motivate students to learn the important implications and solutions to performance problems. In particular, this book is very useful in providing students with the quantitative skills required to analyze the behavior of Web systems. At the graduate level, it can be used in System Performance Evaluation courses. This book offers a theoretical and practical foundation in performance modeling. The book can also be used as a supplement for systems courses, including Operating Systems, Distributed Systems, and Networking, both at the undergraduate and graduate levels. A series of exercises and short projects is available at the Web site associated with this book (www.cs.gmu.edu/~menasce/webservices/).

Book Organization

Chapter 1 introduces, through a series of examples, the importance of performance and availability considerations for Web services. The concepts of capacity planning, service levels, and workload evolution are defined and illustrated.

Chapter 2 presents a brief discussion on local and wide area networks and their protocols including TCP/IP, Ethernet, IEEE 802.11, Token Ring, and FDDI. The chapter revisits the client server (C/S) computing paradigm and discusses several kinds of servers, such as file servers, database servers, application servers, groupware servers, object servers, and Web servers. Various architectural C/S issues, including two-tier versus three-tier C/S architectures, are presented. The HTTP protocol is described in this chapter. The Peer-to-Peer model is also discussed as an alternative to the C/S paradigm used to support Web services. Standards-based technologies for Web services, such as Simple Object Access Protocol (SOAP) and Web Service Description Language (WSDL) are also presented. The concepts here are presented in light of performance considerations and tradeoffs.

Chapter 3 investigates, in detail, the nature of the delay incurred by a typical Web request. A complete analysis of the time to download a Web page is presented. This chapter shows how service times can be computed at single disks, disk arrays, networks, and routers. Queues and contention are defined more formally and some very basic and important performance results from Operational Analysis are introduced.

Chapter 4 discusses issues that affect performance of Web services. The chapter starts by looking at the sources of delay in Web environments. After discussing the end-user perspective to Web service performance, the chapter provides an assessment. It examines the components and protocols involved in the execution of Web services and analyzes their capacity and performance issues. New concepts such as heavy-tailed characteristics, traffic spikes, and network caching are analyzed through the use of simple performance models. The Wireless Application Protocol (WAP) is also presented in this chapter.

Chapter 5 introduces a step-by-step methodology to determining the most cost-effective Web service infrastructure. The main steps of the methodology are: understanding the environment, workload characterization, workload model validation and calibration, performance and availability model development, model validation and calibration, workload forecasting, performance and availability prediction, cost model development, cost prediction, and cost/performance-availability analysis.

Chapter 6 describes and illustrates with examples the major steps required for the construction of workload models. The common steps to be followed by any workload characterization project include specification of the standpoint from which the workload will be analyzed, choice of the set of parameters that capture the most relevant characteristics of the workload for the purpose of the study, monitoring the system to obtain the raw performance data, analysis and reduction of performance data, and construction of a workload model. Some characteristics of Web workloads are discussed and power-laws models are introduced.

Chapter 7 presents several different standard industry benchmarks—such as TPC-C and TPC-W, SPECCPU, SPECWEB, and WebStone—and shows how to use benchmark results as a complementary source of information to support the capacity planning methodology. Mathematical models that represent characteristics of actual Web workloads are studied in this chapter. This chapter also examines performance testing, which is commonly used to determine how users will experience the performance of a Web service.

Chapter 8 starts by introducing very simple models of Web-based systems. Complexity is progressively introduced and the solution to each model is presented using first principles and intuitive concepts. After a few models are presented, the approach is generalized. The models presented in this chapter are called system-level performance models since they view the system being modeled as a "black box."

Chapter 9 introduces powerful techniques to analyzing the performance of intranets and Web sites. The chapter considers the components that make up a Web-based system. Component-level models account for the different resources of the system and the way they are used by different requests. The solution techniques for component-level models are based on Queuing Networks (QN). Solution methods for both open and closed QNs with multiple classes of customers are presented in this chapter. The chapter also shows how system- and component-level models can be combined to address more complex modeling situations.

Chapter 10 shows how the performance models discussed in previous chapters can be specialized to handle specific Web performance issues. The chapter also shows how certain special features common in Web workloads, such as burstiness and heavy-tail distributions of file sizes, can be accounted for in performance models for the Web.

Chapter 11 introduces availability, reliability and performability as important metrics that define the quality of service provided by Web-based applications. A quantitative framework, based on the state transition diagram, is developed to model availability, reliability, performability, software aging and rejuvenation.

Chapter 12 shows how to apply existing forecasting methods and techniques to predict the future workload for Web services. Forecasting techniques includes linear and nonlinear regression models, moving averages, and exponential smoothing. A strategy and a methodology for workload forecasting is discussed here. It encompasses selection of the workload to be forecast, analysis of historical data and estimation of workload growth, selection of a forecasting technique, application of the forecasting technique to the historical data, and analysis and validation of forecast results.

Chapter 13 presents a framework for collecting performance data in Web environments. Next, it discusses the main issues in the process of measuring the performance of Web-based systems. The chapter does not focus on any specific product or manufacturer. Instead, it presents general procedures for transforming typical measurement data into input parameters. The procedures can be thought of as a set of major guidelines for obtaining input parameters for performance models.

Chapter 14 wraps up the book by emphasizing the approach and methods used to develop and solve analytical performance models of Web services. It also discusses properties that should be pursued for the design and implementation of large-scale information systems. For any service provider, whether financial services, merchants, or government services, it is necessary to guarantee the quality of service, which is represented by key issues such as trustworthiness and security, performance, and availability. The chapter discusses the importance of modeling to address these key issues.

Appendix A contains a glossary of the important terms introduced in the book.

Appendix B provides a description of the Microsoft Excel workbooks that accompany this book and describes the C program provided to derive burstiness parameters for HTTP logs.

Acknowledgments

The authors would like to thank their many colleagues for discussions that contributed substantially to this book. Special thanks go to our co-author in the first book of this series, Larry Dowdy of Vanderbilt University, for his enthusiasm and dedication to the field. Particular thanks go to Jeff Buzen of the Computer Measurement Group and BMC Software, Mark Crovella of Boston University and Network Appliance, Peter Denning of George Mason University, Jim Gray of Microsoft Research, and Leonard Kleinrock of UCLA and Nomadix, Inc., for their praise of our work and permission to quote them in the book. Jim Gray's suggestions on the manuscript are deeply appreciated. This book started as a revised edition of our *Capacity Planning for Web Performance* book. However, as time went by, we realized that significant new material had been incorporated and our editor decided that this should be a new book. Many readers of *Capacity Planning for Web Performance* offered important suggestions that helped improve the quality of this work. We are thankful to all. In particular, we would like to thank Professor Richard J. Coppins of the Virginia Commonwealth University for his very detailed comments. We would also like to thank Harry Foxwell for providing useful links to interesting material. Special thanks go to our Acquisitions Editor at Prentice Hall PTR, Tim Moore; his assistant Allyson Kloss; our Production Editor, Nick Radhuber; our Copyeditor, Ian Lamont; and PTR's LaTeX expert Lori Hughes for their support during the preparation and production of this book.

Daniel Menascé would like to thank his students and colleagues at George Mason University for providing a stimulating work environment. He would also like to thank his mother and late father for their love and guidance in life. Special recognition goes to his wife, Gilda, for a life full of love, tenderness, and companionship, and to his children, Flavio and Juliana, who do not cease to bring joy to his heart.

Virgilio Almeida would like to thank his colleagues and students at UFMG and his colleagues at HP Research Laboratory in Palo Alto. Special thanks go to Martin Arlitt, Jerry Rolia, Rodrigo Fonseca, Flavia Ribeiro, Wagner Meira Jr., and Rudolf Riedi. Finally, Virgilio would also like to express his gratitude to his family, parents (in memoriam), brothers, and many relatives and friends. His wife, Rejane, and sons, Pedro and André, have always been a source of continuous encouragement and inspiration.

Book's Web Site and Authors' Addresses

The Web site at www.cs.gmu.edu/~menasce/webservices/ will be used to keep the readers informed about new developments related to the book and to store the various Excel workbooks described in the book.

The authors' e-mail, postal addresses, and Web sites are:

Professor Daniel A. Menascé
Department of Computer Science, MS 4A5
George Mason University
Fairfax, VA 22030-4444
United States
(703) 993-1537
menasce@cs.gmu.edu
www.cs.gmu.edu/faculty/menasce.html

Professor Virgilio A. F. Almeida
Department of Computer Science
Universidade Federal de Minas Gerais
P.O. Box 920
31270-010 Belo Horizonte, MG
Brazil
+55 31 3499-5860
virgilio@dcc.ufmg.br
www.dcc.ufmg.br/~virgilio

About the Authors

DANIEL A. MENASCÉ is a Professor of Computer Science at George Mason University and a Fellow of the Association for Computing Machinery. He has consulted extensively on Web performance and e-commerce scalability. Menascé holds a Ph.D. in Computer Science from the University of California at Los Angeles.

VIRGILIO A. F. ALMEIDA is a Professor of Computer Science at the Federal University of Minas Gerais, Brazil. He holds a Ph.D. in Computer Science from Vanderbilt University. Almeida was formerly a visiting Professor at Boston University and a visiting researcher at Xerox PARC and at HP Research Laboratories in Palo Alto.

Menascé and Almeida co-authored *Scaling for E-Business: Technologies, Models, Performance, and Capacity Planning* (Prentice Hall PTR, 2000) and *Capacity Planning and Performance Modeling: From Mainframes to Client-Server Systems* (Prentice Hall PTR, 1994), with Larry Dowdy.

Chapter 1

When Web Performance is a Problem

1.1 Introduction

The Web is an evolving system that incorporates new components and services at a very fast rate. Applications such as e-commerce, digital libraries, video on-demand, and distance learning increase Internet and Web traffic at even higher rates. Virtual stores on the Web allow one to buy cars, books, computers, and many other products and services [3]. Many Government agencies are using Web sites to disseminate documents and forms to individuals, public interest groups, private companies, and other Government agencies. Interactions between Government agencies and between them and citizens are being streamlined through Web-based services. Virtual public

1

hearings on Government policies can be conducted through the Web.

Some popular Web sites receive millions of requests per day. It is not uncommon for these sites to exhibit extremely high response times. This has been a source of frustration for many Web users and of concern to the management of many Web sites.

One of the most pressing problems faced by Web site administrators is the adequate sizing of their Information Technology (IT) infrastructure so that they can provide the quality-of-service required by their users. This challenge requires them to be able to monitor the performance of their Web sites and of the Web services offered by them. One has to be able to track the intensity of the workload, detect bottlenecks, predict future capacity shortcomings, and determine the most cost-effective way to upgrade Web-enabled systems to overcome performance problems and cope with increasing workload demands. Traffic to Web sites is expected to increase even more with the widespread use of wireless technology and the increasing number of handheld devices, personal digital assistants (PDA), and Web-enabled cell phones. More and more, people will be able to interact with e-commerce sites through mobile devices (m-commerce).

The Web evolved from a publishing medium used to quickly disseminate information into an ubiquitous infrastructure that supports transaction processing. A large number of legacy applications have now been ported to the Web. Current Web systems are characterized by a) complex and dynamically generated Web pages; b) personalized contents; c) integration with databases and with planning, scheduling, and tracking systems; d) high-performance and high-availability quality of service (QoS) requirements; and e) deployment in mission-critical applications [2].

Most Web sites today offer *Web services* that fall into one or more of the following categories [2]:

- informational: online newspapers, products catalogs, newspapers, manuals, online classified ads, white papers, and online books

- interactive: registration forms and online games

- transactional: electronic shopping, ordering goods and services, and online banking

- workflow: online planning and scheduling systems and inventory management

- collaborative environments: distributed authoring systems and collaborative design tools

- online communities: online discussion groups, recommender systems, online marketplaces, and online auctions

- Web portals: electronic infomediaries, electronic shopping malls, search engines, and e-mail services

When Internet technologies and protocols are used to build an internal corporate network not accessible to outside users, it is referred to as an *intranet*. Through the use of a variety of Transmission Control Protocol/Internet Protocol (TCP/IP) development tools, intranets can easily bring information services to the desktop in a platform-independent manner through Web browsers, FTP clients, and Internet Relay Chat (IRC) clients. Intranets have been increasingly used for multimedia-based delivery of computer-based training. Many large companies with thousands of geographically dispersed employees are making the transition from disks and CD-ROMs to Web-accessible training.

The Web and almost all intranet applications are special cases of client/server (C/S) computing. In this paradigm, work is split between two processes—the client and the server—usually running on separate interconnected machines, called the client and server machines. Many organizations converted mainframe-based applications to C/S environments, and many are integrating their existing mainframe applications with new C/S environments. Other organizations are Web-enabling the services they provided through more conventional C/S systems.

This book uses a quantitative approach to analyzing Web services. This approach lends itself to the development of performance predictive models for capacity planning. Instead of relying on intuition, ad hoc procedures, and rules of thumb, we provide a uniform and formal way for dealing with performance problems. The performance models discussed here are based on the theory of queuing networks (QN).

Although some of the concepts about the architecture of Web services and the underlying technologies may be familiar to some of the readers, these concepts are revisited here in light of quantitative and performance issues. A large number of numeric and practical examples help the reader understand the quantitative approach adopted in this book. Several Microsoft Excel workbooks supported by Visual Basic^R modules that can be found at the book's Web site. These workbooks allow the readers to immediately put into practice the methods and models discussed here.

This chapter presents situations where performance is a problem in the context of Web sites, C/S environments, corporate portals, and Internet Service Providers (ISP). These examples are used to illustrate concepts such as capacity planning, saturation, service levels, and workload intensity. The presentation in this chapter assumes that the reader is familiar, at least at a very superficial level, with the Internet, C/S systems, networking, and computer systems in general. The next chapter provides a more detailed discussion of these issues for readers who need this background knowledge to read the remaining chapters.

1.2 Web Site Performance

A virtual car dealership provides users with a Web site they can visit to search and submit purchase requests for new and used cars available at the parking lots of 1,300 affiliated car dealers. A full description of each vehicle, including make, model, year, accessories, mileage, price, and a photo are stored in a database accessible through the Web site, which receives three types of requests:

- requests for documents and images

- requests to search the database according to the following criteria: make, model, and distance of dealer from buyer

- purchase requests

It is important that response time at the Web site be acceptable, otherwise users will not use the service and the virtual dealership and affiliated car dealers will lose business. The virtual car dealership wants to negotiate additional partnership agreements with car dealers. This will increase the availability of makes and models and will increase the number of requests submitted to the Web site. The new agreements will be phased in gradually and are expected to increase the current arrival rate of requests by 10% at the first stage, then by 20%, and finally by 30% with respect to the current rate.

The critical request is the search transaction. It was observed that if the response time for this transaction exceeds 4 seconds but remains below 6 seconds, then 60% of the search transactions will be lost because users will abort the search and potential sales will be lost. If the response time exceeds 6 seconds at the Web server, then 95% of the search requests will be aborted. These upper bounds on the response time are called *service levels*. Other examples of service levels include: minimum throughput exhibited by a server (e.g., at least 100 Web requests processed per second), minimum Web site availability (e.g., the Web site must be available at least 99.9% of the time), percent of transactions that exhibit a response time less than or equal to a certain value (e.g., 95% of the transactions must exhibit a response time not exceeding 2 seconds).

Assume that 5% of the search transactions generate a car sale at an average price of $12,000. The virtual dealership gets 3% in sales commission. So, each sale generated through the site brings $360 in revenue on average.

Management wants to answer the following questions:

- Will the Web site support the load increase while preserving the response time below 4 seconds?

- If not, at which point will its capacity be saturated and why?

- How much money could be lost daily if the Web site saturates when the load increases?

These are typical *capacity planning* questions. Table 1.1 summarizes the results obtained by the capacity planner by using performance models such as the ones presented later in this book. The table shows results for the current load intensity and for loads intensities 10, 20, and 30% higher than the current load. The first row shows the number of search requests submitted to the Web site per day. This number includes the searches that are aborted due to high response times. The second row indicates the predicted response time for each scenario. Note that when the load is 20% higher, the response time is in the range between 4 and 6 seconds, and therefore 60% of the transactions are lost as indicated in the third row. When the load is 30% higher the response time exceeds 6 seconds and 95% of the transactions are lost. Row four shows the actual number of vehicles sold per day, taking into account the increase in the number of search requests and the loss of sales due to aborted transactions. Row five shows the daily revenue. These values should be compared with the revenue that would be potentially obtained if the response time stayed below 4 seconds (see row six). Finally, the last row shows the lost daily revenue caused by the very high response times.

Over two million dollars will be lost daily when the load increases by 30%. As the example illustrates, the consequences of not being able to predict the future performance of the Web site under a load increase can bring undesirable financial consequences.

1.3   Client/Server Performance

Consider the example of a major car rental company that decides to migrate its operations from a mainframe-based environment to a C/S operation in

Table 1.1. Capacity Planning Results for Virtual Car Dealer

	Current	Current + 10%	Current + 20%	Current + 30%
Searches per day	92,448	101,693	110,938	120,182
Response time (sec)	2.9	3.8	5.7	11.3
Sales lost (%)	0	0	60	95
Sales per day	4,622	5,085	2,219	300
Daily revenue (in $1,000)	1,664	1,831	1,997	2,163
Potential daily revenue (in $1,000)	1,664	1,831	799	108
Lost daily revenue (in $1,000)	—	—	1,198	2,055

which regional servers will handle regional transactions. The company has a total of 500,000 vehicles available in 3,500 locations all over the country. Reservations are taken 24 hrs/day and 7 days/week by 1,800 customer representatives. An average of 360,000 reservations are made daily. Sixty percent of these reservations (216,000 = 0.6 x 360,000) are made during a peak period of 12 hours. So, the average number of reservations per hour during the peak period is equal to 21,667 $(260,000 \div 12)$, or 6 $(21,667 \div 3,600)$ transactions per second (tps). A mainframe-based environment supports the operations of the car rental company. Each of the 3,500 car pickup locations has a certain number of terminals connected to a concentrator. The concentrator is connected to the mainframe by a serial communications link. The reservation center has 1,800 terminals, one per customer service representative, connected to the mainframe.

The company decided to replace the aging mainframe-based system to reduce the high maintenance costs they were incurring. They also wanted the new application to be user-friendly and have a well-designed Graphical

User Interface (GUI) to increase the productivity of the customer service representatives and improve customer satisfaction. These motivations led the company to consider a C/S system such as the one depicted in Fig. 1.1.

Each car rental location has a server that stores local databases and runs the transactions submitted by the location attendants. These transactions access both local data and data stored at the database servers located at the car reservation center. Each car rental location has a local area network (LAN) connecting the various attendant workstations to the local server. A router connects the LAN at a car rental location to a Wide Area Network (WAN). The designers of the new C/S system need to ensure that the new environment will exhibit at least the same performance as the current mainframe-based platform.

The reservation center handles two types of transactions: reservations and road assistance requests. Company guidelines require that the average response time for reservation and road assistance transactions does not exceed two seconds and three seconds, respectively. Car rental locations handle two major types of transactions: car rental and reservations. Average response time requirements for both types of transactions must not exceed three seconds.

The following are some examples of important questions to be answered by the system designers to ensure that the C/S system performance will be as expected:

- What kind of servers should be used at the car rental locations? Answering this question amounts to specifying the number and type of processors to be used, the number and type of disks, and the type of operating system (e.g., UNIX or Windows NT^{TM}).

- Should a transaction processing monitor (e.g., BEA's Tuxedo^{TM}, Compaq's Pathway, Microsoft's Transaction Server^{TM}, IBM/Transarc's Encina, and AT&T's TopEnd^{TM}) be used?

- What type of servers and storage boxes should be used to support the

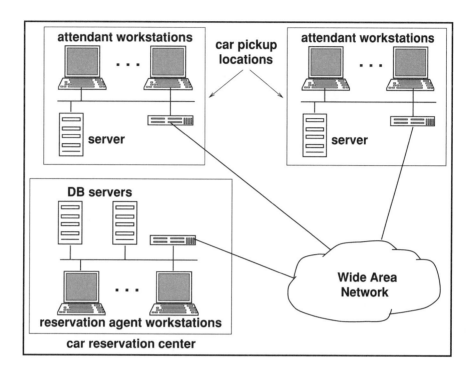

Figure 1.1. C/S environment for the car rental example.

database servers at the reservation center? Issues such as number and type of processors, amount of main memory, number and type of disks, database management system (e.g., Oracle^{TM}, Sybase^{TM}, DB/2, and MS SQL Server) to be used, and operating system must be specified.

- What kind of networking technology and bandwidth should be used at the car rental location and reservation center LANs? Some alternatives include Ethernet (10 Mbps), Token Ring (4 or 16 Mbps), and Fast Ethernet (100 Mbps).

- What should be the bandwidth of the Wide Area Network?

The answer to these and other questions may strongly impact the performance of the C/S system. It is also important to understand how a transaction's response time is composed and to identify bottlenecks for each

type of transaction. Table 1.2 illustrates the percentage of the response time
seen by an agent at a car rental location that is attributed to each major
system component. In this example, more than 50% of the response time is
dominated by the database server—the bottleneck for this type of transaction. The *bottleneck* is the component where a transaction spends most of
its time. Response time improvements are limited by the time spent at the
bottleneck.

Imagine now that the rental car company decides to launch a new pro-
motional campaign designed to boost car rentals by 5, 10, and then 15%
with respect to the current level. As a performance analyst, you are asked if
the system will support the corresponding increase in the number of transactions being submitted to the system, while maintaining the response time
within the desired levels. Using the models and techniques discussed in later
chapters of this book, you would be able to predict the response time of each
of the major types of transactions: reservations made at car rental locations
(local reservations), road assistance requests, car pickup, and phone reservations. Table 1.3 shows these response times, in seconds, for the current load
and for increases of 5, 10, and 15% of the current load. Load is defined in
this case as the average transaction arrival rate measured in tps.

Table 1.2. Response Time Breakdown for Reservation Transactions Submitted by Car
Rental Locations

Component of Response Time	Percentage of Total (%)
Client workstation at car rental location	5
LAN at car rental location	5
Application server at car rental location	25
Wide Area Network	10
LAN at the reservation center	4
Database server at reservation center	51

Table 1.3 shows that the increase in response time is not linear with the load increase as depicted in Fig. 1.2. For example, a 15% increase in the arrival rate of phone reservations generates a fivefold increase in response time. In Chapters 8 and 9 you will understand why performance of computer systems does not vary linearly with the load. An analysis of the graph of Fig. 1.2 shows that local reservations will exceed their maximum acceptable response time of 2 seconds at around a 7% increase in the current load; phone reservations will be able to support a 10% increase in the current load before the 2-second response time service level is violated; car pickup transactions will not get near their 3-second threshold, even when the load increases by 15%; and road assistance transactions will exhibit a response time slightly higher (about 7% higher) than its 3-second threshold when the arrival rate increases by 15%.

We say that if any of the service levels has been violated, as in the case of the reservation transactions at a 15% higher load, the capacity of the system reaches *saturation*. The term saturation should not be used to indicate that the utilization of a device (e.g., CPU, disk) reaches 100%, because service levels can be violated well before the utilization of any device reaches 100%.

Besides predicting if performance requirements will be met by either a new system or an existing system under a higher load situation, we have to be able to determine why performance will not be met. For instance, the

Table 1.3. Response Times (sec) for Various Load Values

Transaction	Current Load	Current Load + 5%	Current Load + 10%	Current Load + 15%
Local reservation	1.28	1.67	2.45	5.06
Road assistance	0.64	0.87	1.37	3.20
Car pickup	0.64	0.76	0.94	1.23
Phone reservation	0.85	1.16	1.82	4.24

predictive model we used to obtain the curves of Fig. 1.2 tells us that local reservation transactions spend 83% of their time doing Input/Output (I/O) at the database (DB) server located at the reservation center. Improving the DB server performance should be the first step toward ensuring that reservation transactions will meet their service level requirement of two-second response time. This can be accomplished in many ways, including spreading the same I/O load among more disks, using faster disks, or increasing the cache size at either the storage box or at the DB server.

1.4   The Capacity Planning Concept

The questions and analyses presented in the examples of Sections 1.2 and 1.3 are typical of capacity planning activities. Let us now introduce the concept of capacity planning in more general terms.

Capacity planning is the process of *predicting* when future load levels will

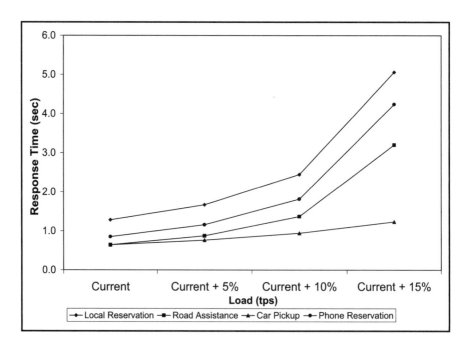

Figure 1.2. Response time vs. load for the car rental C/S system example.

saturate the system and determining the most cost-effective way of delaying system saturation as much as possible. The prediction must consider the evolution of the workload, due to existing and new applications, and the desired *service levels* [6].

We would like to emphasize the importance of the term *prediction* in the definition of capacity planning. In the car rental company example, we were asked to predict what the response time would be if more reservations arrived at the system per time unit. It would not be wise to use the "wait-and-see" approach, namely let the workload intensity increase and then find out what happens to the response time.

The lack of a proactive and continuous capacity planning procedure may lead to unexpected unavailability and performance problems caused by bogged-down routers, LAN segments, servers, or other components. Down times may be financially devastating to a company. The average down time cost per hour may range from thousands to millions of dollars depending on the type of industry [4]. For instance, the average hourly down time cost in credit card transactions is estimated to be $6.5 million. It should be noted that QoS delivered by a computer system such as a Web or e-commerce site has a strong correlation with the cost of the infrastructure needed to provide the service. This is an important concept and is at the core of capacity planning. It has been suggested [8] that marginal costs in the Internet are nearly zero. In other words, that the once a data files are stored, applications developed and communications network built, the cost of sending a file or processing a request to one more user is trivial. This assertion is not true if one needs to guarantee QoS levels. As the number of users of a computer system increases, more resources (e.g., servers, communication links, storage devices) need to be used to provide the same quality of service. Therefore, the cost of providing services through the Internet increases with the number of users if QoS is not to be degraded.

Poor performance of a computer system may generate customer dissatisfaction and damage the external image of the company, leading to loss of business. Another reason for planning ahead is that solving a performance problem may not be instantaneous. Even if a company has the financial resources to buy the needed hardware and/or software to solve a capacity problem, it may take awhile until a decision is reached on the best technical approach to solve the problem, obtain quotes from vendors, go through the procurement cycle, wait for component delivery, install, and test the new components. It may also be the case that the performance problems stem from a poorly designed architecture, in which case the solution is more difficult and generally more time-consuming. This observation contradicts some people's erroneous belief that capacity planning is not needed, provided one has enough money to add more hardware to the system when needed. In summary, capacity planning is important:

- to avoid financial losses
- to ensure customer satisfaction
- to preserve a company's external image
- because capacity problems cannot be solved instantaneously

The use of capacity planning techniques should not be restricted to situations where major changes are anticipated in the workload intensity or even when new applications will be deployed. There is a lot to be gained by making capacity planning a routine process carried out on a continuous basis. Many times, significant performance gains can be obtained by just reallocating servers to different LAN segments, rewriting critical portions of the applications, or even creating indexes on some critical DB tables. These performance gains do not require spending money on new or faster components. However, as with any capacity planning analysis, it is important to predict ahead of time what the benefits of each alternative will be before implementing them. Prediction requires simulation or analytic models, as discussed later. The importance of capacity planning in this context is illustrated in the next sections.

The next section shows how performance is an important issue in intranet design and operation.

1.5   Corporate Portal Performance

A major airplane manufacturer has 60,000 employees, including engineers, computer scientists, managers, technicians, and administrative staff. The company intends to implement a corporate portal to conduct business in a more efficient manner. Portals are a single, integrated point of access to useful information, applications, and other resources including people [7]. The portal will be used to a) support corporate training, b) provide access to human resource records, c) support travel planning and reimbursement requests, d) streamline help desk support, e) disseminate internal corporate news, and f) handle personnel forms and memos. The first application to be implemented is help desk support.

The help desk application will be supported by a site where frequently asked questions (FAQ) about common hardware and software problems will be posted. The site will also have a database of common problems and solutions to be searched via the Web. Finally, users will be able to submit, through the Web, their problem description if they cannot solve it through the FAQs or through the database of common problems. It is assumed that 10% of the employees, on average, submit a request to the help desk application site every day. Seventy percent of these requests fall during the peak period between 10:00 a.m. and 12:00 p.m. and then from 2:00 to 4:00 p.m. Thus, the help desk server will get $4,200$ ($= 0.7 \times 60,000 \times 0.1$) requests during the peak period. Since these requests come in a 4-hour period, the average arrival rate is 0.29 ($= 4,200/4/3,600$) requests/sec.

The company intends to change the operating system on all its client Personal Computers (PC). This upgrade is likely to create a surge in the number of requests submitted to the help desk application. The company wants to predict the performance of the portal for the help desk application as a function of the arrival rate of requests. Figure 1.3 shows that when the arrival rate of requests doubles from the current value of about 0.3 tps to 0.6 tps, the response time approaches 50 seconds, more than a threefold increase from the 16-second response time at the current load.

At about 0.6 tps, we start to see a saturation on the response time value due to the fact that the number of requests in the system reaches its maximum value. Connections start to be refused, showing a very poor performance of the help desk application.

There are many possible alternatives to solve the performance problem experienced by the help desk site, including upgrading the server's CPU, adding more CPUs, more disks, or even splitting the load among more servers. These and other alternatives can be investigated with the models discussed in later chapters.

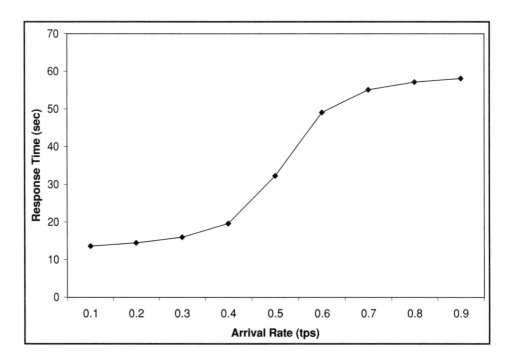

Figure 1.3. Response time at the intranet help desk server.

The next section presents performance issues from the perspective of an ISP.

1.6   ISP Performance

An ISP has 100,000 users. On the average, each one establishes a session twice per day lasting for 12 minutes. Customers who do not find an available modem to connect get a busy signal. The current rate structure used by the ISP is volume-based—customers have 2 hours of free time per month, after which they pay by the minute of connected time. The ISP intends to change the rate structure to one in which customers will pay a flat fee independent of the amount of time they spend connected to the service. The ISP expects that when they make the announcement, they will get a significant boost in the number of users. They also expect users to spend more time using the service since they will not be charged by connection time.

The management of the ISP wants to know how many modems it should have in order to guarantee that the probability of a customer finding all modems busy is less than 5%. The ISP currently has 1,500 modems. Using models to be discussed in later chapters of this book, the performance analyst was able to show what would happen with the probability that a user gets a busy signal as the number of users varies. Figure 1.4 shows this probability for two values of the session duration: 12 minutes and 18 minutes. As the graph shows, if the number of users doubles, the busy probability increases to 55% for 12-minute sessions and to 70% for 18-minute sessions.

At this point, users would start to complain bitterly about the QoS they are getting. Many would likely close their accounts and some might even consider suing the ISP. Figure 1.5 shows how the busy probability varies as a function of the number of modems. It shows that if the ISP wants to keep a 5% busy probability, it needs 2,400 modems when sessions last 18 minutes on average.

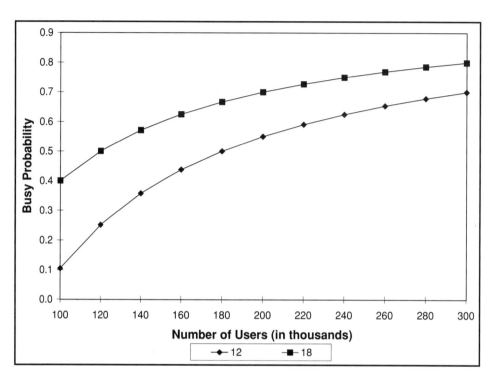

Figure 1.4. Busy probability vs. number of users for an ISP with 1,500 modems.

1.7   Concluding Remarks

Modern computer systems are becoming increasingly complex and dependent on networking technologies such as the ones available on the Internet. Deploying applications that rely on Web sites, intranets, and C/S technologies is a challenge both in assuring that the functionality will be present and in guaranteeing that the functionality will be delivered with an acceptable performance. Providing scalable services on the Web is particularly challenging due to the large gap between average and peak workloads [1]. A service configured to handle well the peak load tends to be oversized and wasteful of resources. On the other hand, if only the average load can be adequately handled, very poor performance will be provided when too many customers request the service.

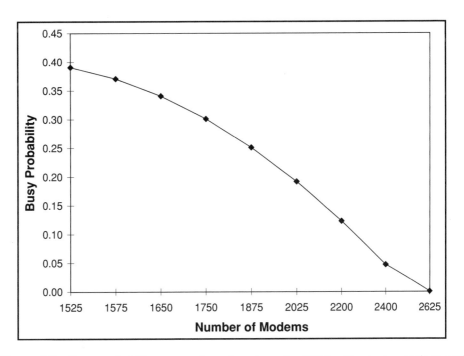

Figure 1.5. Busy probability vs. number of modems for ISP for 18-minute sessions and 100,000 users.

A very nice Web site with numerous functions is of no use if it takes forever to connect or get useful information from it. Users tend to avoid these sites. As illustrated in some of the examples in this chapter, performance problems can bring all sorts of undesired consequences, including financial and sales losses, decreased productivity, and a bad reputation for a company.

The situations presented in this chapter emphasize the importance of being able to plan ahead for the capacity of networked systems. Capacity planning involves being able to predict when the existing applications will fail to meet the required performance levels. Performance prediction is accomplished through the performance models presented in later chapters.

Capacity planning is also important when predicting the performance of a new application under development or when predicting the performance of applications that are being downsized to C/S environments [5]. An increasing number of organizations are moving mission-critical applications into C/S systems. Application designers are faced with a large number of software architectural choices that severely impact performance and cost. Examples include the distribution of work between client and server, use of three-tiered C/S architectures, distribution of functions and database tables among servers, types of clients and servers, and network connectivity. Waiting until the application goes into production may be disastrous and may require costly code redesign and rewrite. Performance models can also be applied in this context to ensure that new C/S applications meet performance requirements.

Bibliography

[1] F. Douglis and M. F. Kaashoek, "Scalable Internet Services," *IEEE Internet Computing*, July/Aug., 2001, pp. 36–37.

[2] A. Ginige and S. Murugesan, "Web Engineering: An Introduction," *IEEE Multimedia*, vol. 8, no. 1, Jan.–March, 2001, pp. 14–17.

[3] S. Hamilton, "E-Commerce for the 21st Century," *Computer*, IEEE Computer Society, pp. 44–47, May 1997.

[4] V. McCarthy, "Performance Tools Kill the Gremlins on Your Net," *Datamation*, Sept. 1996.

[5] D. A. Menascé and H. Gomaa, "A Method for Design and Performance Modeling of Client/Server Systems," *IEEE Tr. Software Eng.*, vol. 26, no. 11, Nov. 2000, pp. 1066–1085.

[6] D. A. Menascé, V. A. F. Almeida, and L. W. Dowdy, *Capacity Planning and Performance Modeling: From Mainframes to Client-Server Systems*, Prentice Hall, Upper Saddle River, New Jersey, 1994.

[7] A. Saha, "Application Framework for e-business: Portals," IBM Software Strategy, Nov. 1999, http://www-4.ibm.com/software/developer/library/portals/

[8] R. J. Samuelson, "The Internet Predicament," Washington Post, Feb. 22, 2001, page A9.

Chapter 2

Protocols and Interaction Models for Web Services

2.1   Introduction

With the advent of computer networks in the early 1970s, the computer and communication industries started to converge, and computing paradigms started to change as a result. Several factors, such as the sharp decline in the cost per millions of instructions per second (MIPS) and megabytes of RAM helped bring computing from remote mainframes to people's desktops. Moore's Law, an empirical observation, has been quite accurate at predicting that the speed of microprocessors doubles every 18 months. If this rate of growth were sustained, computers would be 11 billion times faster in 2047 when compared with 1997 performance! More conservative estimates say that computers will be 100,000 times faster in 2047 than in 1997 [3]; still quite an impressive improvement. Computers will be everywhere, including in the human body and in every single appliance. And, they will all be interconnected [7].

The client/server (C/S) model emerged out of the convergence of computers and communications, the availability of inexpensive and powerful desktop computers with Graphical User Interfaces (GUI) and multimedia presentation devices and advanced forms of data input, including voice input.

One of the most widely deployed examples of the C/S paradigm is the World Wide Web, which allows users to obtain Web services from Web servers located anywhere in the world. This chapter discusses the communications infrastructure on top of which the Web is built. The discussion in this chapter includes wired and wireless LANs and WANs and their protocols, including TCP/IP, Ethernet, IEEE 802.11, Token Ring, and Fiber Distributed Data Interconnect (FDDI). The chapter also defines the C/S computing paradigm and discusses various kinds of servers, such as file servers, database servers, application servers, groupware servers, object servers, and Web servers. The Hyper Text Transfer Protocol (HTTP), used by browsers to interact with Web servers, is presented in this chapter.

The Peer-to-Peer (P2P) model is also discussed here as an alternative to the C/S paradigm used to support Web services. The main components of a Web service architecture are also discussed in this chapter. Standards-based technologies such as Simple Object Access Protocol (SOAP), Web Services Description Language (WSDL), and Universal Description, Discovery and Integration Services (UDDI) are key elements of Web service environments and are presented here. Readers who wish to know more about computer networks are referred to more detailed references [8, 21, 37, 38].

2.2   The World of Networks

This section provides a brief introduction to computer networking. The origins of networking, the various types of networks, and their protocols are discussed. The common thread throughout the discussion is *performance*.

2.2.1   Genesis

The computer networks we use today have their origin in the ARPANET, a packet-switched computer network, developed in the late 1960s under the leadership and sponsorship of the then Advanced Research Projects Agency (ARPA), now DARPA, of the United States Department of Defense. The first nodes of the ARPANET were delivered by Bolt, Beranek & Newman (BBN) in the early 1970s [2]. The motivation for building the ARPANET was to share resources such as the timesharing systems developed in the 1960s. However, one of the major accomplishments of the ARPANET was to demonstrate the usefulness of a computer network as a powerful tool to enhance human communication and interaction through e-mail.

Performance concerns have been present since the early days of the ARPANET. Leonard Kleinrock at UCLA led the research that developed queuing models of packet-switched networks and established the measurement and network management facilities that collected and interpreted a vast array of extremely useful data used to understand and redesign the network and its protocols [19, 20].

The term *Internet* was introduced in 1983 when the ARPANET was split into two networks, a military one—MILNET—and a reduced version of the ARPANET. The Internet as we know it today is a large collection of interconnected WANs worldwide. The cornerstones of the Internet are its networking protocol, IP, and its process-to-process protocol, TCP, invented by Vint Cerf and Bob Kahn. The TCP/IP suite of protocols is discussed in Section 2.2.3.

The Internet has experienced exponential growth since its inception. The number of computers connected to the Internet grew from about 10 nodes in the early days of the ARPANET to almost about 100 million nodes in less than 30 years. Currently, virtually all major companies, educational and research institutions at all levels, hospitals, and governmental agencies at the local, state, and federal levels are connected to the Internet. The number of households with access to the Internet is growing at amazing rates worldwide. As more and more people become users of the Internet and participate in communications with others, and become information providers, the value of the Internet grows. Bob Metcalfe has stated, in what is known as Metcalfe's Law, that the value of a network is proportional to the square of the number of its subscribers and the value of a network to a subscriber is proportional to the number of subscribers [3].

2.2.2 Types of Networks

Networks are usually classified as WANs or LANs, according to the size of the geographical area covered by the network.

2.2.2.1 WANs

WANs can span a city, multiple cities, countries, or continents [8]. The basic technology used by WANs is *packet switching*. In this technology, messages transmitted between two computers, also called *hosts*, are broken down into units called *packets*. Packets have a maximum size and have a header with fields containing the necessary addressing information to allow a packet to be routed from its source to its destination, as well as sequencing information needed to reassemble the message at the destination from its constituent packets.

The building blocks of a WAN are the *packet switches* or *routers* and high-speed (e.g., from 45 Mbps to several Gbps) links connecting the switches. Routers are communication computers that store incoming packets, examine their headers, look up routing tables to make decisions for the next router to send the packet on its way to the destination, and place the packet on the output queue for the selected outgoing link. This method is called *store and forward*. Some of the technologies used to build WANs include *X.25*, a standard of the International Telecommunications Union (ITU), Integrated Services Digital Network (ISDN), a service offered by many telephone companies that integrates voice and data over ordinary telephone lines, *Frame Relay*, a high-speed WAN service offered by long-distance carriers, *Switched Multi-megabit Data Service (SMDS)*, another high-speed wide area network offered by long-distance carrier, and Asynchronous Transfer Mode (ATM), a packet-switched technology that uses fixed-size small packets (53 bytes), called *cells*, to provide fast switching to voice, video, and data over WANs [8].

2.2.2.2   LANs

LANs are typically confined to a building or a set of closely located buildings such as in a university campus. There are many different LAN technologies including wired and wireless. The most popular wired LAN technologies are 10-Mbps Ethernet [13], 100-Mbps Ethernet [14], 4- or 16-Mbps Token Ring [15], and 100-Mbps FDDI [36].

The Ethernet technology was invented by Metcalfe in the early 1970s and constitutes a milestone in local area networking [23]. Ethernet LANs have a bus topology (see Fig. 2.1a). All computers connect to a shared coaxial cable through a Network Interface Card (NIC). Packets transmitted by one NIC can be received by all others. This is called broadcast communication. Since packets contain the address of the destination, only the destination NIC will copy the packet to the computer's main memory. Since there is no central coordinator to decide which computer can use the shared medium, a distributed approach, called Carrier Sense with Multiple Access/Collision Detection (CSMA/CD), is used. If a NIC wants to transmit a packet it "listens" to the medium to check if there is a transmission in progress—this

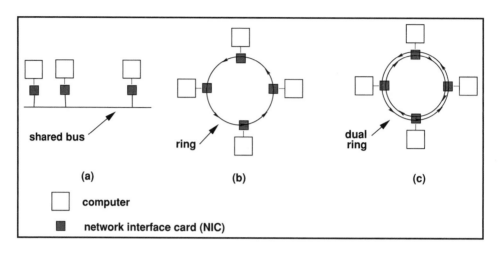

Figure 2.1. (a) Bus-based LAN. (b) Ring-based LAN. (c) Dual ring-based LAN.

is called *carrier sensing*. If a transmission is in progress, the NIC waits before attempting again.

It is possible, however, for two NICs that are far apart in the cable to attempt a transmission at about the same time, detect a free medium, transmit their packets and interfere with each other. This interference is called a *collision*. Ethernet NICs are equipped to detect collisions and stop transmitting a packet when collisions are detected. NICs wait for a randomly selected time period before attempting to retransmit their packets.

As traffic on an Ethernet network increases, the probability of a collision increases and the network throughput decreases as more of the bandwidth is spent on collisions and retransmissions.

Token Ring was invented at IBM Research Labs and, as the name indicates, is based on a ring topology as shown in Fig. 2.1b. A sender inserts the bits of its packet into the ring. The packet goes around the ring and is copied by the NIC specified in the destination address field of the packet. The packet continues its flow around the ring back to the sender which removes the packet and compares the received packet with the packet sent for error control. If two or more NICs attempt to transmit simultaneously, interference would occur. In a Token Ring LAN, access to the ring is controlled by a *token*, a special bit pattern that circulates through the ring. The NIC with the token transmits. When it is done, it passes the token to the next NIC in the ring. If a NIC does not have any packets to transmit, it just passes the token to the next station.

As more stations are added to a Token Ring, the delay in obtaining a token increases because the token will have to circulate through more NICs, and the probability that the token is seized by other stations increases.

Another type of ring LAN technology is FDDI. This technology uses optical fibers and a token-passing mechanism, and improves on Token Ring reliability by adding a second ring (see Fig. 2.1c). Data flow in opposite directions in the two rings so that if a station fails, the hardware can reconfigure the ring and turn it into a single functioning ring, bypassing the malfunctioning station [8].

There are two types of limits on the number of stations that can be connected to a LAN: physical and performance limits. For example, the Ethernet standard limits an Ethernet cable to 500 meters in length and requires a minimum separation of 3 meters between stations [8]. Performance considerations may limit the number of stations on a LAN. To reduce traffic on a LAN and improve performance, LAN administrators divide larger LANs into LAN segments with fewer stations each. These segments are joined by connecting devices such as routers and bridges [32]. Stations that communicate more often should be in the same segment in order to decrease the load on routers and bridges. Analytic expressions for LAN performance can be found in [5].

Wireless LANs use radio frequency (RF) as a medium through which stations communicate. The sequence of zeroes and ones generated by stations are used to modulate the wave transmitted by the RF transmitters used in wireless LANs. We briefly describe here the IEEE 802.11 protocol, an IEEE standard for wireless LANs [16]. Depending on the modulation technique used at the physical layer of the IEEE 802.11 protocol, data can be transmitted at 1 or 2 Mbps. The important features of the physical layer to be considered here are: i) provides a carrier sense signal which indicates if there is a transmission in progress, ii) data sent by one station can be received by all stations in its area of coverage, and iii) communication may suffer from the "hidden terminal problem." This problem arises when walls or other structures obstruct the RF signals. If that happens, it is possible for station C to receive signals from A and B, but for A and B to be unable to hear each other's transmission due to the existence of an obstacle between A and B.

Figure 2.2 displays the architecture of the IEEE 802.11 protocol. Stations communicate, within their cells or *basic service set (BSS)*, with one another and with a base station called an *access point (AP)*. The access point is used to allow stations in different BSSs to communicate with one another. Stations may also organize themselves into *ad hoc* networks, i.e., networks without an access point (see Fig. 2.3). Access points may be connected through a wired LAN, as shown in the figure, or through a wireless LAN.

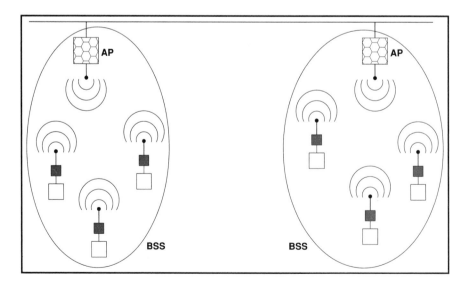

Figure 2.2. Architecture of an IEEE 802.11 wireless LAN with APs.

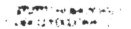

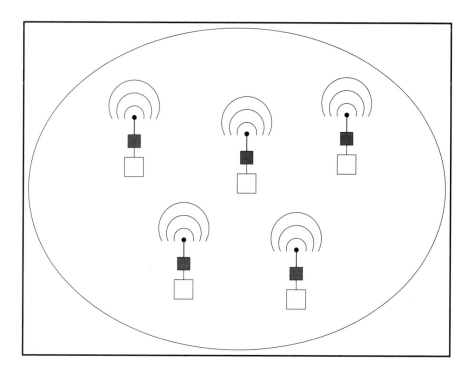

Figure 2.3. Architecture of an ad-hoc IEEE 802.11 wireless LAN.

Similar to transmission in an Ethernet, wireless stations may interfere with one another if they transmit at the same time. The IEEE 802.11 protocol uses a Carrier Sense Multiple Access/Collision Avoidance (CSMA/CA) protocol that works basically as follows: If the channel is sensed idle for an amount of time equal to the Distributed Inter Frame Space (DIFS), a station may transmit. The receiver of a correct frame sends an acknowledgement frame to the sender after a short period of time called the Short Inter Frame Spacing (SIFS). Acknowledgements (ACK) in IEEE 802.11 LANs are required, but not in Ethernet LANs since the sender can hear its own transmission.

If the channel is busy, the sender defers access until the channel is sensed idle for an amount of time equal to DIFS. Then, to avoid interference with all other stations that had to defer their transmissions, a random backoff time is determined. After that time expires, a station sends its frame. The IEEE 802.11 protocol does not use collision detection, as Ethernet does, but aims at avoiding collisions. Any transmitted frame contains the duration of the transmission, so that other stations can avoid transmitting during that time. However, collisions can occur because of the hidden terminal problem. It is possible for two stations hidden from one another to collide when transmitting to the same destination at about the same time. To solve this problem, IEEE 802.11 provides for the optional use of a Request To Send (RTS) and Clear To Send (CTS) exchange of frames before the actual data transmission. Before a sender transmits its data frame, it sends a short RTS frame to the receiver indicating the entire duration of the transmission, including the time to send the ACK. If the RTS is received correctly, then a short CTS is sent by the intended receiver to the sender, which may now proceed with the actual transmission. All other stations hear this exchange and avoid interfering with the data transmission.

2.2.2.3 The LAN to WAN Connection

LANs usually connect to WANs through dedicated leased lines at T1 (1.544 Mbps) or T3 (45 Mbps) speeds. The adequate sizing of the LAN-to-WAN link will be discussed in Chapters 9 and 10, in light of performance models. Figure 2.4 shows the networking topology for a company headquartered in Los Angeles, with branches in Chicago and New York. The three locations are connected through a Frame Relay WAN. The headquarters has an Ethernet and a Token Ring LAN connected to a 100-Mbps FDDI ring backbone. The backbone connects to the Frame Relay WAN through a T1 link. The Chicago branch has two LAN segments connected by a bridge. The router to the WAN is located in one of the LAN segments. Finally, the New York branch has a single 16-Mbps Token Ring LAN connected to the WAN by a router.

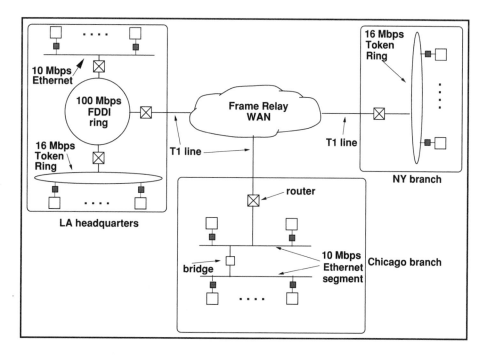

Figure 2.4. Example of LAN-WAN connectivity.

2.2.2.4   The Home to WAN Connection

Currently, there are many alternatives for individuals to connect their home computers, and even their home LANs, to a WAN. The simplest and cheapest is the use of dial-up analog modems at speeds ranging from 14.4 to 56 Kbps. The next fastest alternative is ISDN Basic Rate Interface (BRI). It requires a dial-up digital modem and provides speeds of 128 Kbps. If higher speeds are required from ISDN services, one can use ISDN Primary Rate Interface (PRI) that delivers 1.544 Mbps. The same speed can be obtained by leasing a T1 line. T1-like speeds can also be obtained with High-Bit-Rate Digital Subscriber Line (HDSL) but with more flexibility. An asymmetric version of HDSL, Asymmetric Digital Subscriber Line (ADSL), provides 640 Kbps outbound and 6 Mbps inbound. This asymmetry is advantageous for Web access, since the bandwidth requirements for fast image and video downloads are higher than for sending requests to Web servers.

Finally, cable TV companies offer cable modems that allow high-speed access to the Internet. The cable is a shared medium and the actual bandwidth seen by a customer depends on the load on the network. Most cable modems are asymmetric. Typical speeds range from 1 to 10 Mbps downstream and 128 Kbps upstream. Digital Subscriber Line (DSL) access has a dedicated local loop and therefore offers a more consistent download time than cable modems as shown in various measurements [39].

2.2.3   Protocols

The communication between two computers or two processes over a computer network is governed by a set of rules called a *protocol*. Let A and B be two entities that need to communicate over a computer network by exchanging a series of messages. A needs to address B properly so that messages from A to B arrive at the correct destination. This is accomplished by the *addressing* and *routing* functions of the protocol. Messages from A to B may be lost or become corrupted due to noise or failures in the network. The protocol must then provide *error detection*, *error recovery*, and *sequence control* functions. If A sends messages at a much faster rate than can be consumed by B, the protocol must provide *flow control* mechanisms to regulate the relative speeds of senders and receivers to avoid buffer overflows or discarded messages. So, the main functions of a protocol are: addressing, routing, error detection and recovery, sequence control, and flow control.

The interaction between two entities A and B can be *connectionless* or *connection-oriented*. In the first case, messages from A to B are independent from one another and may arrive at the destination in an order different from the order in which they were transmitted. This type of protocol is good when the data to be exchanged between the two entities fit into the maximum data unit allowed by the protocol. This way, the message does not have to be fragmented into more than one data unit, and sequencing is not an issue. Connection-oriented protocols are used when messages that are much larger than the maximum data unit are to be transmitted. In this case, sequencing and error recovery are important. Before A and B start to exchange messages, a connection between them has to be established, much like when you need to talk to someone over the phone. You first dial the number of the party you want to talk to. A signal travels through the telephone network to establish a connection. If the line at the other end is not busy, a signal travels back to indicate that the conversation may start. Connection-oriented protocols are useful when large files need to be transferred between the communicating entities, because sequencing, error recovery, and flow control are important considerations for this type of application.

A protocol specification consists of two elements: the syntax and semantics. The *syntax* of the protocol specifies all messages exchanged between the entities, their formats, and the meaning of each field of the message. The *semantics* of a protocol specifies the actions taken by each entity when specific events, such as arrival of messages or timeouts, occur.

The design of a computer communication protocol may be a complex task. For this reason, protocol designers use a *layered* architecture in protocol construction. The International Organization for Standardization (ISO) defined a seven-layer model called *Reference Model for Open Systems Interconnection* [36]. The seven layers from 1 to 7 are: physical, data link, network, transport, session, presentation, and application. Each entity at layer n communicates only with remote nth-layer entities. An nth layer entity uses services provided by $(n-1)$th entities as illustrated in Fig. 2.5.

As shown in the picture, data units exchanged between nth-layer entities have to be physically processed by layers n to 1 at the sending computer, transported through the network and moved from layer 1 to n at the receiving end. Each entity at layer n exchanges a Protocol Data Unit (PDU) with a remote layer n entity. A PDU has a layer n header and layer n data. The layer n PDU becomes layer $(n-1)$ data as shown in Fig. 2.6.

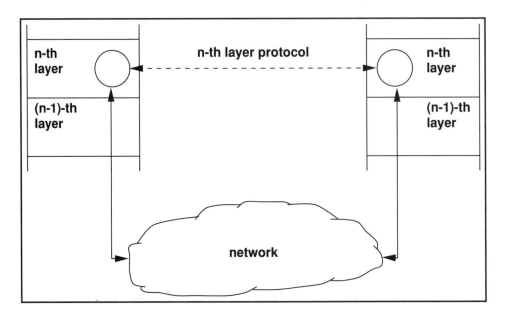

Figure 2.5. Layered approach to protocol design.

The next subsections present a brief description of the two most important protocols in the Internet: the Internet Protocol (IP) and the Transmission Control Protocol (TCP). This suite of protocols is known as TCP/IP and is at the core of the Internet. Figure 2.7 shows the layering of important TCP/IP-based protocols. The figure shows that IP is a network layer protocol on top of which we find two transport layer protocols: TCP—a connection-oriented protocol—and User Datagram Protocol (UDP)—a connectionless protocol.

HTTP (the Web protocol), the File Transfer Protocol (FTP), SMTP

layer (n-1) header	layer n header	layer n data

layer (n-1) data

Figure 2.6. Encapsulation of Protocol Data Units.

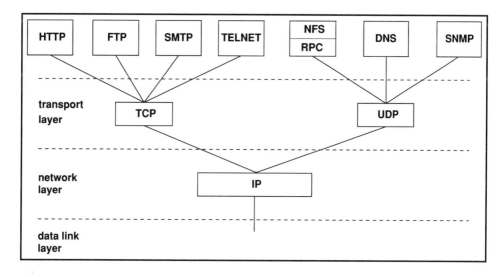

Figure 2.7. Layering of TCP/IP-based protocols.

(the Simple Mail Transfer Protocol used to send e-mail), and Telnet (an interactive login protocol) use TCP. Network File System (NFS) [8], Domain Name Server (DNS), and Simple Network Management Protocol (SNMP) are built on top of UDP. Note that NFS uses a Remote Procedure Call (RPC) protocol.

2.2.3.1   The Internet Protocol (IP)

IP specifies the formats of packets sent across the Internet, the mechanisms used to forward these packets through a collection of networks, and routers from source to destination [8].

Every host connected to the Internet has a unique address, called *IP Address*. This address, a 32-bit number, is usually represented by a dotted decimal notation such as 129.2.0.37, where each of the four numbers (in the range from 0 to 255) represents the value of 8 bits in the 32-bit address. The 32 bits are divided into two parts: a prefix and a suffix. The prefix is used to indicate a network and the suffix a host within the network. The number of bits allocated to the prefix determines the number of unique network numbers and the number of bits in the suffix determines the number of hosts per network.

The data unit transported by IP is called an *IP datagram*. IP is a connectionless protocol that provides no end-to-end guarantee of delivery; datagrams may be lost. This is called a best-effort service. IP datagrams can be delivered out of order—two datagrams sent in sequence from a source host to the same destination are routed independently, may take different routes, and may arrive out of order at the destination [37]. IP lets TCP take care of end-to-end error recovery and sequencing.

The IP header is 20 bytes long. Of these, four bytes are used for the IP address of the source host and four bytes for the IP address of the destination host. An important function of IP is *routing* of datagrams from source to destination. Every host and every router on the Internet implements IP. The IP implementation at a router maintains an in-memory routing table that is used to search for the next router or host (if final destination) to forward the datagram (see Fig. 2.8).

The most widely deployed version of IP, IP version 4 (IPv4), with its 32-bit address field is reaching its limitations as the number of hosts connected to the Internet grows exponentially. The new version of IP, IP version 6 (IPv6), extends the source and destination address fields from 32 to 128 bits, among other improvements including support for audio and video [8].

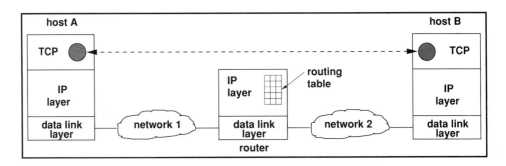

Figure 2.8. IP at hosts and routers.

2.2.3.2   TCP

TCP provides a connection-oriented reliable, flow-controlled, end-to-end communication service between processes running at hosts connected through a network. TCP guarantees that data is delivered in the order it was transmitted, with no missing data. TCP allows the two end points of a connection to exchange data simultaneously; that is, in full-duplex mode (see Fig. 2.8). TCP provides a stream interface, which means that it accepts a continuous stream of bytes from the application to be sent through the connection. The PDU exchanged at the TCP level is called a *segment*. The header of a TCP segment is 20 bytes long. TCP sends segments within IP datagrams.

Before data can be sent between two hosts, a connection has to be established between them. TCP implements a reliable connection establishment mechanism, called *three-way handshake* [8, 37]. Figure 2.9 shows the exchange of segments that takes place for connection establishment, data transmission, and connection termination. The vertical lines are time axes at hosts A and B. Time increases from top to bottom. Diagonal arrows indicate segments being sent between A and B.

Assume that host A establishes a connection with host B, exchanges data with B, and then closes the connection. Host A starts by sending a synchronization segment (SYN) to host B, which replies with another SYN segment. This exchange of SYN segments takes 1 round-trip time (RTT). The connection at host B is not considered complete until an ACK segment from host A arrives. During the time interval elapsed since host B sent its SYN segment to A and until it receives the ACK from A, the connection stays in a queue of incomplete connections. A connection stays in this queue for 1 RTT. If a host receives many requests to open connections from very remote servers, the incomplete connection queue may fill up, preventing the host from accepting new connections. This problem is faced by busy HTTP servers that receive many connections from remote clients [38]. This feature is exploited during Denial of Service (DoS) attacks. When the ACK

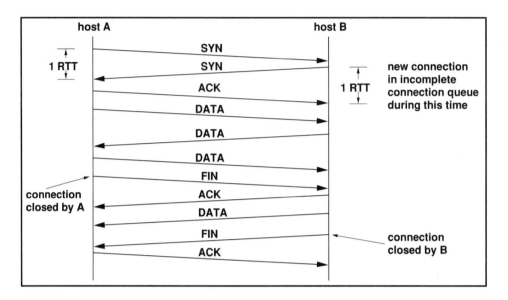

Figure 2.9. TCP connection establishment and termination.

is received at host B, the three-way handshake process is complete and the connection is established. Now, data may be exchanged in both directions.

TCP connection closing is called *half-close* because when a host closes a connection, it is indicating it will no longer send data to the other host, but it is still willing to accept data. For example, in Fig. 2.9, host A closes the connection from A to B by sending a FIN segment to B, which is acknowledged by an ACK segment. When host B wants to terminate the connection from B to A, it sends a FIN segment to A, which is acknowledged with an ACK segment. So, three segments are needed to establish a TCP connection and four are needed to terminate it in both directions.

TCP uses ACKs, timeouts, and retransmissions for error control. Flow control is implemented by TCP through a *sliding window* mechanism [8, 37]. The window size is the maximum number of bytes that can be sent before an acknowledgement is received and is limited by the buffer size at the receiver and by network congestion as perceived by the sender. When a connection is established, the receiver advertises its maximum window size, W_m. The window size used by the sender cannot exceed W_m to prevent the receiver's buffer from overflowing. When network congestion occurs, packets will be dropped at some router or not acknowledged before a timeout occurs. The sender will reduce the current window size W_c to reduce its transmission rate in order to mitigate network congestion.

Figure 2.10 illustrates the evolution of the sliding window. Each number represents a TCP segment. Assume, as in the figure that the current window size W_c is eight segments. In Fig. 2.10a, all the segments up to and including segment 2 have been sent and acknowledged by the receiver. Segments 3 through 5 were sent but not yet acknowledged. So, the sender is allowed to send five more segments in the current window. Figure 2.10b shows the case in which two additional segments, 6 and 7, were sent. No ACKs for segments 3 through 7 were received. In Fig. 2.10c, the window opens, i.e., slides to the right as ACKs are received for segments 3 and 4.

The operation of a TCP connection can be divided into two phases: *slow start* and *congestion avoidance*. These phases will be explained with the help of Fig. 2.11. During slow start, the window size W_c is initialized to one segment and is increased by one for each ACK received. ACKs in TCP are cumulative, i.e., an ACK acknowledges receipt of all segments up to and including the most recent segment received. So, if the window size is W_c, the sender can send W_c segments which will all be acknowledged after RTT units, assuming no packets are dropped. So, in the slow start phase, the sender sends one segment and receives an ACK after one RTT. The window size increases to two and two segments can be sent. After one RTT, these two segments are acknowledged and W_c is incremented by two, one for each of the acknowledged segments (W_c is now equal to four). Then, four segments are sent and four ACKs received after one RTT. W_c is incremented by four (W_c is now eight). Thus, during the slow start phase, W_c doubles every RTT, but cannot exceed the receiver's window W_m. In Fig. 2.11, W_c increases to 16 during the first slow start phase. This figure assumes that $W_m \geq 16$.

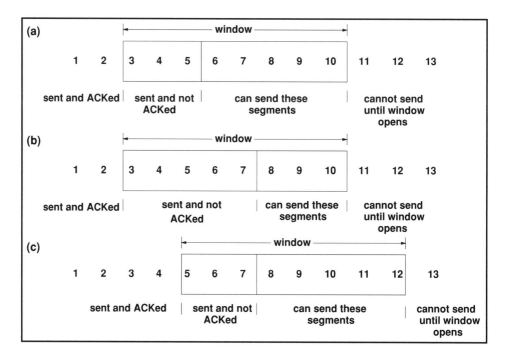

Figure 2.10. Window mechanism.

Network congestion can be detected by TCP through the receipt of a duplicate ACK, which indicates that the receiver received an out-of-sequence segment, or by a timeout at the sender. In any event, the current value of the window size is saved in a variable called slow start threshold window size, W_{ssthr}, and W_c is reduced. In TCP Reno, one of the most common versions of TCP, this reduction works as follows. If a duplicate ACK is received, W_c is divided by two and TCP enters the congestion avoidance phase described in what follows. In the example of Fig. 2.11, a duplicate ACK is received at time 5. Then, half of the current value of W_c, i.e., 8, is stored in W_{ssthr} and the TCP connection enters a congestion avoidance phase. Another duplicate ACK is received at time 20. The value of W_{ssthr} is set to 7 ($14 \div 2$).

If a timeout occurs, then W_c is set to one and TCP goes back to slow start. In Fig. 2.11, a timeout occurred at time 10 and the TCP connection enters a slow start phase. When W_c reaches W_{ssthr} during slow start, TCP

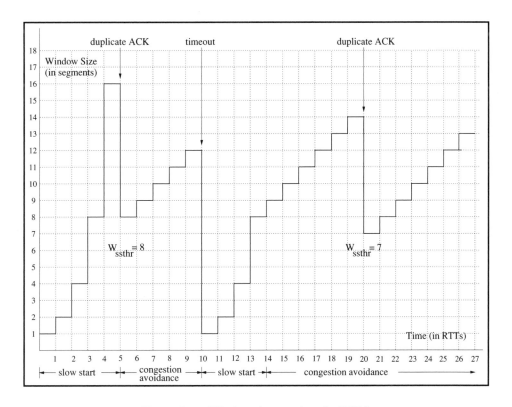

Figure 2.11. Window size vs. time (in RTTs).

switches to congestion avoidance. For example, at time 13 in Fig. 2.11, W_c reaches the current value of W_{ssthr}, which is 8, and the connection enters a congestion avoidance phase.

Let us now explain the operation of TCP during congestion avoidance. In this case, the window size W_c is increased by $1/W_c$ for every ACK received. This is equivalent to saying that W_c is incremented by one every RTT.

The throughput X_{TCP} of a TCP connection, measured in segments per second, decreases with RTT, decreases with the probability p that packets are dropped, increases with the receiver advertised window size W_{m} measured in segments, and decreases with the value of the TCP timeout T_0. An expression for X_{TCP} for a TCP Reno connection was derived by Padhye et al. [29]. This model is implemented in the `TCPModel.XLS` Microsoft Excel worksheet that can be found in this book's Web site. Another model of TCP can be found in [10].

We show in Fig. 2.12 the variation of the TCP throughput in KB/sec as a function of p and for four values of W_m: 10, 20, 30, and 40 segments. The other parameters assumed in these curves are: $T_0 = 2$ seconds, maximum segment size of 1,460 bytes, limiting bandwidth of the connection between sender and receiver equal to 12,500 KB/sec, and $RTT = 0.04$ seconds. The figure shows that as W_m increases, the throughput increases. However, the benefits of a larger window decrease as the packet loss probability increases because more data has to be retransmitted in case of packet losses.

The best-case throughput of a TCP connection is obtained when the window size W_c reaches the receiver maximum window size W_m and no congestion occurs. In this case, the throughput is given by W_m/RTT segments per second or $(W_\mathrm{m}/RTT) \times MSS$ bytes/sec where MSS is the maximum

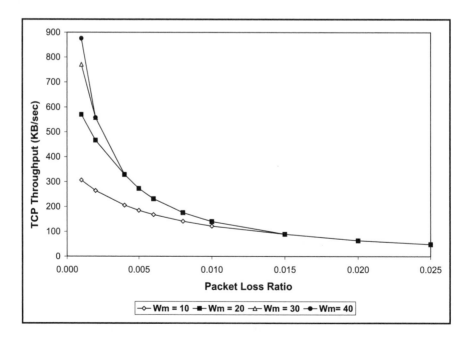

Figure 2.12. Variation of TCP throughput vs. packet loss ratio.

segment size. But, the throughput of a TCP connection cannot exceed the limiting bandwidth B, in bytes/sec, of the network connecting the sender and receiver. So,

$$X_{\text{TCP}} \leq min\{B, (W_{\text{m}}/RTT) \times MSS\} \qquad (2.2.1)$$

So, from Eq. (2.2.1) we get that the maximum throughput is achieved when the windows size W_{m}, given in segments, is equal to

$$W_{\text{m}}^* = \left\lceil \frac{B \times RTT}{MSS} \right\rceil . \qquad (2.2.2)$$

The numerator of Eq. (2.2.2) is called the bandwidth-delay product.

During slow start, TCP operates with windows that are below the window size that would be achieved during congestion avoidance. This may pose a problem for short-lived connections that may never achieve the maximum throughput under an optimal window size [11].

Table 2.1 shows the bandwidth-delay product, and the optimum receiver window size, W_{m}^*, in segments, assuming a segment size of 1,460 bytes, for various types of networks. The values of RTT and bandwidth are from [11]. As shown by the table, high-bandwidth, low-latency networks require large window sizes for the throughput of the TCP connection to use as much of the network bandwidth as possible.

Table 2.1. Throughput and Window Size in TCP

Network	Bandwidth (bytes/sec)	RTT (sec)	Bandwidth-delay (bytes)	W_{m}^* (segments)
Ethernet	1,090,000	0.0007	763	1
Fast Ethernet	12,500,000	0.0007	8,750	6
Slow Internet	12,750	0.1610	2,053	2
Fast Internet	127,500	0.0890	11,348	8

2.3   The World of Clients and Servers

The next subsections describe the main features of the C/S model, discusses server types, and issues regarding C/S architectures.

2.3.1   The C/S Paradigm

The C/S computing model used on the Web is predicated on the notion of splitting the work to be performed by an application between two processes—the *client* and the *server*. The term server should not be confused with the computer that runs the server process. We will use the term *server-class* machine or computer to designate the hardware and operating system platform used to run server processes.

A *client* process, or simply client

- runs on a desktop or user workstation and provides the GUI code for data capture and display

- makes requests for specific services to be performed by one or more server processes usually located at remote machines

- executes a portion of the application code

A *server* process, or simply server, runs on machines that are usually faster, have more main memory and disk space than client machines. A server

- executes a set of functionally-related services that usually require a specialized hardware/software component

- never initiates a message exchange with any client; servers are passive entities that listen to client requests, execute them, and reply to the clients

The protocol implemented between clients and servers is a *request-reply* protocol in which clients send requests and servers reply to client's requests (see Fig. 2.13). Clients and servers may run on top of TCP or on top of a connectionless protocol such as UDP.

Since a server may receive requests from many clients, a queue of requests is formed at the server. If only one request is served at a time, the resources at the server machine may be underutilized, the server throughput (number of requests served per time unit) may be low, and response time to clients will increase as the load on the server increases (see Fig. 2.14a). Most servers create multiple processes or multiple threads of execution in a single process to handle the queue of incoming requests (see Fig. 2.14b).

Using multiple threads or processes has an interesting effect on response time as shown in Fig. 2.15. The figure shows two response time curves: one for an arrival rate of 2.5 requests/sec and the other for 3.6 requests/sec. It is assumed that each request uses 0.07 sec of CPU time and 0.2 sec of disk time. As the curves illustrate, when the number of threads increases from one to two, the response time decreases because of the decrease in the time spent by a request waiting for an available thread. However, as the number of threads increases beyond this point, the additional time spent by a request

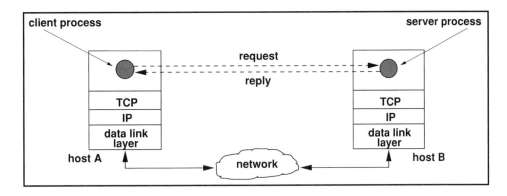

Figure 2.13. Client/server protocol: request/reply.

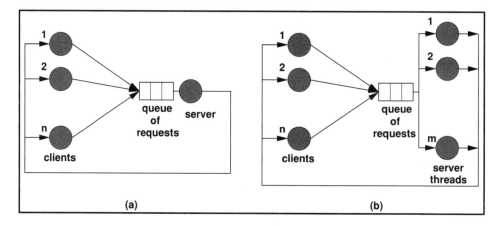

Figure 2.14. (a) Single process server. (b) Multiple process server.

contending for the same hardware resources (e.g., CPU, memory, and disks) dominates the decrease in thread waiting time, leading to a net increase in response time. For a fixed value of the arrival rate, when the number of

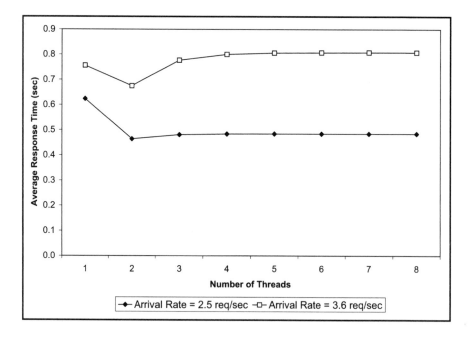

Figure 2.15. Average response (in sec) of a C/S system vs. number of threads.

threads becomes large enough, the thread waiting time becomes negligible and the time spent by a request contending for hardware resources becomes constant because the average number of active threads will not increase with the maximum number of active threads. Then, the response time does not vary any longer with the number of threads.

A common question when designing C/S architectures is whether a two-tier or three-tier architecture should be used. In two-tier architectures, the GUI and application logic runs at the client while the SQL server runs at the server. In a three-tier organization, the GUI runs at the client, and the application logic runs at an application server that acts as a client to an SQL server.

Another important architectural consideration is how "fat" or "thin" the client should be. Fat clients incorporate more of the transaction logic than thin clients and tend to require less interactions with the server at the expense of higher computing requirements for the client.

Requests generated from clients to servers as well as the replies that these requests generate use network bandwidth, processing, and I/O resources at the servers involved. As the load on a system increases, performance may deteriorate very fast. To improve performance and increase system scalability, one may use caches at various levels to significantly enhance the performance of C/S systems. Caches are copies of data stored at servers but kept closer to the client, sometimes at the client itself and sometimes at closer cache servers. This reduces the number of interactions needed with the server and decreases the response time. Clients may keep a cached copy of file or blocks of a file so that they do not need to access the server at every read. Servers may keep main memory caches holding copies of files or database records. Web servers closer to a set of clients may hold popular documents to avoid requesting them from remote servers, thus reducing response times and bandwidth requirements. When data are found at a cache, a *cache hit* is said to occur, otherwise we have a *cache miss*. Consider, for example, a file server that receives requests to read 8-KB file blocks at a rate of

900 requests/sec. If 30% of these requests generate a cache hit at the client, the server will be actually receiving $(1-0.3) \times 900 = 630$ requests/sec. If 25% of these requests can be satisfied from the file server's main memory cache, then only $(1 - 0.25) \times 630 = 472.5$ requests/sec reach the file server's disk subsystem. A price to be paid for the use of caching is that the consistency of the cached data has to be maintained. Additionally, extra processing is required in case of cache misses.

2.3.2   Server Types

The are various types of servers used in networked environments: file servers, database servers, application servers, groupware servers, object servers, Web servers, and software servers [28].

File servers provide networked computers with access to a shared file system (see Fig. 2.16a). Clients make requests to look up directories, retrieve file attributes, and read and write blocks from files. One of the most popular file servers is the Network File System (NFS), which allows easy sharing of data on heterogeneous networks. The NFS protocol allows both UDP and TCP/IP to be used as a transport protocol. However, most NFS implementations use UDP.

Database servers provide access to one or more shared databases. Client requests are in the form of SQL statements—a standard language for accessing relational databases [27]. The database server receives the SQL

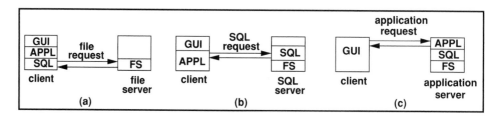

Figure 2.16. (a) File server. (b) SQL server. (c) Application server.

statements and submits them to a database engine that either queries the database or updates the database, depending on the type of request. Even if the database engine has to read hundreds of records to satisfy a client query to retrieve just a few records, only the result is sent back to the client. This cuts down significantly on network traffic and reduces the number of interactions between clients and servers (see Fig. 2.16b).

Application servers provide access to remote procedures invoked by the clients through Remote Procedure Call (RPC) mechanisms. These remote procedures implement the business logic of the application and issue SQL calls to a back-end database engine. So, instead of one C/S interaction per SQL call, this approach requires a single interaction per procedure invocation (see Fig. 2.16c).

As we go from Fig. 2.16a to c, we decrease the rate at which requests are sent to the server but increase the complexity of each request. There is a performance tradeoff that depends on specific values of the relevant parameters. Transaction Processing Monitors (TPM) [1, 9] can be used to balance the load among several servers that implement the same service, provide dynamic server replication, and funnel access to database servers to improve performance. Other systems, such as Microsoft's Transaction Server, further improve performance and scalability by (1) managing a pool of threads that are allocated to service requests and returned to the pool when the service completes, and (2) establishing, at initialization time, a pool of DB connections between the Transaction Server environment and the various databases used by the applications. This pool of pre-connected DB sessions eliminates the time required to connect to the DB during the execution of a service request.

Groupware servers provide access to unstructured and semistructured information such as text, images, mail, bulletin boards, and workflows [28]. Object servers support remote invocation of methods in support of distributed object oriented application development. Object request brokers (ORB) acts as the glue between clients and remote objects.

Software servers are used to provide executables to Network Computers (NC). NCs do not have hard drives, are connected to a network, and obtain the executables of commercial software packages from a software server that always has the latest version of the software.

Web servers provide access to documents, images, sound, executables, and downloadable applications (e.g., Java applets) through the HTTP, described in the next subsection.

2.3.3   HTTP

Documents on the Web are written in a simple "markup language" called Hypertext Markup Language (HTML) [4]. HTML is the system used to create hypertext documents. HTML allows one to describe the structure of documents by indicating headings, emphasis, links to other documents, and so forth. Images and other multimedia objects can be included in HTML documents. Thus, HTML allows one to integrate video, software applications, and multimedia objects on the Web. Most HTML documents consist of text and inline images. Special links point to inline images to be inserted in a document.

Inline images have a great impact on server performance. When a browser parses the HTML data received from a server, it recognizes links associated with inline images and automatically requests the image files pointed to by the links. Actually, an HTML document with inline images is a combination of multiple objects, which generates multiple separate requests to the server. Whereas the user sees only one document, the server sees a series of separate requests for that document. In order to improve end user performance perception, some browsers start requesting images before the whole text has arrived at the client. In terms of system performance, it is important to understand that a single click by a user may generate a series of file requests to a server.

2.3.3.1   The Combination of HTTP and TCP/IP

HTTP [43] is an application-level protocol layered on top of TCP used in the communication between clients and servers on the Web. HTTP defines a simple request-response interaction, which can be viewed as a "Web transaction." Each HTTP interaction consists of a request sent from the client to the server, followed by a response sent back by the server to the client. An HTTP request includes several pieces: the method which specifies the legal action (e.g., GET, HEAD, PUT, and POST), the Uniform Resource Locator (URL) that identifies the name of the information requested, and other information, such as the type of document the client is willing to accept, authentication, and payment authorization.

When a server receives a request, it parses the request and takes the action specified by the method. The server then replies to the client with a response consisting of a status line indicating the success or failure of the request, meta-information describing the type of object returned and the information requested, and a file or an output generated by a server-side application (e.g., CGI). The main steps involved in an HTTP request-response interaction are:

- map the server name to an IP address (e.g., www.performance_book.com to 199.333.111.0)

- establish a TCP connection with the server

- transmit the request (URL + method + other information)

- receive the response (HTML text or image or other information)

- close the TCP/IP connection (in HTTP 1.1 the connection remains open for embedded images as seen later)

Each of these steps has an inherent cost that depends on the server and network performance, as we will see in this section.

HTTP is referred to as a "stateless protocol" because it does not include the concept of a session or interaction beyond delivery of the requested document. In the original HTTP protocol, a conversation is restricted to the transfer of one document or image. Each transfer is totally isolated from the previous or next request. Considering that a Web site is accessible to millions of clients, the stateless nature of the HTTP protocol brings efficiency to the system, because servers do not need to keep track of who the clients are or what requests were serviced in the past.

The other side of the coin of the stateless nature of the HTTP protocol is the performance cost. The original version of the protocol, HTTP 1.0, has several inherent performance inefficiencies. For instance, a new connection is established per request. A page with text and many small images generates many separate connections: one for the HTML page and one for each image. Since most Web objects are small, a high fraction of packets exchanged between client and server are simply TCP control packets used to open and close connections, as shown in Fig. 2.17a.

A key element to understanding the performance of the HTTP and TCP/IP pair is the nature of the mandatory delays imposed by the protocols. These delays can be decomposed into connection delay and request delay. The former is the time (measured in RTTs) it takes to establish a connection. The latter refers to the time it takes to complete a data transfer over an already established connection. Let us analyze the delays involved in the execution of a Web transaction.

Figure 2.17 illustrates the packets exchanged between a client and a server for an HTTP interaction over TCP [8, 30]. Figure 2.17a shows the exchange of packets that occurs in version 1.0 of the HTTP protocol, while Fig. 2.17b displays the equivalent exchange for the persistent version of the protocol, HTTP 1.1, which maintains TCP connections across HTTP requests. Horizontal dashed lines on the client side represent the mandatory RTTs through the network, imposed by a combination of TCP/IP and HTTP. Packets represented by dotted lines are required by TCP but do

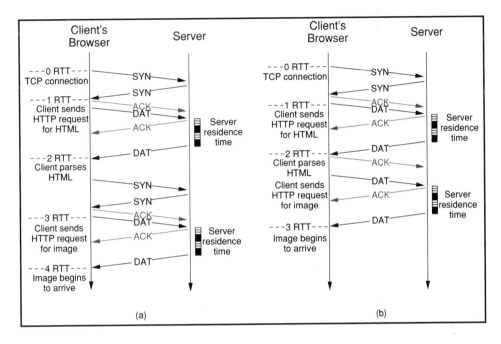

Figure 2.17. (a) HTTP interaction in HTTP 1.0. (b) HTTP interaction in HTTP 1.1.

not interfere with latency, because the receiver does not need to wait for them to proceed execution. The mandatory delays involved in an HTTP request-response interaction are as follows.

- The client opens a TCP connection, which results in an exchange of SYN and ACK segments (see Section 2.2.3.2).

- The client sends an HTTP request to the server, which parses it, executes the action requested, and sends back the response. In the case of a retrieval operation, the server has to move data from disk or cache to the client through the network. Afterward, the server is responsible for closing the connection. The FIN segments exchanged by the server and client to close the connection are not represented in Fig. 2.17, because the client does not have to wait for the connection termination to continue.

- The client parses the HTML response to look for the URL of the inline image. The client then opens a new TCP connection, that involves another three-way handshake.

- The client sends an HTTP request for the first inline image again and the process repeats itself.

For each additional request, a new TCP connection must be established and the system incurs again in a connection setup overhead. As a consequence of the combination of HTTP and TCP/IP, a client has to wait at least four network RTTs before a document with one inline image is displayed by the browser. Each additional image requires at least two other round trips: one to establish a TCP connection and another to obtain the image. Because of TCP's slow start, most HTTP 1.0 operations use TCP inefficiently, resulting in poor performance performance due to congestion and overhead.

A new version of HTTP (also known as HTTP 1.1, persistent-connection HTTP, or HTTP-NG) includes features that solve part of the performance problems of version 1.0. HTTP 1.1 leaves the TCP connection open between consecutive operations, as depicted in Fig. 2.17b. This technique, called "persistent connection," uses one TCP connection to carry multiple HTTP requests, eliminating the cost of several opens and closes and minimizing the impact of slow start. Thus, multiple requests and responses can be contained in a single TCP segment. This feature also avoids many round trip delays, improving performance and reducing the number of packets exchanged. Looking at Fig. 2.17, one can see how the new HTTP protocol affects network latencies. In the case of a request for an HTML document and one inline image, the document is available to the browser after three round trips, instead of the four round trips required by the original version of HTTP.

Another feature of HTTP 1.1 relevant to performance is known as "pipeline of requests." The pipelining technique in HTTP allows multiple requests to be sent without waiting for a response. It means that many requests are sent by the client over a single TCP connection, before the answer of the previous ones are received. Experimental results [26] indicate that a pipelined HTTP 1.1 implementation outperformed HTTP 1.0, even when the original version of HTTP used multiple connections in parallel over different TCP connections. A more detailed analysis of the delays involved in downloading Web pages will be given in Chapter 3.

2.4   The Peer-to-Peer Model

The Web, as we know it, uses essentially a C/S paradigm of computation. As discussed previously, the C/S protocol follows a request-reply model in which the server listens for requests from clients and then replies to them. In a sense, a server (or collection of servers of a site) is a central repository of resources (e.g., files or transaction processing capability). The central nature of the server or set of equivalent servers in the C/S model is a potential impediment to scalability and reliability. Recently, a more collaborative and distributed approach, known as *peer-to-peer (P2P)* [31, 34], has been used to support many different applications such as compressed music file sharing [25], disk-space sharing [6], file sharing [12], or even computing cycle sharing [33]. This trend has become possible in part by the fact that personal computers have become increasingly faster, they have much more disk space than in the past, and are connected to the Internet at higher speeds than before. The P2P computing model is also feasible because a significant portion of the resources of personal computers and workstations are not used by their owners. For example, a study conducted at a major company having about 10,000 file systems showed that around 50% of the total disk space was free [6]. Another study showed that up to 75% of the cycles in a network of workstation are idle [24].

We discuss here two common architectures for the P2P model. A more detailed classification and preliminary performance analysis of P2P computing can be found in [17, 18]. We distinguish here the resources to be shared from the meta-data, i.e., the data that describe the resources. For example, in a music sharing application, the meta-data is typically composed of the title, artist, album, and any other information needed to describe and locate the music file.

In Fig. 2.18a, there is a meta-data server that has to be queried by any machine that needs access to a resource (e.g., a file). For example, machine C queries the meta-data server and obtains a list, (I, J, H) in the example, of peer sites that have a copy of the desired resource. Then, C selects one peer machine—machine I in the example—and holds a session with it. During the session, C obtains access to the resource. So, the meta-data server is involved in registering sites and their resources and replying to queries for resource location. The actual access is done on a peer-to-peer basis. This is how Napster works.

Figure 2.18b illustrates the case in which there is no meta-data server. Here, each machine holds information about the resources located in its neighboring peers. For example, machine C queries its peers A, B, and D. Machine D does not know the location of the resource but sends a query to peers E and F. The latter queries machine I, which happens to have the resource. The answer propagates back to C, through peers F and D. Then, as before, C establishes a session with I. In some cases, the desired resource may also move back along with the information about its location so that copies of the resource end up stored closer to the point where they are accessed most frequently.

There are performance tradeoffs between the centralized meta-data server approach (Fig. 2.18a) and the purely distributed one (Fig. 2.18b). In the former case, there is a constant overhead of the order of two RTTs to obtain the information from the meta-data server. Also, since the meta-server is a centralized resource, it could become overloaded and add a significant delay to the interaction. In the latter case, the number of peers to be contacted before a session starts is not fixed and may exceed two. In this case, the

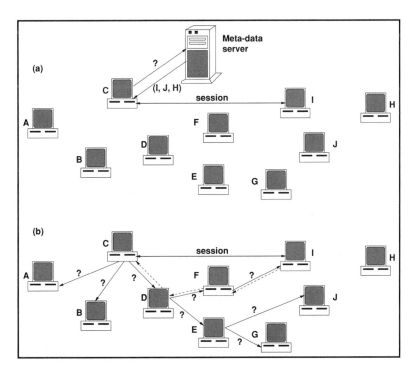

Figure 2.18. (a) P2P architecture with centralized meta-data server (b) P2P architecture with no meta-data server.

distributed approach involves more network messages than the centralized one. However, since there is no centralized server, scalability is less of a concern in the distributed case.

2.5   Web Service Protocols

The Web is evolving into a provider of services. Applications, databases, and a variety of devices perform Web services. Although there is no standard definition of what a "Web service" is, we can simply say that these are services provided to users via the Web. The term "Web service" describes specific business functionality exposed by a company, usually through an Internet connection, for the purpose of providing a way for another company or software program to use the service [40].

The main components of a Web service architecture are the service provider, the service registry, and the service requester. A service is an application available for use by requesters that fit the prerequisites specified by the service provider. Web services can be composed with other services into new services and applications. Services are deployed somewhere on the Web by service providers. A special service called registry provides support for publishing and locating services. It is a searchable repository of service descriptions where service providers publish their services. Service requesters query the service registry and find appropriate services. A description language is used to describe Web services. Its functionality and access policies are registered and published with a registry. Services are invoked over a network by using the information contained in the service description.

Examples of Web services vary from simple requests such as a stock quote, a user authentication, or a payment authorization to complex tasks such as "Buy me an airline ticket from San Francisco to New York on May 14th." The architecture of Web services should enable the automation of tasks such as service discovery, execution, composition, and interoperation. Web service discovery involves automatically locating services that perform a given task and exhibit the requested properties. Web service execution refers to a program or agent automatically executing an identified service on the Web. Service composition and interoperation refers to the automatic selection, composition, and interoperation of adequate Web services to perform a given task [22]. Industry efforts have been developed to establish Web services standards and technologies in aspects of service discovery and execution.

Figure 2.19 shows a layered view of an emerging stack of protocols and standards that enable Web services. Standards-based technologies such as TCP/IP, HTTP, Extended Markup Language (XML) and Simple Object Access Protocol (SOAP) are used to create a uniform service description format and service discovery protocols [40]. The upper layers of the figure represent service interoperability protocols and standards not yet developed.

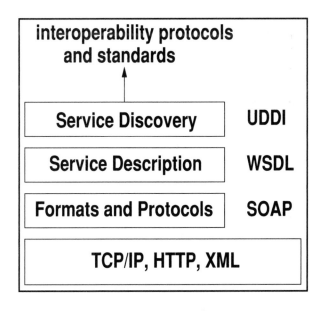

Figure 2.19. Web service protocols.

2.5.1   SOAP

The Simple Object Access Protocol (SOAP) is a World Wide Web Consortium (W3C) [42] draft note describing a way to use XML and HTTP to create information delivery and remote procedure mechanisms [35]. SOAP is a lightweight protocol for the exchange of information in a decentralized, distributed environment. It is a specification that defines a uniform way of passing XML-encoded data. SOAP consists of three parts: an envelope that defines a framework for describing what is in a message and how to process it, a set of encoding rules for expressing instances of application-defined datatypes, and a convention for representing remote procedure calls and responses. SOAP builds on HTTP and XML. SOAP outlines a framework that allows one program to invoke service interfaces across the Internet, without the need to share a common programming language or distributed object infrastructure.

2.5.2 WSDL

The Web Service Description Language (WSDL) is an XML format for describing network services as a set of endpoints operating on messages containing either document-oriented or procedure-oriented information. The operations and messages are described abstractly, and then bound to a concrete network protocol and message format to define an endpoint [41]. In short, WSDL is used to describe what a service does, where it resides and how to invoke it.

2.5.3 UDDI

The Universal Description, Discovery, and Integration (UDDI) specifications define a way to publish and discover information about Web services [40]. The specification consists of several related documents and an XML schema that defines a SOAP-based programming protocol for registering and discovering Web services. UDDI is a framework for Web services integration. It provides a mechanism for clients to dynamically find services on the Web. The core component of the UDDI project is the UDDI business registration, an XML file used to describe a business entity and its Web services [40]. It can be thought of as a DNS service for business applications and services.

2.6 Concluding Remarks

This chapter introduced the concepts of computer networking, protocols, wired and wireless LANs, WANs, and described the most important features of the protocols that are at the core of the Internet and internets: TCP/IP.

The C/S model was discussed along with important architectural issues of these systems and their performance impacts. HTTP, an important example of the C/S protocol, was presented here. Other models of Web interactions were also discussed. These include P2P and Web services. The remaining chapters of this book take a quantitative analysis of Web services.

More details about TCP/IP can be found in [8, 21, 37, 38]. A nice description of C/S systems can be found in [28]. Web servers are described in [43].

Bibliography

[1] J. M. Andrade, M. T. Carges, T. J. Dwyer, and S. D. Felts, *The Tuxedo System*, Addison Wesley, Reading, Massachusetts, 1996.

[2] BBN, "A History of the ARPANET: The First Decade," *Tech. Rep.*, Bolt, Beranek, and Newman, Massachusetts, 1981.

[3] G. Bell and J. Gray, "The Revolution Yet to Happen," *Beyond Calculation: The Next Fifty Years of Computing*, P. J. Denning and R. M. Metcalfe, eds., Copernicus Springer-Verlag, New York, 1997.

[4] T. Berners-Lee, R. Cailliau, H. Nielsen, and A. Pecret, "The World Wide Web," *Comm. ACM*, vol. 37, no. 8, pp. 76–82, Aug. 1994.

[5] D. Bertsekas and R. Gallager, *Data Networks*, 2nd ed., Prentice Hall, Upper Saddle River, New Jersey, 1992.

[6] W. J. Bolosky, J. R. Douceur, D. Ely, and M. Theimer, "Feasibility of a Serverless Distributed File System Deployed on an Existing Set of Desktop PCs," *Proc. ACM Sigmetrics 2000 Int. Conf. on Measurement and Modeling of Comp. Syst.*, June 17-21, 2000, Santa Clara, California, pp. 34–43.

[7] V. Cerf, "When They're Everywhere," *Beyond Calculation: The Next Fifty Years of Computing*, P. J. Denning and R. M. Metcalfe, eds., Copernicus Springer-Verlag, New York, 1997.

[8] D. E. Comer, *Internetworking with TCP/IP Vol. I: Principles, Protocols, and Architecture*, 4th ed., Prentice Hall, Upper Saddle River, New Jersey, 2000.

[9] J. Gray and A. Reuter, *Transaction Processing: Concepts and Techniques*, Morgan Kaufmann, San Francisco, California, 1993.

[10] O. Gusak and T. Dayar, "A Generalization of a TCP Model: Multiple Source-Destination Case with Arbitrary LAN as the Access Network," Chapter 3 of *System Performance Evaluation: Methodologies and Applications*, Erol Gelenbe, ed., CRC Press, Boca Raton, Florida, pp. 39–49, 2000.

[11] J. Heidmann, K. Obraczka, and J. Touch, "Modeling the Performance of HTTP Over Several Transport Protocols," *IEEE/ACM Trans. Networking*, vol. 5, no. 5, pp. 616–630, Oct. 1997.

[12] Enhanced Storage Solution, www.idrive.com

[13] Institute of Electrical and Electronics Engineers, "Carrier Sense Multiple Access with Collision Detection (CSMA/CD) Access Method and Physical Layer Specifications (ANSI)," *IEEE, Standard 8802-3: 1996 (ISO/IEC) [ANSI/IEEE Std 802.3, 1996 Edition]*.

[14] IEEE, "Supplement to Carrier Sense Multiple Access with Collision Detection (CSMA/CD)," *IEEE, Standard 802.3u-1995*.

[15] IEEE, "Token Ring Access Method and Physical Layer Specification," *IEEE, Standard 8802-5: 1995 (ISO/IEC) [ANSI/IEEE 802.5, 1995 Edition]*.

[16] IEEE, "IEEE 802.11 Standard for Wireless LAN Medium Access (MAC) and Physical Layer (PHY) Specifications," 2001.

[17] K. Kant, R. Iyer, and V. Tewari, "On the Potential of Peer-to-peer Computing: Classification and Evaluation," Enterprise Architecture Lab, Intel Corporation, Oregon, 2001.

[18] K. Kant and R. Iyer, "A Performance Model for Peer-to-peer File Sharing Services," Enterprise Architecture Lab, Intel Corporation, Oregon, 2001.

[19] L. Kleinrock, *Queueing Systems, Vol. I: Theory*, John Wiley and Sons, New York, 1975.

[20] L. Kleinrock, *Queueing Systems, Vol. II: Computer Applications*, John Wiley and Sons, New York, 1976.

[21] J. F. Kurose and K. W. Ross, *Computer Networking: A Top-Down Approach Featuring the Internet*, Addison Wesley, Boston, Massachusetts, 2001.

[22] S. McIlraith, T. Son, and H. Zeng, "Semantic Web Services," *IEEE Intelligent Systems*, March/April 2001.

[23] R. M. Metcalfe and D. R. Boggs, "Ethernet: Distributed Packet Switching for Local Computer Networks," *Comm. ACM*, pp. 395–404, 1976.

[24] M. W. Mutka and M. Livny, "The Available Capacity of a Privately Owned Workstation Environment," *Performance Evaluation*, vol. 12, pp. 269–284, 1991.

[25] Napster, www.napster.com

[26] H. Nielsen, J. Gettys, A. Bair-Smith, E. Prud'Hommeaux, H. Lie, and C. Lilley, "Network Performance Effects of HTTP/1.1 CSS1, and PNG," *Proc. ACM SIGCOMM'97*, Cannes, France, Sept. 16–18, 1997.

[27] P. O'Neil and E. O'Neil, *Database: Principles, Programming, Performance*, 2nd ed., Morgan Kauffman, San Francisco, California, 2000.

[28] R. Orfali, D. Harkey, and J. Edwards, *Client/Server Survival Guide*, 3rd ed., John Wiley and Sons, New York, 1999.

[29] J. Padhye, V. Firoiu, D. Towsley, and J. F. Kurose, "Modeling TCP Reno Performance: A Simple Model and Its Empirical Validation," *IEEE/ACM Tr. Networking*, vol. 8, no. 2, pp. 133–145, April 2000.

[30] V. Padmanabhan and J. Mogul, "Improving HTTP Latency," *Comput. Networks ISDN Syst.*, vol. 28, nos. 1,2, Dec. 1995.

[31] M. Parameswaran, A. Susarla, and A. B. Whinston, "P2P Networking: an Information-Sharing Alternative," IEEE Computer, July 2001.

[32] R. Perlman, *Interconnections*, 2nd. ed., Addison Wesley, Reading, Massachusetts, 1999.

[33] SETI, the Search for Extraterrestrial Intelligence, www.setiathome.ssl. berkeley.edu

[34] M. P. Singh, "Peering at Peer-to-Peer Computing," *IEEE Internet Computing,* vol. 5, no. 1, pp. 4–5, 2001.

[35] Simple Object Access Protocol (SOAP), www.w3.org/TR/SOAP

[36] W. Stallings, *Networking Standards: A Guide to OSI, ISDN, LAN, and MAN Standards*, Addison Wesley, Reading, Massachusetts, 1993.

[37] W. R. Stevens, *TCP/IP Illustrated, Vol. 1*, Addison Wesley, Reading, Massachusetts, 1994.

[38] W. R. Stevens, *TCP/IP Illustrated, Vol. 3*, Addison Wesley, Reading, Massachusetts, 1996.

[39] T. Tu, "Analysis of Broadband Performance," *J. Comp. Resource Management*, Computer Measurement Group, pp. 35–39, Spring 2001.

[40] Universal Description, Discovery, and Integration of Business for the Web, www.uddi.org

[41] Web Services Description Language (WSDL), www.w3.org/TR/wsdl

[42] World Wide Web Consortium, www.w3.org

[43] N. Yeager and R. McCrath, *Web Server Technology*, Morgan Kaufmann, San Francisco, California, 1996.

Chapter 3

Basic Performance Concepts

3.1 Introduction

The infrastructure that supports Web services comprises many different hardware resources including client workstations, servers with their processors and storage subsystems, LANs, WANs, load balancers, and routers. Various types of software processes including Web and application servers, middleware, database management systems, protocol handlers, and operating systems share hardware resources. The shared use of these resources gives rise to contention that generates waiting queues. A request for a Web service spends a portion of its time receiving service at various resources as well as queuing for these resources.

The delays encountered by a Web request may be decomposed into (1) service times: time spent using various resources such as processors, disks, and networks; and (2) waiting times: time spent waiting to use resources that are being held by other requests. In this chapter, we investigate, in detail, the nature of the delay incurred by a typical Web request with emphasis on the service times at single disks, disk arrays, networks, and routers. We also provide an analysis of the time to download a Web page. Queues and contention are defined more formally, and some very basic and important performance results are introduced. The formulas presented in this chapter are implemented in the Microsoft Excel workbooks `ServTime.XLS` and `PageDownloadTime.XLS` that can be found in the book's Web site.

3.2   The Big Picture of Response Time

The time perceived by a customer to obtain a reply for a request for a Web service, the *end-to-end response time*, can be broken down into two major components: network time and Web site time (see Fig. 3.1). The network time includes all the time spent by the various messages traveling between the user browser and the Web site. The network time can be decomposed into two major components: latency and transmission time. *Latency* indicates the number of round trip times (RTT) involved in the exchange of messages between the client browser and the site. Latency is a function of the nature of the protocols used and, in the case of Web pages, of the Web page design, as discussed later in the chapter. *Transmission time* is the time needed to transmit all the bytes exchanged between the browser and the Web site and depends on the bandwidth of the slowest link connecting the browser to the Web site.

A request for a Web service may visit one or more Web sites. The time spent by a request at a Web site may be decomposed into two major components as indicated in Fig. 3.1: service time and queuing time. *Service time* is the period of time during which a request is receiving service from

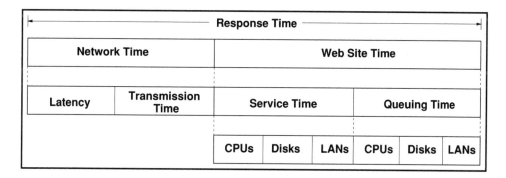

Figure 3.1. Response time breakdown.

a resource such as a CPU, disk, LAN segment, or a communication line. A request may have to visit a resource several times (e.g., more than one I/O to a disk or many visits to the CPU as the request is context-switched by the operating system) before it completes. The notation S_i^j is used to indicate the service time at resource i during the jth visit to the resource. The time spent by a request waiting to get access to resource i during the jth visit to the resource is called *waiting time* and is denoted by W_i^j.

The sum of all service times for a request at resource i is called *service demand* and is denoted by D_i. For example, if requests to a Web site perform 3.5 I/Os on average on a certain disk for which the average service time is 10 msec, the service demand of these requests at that disk is 35 msec ($= 3.5 \times 10$). The sum of all waiting times at resource i for a given request is called *queuing time* and is denoted by Q_i. Let V_i be the average number of visits made by a request to resource i, and let S_i be the average service time per visit at the resource. The average service demand D_i is then the product of the average number of visits to the resource multiplied by the average time spent per visit at the resource. Thus, $D_i = V_i \times S_i$.

The sum of the service demand plus the queuing time for a request at resource i is called *residence time* and is denoted by R_i'. The residence time of a request at a resource is the total time spent by the request at the resource, queuing and receiving service.

Finally, the response time R of a request is the sum of that request's residence time at all resources assuming that a Web request uses one resource at a time.

In summary, we can write that

$$D_i = \sum_{\text{visits } j} S_i^j = V_i \, S_i \qquad (3.2.1)$$

$$Q_i = \sum_{\text{visits } j} W_i^j \qquad (3.2.2)$$

$$R_i' = D_i + Q_i \qquad (3.2.3)$$

$$R = \sum_{\text{resources } i} R_i'. \qquad (3.2.4)$$

Figure 3.2 illustrates the concepts of service time, service demand, waiting time, queuing time, residence time, and response time for a server with one CPU and one disk. A request alternates between the use of the CPU and the disk. At every visit to one of these resources, the request spends some time waiting for the resource and some time using the resource.

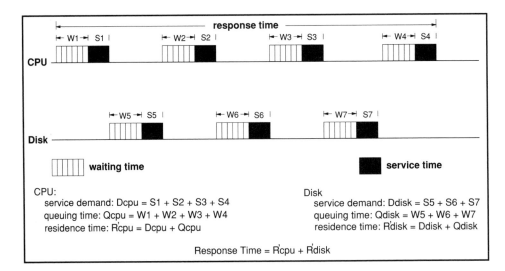

Figure 3.2. Example of service time, service demand, waiting time, queuing time, residence time, and response time.

Consider that a request to a Web site uses 10 msec of CPU at the Web server, and reads ten 2,048-byte blocks from the server's disk. So, $D_{\text{cpu}} = 0.010$ sec. The average seek time at the server's disk is 9 msec, the average latency is 4.17 msec, and the transfer rate is 20 MB/sec. Thus, the average service time, S_d, at the disk is

$$S_d = \text{AvgSeek} + \text{AvgLatency} + \text{TransferTime}$$
$$= \text{AvgSeek} + \text{AvgLatency} + \frac{\text{BlockSize}}{\text{TransferRate}}$$
$$= 0.009 + 0.00417 + 2048/20,000,000 = 0.0133 \text{ sec.}$$

Subsection 3.3.1 provides more details on the computation of service times at magnetic disks. The service demand at the server's disk, D_d, is then equal to $10 \times S_d = 10 \times 0.0133 = 0.133$ sec. Consider that the client and the server are connected by a network that has an effective bandwidth of 0.5 Mbps and an RTT of 80 msec. One RTT is needed to establish the TCP connection. The HTTP request is piggybacked on the ACK TCP segment during TCP connection establishment. Assume that a request going from the client to the server takes a full Ethernet packet (1,518 bytes), and that the reply from the server requires eight packets. Assuming that the sender window at the server allows for all packets of the reply to be sent before an ACK is received, the total latency is equal to 2 RTTs (one for TCP connection establishment, 0.5 RTT for the HTTP request to reach the server, and 0.5 RTT for the first byte of the reply to reach the client browser). The total transmission time, i.e., network service demand D_{net}, is equal to the number of bits transmitted divided by the network bandwidth. So,

$$D_{\text{net}} = [8 \times (1 + 8) \times 1,518]/500,000 = 0.22 \text{ sec.}$$

A detailed description of how service times are computed on networks is provided in Section 3.3.2. The minimum possible value for the response time for the request is obtained by ignoring all waiting times. So,

$$R \geq \text{Latency} + D_{\text{net}} + D_{\text{cpu}} + D_d = 0.16 + 0.22 + 0.01 + 0.133 = 0.523 \text{ sec.} \quad \blacksquare$$

The reader should note that we have not taken into account the waiting times experienced by the request to get access to the network and to use the CPU and the disk at the server. The models presented in the remaining chapters of this book allow us to compute these waiting times.

3.3   Service Times and Service Demands

This section explores, in greater detail, how service times can be computed for various categories of resources found in Web systems.

3.3.1   Service Times at Single Disks and Disk Arrays

This section reviews the major elements of modern disk subsystems and identifies the contributions made by these elements to the overall service time at a disk.

3.3.1.1   Single Disks

Magnetic disks are an important component of any server and client workstation. Access times to information stored on magnetic disks is several orders of magnitude greater than access times to information stored in random access memory (RAM) due to the disk's mechanical components. A disk (see Fig. 3.3) is composed of one or more platters that rotate in lockstep, attached to a spindle. Information is magnetically recorded on both the upper and lower surfaces of each platter. The surface of a platter is divided into concentric circles called *tracks*. A read/write head, mounted at the end of an arm, is associated with each surface. Only one read/write head can be active at any time. An actuator moves all the arms together along the radius of the platters. The set of tracks located at the same distance from the center is called a *cylinder*. Tracks are divided into sectors of the same size.

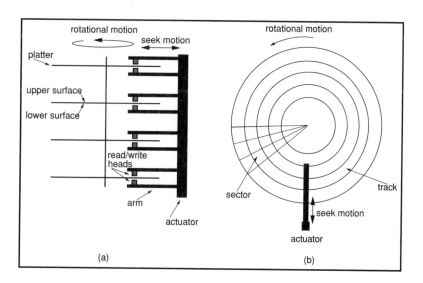

Figure 3.3. (a) Side view of a magnetic disk. (b) Top view of a magnetic disk.

To read/write to/from a magnetic disk, the actuator has to be moved to the proper cylinder. This is called a *seek*. The read/write head corresponding to the desired track has to be activated. The disk mechanism has to wait until the disk rotation brings the desired sector below the read/write head. This is called *rotational latency*. At this point, data transfer can start.

I/O subsystems involve more components than just the disks used to store information. Figure 3.4 shows the typical architecture of the I/O subsystem of a server. I/O requests are submitted to the file system. A cache at the file system stores file blocks that have been used most recently. If the desired block is in the file system cache, no disk access is needed and the request is satisfied directly from the cache. This event is called a file system *cache hit*. Otherwise, a file system *cache miss* is said to occur, and the request is sent to the device driver. The request is then queued at the device driver, which may reorder requests to optimize performance. The request is then sent to the disk controller. A cache at the disk controller (also called a disk cache) is used to match the speed between the disk and the I/O bus. The disk cache may be used for prefetching blocks that may

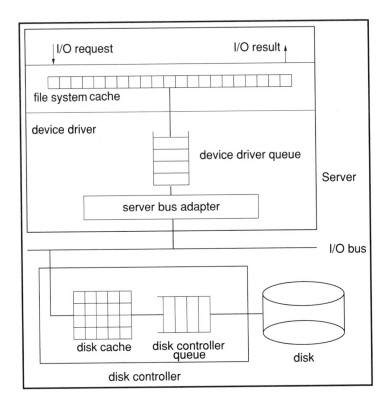

Figure 3.4. Architecture of typical I/O subsystem.

be needed in the near future. For example, if a file is being accessed sequentially, it makes sense to bring to the cache a certain number of blocks that follow the block just requested so that a cache hit occurs when these blocks are requested. This technique is called *read-ahead*, or *pre-fetch*. The disk controller uses a disk-scheduling discipline in its queue aimed at minimizing the average number of cylinders traversed by the arm to serve disk requests. These disk-scheduling disciplines use information about the position of the disk arm. Examples of disk-scheduling disciplines include LOOK, CSCAN, Shortest Seek Time First (SSTF), and Shortest Positioning Time First (SPTF) [6, 14, 15].

We now provide expressions for the average service time at a disk subsystem including the disk controller and the disk itself. More detailed models of disk access can be found in [15]. Let

- $\overline{S}_d$: average time, in seconds, spent at the controller plus disk to access a block from a disk

- SeekTime: average seek time in seconds. That is, the average time to position the arm at the proper cylinder

- Seek$_{rand}$: average seek time, in seconds, for a request to a random cylinder, provided by the disk manufacturers. Sometimes, the average seek times for read and write requests are slightly different

- DiskSpeed: disk rotation speed, in revolutions per minute, provided by the disk manufacturer

- DiskRevolutionTime: time, in seconds, for a disk to complete a full revolution, equal to 60/DiskSpeed

- RotationalLatency: average rotational latency in seconds; i.e., the average time elapsed since the end of the seek until data transfer starts. This time is spent waiting for the disk to rotate until the desired sector lies under the read/write head

- BlockSize: block size in bytes

- TransferRate: rate at which data is transferred to/from a disk, in MB/sec

- TransferTime: time, in seconds, to transfer a block from the disk to the disk controller

- ControllerTime: time, in seconds, spent at the controller processing an I/O request. This includes the time to check the cache plus the time to read/write a block from/to the cache

- P_{miss}: probability that the desired block is not in the disk cache

The average access time at the controller plus disk can be written as

$$\overline{S}_d = \text{ControllerTime} +$$

$$P_{\text{miss}} \ (\text{SeekTime} + \text{RotationalLatency} + \text{TransferTime}) \ (3.3.5)$$

The transfer time is simply the ratio between the block size and the transfer rate converted to bytes/sec. Hence,

$$\text{TransferTime} = \frac{\text{BlockSize}}{10^6 \times \text{TransferRate}}. \qquad (3.3.6)$$

The cache miss probability, the average seek time, and the average rotational latency depend on the type of workload submitted to the disk subsystem. A disk workload is defined as a sequence of disk block numbers submitted to the disk subsystem. We consider two types of workloads: random and sequential. A *random* workload is one in which the blocks requested are randomly spread over the blocks on the disk. A *sequential* workload is one that exhibits subsequences, called *runs*, of requests to consecutive blocks on the disk. The workload 10, 201, 15, 1,023, 45, 39, 782 is an example of a random workload and 4, 350, 351, 352, 353, 80, 104, 105, 106, 107, 108, 243 is an example of a sequential workload with two runs of length greater than one. The first (350, 351, 352, 353) has length four blocks and the second (104, 105, 106, 107, 108) has length five. Let RunLength be the average run length observed in a workload. Random workloads have RunLength = 1.

For random workloads we have that

$$P_{\text{miss}} = 1 \qquad (3.3.7)$$

$$\text{RunLength} = 1 \qquad (3.3.8)$$

$$\text{SeekTime} = \text{Seek}_{\text{rand}} \qquad (3.3.9)$$

$$\text{RotationalLatency} = \frac{1}{2} \times \text{DiskRevolutionTime}. \qquad (3.3.10)$$

Equation (3.3.10) comes from the fact that a random request may have to wait anywhere between no revolution and a full revolution. On average, the rotational latency for a random request is a half revolution.

The equations for sequential workloads are given below and discussed in the following paragraphs.

$$P_{\text{miss}} = 1/\text{RunLength} \qquad (3.3.11)$$

$$\text{SeekTime} = \text{Seek}_{\text{rand}}/\text{RunLength} \qquad (3.3.12)$$

$$\text{RotationalLatency} = \frac{1/2 + (\text{RunLength} - 1)[(1 + U_d)/2]}{\text{RunLength}}$$
$$\times \text{DiskRevolutionTime.} \qquad (3.3.13)$$

Assuming that read-ahead requests are only performed on disk cache misses and that only the first request of a run will not be served out of the cache, the cache miss probability can be approximated by Eq. (3.3.11).

Equation (3.3.12) can be easily proved as follows. Consider first the following trivial relationship:

$$\text{RunLength} = \text{NumberRequests}/\text{NumRuns} \qquad (3.3.14)$$

where NumberRequests and NumRuns are the number of requests submitted to the disk in a given time interval and the total number of runs observed in the same interval, respectively. The average seek time is equal to the sum of the seek times for all requests in an interval divided by the number of requests in that interval. Only the first request of a run will require a random seek. The remaining requests of a run require a seek of length zero. So, the sum of the seek times for all requests is equal to the number of runs multiplied by the time of a random seek. Dividing the sum by the number of requests to get the average seek time per request and using Eq. (3.3.14) we get that

$$\begin{aligned}
\text{SeekTime} &= \frac{\text{NumRuns} \times \text{Seek}_{\text{rand}}}{\text{NumberRequests}} \\
&= \frac{\text{Seek}_{\text{rand}}}{\text{NumberRequests}/\text{NumRuns}} \\
&= \text{Seek}_{\text{rand}}/\text{RunLength.} \qquad (3.3.15)
\end{aligned}$$

Example 3.2

What is the average seek time for the workload (4, 350, 351, 352, 353, 80, 104, 105, 106, 107, 108, 243) considering that the average random seek time Seek$_{\text{rand}}$ for the disk is 9 msec?

The workload has three runs of length one—the accesses for blocks 4, 80, and 243—and two runs of length four and five: (350, 351, 352, 353) and (104, 105, 106, 107, 108). So, the average seek time for the entire workload is

$$\text{SeekTime} = \frac{3}{12} \times \text{Seek}_{\text{rand}} + \frac{4}{12} \times \frac{\text{Seek}_{\text{rand}}}{4} + \frac{5}{12} \times \frac{\text{Seek}_{\text{rand}}}{5}$$
$$= \frac{5}{12} \times \text{Seek}_{\text{rand}} = 3.75 \text{ msec.}$$

∎

Equation (3.3.13) is slightly more complex and is a very interesting result derived in [15]. Consider two extreme load scenarios for the disk: light load and heavy load. Under light load, i.e., a very low arrival rate of requests to the disk and therefore a very low disk utilization U_d, two consecutive requests to consecutive blocks on the disk arrive at the disk sufficiently far apart that the second request sees a random rotational latency (i.e., a half revolution). Under heavy load, the second of two consecutive requests will be already in the queue waiting for the first request to finish. The time needed to process a request at the controller will make the second request miss a full revolution before it is able to start transferring its block. The probability that a request finds a busy disk is equal to its utilization, U_d, also defined as the fraction of time the disk is busy. Thus, a request will find an idle disk with probability $(1 - U_d)$. The fraction of a revolution seen by a request in a run is one if the request arrives at a busy disk and one-half if the request arrives at an idle disk. So, the average fraction of a revolution seen by requests in a run is

$$1 \times U_d + \frac{1}{2} \times (1 - U_d) = \frac{1 + U_d}{2}. \tag{3.3.16}$$

The average rotational latency, measured in number of revolutions, for a sequential workload can be computed as the sum of the latencies for all requests divided by the number of requests. This can also be computed as the average latency per run multiplied by the number of runs divided by the number of requests. The average latency in revolutions per run is given by

$$1/2 + (\text{RunLength} - 1)(1 + U_d)/2. \tag{3.3.17}$$

The first term in Eq. (3.3.17) corresponds to the first request of a run, which sees a random rotational delay. The remaining (RunLength − 1) requests of a run see a latency given by Eq. (3.3.16). Finally, the average rotational latency is

$$
\begin{aligned}
\text{RotationalLatency} &= \frac{\text{NumRuns } [1/2 + (\text{RunLength} - 1)(1 + U_d)/2]}{\text{NumberRequests}} \\
&\qquad\qquad\qquad\qquad\qquad \times \text{DiskRevolutionTime} \\
&= \frac{1/2 + (\text{RunLength} - 1)(1 + U_d)/2}{\text{NumberRequests}/\text{NumRuns}} \\
&\qquad\qquad\qquad\qquad\qquad \times \text{DiskRevolutionTime} \\
&= \frac{1/2 + (\text{RunLength} - 1)(1 + U_d)/2}{\text{RunLength}} \\
&\qquad\qquad\qquad\qquad\qquad \times \text{DiskRevolutionTime}
\end{aligned}
\tag{3.3.18}
$$

as given in Eq. (3.3.13). Equation (3.3.18) correctly reduces to the random case equation, Eq. (3.3.10), when RunLength $= 1$ and when the disk utilization approaches zero. Also, as the load on the disk increases, i.e., the utilization U_d approaches 100%, the rotational latency approaches a full revolution as illustrated in Table 3.1.

Note that Eqs. (3.3.12) and (3.3.13) already take into account the effect of the disk cache. Therefore, when using Eq. (3.3.5) for sequential workloads, we should only multiply the transfer time by the cache miss probability.

The curious reader may have noticed that Eq. (3.3.18) requires the disk utilization U_d. As we shall see in Section 3.6, the disk utilization is equal to the average arrival rate of requests to the disk multiplied by the disk average

Table 3.1. Average Rotational Latency in Full Revolutions

RunLength	U_d	Rotational Latency (in revolutions)
4	0.1	0.54
4	0.5	0.69
4	0.8	0.80
8	0.1	0.54
8	0.5	0.72
8	0.8	0.85
16	0.1	0.55
16	0.5	0.73
16	0.8	0.88

service time. But the disk average service time is a function of the average rotational latency, which depends on the utilization! It looks like we are faced with an impasse. It turns out that there is an easy way out. To compute the disk utilization, we start by using Eq. (3.3.10) for the rotational latency for random workloads. This gives, in general, a very good approximation for the average disk service time. The approximation can be improved by using the value of the service time computed this way to obtain a more accurate value for the disk utilization. This new value is used, in turn, to compute a new value for the rotational latency and therefore a new value for the disk service time. The process is repeated until successive values of the disk service time are close enough within a certain tolerance. This kind of iterative procedure is very common in solving this type of problems known as *fixed-point equations* [2].

Figure 3.5 summarizes the formulas discussed above. The worksheet `SingleDisks` in the Microsoft Excel workbook `ServTime.XLS`, found in the book's Web site, implements these formulas as well as the iterative procedure to solve the fixed point equation for the utilization.

$$\text{TransferTime} = \frac{\text{BlockSize}}{10^6 \times \text{TransferRate}} \qquad (3.3.19)$$

Random workloads:

$$\overline{S}_d = \text{ControllerTime} + \text{Seek}_{\text{rand}} + \frac{\text{DiskRevolutionTime}}{2} + \text{TransferTime}$$
$$(3.3.20)$$

Sequential workloads:

$$\overline{S}_d = \text{ControllerTime} + \frac{\text{Seek}_{\text{rand}}}{\text{RunLength}} +$$
$$\frac{[1/2 + (\text{RunLength} - 1)(1 + U_d)/2] \times \text{DiskRevolutionTime}}{\text{RunLength}} +$$
$$\text{TransferTime}/\text{RunLength} \qquad (3.3.21)$$

Figure 3.5. Disk service times equations.

Example 3.3

The disk of a DB server receives requests at a rate of 20 requests/sec (0.020 requests/msec). An analysis of a trace of the requests revealed that 20% of the requests are for random blocks and 80% are for sequences of blocks or runs. The block size is 2,048 bytes. The average measured run length for this workload is 24 requests. The disk rotates at 7,200 RPM, has an average seek for random requests equal to 9 msec, and a transfer rate of 20 MB/sec. The controller time is equal to 0.1 msec. What is the average disk service time?

We start by computing the average service time for random requests. Using Eqs. (3.3.8)–(3.3.10) for random requests, SeekTime = 9 msec, RotationalLatency = $1/2 \times 60/7,200 \times 1,000 = 4.17$ msec, and TransferTime = $2,048/(10^6 \times 20) \times 1,000 = 0.1$ msec. So, using Eq. (3.3.5), we get the average service time for random requests as $0.1 + 9 + 4.17 + 0.1 = 13.4$ msec.

The service time for the sequential portion of the workload can be computed using Eqs. (3.3.11)–(3.3.13). We can approximate the disk utilization

U_d by the arrival rate multiplied by average random seek + average latency + average transfer time. Thus,

$$U_d = 0.020 \times (9 + 4.17 + 0.1) = 0.27. \qquad (3.3.22)$$

The cache miss probability is $P_{\text{miss}} = 1/24 = 4.2\%$. The average seek time is $9/24 = 0.38$ msec. The average rotational latency is

$$\frac{1/2 + 23\,(1 + 0.27)/2}{24} \times \frac{60 \times 1{,}000}{7{,}200} = 5.25 \text{ msec.} \qquad (3.3.23)$$

Hence, the average service time for sequential requests is $0.1 + 0.38 + 5.25 + 0.042 \times 0.1 = 5.73$ msec. So, the average service time, considering both random and sequential requests, is $0.2 \times 13.4 + 0.8 \times 5.73 = 7.26$ msec.

If we use the iterative approach discussed before to refine the service time value for the sequential workload, the procedure would converge to a value of 7.02 msec in three iterations with an absolute error of 0.01%. See the worksheet **SingleDisks** in the Microsoft Excel workbook **ServTime.XLS** for details.   ∎

3.3.1.2   Disk Arrays

Reliability and increased performance in disk access can be obtained by using disk arrays, also known as Redundant Arrays of Independent Disks (RAID). Disk arrays can be organized in several ways. Figure 3.6 shows a disk array composed of five independent disks with their disk controllers.

An array controller, with its cache and queue, controls access to the disk array. We focus here on RAID-5 disk organizations. In this case, data is distributed, or striped, across $N-1$ physical disks. Large chunks of data are broken down into $N-1$ pieces, called *stripe units*, stored into the $N-1$ disks. The set of these $N-1$ stripe units is called a *stripe group*. To increase reliability, a parity block is associated with each stripe group. The parity block is stored in a disk different from the $N-1$ disks used to store the stripe group. If any disk is lost due to a failure, the stripe units stored in

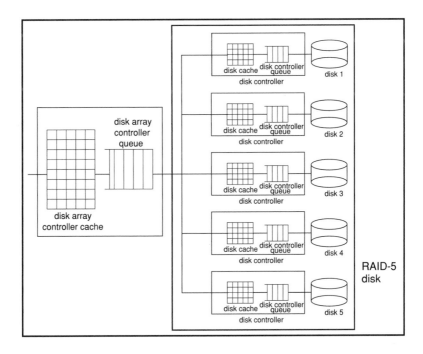

Figure 3.6. Disk array.

this disk can be rebuilt from the other $N - 2$ stripe units in the stripe group and from the parity block.

In RAID-5 organizations, the parity block is uniformly distributed, or rotated, among the physical disks to avoid bottlenecks. The minimum number of physical disks for RAID-5 is three, i.e., $(N \geq 3)$. Figure 3.7 shows how records A–E are stored in a disk array under a RAID-5 organization with five physical disks. Each record is striped into four stripe units. For example, record A is striped into stripe units A1 through A4 and has a parity block PA. The figure illustrates how the parity blocks are rotated among the five disks. By looking at this figure, we can derive some important performance features of RAID-5 disks:

- RAID-5 requires $N/(N-1)$ more disk space than a non-redundant disk organization. For five physical disks, 25% more disk space is required.

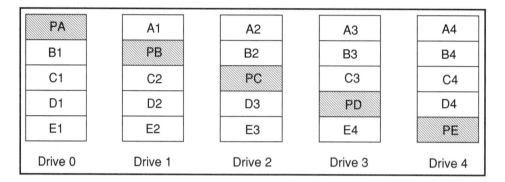

Figure 3.7. Example of RAID-5 organization with five disks.

- Large reads, i.e., reads of a full stripe group (e.g., block A in Fig. 3.7), can be done in parallel, by reading from all disks that contain the stripe group.

- Small reads, i.e., reads of one stripe unit, exhibit good performance because they only tie up one disk, therefore allowing other small reads to other disks to proceed in parallel. For example, A1, B1, C4, D3, and E4, can all be read in parallel from drives 1, 0, 4, 2, and 3, respectively.

- Large writes, i.e., writes of a full stripe group require writing into all physical disks: $N-1$ data disks and the parity disk for the stripe unit.

- Small writes, i.e., writes to one stripe unit, require that the parity block for the entire stripe unit be recomputed. The new parity block can be computed from the old parity block, the old and the new values of the stripe unit being modified. Thus, a small write to a RAID-5 requires reading the stripe unit and the parity block in parallel, computing the new parity block, and writing the new stripe unit and the new parity block in parallel.

For example, modifying stripe unit A2 in Fig. 3.7 requires reading blocks A2 and PA from drives 2 and 0, in parallel, recomputing the new value of PA, and writing the new value of blocks A2 and PA into drives 2 and 0, in parallel. Thus a write of one stripe unit requires four I/Os: two reads and two writes. This is known as the small write penalty for RAID-5 disks.

Consider the following notation for RAID-5 disk arrays.

- StripeUnit: size in bytes of a stripe unit
- StripeGroupSize: size in bytes of the stripe group assumed to be a multiple of StripeUnit
- n_r: number of stripe units read by a read request
- n_w: number of stripe units modified by a write request
- λ_{array}^r: arrival rate of read requests to the disk array
- λ_{array}^w: arrival rate of write requests to the disk array
- λ_{disk}^r: arrival rate of read requests to any of the disks in the array
- λ_{disk}^w: arrival rate of write requests to any of the disks in the array
- N: number of physical disks in the array ($N \geq 3$ for RAID-5)
- S_{array}^r: average service time at a disk array for read requests
- S_{array}^w: average service time at a disk array for write requests

Each read request presented to the disk array generates requests to n_r disks. The number of possible groups of n_r disks is

$$\binom{N}{n_r} = \frac{N!}{(N - n_r)!\, n_r!}.$$

Each disk in the array belongs to

$$\binom{N-1}{n_r - 1} = \frac{(N-1)!}{(N - n_r)!\, (n_r - 1)!}$$

groups of n_r disks. So, the fraction of read requests to the array that goes to any of the disks, assuming that requests are uniformly distributed to all disks, is given by

$$\frac{\binom{N-1}{n_r-1}}{\binom{N}{n_r}} = \frac{n_r}{N}.$$

Let $rw\ (n_w)$ be the number of stripe units read as a result of a request to write n_w stripe units. Table 3.2 shows the values of $rw\ (n_w)$ for $n_w = 1, \cdots, 4$.

Counting the reads due to read and write requests, one can write the arrival rate of disk requests at a disk as a function of the arrival rate of read and write requests to the array as,

$$\lambda^r_{\text{disk}} = \frac{n_r}{N} \times \lambda^r_{\text{array}} + \frac{rw\ (n_w)}{N} \times \lambda^w_{\text{array}}. \qquad (3.3.24)$$

Each request to write n_w stripe units in the array requires that writes be done at $n_w + 1$ disks because the parity block has to be updated. So, the arrival rate of write requests to any disk in the array is

$$\lambda^w_{\text{disk}} = \frac{n_w + 1}{N} \times \lambda^w_{\text{array}}. \qquad (3.3.25)$$

The service time at the array is equal to the maximum time spent at all disks involved in the request. The time spent at each disk of the array includes queuing plus service. So, the average service time, S^r_{array}, of read

Table 3.2. Number of Reads Generated by Writes on a RAID-5 Device

n_w	$rw\ (n_w)$	Explanation
1	2	Read one stripe unit and the parity block
2	2	Read two additional stripe units to compute the parity
3	1	Read one more stripe unit to compute the parity
4	0	No additional reads needed

requests at a disk array is

$$S^r_{\text{array}} = \max_{i=1}^{n_r}\{R^r_{\text{disk } i}\} \tag{3.3.26}$$

where $R^r_{\text{disk } i}$ is the average response time of read requests at disk i. Expressions to compute the average response time at single disks are provided in Chapter 9. The average service time, S^w_{array}, of write requests at a disk array is

$$S^w_{\text{array}} = \max_{i=1}^{rw(n_w)}\{R^r_{\text{disk } i}\} + \max_{i=1}^{n_w+1}\{R^w_{\text{disk } i}\} \tag{3.3.27}$$

where $R^w_{\text{disk } i}$ is the average response time of write requests at disk i.

Example 3.4

Consider a medical information retrieval system that stores X-ray images as low-resolution .gif files in a RAID-5 disk with five physical disks on its server. We want to compute the maximum number of X-ray images that can be retrieved from the image server per second. Files are 80 KB long on average. Each disk of the RAID-5 array has an average random seek time of 9.0 msec, a speed of 7,200 RPM, and a transfer rate of 20 MB/sec. The stripe unit size is 16 KB; therefore the stripe group size is 64 KB ($= 4 \times 16$ KB). This means that each request to read a file generates an average of 1.25 ($= 80/64$) requests to the disk array. Since this number is small, i.e., close to 1, we can consider that requests to individual disks behave as random requests. This means that the average service time, S_d, to read a stripe unit at each disk is $0.009 + 0.5 \times 60/7{,}200 + 16{,}384/20{,}000{,}000 = 0.014$ sec, according to Eq. (3.3.20). The system is read-only, that is, there are no writes ($\lambda^w_{\text{array}} = 0$). Each request to retrieve a file of average size from the image server retrieves a full stripe group plus one stripe unit. So, half of the read requests to the disk array are for stripe groups ($n_r = 4$) and half for stripe units ($n_r = 1$). Using Eq. (3.3.24), we can compute the arrival rate of read requests to each individual disk as

$$\lambda^r_{\text{disk}} = (4/5 \times \lambda^r_{\text{array}})/2 + (1/5 \times \lambda^r_{\text{array}})/2$$
$$= \lambda^r_{\text{array}}/2.$$

The utilization, U_d, of each individual disk is $\lambda_{\text{disk}}^r \times S_d = \lambda_{\text{array}}^r \times S_d/2 = 0.007 \times \lambda_{\text{array}}^r$. Since the maximum utilization of any device is 100%, the maximum arrival rate of requests to the disk array is $1/0.007 = 143$ requests/sec. Since each file read corresponds to an average of 1.25 read requests to the disk array, the maximum number of X-ray images retrieved from the image server per second is equal to $143/1.25 = 114$ images/sec.   ■

Example 3.5

An Online Transaction Processing System (OLTP) is served by a DB server that uses a RAID-5 disk with five physical disks. Ninety percent of the requests to the DB server are for short read requests of 2-KB blocks. The remaining 10% are for write requests of 16 KB blocks. Since most RAID-5 disks allow the user to tune the stripe unit size to best fit the needs of the application, we want to investigate the influence of different stripe unit sizes on the utilization of the disks of the disk array. Assume that the component disks are the same as in Ex. 3.4. Assume that read requests to the DB server arrive at a rate of 36 requests/sec and therefore write requests arrive at 4 requests/sec. Table 3.3 shows the individual disk utilizations for several values of the stripe unit size. Before we discuss the results in the table, let us understand how the values in the table were obtained.

The number of stripe units read, n_r, is equal to the size of a DB read request divided by the stripe unit size. Since one can only read multiples of a stripe unit,

$$n_r = \lceil \text{DB read request size (in KB)/StripeUnit (in KB)} \rceil$$
$$= \lceil 2/\text{StripeUnit (in KB)} \rceil.$$

So, if StripeUnit = 8 KB, $n_r = \lceil 2/8 \rceil = \lceil 0.25 \rceil = 1$. The number of stripe units accessed per write request to the disk array is equal to the database update request size divided by the stripe unit size. However, one cannot update more than four stripe units at a time in a RAID-5 disk. So

$$n_w = \min[4, \lceil 16/\text{StripeUnit (in KB)} \rceil].$$

So, when StripeUnit $= 2$ KB, $n_w = \min(4, \lceil 16/2 \rceil) = \min(4, 8) = 4$.

The value of λ^w_{array} is obtained by multiplying the arrival rate, λ^w_{DB}, of updates to the DB (4 updates/sec) by the number of stripe groups involved in each update. The number of stripe groups per database update is equal to 16 KB divided by the number of KB accessed per write request to the disk array. This number is equal to $n_w \times$ StripeUnit (in KB). Note the we need to use the ceiling function to obtain an integer number of stripe groups. So

$$\lambda^w_{\text{array}} = \lambda^w_{\text{DB}} \left\lceil \frac{16}{n_w \times \text{StripeUnit (in KB)}} \right\rceil .$$

The values for λ^r_{disk} and λ^w_{disk} are obtained using Eqs. (3.3.24) and (3.3.25). Finally, the disk utilization is computed by multiplying the total arrival rate of requests to the disk, that is, $\lambda^r_{\text{disk}} + \lambda^w_{\text{disk}}$, by the average disk service time. Note that the proper stripe unit size must be used to obtain the transfer size in each case.

Table 3.3 shows that the best stripe unit size is 16 KB because it provides the smallest utilization for each individual disk. It should be noted that as the stripe unit size increases, the total arrival rate of requests to the disks decreases or stays constant. A stripe unit size of 8 KB is worse than one of

Table 3.3. Disk Utilization vs. Stripe Unit Size for RAID-5 Example for $\lambda^r_{\text{array}} = 36$ req/sec

λ^w_{array} (req/sec)	StripeUnit (in KB)	n_r	n_w	λ^r_{disk} (req/sec)	λ^w_{disk} (req/sec)	Percent Disk Utilization
16.00	1	2	4	14.4	16.0	40.2
8.00	2	1	4	7.2	8.0	20.2
4.00	4	1	4	7.2	4.0	15.0
4.00	8	1	2	8.8	2.4	15.2
4.00	16	1	1	8.8	1.6	14.6
4.00	32	1	1	8.8	1.6	15.4
4.00	64	1	1	8.8	1.6	17.1

4 KB because even though the total arrival rate is the same for both cases, the transfer time is bigger for the 8-KB case. The total arrival rate for 16-KB stripe units is smaller than for 8-KB stripe units. The total arrival rate is the same for stripe units of 16, 32, and 64 KB. However, since the transfer time increases with the stripe unit size, the disk utilization increases.   ■

The expressions for disk arrays are summarized in Fig. 3.8 and are implemented in the worksheet `DiskArrays` in the Microsoft Excel workbook `ServTime.XLS`.

3.3.2   Service Times in Networks

A message from a client to a server has to go through several protocol layers and may have to be transmitted through one or more networks as depicted by

---

Arrival rate of read and write requests to component disks:

$$\lambda^r_{\text{disk}} = \frac{n_r}{N} \times \lambda^r_{\text{array}} + \frac{rw\,(n_w)}{N} \times \lambda^w_{\text{array}} \qquad (3.3.28)$$

$$\lambda^w_{\text{disk}} = \frac{n_w + 1}{N} \times \lambda^w_{\text{array}} \qquad (3.3.29)$$

Service times for reads and writes for the disk array:

$$S^r_{\text{array}} = \max_{i=1}^{n_r}\{R^r_{\text{disk }i}\} \qquad (3.3.30)$$

$$S^w_{\text{array}} = \max_{i=1}^{rw(n_w)}\{R^r_{\text{disk }i}\} + \max_{i=1}^{n_w+1}\{R^w_{\text{disk }i}\} \qquad (3.3.31)$$

Utilization of individual disks:

$$U_d = (\lambda^r_{\text{disk}} + \lambda^w_{\text{disk}}) \times$$
$$\left[\text{Seek}_{\text{rand}} + \frac{\text{DiskRevolutionTime}}{2} + \frac{\text{StripeUnit (in bytes)}}{10^6 \times \text{TransferRate}}\right]$$
$$(3.3.32)$$

Figure 3.8. Disk array equations.

Fig. 3.9. In this figure, a message from a client to the Web server has to cross a 10-Mbps Ethernet network, a 100-Mbps backbone FDDI network, and a 16-Mbps Token Ring LAN. Messages generated by an application have to go through a protocol stack that involves, at least, a transport layer protocol (e.g., TCP or UDP), an internet protocol (e.g., IP), and a network protocol (e.g., Ethernet or Token Ring). Protocol entities at each layer communicate with each other by exchanging PDUs composed of a header and a data area. PDUs receive different names for different protocols and usually have a maximum size for the data area. At the network layer, the maximum size of the data area is called maximum transmission unit (MTU). As indicated in Fig. 3.9, the MTU is 1,500 bytes for an Ethernet network, 4,472 bytes for a FDDI ring, and 4,444 bytes for a Token Ring LAN. So, routers have to be able to fragment datagrams as they go through networks of decreasing MTUs. Fragments are reassembled at the IP level by the destination host. For example, a 2,500-byte packet crossing from the FDDI network in Fig. 3.9 to the Ethernet has to be fragmented into two *fragments* by router 1.

Each protocol layer adds its own header and sometimes a trailer, as explained in Chapter 2. Table 3.4 lists the PDU name, maximum size of the PDU, header plus trailer overhead, and the maximum size of the data area, which is equal to the maximum size of the PDU minus the overhead,

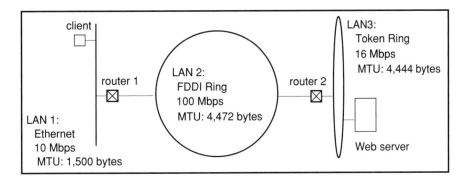

Figure 3.9. Connectivity between a client and a server.

Table 3.4. Characteristics of Various Network Protocols

Protocol	PDU Name	Max. PDU Size (bytes)	Overhead (bytes)	Max. Data Area (bytes)
TCP	Segment	(*)	20	(*)
UDP	Datagram	(*)	8	(*)
IP version 4	Datagram	65,535	20	65,515
IP version 6	Datagram	65,535	40	65,495
ATM	Cell	53	5	48
Ethernet	Frame	1,518	18	1,500
IEEE 802.3	Frame	1,518	21	1,497
IEEE 802.5 Token Ring	Frame	4,472	28	4,444
FDDI (RFC 1390)	Frame	4,500	28	4,472

(*): limited by IP datagram size.

for various important protocols [1, 3, 9].

The service time of a message at a network is the time it takes to transmit the message over the network. This time is equal to the ratio of the number of bytes needed to transmit the message—including protocol header and trailer overhead—divided by the network bandwidth. The protocol overhead depends on the protocols involved and on the fragmentation that may be needed at the network layer.

To illustrate how a message service time is computed, let us consider the following example.

Example 3.6

The client of Fig. 3.10a sends a 300-byte request to the Web server and receives a 10,000-byte reply. The interaction between the client and the server takes place over a TCP connection (see Fig. 3.10a).

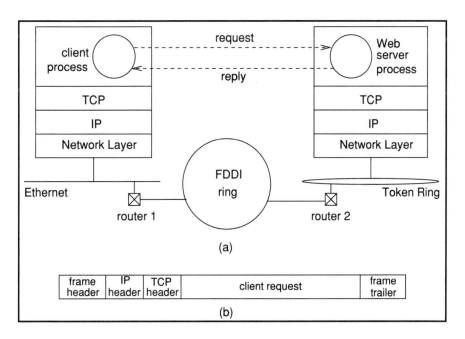

Figure 3.10. (a) Interaction between client and server over a TCP connection. (b) Frame format.

The request from the client to the server is placed into the data area of a TCP segment, which travels in the data area of an IP datagram. The IP datagram is encapsulated by an Ethernet frame, by a FDDI frame, and by a Token Ring frame as it travels in LANs 1, 2, and 3, respectively, as shown in Fig. 3.10b. So, the 300-byte request receives 20 bytes of TCP and 20 bytes of IP header, plus 18 bytes of frame overhead in LAN 1, 28 bytes of frame overhead in LAN 2, and 28 bytes of frame overhead in LAN 3. So, the 300-byte request becomes a 358 ($= 300 + 20 + 20 + 18$)-byte frame in LAN 1 and a 368 ($= 300 + 20 + 20 + 28$)-byte frame in LANs 2 and 3. The time to transmit a frame over a network is equal to the size of the frame in bits divided by the network's bandwidth in bits per second. So, the frame transmission time for the frames containing the client request at LANs 1, 2, and 3 are given by

$$\frac{358 \times 8}{10,000,000} = 0.000286 \ \text{sec}$$

$$\frac{368 \times 8}{100,000,000} = 0.00002944 \ \text{sec}$$

$$\frac{368 \times 8}{16,000,000} = 0.000184 \ \text{sec}.$$

Let us now turn our attention to the reply from the server to the client. Assume that when the TCP connection was established, the Maximum Segment Size (MSS) used is 1,460 bytes. This means that the server will have to send seven TCP segments to the client in order to send its ten-thousand-byte reply. The first six segments have 1,460 bytes of data each plus the 20-byte TCP header. The last segment has 1,240 ($= 10,000 - 6 \times 1,460$) bytes of data. Each segment receives an IP header and a frame header in each of the networks it travels from the server to the client.

We compute now the service times of the reply in LANs 1, 2, and 3. We start with LAN 3, the Token Ring LAN. Each of the first six segments generates 1,528-byte frames because each of these frames has 1,460 bytes worth of TCP data, 20 bytes of TCP header, 20 bytes of IP header, and 28 bytes of Token Ring frame overhead. The last segment generates a 1,308-byte frame. Thus, the service time of the reply in LAN 3 is

$$\frac{(6 \times 1,528 + 1,308) \times 8}{16,000,000} = 0.00524 \ \text{sec.} \tag{3.3.33}$$

The frame overhead and bandwidth in LANs 1 and 2 are different than in LAN 3. So, the service times in these LANs is different and equal to

$$\frac{[6 \times (1,460 + 20 + 20 + 18) + (1,240 + 20 + 20 + 18)] \times 8}{10,000,000} = 0.00832 \ \text{sec}$$

and

$$\frac{[6 \times (1,460 + 20 + 20 + 28) + (1,240 + 20 + 20 + 28)] \times 8}{100,000,000} = 0.000838 \ \text{sec,}$$

respectively.   ∎

Note that since the MSS is smaller than or equal to the MTU of all networks involved, there is no fragmentation. Current IP standards recommend that a source host discovers the minimum MTU along a path before choosing the initial datagram size [3]. This avoids fragmentation and reassembly altogether and speeds up packet processing time at intermediate routers and at the destination host.

In what follows, we provide general equations for the average service time of a message at a network for the case when there is no fragmentation.

Let

- N $=$ number of networks between the client and the server,

- MessageSize $=$ size, in bytes, of a message exchanged between client and server,

- MTU_n $=$ MTU, in bytes, of network n,

- TCPOvhd $=$ overhead, in bytes, of the TCP protocol,

- IPOvhd $=$ overhead, in bytes, of the IP protocol,

- MSS $=$ maximum segment size in bytes (since there is no fragmentation, we assume that $\text{MSS} \leq \min_{n=1}^{N} \text{MTU}_n - \text{TCPOvhd} - \text{IPOvhd}$),

- FrameOvhd_n $=$ overhead, in bytes, of the frames in network n,

- Overhead_n $=$ total overhead (TCP + IP + frame), in bytes, for all frames necessary to carry a message on network n,

- Bandwidth_n $=$ bandwidth, in Mbps, of network n, and

- NDatagrams_n $=$ number of IP datagrams transmitted over network n to carry a message.

In the case of no fragmentation, the sender host (client or server) generates datagrams whose size is less than or equal to the minimum MTU over all N networks. Each datagram only carries MSS bytes worth of message data. Thus, the number of datagrams needed to transmit the message over any of the N networks is

$$\text{NDatagrams} = \left\lceil \frac{\text{MessageSize}}{\text{MSS}} \right\rceil. \tag{3.3.34}$$

The total protocol overhead involved in transmitting a message over network n is given by

$$\text{Overhead}_n = \text{NDatagrams} \times (\text{TCPOvhd} + \text{IPOvhd} + \text{FrameOvhd}_n). \tag{3.3.35}$$

Finally, the service time at network n for a message is equal to the total number of bits needed to transmit the message (including overhead) divided by the bandwidth in bps. Hence,

$$\text{ServiceTime}_n = \frac{(\text{MessageSize} + \text{Overhead}_n) \times 8}{10^6 \times \text{Bandwidth}_n}. \tag{3.3.36}$$

The utilization of network n is given by the arrival rate of messages to the network multiplied by the average service time of a message in the network, as shown in Section 3.6.1.

Example 3.7

The client in Fig. 3.9 submits requests to the Web server at a rate of three requests per minute, i.e, 0.05 requests/sec. The average size of the request message is 400 bytes. Eighty percent of the replies are 8,092 bytes long and the remaining 20% are 100,000-bytes long on average. Assuming there is no fragmentation, we want to compute the average service time of requests and replies at each of the three networks, as well as the utilization of each network assuming an MSS of 1,460 bytes.

Using Eq. (3.3.34), we compute the number of datagrams for requests, short replies, and long replies, as

$$\lceil 400/1,460 \rceil = 1 \text{ for requests,}$$
$$\lceil 8{,}092/1{,}460 \rceil = 6 \text{ for short replies, and}$$
$$\lceil 100{,}000/1{,}460 \rceil = 69 \text{ for long replies.}$$

The overhead per network, computed using Eq. (3.3.35), and the average service time, computed from Eq. (3.3.36), for the request and the two types of replies are shown in Table 3.5. The average network utilization at each network is obtained by multiplying the average arrival rate of requests by the average service time for the messages involved in a request. The average service time per request at any network is equal to the average service time for the request plus the average service time for the reply. The average service time for the reply is 0.8 times the average service time for short replies plus 0.2 times the average service time for long replies. Using the values of Table 3.5, we can compute the utilization of each network. The results are shown in Table 3.6. Network utilization values are given for various values of the number of clients. The overall arrival rate of requests at each network is equal to the number of clients multiplied by the arrival rate of requests per client.   ■

The expressions for network service times and utilizations are summarized in Fig. 3.11. and are implemented in the worksheet `Networks` in the Microsoft Excel workbook `ServTime.XLS` found in the book's Web site.

Table 3.5. Network Computations for Ex. 3.7.

		Request	Short Reply	Long Reply
	NDatagrams	1	6	69
LAN 1	Overhead (bytes)	58	348	4002
	ServiceTime (msec)	0.366	6.75	83.2
	NDatagrams	1	6	69
LAN 2	Overhead (bytes)	68	408	4692
	ServiceTime (msec)	0.0374	0.680	8.38
	NDatagrams	1	6	69
LAN 3	Overhead (bytes)	68	408	4692
	ServiceTime (msec)	0.234	4.25	52.3

Table 3.6. Network Utilizations for Ex. 3.7.

	Service Times (sec)		
	LAN 1	LAN 2	LAN 3
	0.0224	0.00223	0.0141
	Percent Utilization		
No. Clients	LAN 1	LAN 2	LAN 3
40	4.5	0.4	2.8
80	9.0	0.9	5.6
120	13.4	1.4	8.5
160	17.9	1.8	11.3
200	22.4	2.3	14.1
240	26.9	2.7	16.9
280	31.4	3.2	19.7

3.3.3   Service Times at Routers

A router is a communications processor that is used to determine the route that a datagram will follow from the source host to the destination host. Incoming datagrams are queued up until the router processor is available to inspect the packet. The datagram's destination address is used by the router to determine the next best outgoing link, based on routing tables at the router [13]. The datagram is then placed at the output queue for the next link in its path to the destination (see Fig. 3.12).

The time taken by a router to process a datagram is known as *router latency* and is usually provided by router vendors in microseconds per packet. The total service time of a message at a router is then given by

$$RouterServiceTime = NDatagrams \times RouterLatency \qquad (3.3.41)$$

where NDatagrams is given by Eq. (3.3.34).

Number of datagrams generated by a message (no fragmentation):

$$\text{NDatagrams} = \left\lceil \frac{\text{MessageSize}}{\text{MSS}} \right\rceil \qquad (3.3.37)$$

Total protocol overhead of a message over network n:

$$\text{Overhead}_n = \text{NDatagrams} \times (\text{TCPOvhd} + \text{IPOvhd} + \text{FrameOvhd}_n) \qquad (3.3.38)$$

Message service time at network n:

$$\text{ServiceTime}_n = \frac{(\text{MessageSize} + \text{Overhead}_n) \times 8}{10^6 \times \text{Bandwidth}_n} \qquad (3.3.39)$$

Utilization of network n:

$$U_n = \sum_{\text{messages } j} \lambda_j \times \text{ServiceTime}_n^j, \qquad (3.3.40)$$

where λ_j is the arrival rate of messages of type j and ServiceTime_n^j is the average service time for messages of type j on network n

---

Figure 3.11. Network service time equations.

Example 3.8

Consider Ex. 3.7 and assume that routers 1 and 2 can process 400,000 packets/sec. Thus, the service time per packet at the router is 2.5 μsec ($= 1/400,000$). Therefore, the service demand at the routers for the client request, short reply, and long reply are, respectively, $1 \times 2.5 = 2.5$ μsec, $6 \times 2.5 = 15$ μsec, and $69 \times 2.5 = 172.5$ μsec. ■

3.4   Web Page Download Time

A Web page is composed of various elements, which include the HTML page and embedded objects (e.g., images). In this section we discuss the computation of Web page download time defined as the time necessary to

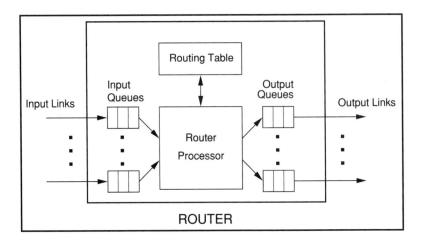

Figure 3.12. Router queues.

download from the server a Web page and all its embedded objects. We do not include here the time needed for the browser to display the page. We make the following assumptions:

- Web server time is not included in the page download time. We consider server delays later in the book.

- No redirection is involved, i.e., the first server contacted is the one that will serve the HTML page.

- We ignore DNS mapping time, i.e., the time to map a URL to an IP address.

- The RTT and effective bandwidth to the HTML page and its embedded objects are the same. This is a reasonable assumption if all embedded objects are served by the same server that provided the HTML page. The expressions discussed here can be adapted if Content Delivery Networks (CDN) [5] are used to serve the embedded images.

The following notation is used in the formulas discussed here:

- HTTPHeader: number of bytes of the HTTP response header (around 290),

- NObj: number of embedded objects in the page,

- O_i: size in bytes of the i-th ($i = 0, \cdots, \mathrm{NObj}$) object of the page; object 0 is the HTML page itself,

- RTT: Round Trip Time in seconds,

- MSS: Maximum Segment Size in bytes, and

- B: effective bandwidth between browser and Web server in bytes/sec. The effective bandwidth is a property of a given network path and may change dynamically due to variations in network and server load. One can measure the effective bandwidth or use measurements obtained in several existing networks as reference [7]. One can also calculate the effective bandwidth for a given network path by dividing the total amount of data transmitted by the total time required by the transmission. Usually, these measurements should be based on large files in order to minimize the effects of latency in the calculation of the transmission time.

We provide formulas for the Web page download time for two cases: nonpersistent HTTP and persistent HTTP (see Chapter 2). These formulas are based on the work of Kurose and Ross [9].

We start our analysis by providing some simple relationships. The total page size including the HTTP header in bytes is

$$\mathrm{PageSize} = \sum_{i=0}^{\mathrm{NObj}} (O_i + \mathrm{HTTPHeader}). \qquad (3.4.42)$$

The number of IP packets needed to transmit the page is

$$\mathrm{NPackets} = \left\lceil \frac{\mathrm{PageSize}}{\mathrm{MSS}} \right\rceil. \qquad (3.4.43)$$

In the case of non-persistent TCP connections, two RTTs are needed before the first byte of each document (HTML page or embedded object) arrives. The first RTT is for the TCP connection establishment. The HTTP request is piggybacked on the ACK of the three-way handshake and the first segment of the response completes the second RTT. So, a lower bound on the page download time, PDT_{NP}, for the non-persistent case is

$$PDT_{NP} < (NObj + 1)\,(2 \times RTT) + \frac{PageSize}{B}. \qquad (3.4.44)$$

For persistent TCP connections, only one RTT is needed for the HTML page for TCP connection establishment. The HTML page and all embedded objects require one RTT each for the object to be requested from the server. So, a lower bound on the page download time, PDT_P, for the persistent case is

$$PDT_P < RTT + (NObj + 1)\,RTT + \frac{PageSize}{B}. \qquad (3.4.45)$$

Example 3.9

A Web designer wants to do a quick evaluation of the download time of two alternative designs. The first design uses an HTML page with 15,650 bytes and ten images of about 4,200 bytes each. The second design, much more elaborate, uses the same HTML page but has twenty higher resolution images of about 20,000 bytes each. Compute a lower bound on the page download time for both persistent and non-persistent connections assuming the following parameters: RTT = 0.05 sec, MSS = 1,460 bytes, and B = 125 KB/sec.

The page size for the simpler Web page is $15,650 + 11 \times 290 + 10 \times 4,200 = 60,840$ bytes. The size of of the more elaborate page, is $15,650 + 21 \times 290 + 20 \times 20,000 = 421,740$ bytes. The minimum page download times for the persistent and non-persistent cases are:

Simpler page :

$$PDT_{NP} < 11 \times 2 \times 0.05 + 60,840/125,000 = 1.59 \text{ sec}$$
$$PDT_P < 0.05 + 11 \times 0.05 + 60,840/125,000 = 1.09 \text{ sec}$$

Elaborate Page :

$$\text{PDT}_{\text{NP}} \; < \; 21 \times 2 \times 0.05 + 421,740/125,000 = 5.47 \text{ sec}$$

$$\text{PDT}_{\text{P}} \; < \; 0.05 + 21 \times 0.05 + 421,740/125,000 = 4.47 \text{ sec.}$$

As we can see, the elaborate page takes at least between three and four times more time to download than the simpler one. If instead of assuming a high-bandwidth connection, we assumed that users only have access to a dial-up line at 56 Kbps, the minimum page download time goes up to around 9 sec for the simple design and to over one minute for the more ellaborate design. The influence of persistent versus non-persistent HTTP connections is negligible in the case of slow dial-up access since most of the page download time will be spent in transmission time.   ∎

The lower bounds on page download time do not consider the time the server is stalled because its window does not allow it to send segments. Figure 3.13 shows the equations needed to compute the page download times for persistent and non-persistent connections, taking into account the dynamic behavior of TCP window size and slow-start. Note that the page download time equations can be divided into three components: latency, transmission time, and the time the server is stalled due to the congestion window being closed. These formulas are implemented in the Microsoft Excel workbook `PageDownloadTime.XLS` found in the book's Web site.

Figure 3.14 shows the variation of page download times versus the number of embedded objects in a page assuming that the HTML page is fixed at 2,200 bytes and that the total page contents is fixed at 112,000 bytes. The number of embedded objects and therefore their size (assuming they are all the same size) varies as follows: 1, 2, 4, 8, 16, 32, and 64. The top curve is for non-persistent HTTP and the lower for persistent HTTP. The number of packets transmitted to download this page is 78. This figure illustrates that despite the fact that the page size is constant for all points in the curves, the page download time can vary significantly as a function of the number and size of objects in the page.

$$\text{PageSize} = \sum_{i=0}^{\text{NObj}} (O_i + \text{HTTPHeader}). \tag{3.4.46}$$

$$\tag{3.4.47}$$

Non-persistent equations:

$$\text{PDT}_{\text{NP}} = (\text{NObj} + 1) \times 2 \times \text{RTT} + \text{PageSize}/B +$$
$$\sum_{i=0}^{\text{NObj}} [\text{P}_i \ (\text{RTT} + \text{MSS}/B) - (2^{\text{P}_i} - 1) \ \text{MSS}/B]$$

$$\tag{3.4.48}$$

where

$$\text{P}_i = \min\{\lceil \log_2(1 + \frac{\text{RTT}}{\text{MSS}/B}) \rceil + 1, \lceil \log_2(\text{O}_i/\text{MSS} + 1) \rceil - 1\} \tag{3.4.49}$$

Persistent equations:

$$\text{PDT}_{\text{P}} = \text{RTT} + \text{PageSize}/B + (\text{NObj} + 1) \times \text{RTT} +$$
$$\text{Q} \ (\text{RTT} + \text{MSS}/B) - (2^{\text{Q}} - 1) \ \text{MSS}/B \tag{3.4.50}$$

where

$$\text{Q} = \min\{\lceil \log_2(1 + \frac{\text{RTT}}{\text{MSS}/B}) \rceil + 1,$$
$$\lceil \log_2(\text{PageSize}/\text{MSS} + 1) \rceil - 1\} \tag{3.4.51}$$

Figure 3.13. Web page download time equations.

Example 3.10

The HTML page for the home page of a Web site has 44,087 bytes and 17 embedded images. The size of these images in bytes are: 19,288, 4,243, 5,362, 3,030, 3,011, 265, 654, 586, 608, 3,913, 7,303, 6,052, 1,195, 640, 1,470, 2,538, and 2,984. You can see what the size of an image in a Web page

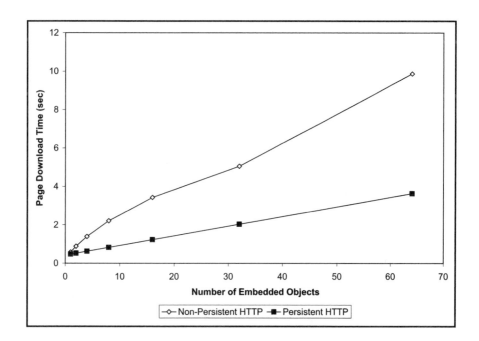

Figure 3.14. Web page download time for persistent and non-persistent HTTP.

is by right-clicking on it. Using the `PageDownloadTime.XLS` workbook, and
assuming a bandwidth of 10 Mbps, a segment size of 1,460 bytes, and an RTT
of 0.05 sec, we see that the page download time for non-persistent HTTP
is 3.02 sec and 1.27 for persistent connections. The page size including the
HTTP header overhead is 112,449 bytes. The transmission time is 0.09 sec
and the latency is 1.8 sec for non-persistent HTTP and 0.95 sec for persistent
HTTP, respectively.   ∎

We did not discuss here the effect that pipelining has on page download time. Some browsers allow more than one object to be requested simultaneously. It has been shown experimentally that browsers connected
via low-speed dial-up connections have little to gain through pipelining
while browsers connected through high-speed connections can benefit significantly [16].

Experimental studies conducted with a large number of servers analyzed
the effects of the various HTTP options: persistent versus non-persistent

and pipelined versus serial [8]. The main conclusion were: i) best end-to-end response time is obtained when servers support persistent connections with pipelining; this effect is more evident for pages with large number of embedded objects, ii) the percentage of servers supporting perfect persistent connections, i.e., a single TCP connection per page decreases with the number of embedded objects in a page, and iii) if clients have a persistent pipelined connection with a base server, retrieving a small amount of content from another server, even if that server is closer to the client than the base server, may increase the overall page download time.

3.5   Queues and Contention

As already discussed, requests to a Web site are served by several types of resources (e.g., processors, disks, networks, and routers). Each time a request visits a resource, it may need to queue for the use of the resource. Figure 3.15a shows the graphical notation used to represent a resource (a circle) and its waiting queue (striped rectangle).

The resource in the case of Fig. 3.15a could be a disk, and the striped rectangle would represent the queue of requests waiting to use the disk. In some cases, there may be multiple resources for the same queue. Consider for example a symmetric multiprocessor used to support a DB server. In this case, there is a common queue of processes waiting to be scheduled to any of the processors as shown in Fig. 3.15b.

There are situations where a resource is dedicated to a request or there is an ample number of resources, so that no queuing takes place. We call these resources *delay resources*, since they only impose a delay to the flow of a request. The graphical representation of a delay resource is a circle without the striped rectangle (the queue). Delay resources can be used to represent the time spent by a request at a client if the client does not generate another request until the previous one is completed.

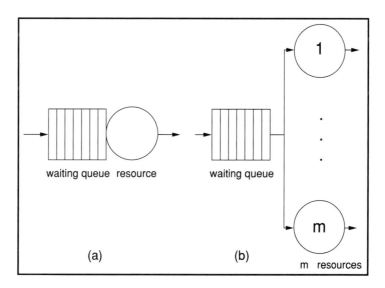

Figure 3.15. (a) Graphical notation for a resource and its queue. (b) Graphical notation for a multiresource queue.

As the load on a resource increases, more requests will be queued for the resource. However, at light loads the total queuing time may be negligible when compared with the service time at the resource. In these cases, we may want to represent the resource as a delay resource to simplify the model.

We now define the notation used throughout this book to represent performance variables for queues in Web systems. Some of the concepts presented here were already introduced, albeit more informally, in the previous sections.

We will call *queue* the waiting queue plus the resource or resources associated with the waiting queue. Let

- V_i: average number of visits to queue i by a Web request

- S_i: average service time of a Web request at resource i per visit to the resource

- W_i: average waiting time of a Web request at queue i per visit to the queue

- R_i: average response time of a Web request at queue i, defined as the sum of the average waiting time plus average service time per visit to the queue. So, $R_i = W_i + S_i$

- λ_i: average arrival rate of requests to queue i

- X_i: average throughput of queue i, defined as the average number of requests that complete from queue i per unit time. We will assume that any queue is observed during a time interval large enough that the number of arrivals and departures to the queue are almost the same. This assumption is known as *Flow Equilibrium Assumption* [4, 12] and implies that $\lambda_i = X_i$

- X_0: average system throughput, defined as the average number of requests that complete per time unit

- N_i^w: average number of requests at the waiting queue of queue i

- N_i^s: average number of requests receiving service at the any of the resources of queue i. In the case of a single resource queue (see Fig. 3.15a), N_i^s is a number between zero and one that can be interpreted as the fraction of time that the resource is busy, or in other words, the utilization of the resource

- N_i: average number of requests at queue i waiting or receiving service from any resource at queue i. So, $N_i = N_i^w + N_i^s$

Section 3.6 establishes some important and fundamental relationships between the performance variables defined above.

3.6   Some Basic Performance Results

The relationships presented in this section are very simple and general and are known as operational results [4]. To understand the validity of these results, we do not need to resort to any complex mathematical formulation.

3.6.1   Utilization Law

Let us start with a very simple relationship called *Utilization Law*. Consider first the single resource queue of Fig. 3.15a. The utilization U_i of the resource is defined as the fraction of time that the resource is busy. So, if we monitor queue i during $\mathcal{T}$ seconds and find out that the resource was busy during B_i seconds, its utilization, U_i, is $B_i/\mathcal{T}$. Assume that during the same interval $\mathcal{T}$, C_0 requests completed from the queue. This means that the average throughput from the queue is $X_i = C_0/\mathcal{T}$. Combining this relationship with the definition of utilization, we get

$$U_i = B_i/\mathcal{T} = (B_i/C_0) \times X_i = X_i \times S_i. \tag{3.6.52}$$

Note that in Eq. (3.6.52) we used the fact that the average time the resource was busy per request, i.e., the average service time S_i per request, is equal to the total time the resource was busy (B_i) divided by the number of requests that were served during the monitoring period. In equilibrium, $\lambda_i = X_i$, and we can write that,

$$U_i = X_i \times S_i = \lambda_i \times S_i. \tag{3.6.53}$$

> **Example 3.11**

A network segment transmits 1,000 packets/sec. Each packet has an average transmission time equal to 0.15 msec. What is the utilization of the LAN segment? From the Utilization Law, the utilization of the LAN segment is $1,000 \times 0.00015 = 0.15 = 15\%$. ∎

The utilization can also be interpreted as the average number of requests in the resource because there is one request using the resource during U_i percent of the time and zero requests during $(1 - U_i)$ percent of the time. For the case of a multiple resource queue, as in Fig. 3.15b, the utilization is defined as the average number of requests using any of the resources normalized by the number of resources. So, the utilization of an m-resource queue is

$$U_i = X_i \times S_i/m. \tag{3.6.54}$$

We will see in the next subsection why $X_i \times S_i$ is also the average number of requests using any resource in a multiple resource queue. Since this number is less than or equal to the number of resources m, the utilization of an m-resource queue must be less than or equal to one.

3.6.2   Forced Flow Law

By definition of the average number of visits V_i, each completing request has to pass V_i times, on average, by queue i. So, if X_0 requests complete per time unit, $V_i \times X_0$ requests will visit queue i per time unit. So, the average throughput of queue i, X_i, is $V_i \times X_0$. This simple result is known as the *Forced Flow Law* and is written as

$$X_i = V_i \times X_0. \tag{3.6.55}$$

Example 3.12

Database transactions perform an average of 4.5 I/O operations on the database server. The database server was monitored during one hour and during this period, 7,200 transactions were executed during this period. What is the average throughput of the disk? If each disk I/O takes 20 msec on average, what was the disk utilization?

The database server throughput, X_0, is $7,200/3,600 = 2$ tps. The average number of visits to the disk, V_d, is 4.5. Using the Forced Flow Law we obtain the disk throughput, X_d, as $4.5 \times 2 = 9$ tps. To compute the disk utilization U_d we use the Utilization Law and obtain $U_d = X_d \times S_d = 9 \times 0.02 = 0.18 = 18\%$.   ■

3.6.3   Service Demand Law

The service demand D_i, previously defined as $V_i \times S_i$, can easily be related to the system throughput and resource utilization by combining the Utilization and Forced Flow laws as follows:

$$D_i = V_i \times S_i = (X_i/X_0) \, (U_i/X_i) = U_i/X_0. \qquad (3.6.56)$$

Example 3.13

What is the service demand of the disk in Ex. 3.12? From the Service Demand Law we get that $D_d = U_d/X_0 = 0.18/2 = 0.09$ sec. Note that this is also equal to $V_d \times S_d = 4.5 \times 0.02$ sec. ∎

3.6.4   Little's Law

Our next result is probably one of the most important things you will learn in this book! It is quite simple and widely applicable. We present in what follows a very simple derivation of the result known as *Little's Law* (see [10] for a more formal derivation).

Consider the box in Fig. 3.16a. This box could contain anything, from a very simple device such as a disk, or something as complex as an entire intranet. For the purpose of this discussion, we assume that "customers"

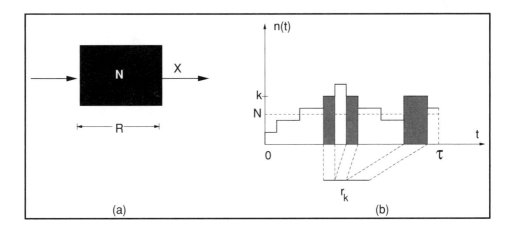

Figure 3.16. (a) Box for Little's Law. (b) Graph of n (t) vs. t.

that arrive at the black box spend an average of R sec in the black box and then leave. The average departure rate, that is, the throughput of the black box, is X customers/sec and the average number of customers in the black box is N. We want to show that $N = X \times R$. Consider Fig. 3.16b that shows a graph of the number of customers, $n(t)$, in the black box at time t. Suppose we observe the flow of customers from time zero to time $\mathcal{T}$. Then, the average number of customers during that interval is simply equal to the sum of all products of the form $k \times f_k$, where k is the number of customers in the black box and f_k is the fraction of time that k customers are in the black box. But f_k is simply $r_k/\mathcal{T}$, where r_k is the total time that there are k customers in the black box (see Fig. 3.16b). So

$$N = \sum_k k \times f_k = \sum_k k \times \frac{r_k}{\mathcal{T}}. \tag{3.6.57}$$

Let us multiply and divide the right-hand side of Eq. (3.6.57) by the number of customers, C_0, that departed from the black box in the interval $[0, \mathcal{T}]$ and rearrange the equation. Hence,

$$N = \frac{C_0}{\mathcal{T}} \times \frac{\sum_k k \times r_k}{C_0}. \tag{3.6.58}$$

Note that $C_0/\mathcal{T}$ is the throughput X. The summation in Eq. (3.6.58) is the total number of (customer $\times$ seconds) accumulated in the system. If we divide this number by the total number C_0 of customers completed, we get the average time, R, each customer spent in the black box. So,

$$N = X \times R. \tag{3.6.59}$$

Example 3.14

An NFS server was monitored during 30 minutes and the number of I/O operations performed during this period was found to be 10,800. The average number of active NFS requests was found to be three. What was the average response time per NFS request at the server?

The throughput X of the server is $10,800/1,800 = 6$ requests/sec. From Little's Law, the average response time R is N/X. So, $R = 3/6 = 0.5$ sec.■

Little's Law is quite powerful and can be applied to any black box provided it does not create nor destroys customers. If we now apply Little's Law to the waiting queue, to the set of m resources, and to the entire queue of Fig. 3.15b, we get, respectively, that

$$N_i^w = X_i \times W_i \qquad (3.6.60)$$

$$N_i^s = X_i \times S_i \qquad (3.6.61)$$

$$N_i = X_i \times R_i. \qquad (3.6.62)$$

Equation (3.6.61) gives the average number of requests at the set of m resources. So, the average number of requests per resource, also defined as the utilization, is $X_i \times S_i/m$.

Example 3.15

Consider that packets spend an average of 4 msec at router 2 of Fig. 3.9. Packets flow from LAN 2 to LAN 3 at a rate of 20,000 packets/sec. What is the average number of packets in the router in transit from from LAN 2 to LAN 3?

From Little's Law, the average number of packets in router 2 in transit from LAN 2 to LAN 3 is $20,000 \times 0.004 = 80$ packets.   ■

3.6.5   Response Time Law

Consider that the request processing system shown in box (1) of Fig. 3.17 receives requests from M sources. The sources could be client workstations submitting requests or applications running on a machine isolated from the request processing system. Let Z, called *think time*, be the average time elapsed between the reply from a request and the submission of a new request by the same source. The throughput of the request processing system is X_0

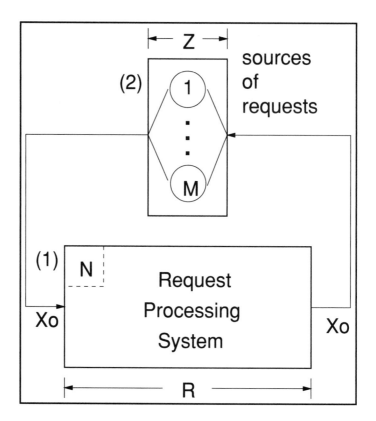

Figure 3.17. Response Time Law.

and its average response time is R. A simple relationship between R, M, X_0, and Z, called the *Response Time Law*, can be derived as follows.

Little Law's applied to the request processing system (box (1) of Fig. 3.17) tells us that

$$N = R \times X_0, \tag{3.6.63}$$

where N is the average number of requests being processed. Let us now apply Little's Law to the box that contains all M requests sources (box (2) in Fig. 3.17). Since each request spends a time Z, the think time, in this box, and the throughput of this box is also X_0, we get that

$$\overline{M} = Z \times X_0, \tag{3.6.64}$$

where $\overline{M}$ is the average number of requests in the "think state." Since a request is either being processed or is in the "think state," the total number of requests in boxes (1) and (2) has to be equal to the total number of request sources, M. So, $M = N + \overline{M}$. Then, combining Eqs. (3.6.63) and (3.6.64) we get that

$$M = N + \overline{M} = R \times X_0 + Z \times X_0 = X_0 \times (R + Z). \qquad (3.6.65)$$

Solving Eq. (3.6.65) for R we get the Response Time Law.

$$R = \frac{M}{X_0} - Z \qquad (3.6.66)$$

Example 3.16

A corporate portal provides Web services to the company's employees. On average, 500 employees are online requesting Web services from the portal. An analysis of the portal's log reveals that 6,480 requests are processed per hour on average. The average response time was measured as 5 seconds. What is the average time since a response to a reply is received and a new request is submitted by an employee?

Using the Response Time Law, we can compute the average think time Z as $M/X_0 - R$. The throughput X_0 is 1.8 ($=6,480/3,600$) requests/sec. Then, $Z = 500/1.8 - 5 = 273$ sec.   ∎

3.6.6   Summary of Basic Results

Figure 3.18 summarizes the main relationships discussed in Section 3.6. These formulas are implemented in the worksheet `BasicResults` of the Microsoft Excel workbook `ServTime.XLS` found in the book's Web site.

3.7   Performance Metrics in Web Systems

The most important metrics used to assess Web systems are *response time*, *throughput*, *availability*, and *cost*. Response time can be defined in two ways,

Utilization of an m-resource queue:

$$U_i = X_i \times S_i/m \qquad (3.6.67)$$

Forced Flow Law:

$$X_i = V_i \times X_0 \qquad (3.6.68)$$

Service Demand Law:

$$D_i = V_i \times S_i = U_i/X_0 \qquad (3.6.69)$$

Little's Law:

$$N = X \times R \qquad (3.6.70)$$

Little's Law applied to queue i:

$$N_i^w = X_i \times W_i, \quad N_i^s = X_i \times S_i, \quad N_i = X_i \times R_i \qquad (3.6.71)$$

Response Time Law

$$R = \frac{M}{X_0} - Z \qquad (3.6.72)$$

Figure 3.18. Basic performance results.

as illustrated in Fig. 3.19. At time t_0, the client finished to receive a reply from the server. Between time t_0 and time t_1, the user is deciding what to do next and prepares to submit the next request . The interval between t_0 and t_1 is called *think time*. At time t_1, the client submits a new request to the server. The reply from the server starts to arrive at the client at time t_2 and finishes arriving at time t_3. Both intervals $(t_2 - t_1)$ and $(t_3 - t_1)$ are usually called *response time*. To distinguish between the two, we will use the term *reaction time* to denote the interval $(t_2 - t_1)$. Consider the case of a user browsing the Web. The moment the user clicks on a link on the browser, a request to the server is submitted. This request may cause several

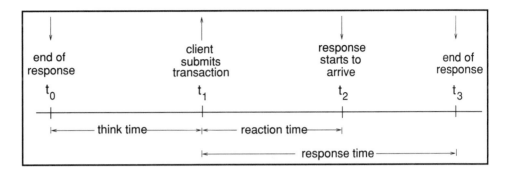

Figure 3.19. Definition of think time, reaction time, and response time.

files, including text and images, to be fetched from the server and displayed by the browser. As soon as the first document starts to be displayed by the browser, the reaction interval ends. When all text and image files are completely displayed, the response time interval ends. A detailed discussion of end-to-end response times in C/S systems is presented in [11].

While response time is a performance metric of interest to users, throughput, defined as the number of requests executed per unit time, is of more interest to system administrators. The unit used to measure throughput depends on the type of request in question. If the server is an NFS server, throughput is usually measured in NFS IOPS (NFS I/O operations per second). For Web servers, throughput is measured in HTTPops/sec (HTTP operations per second) and for database servers, throughput is measured in tps. Chapter 7 discusses other measures of throughput used in industry standard benchmarks.

Availability measures the fraction of time a Web site is operational. A site may be down due to scheduled maintenance or unscheduled and unforeseen failures. Chapter 11 discusses availability of Web sites in further detail.

Cost is usually associated with some measure of performance, i.e., response time or throughput, as a price-performance ratio. For example, the TPC-C benchmark for online transaction processing systems, from the Transaction Processing Performance Council (TPC), provides a dollar per tpm (\$/tpm) metric, which indicates how much needs to be spent per unit of throughput measured in transactions per minute (tpm). The TPC-W benchmark for e-commerce systems, also from TPC, measures dollars/WIPS, where WIPS stands for Web Interactions Per Second. The cost figure includes both hardware and software cost.

3.8   Concluding Remarks

A Web request uses various resources, including processors and disks, at the client and server, networks, and routers. The total response time of a request is decomposed into network time and Web site time. The former can be further decomposed into latency and transmission time. The Web site time can be broken down into service time and queuing time. Service time includes the time a request spends receiving service from any of the resources (e.g., performing an I/O operation at the database server). Queuing time is the time spent waiting for a resource to become available (e.g., waiting for the CPU to become available).

This chapter presented many important concepts, such as service time, service demand, utilization, throughput, and response time. Formulas were given to obtain the average service time at single disks, disk arrays, networks, and routers. The computation of page download times was also discussed. The notion of queues was introduced and formalized. Several important relationships, including the Utilization Law, Service Demand Law, Forced Flow Law, Little's Law, and the Response Time Law were presented. Chapters 8 and 9 present models that allows us to predict the queuing time of a Web request on the various resources.

Bibliography

[1] J. Blommers, *Practical Planning for Network Growth*, Prentice Hall, Upper Saddle River, New Jersey, 1996.

[2] S. C. Chapra and R. P. Canale, *Numerical Methods for Engineers: with*

Software and Programming Applications, 4th ed., McGraw-Hill, New York, New York, 2001.

[3] D. E. Comer, *Computer Networks and Internets*, Prentice Hall, Upper Saddle River, New Jersey, 1997.

[4] P. J. Denning and J. P. Buzen, "The Operational Analysis of Queuing Network Models," *Computing Surveys*, vol. 10, no. 3, pp. 225–261, Sep. 1978.

[5] S. Gadde, J. Chase, and M. Rabinovich, "Web Caching and Content Distribution: A View from the Interior," *Proc. 5th International Web Caching Workshop and Content Delivery Workshop*, Lisbon, Portugal, May 2000.

[6] C. C. Gotlieb and G. H. Macewen, "Performance of Movable-Head Disk Storage Systems," *J. ACM*, vol. 20, no. 4, pp. 604–623, Oct. 1973.

[7] J. Heidmann, K. Obraczka, and J. Touch, "Modeling the Performance of HTTP Over Several Transport Protocols," *IEEE/ACM Trans. Networking*, vol. 5, no. 5, pp. 616–630, Oct. 1997.

[8] B. Krishnamurthy and C. Willis, "Analyzing Factors that Influence End-to-End Web Performance," *Proc. WWW-9 Conf.*, Amsterdam, May 2000.

[9] J. F. Kurose and K. W. Ross, *Computer Networking: A Top-Down Approach Featuring the Internet*, Addison Wesley, Boston, Massachusetts, 2001.

[10] J. C. Little, "A Proof of the Queuing Formula $L = \lambda W$," *Operations Res.*, vol. 9, pp. 383–387, 1961.

[11] M. MacCabee, "Client/Server End-to-end Response time: Real Life Experience," *Proc. 1996 Comput. Measurement Group Conf.*, Orlando, Florida, Dec. 8–13, 1996, pp. 839–849.

[12] D. A. Menascé, V. A. F. Almeida, and L. W. Dowdy, *Capacity Planning and Performance Modeling: From Mainframes to Client-Server Systems*, Prentice Hall, Upper Saddle River, New Jersey, 1994.

[13] R. Perlman, *Interconnections: Bridges and Routers*, 2nd. ed., Addison Wesley, Reading, Massachusetts, 1999.

[14] M. Seltzer, P. Chen, and J. Ousterhout, "Disk Scheduling Revisited," *Proc. Winter 1990 USENIX Conf.*, Washington, DC, Jan. 22–26, 1990, pp. 313–323.

[15] E. Shriver, *Performance Modeling for Realistic Storage Devices*, Ph.D. dissertation, Dep. Computer Science, New York University, New York, May 1997.

[16] J. Zhi, "Web Page Design and Download Time," *J. Comp. Resource Management*, Computer Measurement Group, Spring 2001, pp. 40–55.

Chapter 4

Performance
Issues
of Web
Services

4.1   Introduction

This chapter discusses issues that affect the performance of Web services and provides an overview of performance problems in the Web. The chapter presents a first cut on how to develop simple quantitative models to analyze these problems. As indicated in Chapter 3, Web service performance problems can be mapped onto Web service processing delays and network delays, which include all delays that occur somewhere between the client browser and the Web service provider. As the Web evolves, non-traditional computing devices (e.g., PDAs and mobile phones) add to the number of components in the Internet environment, increasing its complexity. Another challenge in the management of the performance of Web services are the wireless communication networks with their relatively low bandwidth and high latency, and the lack of a permanent relationship between components.

We start out the chapter looking at the concepts associated with Web services. We then look at how users perceive performance in Web environments. After examining the sources of delay in the Web, this chapter discusses the infrastructure and components involved in the execution of Web services and analyzes their capacity and performance issues.

Servers are key components of the Internet and intranets. They deliver information upon request, in the form of text, images, sound, video, and multimedia combinations of these. Web services available on the Internet and intranets are provided by many different servers using a wide variety of computers and software. Servers receive, store, and forward information on the Internet and intranets. Several different types of servers support Web services: Web servers, transaction servers, proxy servers, cache servers, wireless gateway servers, and mirror servers. Internet and intranet clients are foremost Web browsers together with other applications such as e-mail, FTP, and Telnet. Browser software allows a desktop computer to communicate with any other client on a TCP/IP network and any server on the network with a URL. As businesses increase their reliance on Web-based systems, service performance will become very important, even critical. The more information and services a company makes available on a Web site, the more requests it gets. And the more requests a Web site gets, the higher the probability that users will wait too long for a response. And in many cases, Web users or customers will become frustrated and switch to another site.

Performance problems on the Internet are exacerbated by the unpredictable nature of requests for information and services over the Web. At times, sites are almost idle, with no visitors. Suddenly, sometimes without warning, traffic can increase a tenfold. This type of load spike, also known as "flash crowds," is faced by many Web sites. Web performance exhibits enormous variations depending on multiple factors such as the geographical location of clients and servers, day of week and time of day. There are also other characteristics that distinguish Web-based systems from traditional C/S systems. For example, the size of objects (e.g., text, graphics, video, audio) retrieved from Web sites varies from 10^3 to 10^7 bytes. Experimental studies [5, 12] have already identified some WWW workload properties and invariants. These properties are discussed in this section and a detailed characterization of a Web workload is presented in Chapter 6. Compounding the problem, there is a large population of robots, i.e., autonomous software agents that interact with Web sites and consume significant amount of system resources. The combination of these unique characteristics of the Web generates several performance problems, such as server overload and network bottlenecks, that have a tremendous impact on the end user perception of performance. Performance issues are among the top management concerns. There are basically six topics to look at when analyzing the performance of Web services: contents, server software, hardware, application, network bandwidth, and infrastructure. Performance issues associated with these topics are covered in this chapter.

4.2   From Boxes to Services

With the evolution of the Web, users to do not see boxes, nor storage subsystems, nor networks, but rather they see the *services* that these devices enable. Simply stated, a Web service is a service available via the Internet, that complete tasks, or conducts transactions [29]. As explained in Chapter 2, Web services are self-contained, modular applications that can be described, published and invoked over the Internet. A Web service could be a business process, an application or even a computational resource. Examples range from electronic payment services to content distribution services and storage services. Web services can be automatically invoked by application programs, not necessarily by a browser.

A Web service may be executed at one site or may be a result of the combination of several services executed at different sites. In any case, the performance depends on the underlying infrastructure, composed of applications, servers and networks. Many factors can contribute to degrade the performance of a Web service. Some of the most common problems are related to: insufficient bandwidth at peak times, overloaded servers, uneven server loads, delivery of dynamic content, shortage of connections between application servers and database servers, failure of third-party services and delivery of multimedia contents. Thus, it is important to understand the behavior of a Web service provider, in order to identify the correct problems that impair the performance.

In a Web service environment, scalability and performance are major issues. What happens when 10,000 users concurrently demand a single Web service? How will Web service providers guarantee quality of service? How could a service provider differentiate the quality of service offered to various customers based on service level agreements (SLA)? These are typical questions that architects and administrators of Web services have to face.

> ### Example 4.1

Portal B is offering bill payment services on the Web. A customer can pay utility bills, phone bills, and credit card bills through this service. The architecture of the service is illustrated in Fig. 4.1. The bill payment service uses services offered by other providers such as debit authorization, electronic transfer of funds, and customer authentication. These services are offered by providers Y, W, and Z, respectively. The SLA negotiated between company B and the debit authorization provider guarantees that this third party service provider is able to process 100 tps. Management of portal B wants to know its service capacity in tps.

The tasks that make up a service request can be viewed as a sequence of visits by the request to service providers [14]. Each visit to a provider corresponds to a transaction executed by the provider. On average, each bill

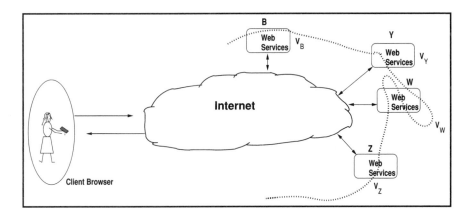

Figure 4.1. Service architecture.

payment transaction requires two visits to the credit authorization service. The average number of visits per request to a particular service provider i is called the visit ratio and denoted by V_i. The throughput of service provider i is represented by X_i. The throughput of service B, denoted by X_0, is related to X_i and V_i through the Forced Flow Law seen in Chapter 3:

$$X_i = V_i X_0.$$

For the debit authorization service, we have $X_Y = 100$ and $V_Y = 2$. Thus, portal B is capable of processing 50 service requests per second ($X_0 = 50$ requests/sec). ∎

4.2.1   Web Server Overview

A Web server is a combination of a hardware platform, operating system, server software, and contents, as illustrated in Fig. 4.2. All of these components have influence on the performance of Web servers and intranets. We present next an overview of Web server's features that affect the operational behavior of Web services.

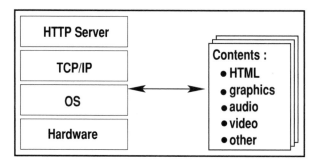

Figure 4.2. Web server elements.

4.2.1.1   HTML and XML

Most documents on the Web are written in a simple "markup language" called HTML [6]. HTML allows one to describe the structure of documents by indicating headings, emphasis, hyperlinks to other documents, and so forth. Images and other multimedia objects can be included in HTML documents. Thus, HTML allows one to integrate video, software applications, and multimedia objects on the Web. Most HTML documents consist of text and inline images. Special hyperlinks point to inline images to be inserted in a document. Inline images have a great impact on server performance. When a browser parses the HTML data received from a server, it recognizes hyperlinks associated with inline images and automatically requests the image files pointed to by the hyperlinks. Actually, an HTML document with inline images is a combination of multiple objects and generates multiple separate requests to the server. Whereas the user sees only one document, the server sees a series of separate requests for that document. To improve end user performance perception, some browsers start requesting images before the entire text has arrived at the client. In terms of system performance, it is important to understand that a single click by a user may generate a series of file requests to a server.

HTML uses tags (instructions bracketed by "<" and ">") and attributes to indicate how a Web page should be rendered by the browser. XML

(Extensible Markup Language) also uses tags and attributes to delimit pieces of data and leaves to the application the interpretation of the meaning of these tags. Thus, XML developers may define their own set of tags for a specific domain. They may even describe the type of documents to be dealt with by their applications in a Document Type Definition (DTD).

4.2.1.2   Hardware and Operating System

Server performance depends primarily on the behavior of its basic elements: the hardware platform and the operating system. From a hardware standpoint, the performance of a server is a function of the number and speed of its processors, the amount of main memory, the bandwidth and storage capacity of its disk subsystem, and the bandwidth of the NIC.

Web servers can run on top of timesharing, multiuser operating systems, such as Unix, Windows NT, Windows 2000, Linux, and others. Reliability, performance, scalability, and robustness are some of the features that one should consider when deciding on an operating system. As described in the previous chapter, the TCP/IP implementation of the operating system is also a key issue for HTTP performance.

4.2.1.3   Contents

The true value of a Web site lies in the relevance and quality of the information it contains. A Web site delivers many forms of content, such as HTML documents, images, video and audio objects. Contents size, structure, and hyperlinks affect the performance of intranets and Web services as discussed in Chapter 3. For example, a popular page with heavy graphics could have a strong impact on the network connection to the site. In other cases, highly popular contents may have to be mirrored on multiple servers to avoid traffic bottlenecks.

4.3   Perception of Performance

Responsive Web services play a critical role in determining user satisfaction. Web service performance can be analyzed from different viewpoints. For instance, a Web user's perception of performance has to do with fast response time and no connections refused. On the other hand, management's perception of performance also includes high throughput and high availability. What is common to both perceptions of performance is the need for quantitative measurements that describe the behavior of a Web service.

Web environments have some unique characteristics that distinguish them from traditional distributed systems. Some of these characteristics have a profound impact on the performance of Web services. First, the number of Web users is in the hundreds of millions and rising. The randomness associated with the way that users visit sites makes the problem of workload forecasting and capacity planning difficult. The Web is also characterized by a large diversity of components; different browsers and servers running on a variety of platforms with different capabilities. The variety of components complicates the problem of monitoring and collecting performance data. Web users may experience long, variable, and unpredictable network delays, which depend on the connection bandwidth and network congestion.

4.3.1   Metrics

Response time and throughput are the two most important performance metrics for Web systems. The rate at which HTTP requests are serviced is a common measure of the throughput of a Web service and is expressed in HTTP operations per second. Due to the large variability in the size of Web objects requested, throughput is also measured in bits per second (bps).

Other metrics have also been used to indicate Web activity. A popular one is known as *hit*, which means any connection to a Web site, including in-line requests and errors. A single page request may generate several hits depending on what types of files are included in the HTML page. Hits are no longer considered a key metric because of the difficulty in comparing their importance across sites. A series of page requests by a user at a single site is called *visit*. A series of consecutive and related requests made during a single visit is also called a *session*. One session or visit is distinguished from the next by a "time-out" period (e.g., 30 minutes). If a user does not interact with the site within the time-out period, the user's next interaction with the site starts a new session.

A number of companies offer services to measure user-perceived response times. These companies periodically poll Web services using a geographically distributed set of agents. Polling can generate an approximation of the actual response time perceived by users at different geographic locations [28]. Increased errors per second are an indication of degrading performance. An error is any failure in attempting an interaction with the server. For example, an overflow on the pending connections queue at the server is an error. This means that an attempt by a client to connect to the server will be ignored. As a consequence, the client will retransmit the connection request until there is available space in the queue or a predefined period of time expires.

In the case of streaming services, user-perceived performance is different. More important than downloading times are metrics such as *startup latency* and *jitter*. While the startup latency impacts user satisfaction, it is a non-continuous one-time factor, i.e., it is measured once per request and does not measure the quality of the whole session.

In summary, the most common measurements of Web service performance are:

- end-to-end response time

- site response time

- throughput in requests/sec

- throughput in Mbps

- errors per second

- visitors per day

- unique visitors per day

Example 4.2

The Web site of a travel agency was monitored during 30 minutes and 9,000 HTTP requests were counted. The server delivered three types of objects: HTML pages, images, and video clips. It was observed that HTML documents represented 30% of the requests with an average size of 11,200 bytes. Images accounted for 65% of the requests, and their average size was 17,200 bytes. Video clips represented only 5% of the total number of requests. The average file size of video files was 439,000 bytes. What is the server throughput?

The throughput expressed in terms of requests/sec is: $9000/(30 \times 60) = 5$ requests/sec. However, this metric does not give any insight on the network bandwidth used during the observation period, nor does it give any clue about the size of the requested objects. So, to size the network bandwidth or the NIC, we need to calculate the throughput in Kbps. To do that, we calculate the throughput for each class of objects as

$$\text{Class throughput} = \frac{\text{total requests} \times \text{class percentage} \times \text{average size}}{\text{observation period}}.$$

Thus,

$$\text{HTML throughput} = 9,000 \times 0.30 \times (11,200 \times 8)/1,800 = 131.25 \text{ Kbps}$$
$$\text{Image throughput} = 9,000 \times 0.65 \times (17,200 \times 8)/1,800 = 436.72 \text{ Kbps}$$
$$\text{Video throughput} = 9,000 \times 0.05 \times (439,000 \times 8)/1,800 = 857.42 \text{ Kbps}.$$

The total throughput is the sum of the class throughputs, given by

$$\text{Throughput} = 131.25 + 436.72 + 857.42 = 1,425.39 \text{ Kbps}.$$

To support the Web traffic, the network connection should be at least a T1 line. ∎

4.3.2   Quality of Service

The QoS of Web service providers plays a crucial role in attracting and re-taining users. For instance, frustrated customers leave e-commerce sites and do not return, causing revenue to be lost. But how does management specify the quality of Web services? To answer this question, let us take an example from a different industry. When one thinks about the QoS provided by a mobile phone company to its customers, the following indicators naturally arise:

- 24 hours/day uninterruptible service
- small call drop index
- large coverage
- short repair time in case of problems
- accurate, detailed, and understandable bill
- cost

From the customer's point-of-view, the above list of service characteris-tics tailors the image of the company. Moreover, these indicators represent the level of service provided to customers at a given cost. The expected service levels rule the relationship between customers and the company. If the call drop index increases more than usual or repair times exceed the ac-ceptable limit, customers will certainly complain about the QoS provided by the phone company. The source of the problems is immaterial to customers. They do not see the switching network, base station transmitter, and the links that constitute the telephone system. Resource utilization, blocking of handoffs, percentage of trunk blockage, and other measures of system capac-ity do not interest customers. What a customer sees is the level of service provided by the company.

In a Web environment, a user does not care about traffic jams, overloaded servers, network bandwidth, or other indicators of system activities. Besides contents and aesthetics, online users want performance, availability, and security. To an online customer, quality of service means fast, predictable user-perceived response time and 24 × 7 (24 hours/day, and 7 days/week) uptime. Any degradation in the service level of a Web site is noted in real time. QoS indicators for Web services should represent response time, availability, reliability, predictability, and cost.

A Web service is said to be available when it is "live" and serving customer requests. Availability is the metric used to represent the percentage of time a service is available. Reliability is defined as the probability that a Web service will perform in a satisfactory manner for a given period of time under specified operating and load conditions. This definition emphasizes the elements of probability, adequate performance, and operating conditions. The need for highly reliable and highly available Web services increases as more and more companies and customers rely on them to satisfy business and personal needs.

Companies must measure traffic, performance, and usage patterns in order to monitor the QoS of their Web sites. After assessing the quality of service, management has to decide if additional capacity is needed to stay ahead of customer demands. As the demand on Web services grows, the technological infrastructure of Web sites and the Internet should have enough capacity to handle changes in demand patterns smoothly. The infrastructure should be designed so that information services scale with demand. For instance, it may be very difficult to access a major newspaper or TV site after some very important breaking news due to site overload. As pointed out by Hennessy [20], "those are the most important times to be able to get the service."

Answering the following questions can help establish the SLAs of Web services.

- Is the objective of the service to provide information and applications to external customers?

- Do the mission-critical business operations depend on Web services?

- Does the company have high-end business needs for which 24 hours/day, 7 days/week uptime and high performance are critical?

If Web services are part of mission-critical applications, then one has to define adequate metrics to quantify the level of service provided to users. Usually, at peak times, metrics exhibit values completely different from average metrics. However, on the Web, customers want to have good services available at any time. This is why capacity planning for peak periods is so important.

4.4   Where Are the Delays?

One needs to pinpoint where the problems are before starting to change software, upgrade equipment, or install faster lines in hope that performance will improve. In this section, we look into the execution of a generic Web transaction to identify the major sources of delays.

The reference model for Web delay, shown in Fig. 4.3, creates a framework for analyzing performance of Web transactions. It groups the delays associated with the execution of a Web service into four categories: 1) DNS lookup phase, 2) TCP connection set-up phase, 3) server execution time, and 4) network time. The first step in the execution of a Web transaction is DNS lookup, where the browser converts the server name given in the URL into an IP address to establish the TCP connection. If the server name cannot be resolved by the local cache, a query is sent to a higher-level DNS server. It has been shown that average DNS lookup falls between 0.01 and 0.11 sec for leading e-commerce sites. The fastest sites achieve DNS lookup times of 0.001 sec [26]. The three other sources of delay are examined in detail in the following section.

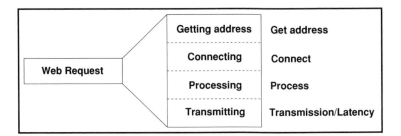

Figure 4.3. Components of the Web delay.

4.4.1   Anatomy of a Web Transaction

In distributed systems, such as the WWW, when something goes wrong, the responsibility for bad performance is so diffuse that there is no one to blame. Thus, to fix performance problems in Web-based systems, the first step is to understand what happens when one clicks on a Web page link. Let us examine the anatomy of a Web transaction, as depicted in Fig. 4.4. We break a typical transaction into the major tasks performed at the three main components of a Web system: browser, network, and server [10].

1. Browser

- The end user clicks on a hyperlink and requests a document.
- The client browser looks for the requested document in the local cache and returns the document in the case of a hit. In this case, the user response time is denoted by $R'_{\text{Browser,hit}}$.
- In the case of a miss:

  - the browser asks the DNS service to map the server hostname to an IP address,
  - the client opens a TCP connection to the server defined by the URL of the link, and
  - the client sends an HTTP request to the server.

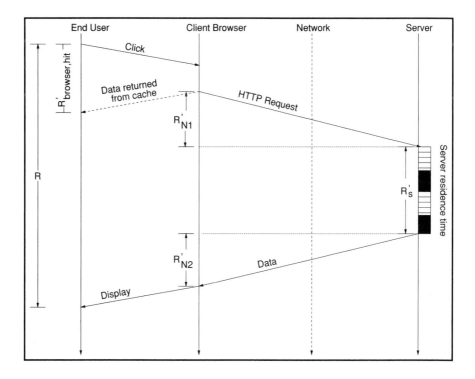

Figure 4.4. Anatomy of an HTTP transaction.

- Upon receiving the response from the server, the browser formats and displays the document and renders the associated images. The returned document is stored in the browser cache. Let $R'_{Browser,miss}$ be the total processing time of a request at the browser in the case of a browser cache miss.

2. Network

- The network imposes delays to deliver information from the client to server (R'_{N1} in Fig. 4.4) and back from the server to client (R'_{N2} in Fig. 4.4). These delays are a function of the various components on the route between the client and the server, such as modems, routers, communication links, bridges, and relays. Let $R'_{Network}$

be the total time an HTTP request spends in the network. So, $R'_{\text{Network}} = R'_{N1} + R'_{N2}$.

3. Server

- A request arrives from the client.
- The server parses the request, according to the HTTP.
- The server executes the method requested (e.g., GET, HEAD, etc.).
- In the case of a GET, the server looks up the file in its document tree by using the file system; the file may be in the cache or on the disks.
- The server reads the contents of the file from disk or from its main memory cache and writes it to the network port.
- When the file is completely sent, the server closes the connection if non-persistent HTTP is used.
- The server residence time, R'_{Server}, is the time spent in the execution of an HTTP request. It includes service time and waiting time at the various components of the server, such as processor, disk, and NIC.

When the document requested is not found in the client's cache, the response time R of a request is the sum of that request's residence time at all resources:

$$R_{\text{miss}} = R'_{\text{Browser,miss}} + R'_{\text{Network}} + R'_{\text{Server}}. \qquad (4.4.1)$$

When there is a hit and data are available at the local client cache, the response time perceived by an end user is given by

$$R_{\text{hit}} = R'_{\text{Browser,hit}}. \qquad (4.4.2)$$

Usually, $R_{hit} \ll R_{miss}$. Let us consider that the browser finds the data requested in the local cache, N_C times out of every N_T requests. The average response time, R, over N_T requests can be written as:

$$R = p_C \times R_{hit} + (1 - p_C) \times R_{miss} \qquad (4.4.3)$$

where $p_C = N_C/N_T$ denotes the fraction of time that the data is found in the local cache, i.e., the probability of a cache hit.

Example 4.3

A user wants to analyze the impact of the local cache size of its browser on the Web response time that he/she perceives. The user noted that 20% of his/her requests were serviced by the local cache, and the average response time was 400 msec. The average response time for requests serviced by remote Web sites was 3 seconds. The average time perceived by the user is given by

$$\begin{aligned} R &= p_C \times R_{hit} + (1 - p_C) \times R_{miss} \\ &= 0.20 \times 0.4 + (1 - 0.20) \times 3.0 \\ &= 2.48 \text{ sec.} \end{aligned}$$

Previous experiments had shown that tripling the size of the browser local cache would raise the hit ratio to 45%. Thus, the new average response time is

$$\begin{aligned} R &= 0.45 \times 0.4 + (1 - 0.45) \times 3.0 \\ &= 1.83 \text{ sec.} \end{aligned}$$

This example illustrates the influence of cache size on Web performance. ∎

4.4.2   Bottlenecks

As the number of clients and servers grows, end-user performance is usually constrained by the performance of some components (e.g., server, network links, and routers) along the path from the client to the server. The components that limit system performance are called *bottlenecks*. Bottleneck identification is a key step in performance analysis because it indicates the component one should upgrade first to boost performance.

Example 4.4

Consider a home user who is unhappy with access times to Internet services. She has been complaining that it takes too long to download a medium-size page, with an average size of 20 KB. To cut down response time, the user is considering upgrading her desktop system, replacing it with one whose processor is twice as fast.

Before spending the money, she wants an answer to the following question, "What will be the response time improvement if I upgrade the speed of my desktop computer?" Let us assume that the network time to bring a medium page across the network is 7.5 sec. The average server residence time is 3.6 sec, and the time spent at the desktop system by the browser (e.g., parsing, formatting, and displaying the response) is 0.3 msec. Using Eq. (4.4.1), we have that

$$R = R'_{\text{Browser,miss}} + R'_{\text{Network}} + R'_{\text{Server}} = 0.3 + 7.5 + 3.6$$
$$= 11.4 \text{ sec}.$$

The browser time is basically CPU time. Thus, after the CPU upgrade, we can expect the browser time to be reduced to half of its original value. Thus,

$$R^{\text{new}}_{\text{Browser,miss}} \approx \frac{1}{2} \times R'_{\text{Browser,miss}} = \frac{1}{2} \times 300 = 150 \text{ msec}.$$

The new average response time will be

$$R = R^{\text{new}}_{\text{Browser,miss}} + R'_{\text{Network}} + R'_{\text{Server}} = 0.15 + 7.5 + 3.6$$
$$= 11.25 \text{ sec}.$$

Therefore, if the speed of the desktop computer were doubled, the response time would decrease from 11.40 sec to 11.25 sec, a 1.3% decrease only! The model clearly indicates that the CPU upgrade does not affect the response time significantly, because the desktop system is not the first bottleneck.   ■

The basis for bottleneck analysis relies on the fact that the overall system throughput is limited by the throughput of the most restrictive component of the system. Thus, we only need to calculate the throughput of each component of the system and select the one that has the lowest throughput. In Chapter 9, we discuss a systematic way to determine bottlenecks as a function of the combination of workload and system configuration.

Example 4.5

A manufacturer of pharmaceuticals intends to use an intranet to disseminate images of molecular structures of chemicals created by the company. The intranet will be used for online training sessions. Each class has 100 employees, and we can consider that an average of 80% of the trainees are active at a time. During the class, each user performs an average of 100 operations per hour. Each operation requests five images on average. The average size of the requested images is 25,600 bytes. What is the minimum bandwidth of the network connection to the image server?

There are 80 ($= 0.8 \times 100$) active users. Each user performs operations $100/3{,}600$ operations/sec. Each operation generates $5 \times 25{,}600 \times 8$ bits of data. So, the minimum bandwidth is

$$(0.8 \times 100) \times \frac{100}{3{,}600} \times (5 \times 25{,}600 \times 8) = 2.28 \;\; \text{Mbps}. \qquad (4.4.4)$$

Therefore, if the network connection is a T1 line (1.544 Mbps), then the network will be the bottleneck of this intranet Web site.   ■

Example 4.5 illustrates some aspects involved in sizing an intranet. First, one needs to estimate the amount of information maintained on the server. This information includes the number of objects (e.g., documents, video, and audio files) and their size. A second factor is the kind of information that the server will deliver. In other words, what is the contents available in your site? Multimedia files are 100 to 10,000 times larger than HTML pages and demand larger portions of network bandwidth. The third factor is the size of the user community. When you think of a public Web site, you may not have an idea of the number of users that will visit your site. However, when you are planning a corporate portal, your community of users is somehow defined by the number of employees of your company that have access to the intranet.

4.5   Web Infrastructure

A Web infrastructure includes ISPs, servers, firewalls, proxies, caches, and networks with adequate bandwidth. From a user perspective, there is noticeable performance difference in accessing the Internet when compared with accessing a corporate network. Usually, intranets are based on LANs, whose bandwidth vary from 10 to 100 Mbps. On the other hand, Internet connections vary from 56.6 Kbps to 45 Mbps. Figure 4.5 illustrates the conceptual infrastructure of the Internet. It represents the three major delays that a Web user may incur when trying to use the Internet: last mile, ISPs, and network. "Last mile" is an imprecise term used to mean the link between an end user and the phone company switch. Most home-based users have access through phone lines that transmit at speeds of no more than 56.6 Kbps. Home users also have access to broadband Internet connections, such as DSL and cable. ISPs and companies that have presence on the Internet represent another potential bottleneck for end users. The capacity of ISPs has been improved by adding additional bandwidth and by improvements in the system architecture. Caching, load balancing and more servers have been used to improve the capacity of ISPs to handle larger amounts of traffic. The backbone is a collection of interconnected network providers. In order to work as a single global network, all of the individual networks must connect

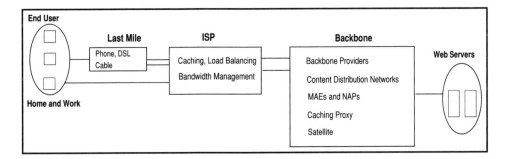

Figure 4.5. Web infrastructure.

to each other to exchange traffic. The process of exchanging traffic is called peering. There are two types of peering: public and private. The latter refers to direct connections between backbone providers to exchange traffic. Public peering occur at major interconnection points, such as Network Access Points (NAP) or Metropolitan Access Points (MAE). Delays may occur at peering points. This section discusses the role and performance implications of the main components of the Web infrastructure.

4.5.1   Basic Components

Servers and browsers are the most popular components of a Web environment. For security reasons, a firewall is also a popular component in corporate environments. A firewall is a security mechanism used to protect data, programs, and computers on a private network from the uncontrolled activities of untrusted users and software on other computers. A firewall is a combination of system software, computers, and network hardware to screen network traffic that passes through it. While a firewall is a central point of access and control, it also represents a potential performance bottleneck because of the extra overhead it imposes on traffic. Intranet servers communicate heavily with proxy servers that act as firewall for Web pages. As a consequence, users may perceive a degradation in response time when accessing Web services via a firewall.

4.5.2   Proxy, Cache, and Mirror

Proxy, cache, and mirror are techniques used for improving Web performance and security. These techniques aim at reducing the access time to
Web documents, the network bandwidth required for document transfers,
the demand on servers with very popular documents, and the security of
electronic services [13].

A proxy server is a special type of Web server. It is able to act as both a
server and a client (see Fig. 4.6). A proxy acts as an agent, representing the
server to the client and the client to the server. A proxy accepts requests from
clients and forwards them to Web servers. Once a proxy receives responses
from remote servers, it passes them to the clients. Originally, proxies were
designed to provide access to the Web for users on private networks, who
could only access the Internet through a firewall.

Proxy servers do more than merely relay HTTP responses. Web proxies
can be configured to cache relayed responses, becoming then a caching proxy.
In large distributed information systems, such as the World Wide Web,
caching is a key issue to good performance. The basic idea in caching is
simple: store the frequently retrieved documents into local files or proxies for

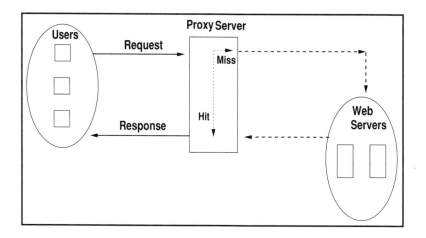

Figure 4.6. Web proxy architecture.

future use, so it will not be necessary to download the documents next time they are requested. Caching minimizes access time by bringing the data as close to its consumers as possible. Thus, caching improves access speed and cuts down on network traffic, as documents often get returned from a nearby cache, rather than from far-away servers. Caching also reduces the server load and increases availability in the Web by replicating documents among many servers. Although caching has many advantages, it also introduces its own set of problems. For example, how can one keep a document in the cache and still be sure it is up-to-date? What documents are worth caching and for how long?

Despite its limitations, caching has a widespread use in the Web. It has been used in the Web in two forms. On the client side, browsers maintain small caches of previously viewed pages on the user's local disk. The cache is useful when a user hits the "back" button or goes to a page she has already seen recently. The other form of use is in the network, where a caching proxy (also known as network caching) is located on a machine in the path from multiple clients to multiple servers, as represented by Fig. 4.6. Caching proxy servers can be located near a large community of users, such as on campus, at a corporate network, or at an ISP server. When a document is first requested by a client, the proxy acts as a Web client and requests the document from a remote server, returning the response to the client. Subsequent requests for the same document from any client serviced by the proxy are satisfied by the cached copy, optimizing the traffic flow and reducing bandwidth consumption.

Caching effectiveness [8] can be measured by three quantities. Hit ratio is defined as the number of requests satisfied by the cache over the total number of requests. Because of the high variability of Web document sizes, it is important to have a metric that includes the size of the requested document. The byte hit ratio is equal to the hit ratio weighted by the document size. The third metric, called *data transferred*, represents the total number of bytes transferred between the cache and the outside world during an observation period. Let us see how to use these new metrics.

Example 4.6

The manager of information technology of a large company decided to install a caching proxy server on the corporate intranet, which has more than 2,000 subscribers. After 6 months of use, management wanted to assess the caching effectiveness. To provide a quantitative answer for management, the system administrator wants to know the resulting bandwidth savings after the caching server is installed. With the purpose of analyzing the use of cache metrics, let us consider two cases. First, we have a cache that only holds small documents, with average size equal to 4,800 bytes. The observed hit ratio was 60%. In the second case, the cache management algorithm was specified to hold medium documents, with average size of 32,500 bytes. The hit ratio was 20%. The proxy server was monitored during one hour and 28,800 requests were handled in that interval. Comparing the efficiency of the two cache strategies by the amount of saved bandwidth, we get

$$
\begin{aligned}
\text{SavedBandwidth} &= \frac{\text{NoOfRequests} \times \text{HitRatio} \times \text{AverageSize}}{\text{MeasurementInterval}} \\
\text{SavedBandwidth } \#1 &= \frac{28,800 \times 0.6 \times 4,800 \times 8}{3,600} = 184 \text{ Kbps} \\
\text{SavedBandwidth } \#2 &= \frac{28,800 \times 0.2 \times 32,500 \times 8}{3,600} = 416 \text{ Kbps}.
\end{aligned}
$$

The above results shows that, in this example, the strategy of holding larger documents saves more bandwidth.   ■

Another information distribution strategy involves mirroring the site at several locations, which implies replicating the site contents at other servers. This requires regular distribution of contents updates, typically done over the Internet itself, and the use of a domain name server to direct browsers to secondary sites when the primary one is busy. For example, if a company has a large base of customers that are geographically dispersed, it is difficult to service them well from a distance. The company would be better off with mirrored remotely hosted sites run by local ISPs around the world. The purpose of site mirroring is to increase availability and to balance server load, improving the quality of service.

Example 4.7

A large manufacturing company, with offices and plants across the globe, created an employee portal that receives a large number of daily visitors. Recently, IT people started receiving mails from employees located in Europe saying: "we like the contents and services provided by the site, but it is way too slow." Site management considered getting more links to increase bandwidth, but was not sure about the effectiveness of this costly alternative. To speed up content delivery to users in Europe, the company decided to analyze the cost-benefit of installing a caching server in the Paris area. What is the estimated bandwidth savings derived from the new cache to be located in Europe? Currently, the average bandwidth consumed is 35 Mbps.

An analysis of the server logs revealed that 40% of the load originates from Europe and that 42% of the total traffic could be served from caching systems. Thus, $0.42 \times 35 = 14.7$ Mbps could be cacheable. The cache hit ratio is estimated at 38%. Then, CacheableTraffic $\times$ CacheHitRatio ($14.7 \times 0.38 = 5.6$ Mbps) is equal to the traffic that could be served from caching systems. But, the traffic from Europe represents 40% of the total traffic. Thus, we could estimate that $0.40 \times 5.6 = 2.24$ Mbps would be served by the cache in Europe. This represents 6.4% of the current bandwidth usage. In addition to the bandwidth savings, the cache would bring a perceived-response time improvement for a large group of users and lighter loads on the origin servers of the company. ∎

4.5.3   Content Delivery Networks

Content Delivery Networks (CDN) cache or replicate content as needed to meet the demand from clients over the Web [18]. CDNs offer their service to content providers, which are their customers. Web clients that access customer's contents are called clients. CDNs can be viewed as coordinated caching systems that are implemented through proprietary networks and data centers.

Basically, CDNs operate through a DNS-redirecting mechanism. When a client requests an URL, the browser generates a DNS request for the IP address corresponding to the domain name in the URL. Since a CDN works as an agent of the customer, i.e., the content provider, it controls the DNS service for the domain name used by the customer. The CDN modifies DNS requests with the IP address of the selected server, rather than the IP address of the original server of the customer. In order to select a server in the CDN network, a routing function is used. This function takes into consideration information such as: client location, identification of the requested content, load of the CDN network and servers, and proximity of the CDN servers to the client. In summary, the routing function tries to obtain the best location from which the requested content will be served.

The architecture of a CDN service should meet the following requirements: scalability, high availability, manageability, and performance. In [22], an experiment was set to measure the performance of two commercial CDNs. The results show the delay experienced when a small GIF file was fetched from various servers of the CDNs. For example, the best server responded in 128 msec or less 95% of the time. The worst server responded within 2 seconds about 70% of the time.

4.5.4   The WAP Infrastructure

The Wireless Application Protocol (WAP) is an open standard designed by the WAP Forum [30], which includes an architecture and set of protocols to allow all sorts of wireless devices, such as Web-enabled phones, PDAs, and pagers, to access Web services at regular Web sites. The basic architecture of WAP is shown in Fig. 4.7. Mobile clients interact with a WAP gateway through a wireless network. The communication between the WAP

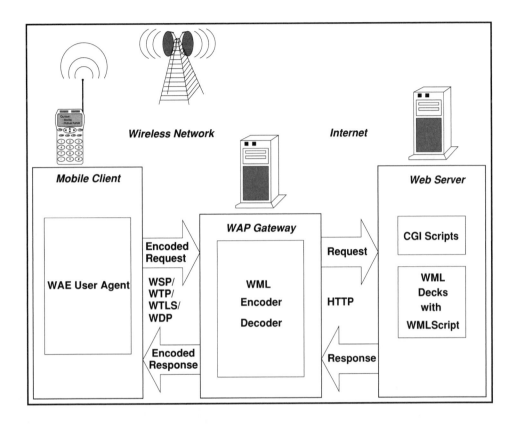

Figure 4.7. WAP architecture.

client and the gateway follows a set of protocols, to be discussed in what follows, aimed at mitigating the various constraints of the wireless environment. These constraints are related to the computing capacity, main memory size, power, and screen size constraints of most wireless devices, and to the high latency, low transmission rates, and low reliability of wireless networks.

Documents for wireless devices are written in a markup language, which adheres to XML, called Wireless Markup Language (WML). A scripting language, called WMLScript, can also be used to build more powerful WAP applications. WML and WMLScript do not assume that a QWERTY keyboard or a mouse are available for user input [31]. WML documents, unlike HTML ones, are structured as a set of units of user-interaction called *cards*.

A set of WML cards is called a *deck*. Users navigate between cards of one or more WML documents. WML decks with WMLSripts are stored in regular Web servers on the Internet and are retrieved by the WAP gateway using HTTP (see Fig. 4.7). The response from the Web server is binary encoded by the WAP gateway for compactness and sent to the wireless device using a lightweight set of protocols to minimize bandwidth requirements.

The layering of the WAP protocols is illustrated in Fig. 4.8 [31]. WAP works with many different wireless bearers at the network layer. The Wireless Datagram Protocol (WDP) provides a connectionless unreliable service. If an IP network is used, WDP is replaced by UDP. WAP provides authentication, data integrity, and privacy through the use of public-key and symmetric key encryption in its Wireless Transport Layer Security (WTLS), which is very similar to common Internet protocols such as Secure Sockets Layer (SSL) and Transport Layer Security (TLS) [15]. WTLS provides end-to-end security between the mobile device and the WAP gateway. Data is decrypted at the gateway, which makes it vulnerable to attack if the gateway is hacked. Several optimizations over TLS are done to cope with the limitations of the wireless environment. Examples include long-lived secure sessions and more efficient handshake procedures for secure session establishment.

Since the transport layer of the WAP stack is an unreliable datagram service, there is a need to provide a reliable data transfer mechanism based on the request/reply C/S paradigm. This is accomplished by the Wireless Transaction Protocol (WTP). WTP is a connectionless protocol that supports packet retransmission, flow control, and packet assembly/re-assembly. WTP conserves wireless bandwidth and reduces the number of RTTs by piggybacking ACK packets on data and data request packets. The wireless environment may require connectivity to be suspended to save network resources or to save battery power. To that end, the Wireless Session Protocol (WSP) allows for sessions to be efficiently suspended and resumed. The

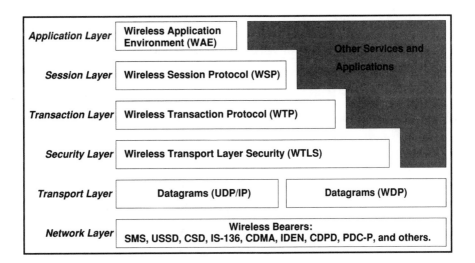

Figure 4.8. WAP protocol stack.

Wireless Application Environment (WAE) includes WML, WMLScript, a Wireless Telephony Architecture Application Programming Interface (API), and a microbrowser.

The WAP gateway can potentially become a bottleneck since all requests for WAP documents have to be mediated by it. Caching is used at the WAP gateway to reduce the need to access remote servers for popular contents.

4.6   Server Architectures

4.6.1   Web Server

Web server software, also known as HTTP server or HTTP daemon, are programs that control the flow of incoming and outgoing data on a computer connected to an intranet or to the Internet. Basically, a Web server software listens for HTTP requests coming from clients over the network. The server program establishes the requested connection between itself and the client, sends the requested file, and returns to its listening mode. In order to speed up the service, HTTP servers handle more than one request at a time.

Usually, this is done in three different ways [33]: by forking a copy of the HTTP process for each request, by multithreading the HTTP program, or by spreading the requests among a pool of running processes.

Most Web sites do more than serve static HTML pages. A Web site becomes alive with dynamic content pages, that offer interactivity and special effects. Dynamic Web pages can be obtained by using either client-side or server-side programs. Java, ActiveX, and Dynamic HTML [21] are client-side Web technologies. With any of these technologies, special effects can be added to Web documents without relying on server-side programs. Client-side programs help reduce response times, avoiding networking and server delays. For example, Dynamic HTML achieves interactivity and special effects by automatically reformatting and redisplaying the current Web document to show modifications. These modifications can be done without the need to reload the document or to load a new document from a remote Web server. In many commercial Web sites, Common Gateway Interface (CGI) programs, including search engines, represent the major part of the workload and are handled by application servers.

Conventional Web servers typically run in user space making a context switch necessary for every disk I/O operation performed by the Web server [4]. To speed up delivery of Web content, some vendors have recently started to integrate a significant portion of the functionality of a Web server with the kernel of the operating system. These Web servers are called *in-kernel* Web servers. They typically handle all requests for static pages as well as requests for simple, often used dynamically generated content that poses little security risks [23]. Requests that cannot be handled directly by the in-kernel Web server (e.g., complex and slow dynamically generated requests or HTTP requests with unrecognized header information) are passed to a user-space Web server. In-kernel Web servers also maintain an in-kernel cache of recently served Web documents.

In-kernel Web servers have less flexibility and more security vulnerabilities than user-space Web servers due to the lack of address space isolation.

But, a combination of in-kernel and user-space Web servers can provide considerable performance gains with the needed flexibility and security.

4.6.2   Application Server

An *application server* is the software that handles all application operations between browser-based customers and a company's back-end databases. For example, an application server in a travel agency Web site translates search requests for flights into scripts that access the back-end database. In general, an application server receives client requests, executes the business logic and interacts with transaction servers and/or database servers. Usually, application servers exhibit the following characteristics: i) host and process application logic written in different programming languages (e.g., Java, C or C++), ii) manage high volumes of transactions with back-end databases, and iii) are compliant with all existing Web standards, including HTTP, HTML, XML, CGI, Netscape[TM] Server API (NSAPI), Microsoft Internet Server[TM] API (ISAPI), and Java, and iv) work with most of the popular Web servers, browsers, and databases.

Application servers can be implemented in many different ways: as CGI scripts, as FastCGIs, server-applications, and server-side scripts. Figure 4.9a shows the CGI approach. In this case, a new process is created to handle each request (part 2 of Fig. 4.9). When the request is complete, the process is killed (part 3 of Fig. 4.9). The advantage of this approach is that there is complete isolation between the application and the Web server.

The drawbacks of using CGI scripts are (1) the overhead involved in creating and killing processes and (2) the fact that it is harder to build persistent applications, i.e., applications that require several interactions with the user. Since the process that implements the CGI script is killed after each interaction, other methods (e.g., cookies) have to be used to pass the application state from one interaction to the next within the same transaction.

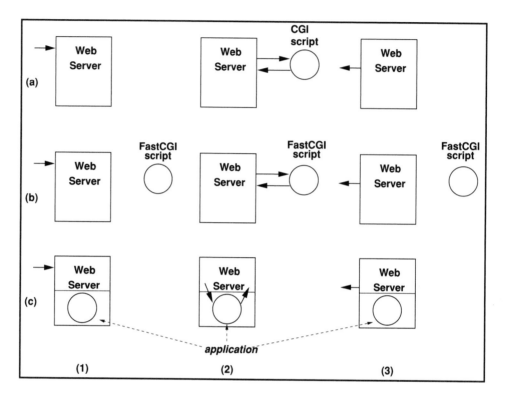

Figure 4.9. (a) CGI scripts (b) FastCGI Scripts (c) Applications within the server context.

To overcome some of the problems of CGI scripts, one can use FastCGI scripts (see Fig. 4.9b), which are persistent processes that communicate with the Web server either through TCP or local interprocess communication mechanisms. FastCGIs provide isolation and persistency as well as better performance than CGI scripts. As shown in Fig. 4.9b, the FastCGI script is present throughout the entire life of one or more requests. The communication between the Web server and FastCGI scripts usually involves system calls.

The third approach, shown in Fig. 4.9c, is of applications that run within the context of the Web server. The application is invoked through APIs provided by the Web server software. Examples include ISAPI for Microsoft's IIS^{TM} Web server and NSAPI for Netscape's Web server.

Example 4.8

The Web site of a virtual bookstore receives an average of twenty visitors per second. Most of the visitors only browse the books available. However, one out of ten visitors places an order for books. Each order transaction generates a CGI script, which is executed on the Web server. The Webmaster wants to know the CPU load generated by the CGI scripts.

We model the CGI load as follows. The average CGI CPU service demand ($D_{\text{cpu}}^{\text{cgi}}$) is 120 msec. Using the Service Demand Law discussed in Chapter 3, we have that

$$U_{\text{cpu}}^{\text{cgi}} = X_{\text{cgi}} \times D_{\text{cpu}} \qquad (4.6.5)$$

where X_{cgi} is the server throughput measured in CGI scripts executed per second and $U_{\text{cpu}}^{\text{cgi}}$ is the utilization of the CPU due to the execution of CGI scripts. The CGI arrival rate (λ_{cgi}) can be calculated as

$$\begin{aligned} \lambda_{\text{cgi}} &= \text{VisitRate} \times \text{PercentageOfOrders} \\ &= 20 \times (1/10) \\ &= 2 \text{ CGI/sec.} \end{aligned}$$

Assuming flow equilibrium, we have that $X_{\text{cgi}} = \lambda_{\text{cgi}}$. Thus,

$$U_{\text{cpu}}^{\text{cgi}} = 2 \times 0.12 = 0.24 = 24\%. \qquad (4.6.6)$$

From the above results, we see that 24% of the CPU utilization is spent processing CGI scripts. Also, it is important to know that CGI scripts and HTTP requests are competing for the same resources: CPU, memory, and disk. Several other questions could be investigated using this simple performance model. For example, some software companies claim that Java servlets (i.e., server-side applets) have performance advantage over CGI. Performance improvement comes from the fact that servlets run in the same process as the Web server, whereas CGI programs must start a new process for every request. Let us then assume that Java servlet transactions are 30%

less resource-intensive than CGI applications. What would be the impact of replacing the CGI script by servlets? The CPU service demand for servlets is $D_{\text{cpu}}^{s} = D_{\text{cpu}}^{\text{cgi}} \times 0.7 = 120 \times 0.7 = 84$ msec. Using Eq. (4.6.5) again, we have that the CPU utilization due to servlets would be 16.8%. Notice the CPU utilization was reduced from 24% to 16.8%. ■

The last approach is the use of server-side scripting. The page, retrieved from the document tree, contains HTML code and a script written in a scripting language. Microsoft's Active Server Pages (ASP)^{TM} allow the use of Javascript and VBscript with ActiveX controls in a page and Netscape's Livewire allow the use of server-side Javascript. A script interpreter at the Web server interprets the script and dynamically generates an HTML page that is returned to the browser (see Fig. 4.10).

4.6.3   Transaction and Database Server

A transaction processing (TP) monitor [19] comprises three major functions: (1) an application programming interface, (2) a set of program development tools, and (3) a system to monitor and control the execution of transaction programs. A TP monitor provides a seamless environment that integrates all the components needed to execute transactions: the database system, operating system, and communication system. The growth of transactions over

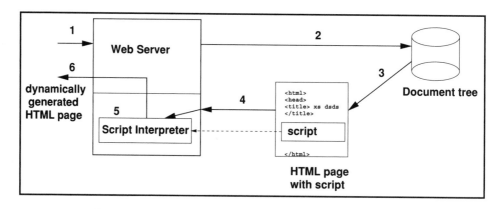

Figure 4.10. Server-Side Scripting.

the Internet makes TP monitors a key component to guarantee performance, reliability, and scalability.

Like a TP monitor, a database server executes and manages transaction processing applications [7]. It can be a relational database system that supports stored procedures that can issue SQL requests to the database, as shown in Fig. 4.11. Database management systems run on medium, high-powered servers or mainframes to provide shared access to data [17]. The data management servers ensure that the data is consistent throughout the distributed environment through the use of features such as data locking, consistency, and replication.

Mainframes and legacy systems are important components of information technology infrastructures. Very large volumes of business data exists on mainframes. Legacy systems with databases (e.g., IBM's IMS and DB2, Oracle, and Sybase) and on-line transaction applications have been used by companies for decades and represent a valuable asset for them. Web-based applications make use of legacy data that reside on back-end mainframes. There exists a number of techniques used to help the integration of Web and mainframes, such as wrapping and back-end scripting. Wrapping refers to hiding the existing legacy applications behind an abstraction layer, representing a programming model [25]. Usually, *wrapping* is done at the business

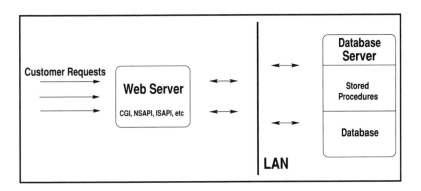

Figure 4.11. Database Server.

logic layer, as discussed in Section 4.6.5. With *back-end scripting*, servers at the application layer take a request for information and decompose it into a script of multiple, discrete tasks, each appropriate for an individual legacy application. Due to their reliability and capacity, mainframes have been also used as Web servers.

4.6.4   Streaming Server

At first, audio and video on the Web was primarily a download-and-play technology. One had to first download an entire media file before it could be played. But media files are usually very large and take a long time to download, which makes this process unattractive to users. The other mode for transmitting stored video over the Internet is the streaming mode [32]. Streaming media files begin playing almost immediately, while the data is being sent, without having to wait for the whole file to download.

Upon the client's request, a streaming server retrieves video and audio data and deliver them over the network. To achieve transmission efficiency, video and audio are compressed. Coding and compression standards, such as Moving Picture Experts Group (MPEG) and MPEG Audio Layer 3 (MP3), specify how a digitized media is represented. Streaming media servers use specialized protocols to improve the streaming experience [11, 32]. Protocols for streaming media provide network addressing, transport and session control. Different transport protocols can be used to deliver streaming media, such as multicast, UDP and TCP. Multicast is used to deliver a single stream to multiple users, such as in Video-on-demand (VoD) and live scheduled programs. Transport protocols are grouped into two layers. UDP and TCP are lower-layer protocols. Real Time Protocol (RTP) and Real Data Transport (RDT) are upper layer transport protocols. Streaming traffic is usually made of a control part and a data part, each of them with a different protocol. Session control protocols define the messages and procedures to control the delivery of multimedia data. They allow users to interactively control the media stream. Examples of such protocols include Real Time Streaming Protocol (RTSP), Microsoft Media Server Protocol (MMS)^{TM} and Session Initiation Protocol (SIP). Streaming objects are usually grouped into media presentations using languages, such as Synchronized Multimedia Integration Language (SMIL) and Advanced Stream Redirector (ASX).

There are several potential performance issues associated with a streaming server given the typically large size of multimedia objects and the strict QoS requirements. This leads to typical questions such as "How many streams can a server send out at once?" "What are the bandwidth constraints to deliver 400 high-speed clips simultaneously?"

Example 4.9

A company is planning to offer multimedia online training from its corporate portal. Basically, an employee retrieves a lecture presentation, composed of video, audio, and slides. Each lecture lasts thirty minutes on average. The capacity planning analyst was asked to answer the following question: "What is the number of streaming servers needed to serve the lecture presentation during the busiest period of the day, from 4:00 to 5:00 p.m.?" The estimated number of employees that will request lecture presentations at this hour is 400. Also, according to product specifications, one multimedia server can stream presentations to 150 viewers simultaneously.

In order to answer the question, one has to estimate the average number N of simultaneous viewers during the peak period. Using Little's Law, we have that

$$N = \lambda \, R$$

where R represents the duration of the presentation and λ the arrival rate of presentation requests, given as

$$\lambda = \frac{\text{NumberOfPresentationRequests}}{\text{TimeInterval}} = 400/60 \text{ viewers/min.}$$

Then, $N = 30$ min $\times$ 400/60 viewers/min $= 200$. Thus, the number of streaming servers needed is $\lceil 200/150 \rceil = 2$.   ■

4.6.5   Multi-Tier Architecture

Web-based applications are usually framed in a three-tier architecture. The first layer, also called the presentation layer, embodies the user interface with the Web services. Via interpretation of HTML or XML by a browser, Web users enter data, edit data, and receive information. New interfaces are available for accessing Web services from mobile devices, such as cellular phones and PDAs. The business logic layer, also known as application layer, encapsulates a collection of rules to implement the application logic. The separation of the business logic from the presentation layer and the data services gives a new level of autonomy to applications and make them more robust [24]. In the case of Web-based applications, this middle tier also contains components displayed by the browser, such as Java applets and ActiveX controls. The data service layer consists of persistent data that are managed by mechanisms that guarantee reliability, stability, and availability.

The architecture of Web service providers consists of multiple layers of servers, or tiers, each handling a particular set of functions as depicted in Fig. 4.12. The three-tier Web site is composed of a load balancer, Web servers in layer 1, application servers in layer 2, and data servers in layer 3. These various elements are interconnected through various LANs, routers, and firewalls. A firewall is a special type of router that can be configured to block flow of packets from one network to another. This is important to shield important internal servers from external attacks. The flow of a request in Fig. 4.12 would be as follows. Requests arrive at the load balancer through the router that connects the site to the Internet. The load balancer then decides which Web server should receive the request. The next section discusses load balancing in more detail. A firewall (firewall 1) isolates LAN 1 from the internal part of the site. The zone which is accessible to the outside world is called the demilitarized zone (DMZ). Firewall 1 ensures that any of the Web servers in Layer 1 only receive requests from the load balancer and not from the outside world. Web servers send requests to application servers. Firewall 2 ensures that application servers are only contacted by

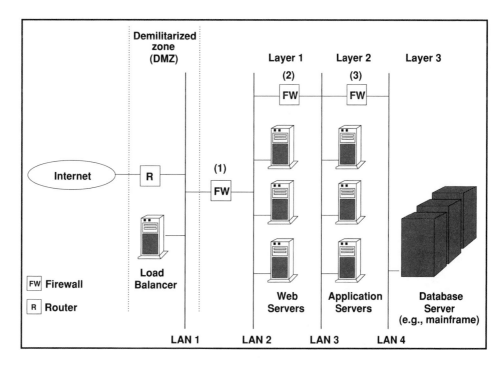

Figure 4.12. Typical multi-tier Web site architecture.

Web servers. Finally, if an application server needs data from a database server, the request has to flow through firewall 3.

Example 4.10

Consider a multi-tier Web site as shown in Fig. 4.12. The application layer was designed to support up to 400 processes simultaneously. Each application process receives a client request, executes the application logic, and interacts with the database servers. After monitoring the application layer, the support analyst got the following information: an application process executes for 150 msec between database requests. The database server handles 550 requests/sec. During the peak period, the application layer will have 400 processes running. The application architect wants to know the average database response time during the peak hour. He also wants to understand the impact on the database servers if the application server boxes are replaced by new ones twice as fast as the current servers.

In order to answer these questions, we use a simple performance model, depicted in Fig. 4.13. Each of the N application processes is characterized by Z, the time between receiving a reply from the database server and submitting a new database request. The database layer performance is represented by its throughput X, measured in requests/sec. Using the Response Time Law from Chapter 3, we have:

$$R = N/X - Z.$$

Plugging the numerical values into the above expression, we obtain the average database response time: $R = 400/550 - 0.15 = 577$ msec $= 0.577$ sec. The application processing time is basically CPU time. Thus, after the CPU upgrade, we can expect the application time to be reduced to half of its original value. Thus,

$$Z_{\text{new}} \approx \frac{1}{2} \times Z_{\text{original}} = 150/2 = 75 \text{ msec.}$$

Using the new value of Z, we obtain the new database response time: $R_{\text{new}} = 400/550 - 0.075 = 652$ msec $= 0.652$ sec.

There are two comments worth mentioning in this example. First, the performance model revealed that an improvement in the application layer may not lead to improving the overall response time, because it would increase the load on the database servers. Second, this example shows that some parameters of performance models may have different meanings, according to the problem being modeled. Usually, Z is used to represent user think time. In this example, application processes are modeled as *users* of the database servers and Z represents the time an application process is executing, before requesting service from the database. ∎

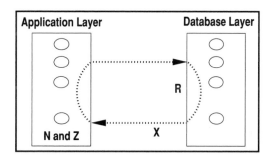

Figure 4.13. Performance model of a multi-tier site.

4.6.6   Dynamic Load Balancing

With many sites getting tens of millions of requests per day, traffic to a Web server may get too high for one machine to handle effectively. The obvious solution to servicing a heavy traffic load is adding more servers or buying a bigger servers. Which one is better is a matter of specific cost-performance analysis.

A locally distributed Web system, also called *Web cluster*, is an architecture consisting of multiple Web servers and mechanisms to route incoming requests among several server nodes in a user-transparent way, as shown in Fig 4.14. A Web cluster is a tightly coupled architecture at a single location, addressed by one URL and a single virtual IP address. A key component of a cluster is the Web switch, which acts as a dispatcher, mapping the virtual IP address to an actual server address. A Web cluster offers the address of the Web switch as the single address of the Web cluster. Client requests are addressed to the switch which, by its turn, dispatches them to a server, according to some scheduling rules (i.e., server load characteristics). In order to make the dispatching transparent to users, the selected server returns the response with the switch address, instead of its own address. Two alternative architectures exist for Web clusters [9]. A *Level 4* Web switch, also called content information blind, works at the TCP/IP layer, assigning packets pertaining to the same connection to a server node. This type of switch determines the server when the client establishes the TCP connec-

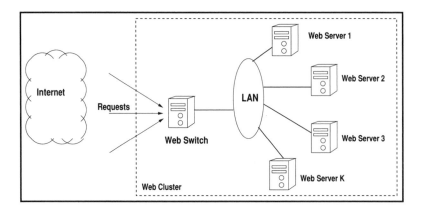

Figure 4.14. Web cluster architecture.

tion, i.e., before the HTTP request is sent to the server. A *Level 7* switch, called content information aware, operates at the application level. The Web switch establishes a connection with the client and examines the HTTP request content to schedule it to a specific server node. Server selection could be based on the content or service requested.

Other scheduling techniques can be used to split the traffic across servers, such as DNS-based, and server-based. The latter is a technique where the server responds to a client with a new server address to which the client will resubmit the request. The redirected URL could be on the same computer as the main server or any one of several back-end mirror computers. The main server redirects the traffic to back-end Web servers, according to some load balancing mechanism. Although the technique is transparent to users, it adds an extra connection to the original request and may, in some cases, increase the user response time and network traffic on the Internet or intranets. The DNS service translates a domain name to an IP address. Thus, when the DNS service receives a mapping request, it selects the IP address of one of the servers in the cluster. In round-robin DNS systems, the Web server name is associated with a list of IP addresses. Each IP address on the list maps to a different server, and each server contains a mirrored version of the Web site or access to a common file system. Whenever a request is received, the Web server name is translated to the next IP address on the list. By translating Web-server names to IP addresses in a round-robin fashion, this technique tries to balance the load among the servers.

4.7   Networks

Web services lure users with new content (e.g., graphics, audio, video), which alter the distribution patterns of network traffic and may cause performance problems. This section discusses network characteristics that affect Web performance.

4.7.1   Bandwidth and Latency

Latency and bandwidth are two fundamental characteristics of networks that can be analyzed quantitatively. Latency indicates the time needed for a bit (or a small packet) to travel across the network, from the client to the server or vice versa. To understand the concept of latency one needs to understand the route a packet takes. Between the client and the server, numerous activities take place, involving communication lines, hubs, bridges, gateways, repeaters, routers, and modems. Network latency is similar to disk seek and rotational latency time: the minimum time between requesting a piece of data and starting to obtain it. A propagation delay is the time an electrical signal takes to travel along a wire or fiber. For example, for a typical LAN within a building, the propagation delay is around 1 msec. Switching delays are introduced by network devices, such as hubs, routers, and modems. In the case of shared media (e.g., Ethernet or Token Ring), packets may experience access delays. Finally, in packet-switched networks (e.g., the Internet), there are queuing delays in the routers. Latency increases with the propagation delay, i.e., with physical distance and with the number of hops connecting the client to the server. Considering that everything else is equal, it is always faster to download Web objects that are "close," rather than far away.

Bandwidth measures the rate at which data can be sent through the network and is usually expressed in bps. For instance, a 56-Kbps line takes 14.3 sec to transfer a 100,000-byte document, whereas the same document can be downloaded in 0.5 sec using a T1 line. Table 4.1 shows the bandwidth for different types of network connections.

Example 4.11

As multimedia application use grows in a network, it becomes necessary to keep track of the link utilization over time, in order to estimate future

Table 4.1. Network Capacity

Network connection	Theoretical bandwidth
56 Kbps modem	56 Kbps
ISDN 1 BRI (phone line)	64 Kbps
ISDN 2 BRI (phone line)	128 Kbps
DS1/T1 (dedicated connection)	1.5 Mbps
DS3/T3 (dedicated connection)	45 Mbps
Ethernet	10 Mbps
Fast Ethernet	100 Mbps
OC-3	155 Mbps
OC-12	622 Mbps
HDTV	1.2 Gbps
OC-48	2.5 Gbps
OC-192	10 Gbps
OC-48 with WDM*	40 Gbps
OC-768	40 Gbps
OC-3072	160 Gbps
OC-768 with DWDM**	6.4 Tbps

(*) WDM: Wave Division Multiplexing; (**) DWDM: Dense Wave Division Multiplexing

needs of additional bandwidth. Consider a streaming service that offers training videos for the employees of a company. Each training session corresponds to a 15-minute video at 300 Kbps. Management wants to know what is the impact on the network, if the session length is increased to 25 minutes. The service supports thirty-five simultaneous sessions, on average. This translates into an average bandwidth need of $35 \times 300,000 = 10.5$ Mbps.

The average number of simultaneous sessions N is given by Little's Law as $N = 35 = \lambda \times R = \lambda \times 15$, where λ is the arrival rate in requests/min. Assuming the same arrival rate of requests, the new average number of simultaneous sessions, N_{new}, will be

$$N_{\text{new}} = \lambda\, 25 = (\lambda\, 15)\, (25/15) = 35\, (25/15) = 58.3. \qquad (4.7.7)$$

Thus, the streaming service will need $58.3 \times 300,000 = 17.5$ Mbps of bandwidth. ∎

Example 4.12

What is the impact of contents on performance and infrastructure requirements? Consider Example 4.5 and assume that the training department is considering the use of video clips for improving online training. The average file size of the training videos is 950 MB (using 1 MB = 10^6 bytes). Classes have 100 students and 80% of them are active at any time. During class, each user requests an average of two video clips per hour. Thus, the minimum network bandwidth needed to support video is $(0.80 \times 100) \times 2 \times (8 \times 950)/\, 3,600 = 337.7$ Mbps. Looking at Table 4.1, we see that a 622 ATM network is required to support the new video objects. ∎

4.7.2   Traffic

Web traffic exhibits a bursty behavior [12]. "Bursty" refers to the fact that data are transmitted randomly, with peak rates exceeding the average rates by factors of eight to ten [27]. It has been also observed that Web traffic is bursty across several time scales. This phenomenon can be statistically described using the notion of self-similarity, which implies the existence of a correlational structure in traffic bursts that is retained over several time scales. A practical consequence of the bursty behavior is that Web site management has difficulty sizing server capacity and bandwidth to support the demand created by load spikes. As a result, users perceive a service performance degradation during periods of burstiness. Spikes can be characterized by the *peak traffic ratio*, defined as the ratio of peak site load to average site traffic. For example, in the Web site of a cable TV network, the peak traffic ratio was 6.5 during a major boxing fight. The consequences of traffic and load spikes are tremendous on the performance of Web sites.

In some special cases, adequate capacity can be planned beforehand to handle traffic spikes. For example, during big events, such as presidential elections, the Olympic Games, the soccer World Cup, new product releases, and the Academy Awards, a large number of people try to visit key Web sites. Servers and Internet connections get overwhelmed with the onslaught of traffic and spikes up to eight times the average values can be observed. Scalability issues in Web services arise largely due to the gap between average and peak workload demands [16]. In an attempt to smooth load spikes, management of Web sites use content delivery services to take some load off their Web servers.

Example 4.13

The manager of the Web site of a large electronic publishing company is planning the capacity of the network connection. Looking at the access logs in retrospect, management noted that the site throughput was one million HTTP operations per day. The average document requested was 10,000 bytes. What will be the network bandwidth needed by this site considering peak traffic?

The required bandwidth (in Kbps) is given by

HTTP operations/sec × average size of requested documents

In our case, we have

$$1 \text{ million HTTP operations/day} = 41,667 \text{ operations/hour}$$
$$= 11.6 \text{ HTTP operations/sec.}$$

The needed bandwidth is then,

$$11.6 \text{ HTTP operations/sec} \times (10,000 \times 8) \text{ bits/operation} = 928 \text{ Kbps.}$$

Let us assume that protocol overhead is 20%. Thus, the actual bandwidth required is $928 \times 1.2 = 1,114$ Kbps = 1.114 Mbps and can be provided by a T1 link. However, management decided to plan for peak load. The hourly peak traffic ratio observed in the past was five for some big news events. Therefore, the required bandwidth at peak hours is also five times bigger and equal to $5 \times 1.114 = 5.57$ Mbps. Considering that each T1 line is 1.5 Mbps, the site will need four T1 connections to support the load spikes. ∎

4.7.3   Special Features

Several studies [3, 5, 12] have shown characteristics that distinguish the behavior of Web environments from traditional distributed systems. The following aspects have a profound impact on the performance of Web services. The Web exhibits extreme variability in workload characteristics. For example, it has been verified in the analysis of some popular Web sites [5] that there are very few documents whose size is less than 100 bytes. Most documents are in the range of 10^2 to 10^5 bytes, while a few files are larger than 100 KB. The distribution of file sizes in the Web, including files stored on servers and files requested by clients and transmitted over the network, exhibits a heavy tail, which declines with some power law (e.g., Pareto distribution). In practical terms, heavy-tailed distributions indicate that very large values (e.g., huge file sizes) are possible with non-negligible probability. Another consequence of heavy tails is that values have a large variability, which reduces the statistical meaning of measurements. The impact of heavy tailed distributions on workload characterization will be quantitatively illustrated in Chapter 6.

A first cut approximation to represent the heavy-tail characteristic of Web workloads in performance models is to use the notion of class. Each class comprises requests that are similar with respect to the size of the document they retrieve. Thus, similar requests in terms of resource usage would be grouped together. This reduces the variability of the measurements and improves the statistical meaning of measurements. For example, one could group the HTTP requests of a workload into three classes: small pages with documents up to 5 KB, medium pages varying from 5 to 50 KB, and large pages for file sizes greater than 50 KB.

The highly uneven popularity of various Web documents is a well-documented phenomenon [5, 12]. In several studies, it was shown that Zipf's Law [34] can be used to characterize access frequency to Web documents. Zipf's Law was originally applied to the relationship between a word's popularity in terms of rank and its frequency of use. It states that if one ranks the popularity of words in a given text (denoted by ρ) by their frequency of use (denoted by f), then

$$f \sim \frac{1}{\rho}. \qquad (4.7.8)$$

The data shown in [3] indicates that Zipf's Law applies quite strongly to documents serviced by Web servers. This means that the nth most popular document is exactly twice as likely to be accessed as the $2n$th most popular document. Results about document popularity can be used to characterize WWW workload and analyze document dissemination strategies, such as caching and mirroring.

Example 4.14

Company X is being created to sell online maps to its customers. The company expects to receive 500,000 visitors per day at the end of its first year of operation. The company anticipates that three maps will be the best sellers. The most popular document will be the site map (i.e., the home page), that shows customers how to walk through the electronic store. New York and Paris are expected to be the second and third most popular documents, respectively. The capacity planning analyst wants to estimate the number of accesses to the most popular maps, in order to place them in different disk storage units, so that I/O time is optimized. According to Eq. (4.7.8) (Zipf's Law), the frequency of accesses to a document is proportional to its popularity. Considering that the home page is hit by each customer that visits the store, we can say that its frequency of access equals one ($f = 1$). In other words, the home page is expected to receive 500,000 hits/day. The frequencies of access to the New York and Paris maps are $f_{NY} \sim 1/2 = 0.5$ and $f_{Paris} \sim 1/3 = 0.333$, according to Zipf's Law. Thus, the number of visits per day to these maps are

$$NumberOfVisits \sim f \times TotalVisits$$
$$NumberOfVisitsToNY \sim f_{NY} \times TotalVisits \sim \frac{1}{2} \times 500,000 = 250,000$$
$$NumberOfVisitsToParis \sim f_{Paris} \times TotalVisits \sim \frac{1}{3} \times 500,000 = 166,667.$$

∎

Another special feature of the Web is the presence of robots in the Internet. A large population of robots, i.e., crawlers, shopbots, pricebots, and autonomous software agents interact with Web sites. For example, search engines demand exhaustive crawling work to maintain and update their indices to the very large collection of documents on the Web. Robots consume significant amount of system resources [1, 2]. They increase server loads as they dig out the information in the Web and require bandwidth for shipping information.

4.8   Concluding Remarks

Performance analysis of intranets and Web servers is unique in many senses. First, the number of WWW clients is in the hundreds of millions and rising. The randomness associated with the way users visit pages and request Web services makes the problem of workload forecasting and capacity planning difficult.

This chapter introduced several important concepts that help users, administrators, and managers understand performance problems in Web environments. Performance metrics and quality of service were discussed. New concepts such as heavy-tailed characteristics, traffic spikes, and network caching and their impact on Web performance were analyzed.

The next chapter presents a capacity planning methodology, where the main steps are: understanding the environment, workload characterization, workload model validation and calibration, performance model development, performance model validation and calibration, performance prediction, cost model development, cost prediction, and cost/performance analysis. Workload characterization and performance models that take into consideration the unique aspects of Web environments are presented in subsequent chapters.

Bibliography

[1] V. A. F. Almeida, D. A. Menascé, R. Riedi, F. P. Ribeiro, R. Fonseca, and W. Meira Jr., "Analyzing Web Robots and their Impact on Caching," *Proc. Sixth Workshop on Web Caching and Content Distribution*, Boston, Massachusetts, June 20-22, 2001.

[2] V. A. F. Almeida, D. A. Menascé, R. Riedi, F. P. Ribeiro, R. Fonseca, and W. Meira Jr., "Characterizing and Modeling Robot Workload on E-Business Sites," *Proc. 2001 ACM SIGMETRICS Conf. Measurement Comput. Syst.*, ACM, Boston, Massachusetts, June 16-20, 2001.

[3] V. A. F. Almeida, A. Bestavros, M. Crovella, and A. Oliveira, "Characterizing Reference Locality in the WWW," *Fourth Int. Conf. Parallel Distrib. Inform. Syst. (PDIS)*, IEEE Comput. Soc., Dec. 1996, Miami Beach, Florida, pp. 92–103.

[4] J. M. Almeida, V. A. F. Almeida, and D. Yates, "Measuring the Behavior of a World-Wide Web Server," *Proc. Seventh Conf. High Perform. Networking (HPN)*, IFIP, Apr. 1997, pp. 57–72.

[5] M. Arlitt and C. Williamson, "Web Server Workload Characterization: the Search for Invariants," *Proc. 1996 ACM SIGMETRICS Conf. Measurement Comput. Syst.*, Philadelphia, Pennsylvania, May 1996, pp. 126–137.

[6] T. Berners-Lee, R. Cailliau, H. Nielsen, and A. Pecret, "The World Wide Web," *Comm. ACM*, vol. 37, no. 8, pp. 76–82, Aug. 1994.

[7] P. Bernstein and E. Newcomer, *Principles of Transaction Processing*, Morgan Kaufmann, San Francisco, California, 1996.

[8] A. Bestavros, R. Carter, M. Crovella, C. Cunha, A. Heddaya, and S. Mirdad, "Application-Level Document Caching in the Internet," *Proc. Int. Workshop Distrib. Networked Environments*, Canada, 1995.

[9] J. Cardellini, E. Casalicchio, and M. Colajanni, "A Performance Study of Distributed Architectures for the Quality of Web Services," *Proc. IEEE Hawaii International Conf. on System Sciences*, Jan. 2001.

[10] J. Charzinski, "HTTP/TCP Connection and Flow Characteristics," *Performance Evaluation*, vol. 42, no. 2-3, Sep. 2000, pp. 149–162.

[11] M. Chesire, A. Wolman, G. Voelker, and A. Levy, "Measurement and Analysis of a Streaming-Media Workload," *Proc. 3rd USENIX Symposium on Internet Technologies and Systems*, San Francisco, California, March 2001.

[12] M. Crovella and A. Bestavros, "Self-Similarity in World-Wide Web Traffic: Evidence and Possible Causes," *Proc. 1996 ACM SIGMETRICS Conf. Measurement of Comput. Syst.*, Philadelphia, Pennsylvania, May 1996, pp. 160–169.

[13] B. D. Davison, "A Web Caching Primer," *IEEE Internet Computing*, July/Aug. 2001, pp. 38–45.

[14] P. J. Denning, "Queueing Networks of Computers," *American Scientist*, May 1991.

[15] T. Dierks and C. Allen, "The TLS Protocol," Version 1.0, *The Internet Engineering Task Force (IETF)*, RFC 2246, January 1999.

[16] F. Douglis and M. F. Kaashoek, "Scalable Internet Services," *IEEE Internet Computing*, July-Aug. 2001, pp. 36–37.

[17] W. Eckerson, "Three-Tier Client/Server Architecture: Achieving Scalability, Performance, and Efficiency in Client Server Applications," *Open Information Systems*, vol. 10, no. 1, Jan. 1995.

[18] S. Gadde, J. Chase, and M. Rabinovich, "Web Caching and Content Distribution: A View from the Interior," *Proc. 5th International Web Caching Workshop and Content Delivery Workshop*, Lisbon, Portugal, May 2000.

[19] J. Gray and A. Reuter, *Transaction Processing: Concepts and Techniques*, Morgan Kaufmann, San Francisco, California, 1992.

[20] J. Hennessy, "The Future of Systems Research," *Computer*, Aug. 1999.

[21] S. Isaacs, *Inside Dynamic HTML*, Microsoft Press, Seattle, Washington, 1997.

[22] K. Johnson, J. Carr, M. Day, and M. F. Kaashoek, "The Measured Performance of Content Distribution Networks," *Proc. 5th International Web Caching Workshop and Content Delivery Workshop*, Lisbon, Portugal, May 2000.

[23] C. Lever, M. A. Eriksen, and S. P. Molloy, "An Analysis of the TUX Web Server," CITI Tech. Rep. 00-8, Center for Information Technology Integration, University of Michigan, Ann Arbor, Michigan, November 16, 2000.

[24] S. Lewandowski, "Frameworks for Component-Based Client/Server Computing," *ACM Computing Surveys*, vol. 30, no. 1, 1998.

[25] P. Lloyd and G. Galambos, "Technical Reference Architecture," *IBM Systems J.*, vol. 38, no. 1, 1999.

[26] C. Loosley, R. Gimarc, and A. Spellmann, "e-commerce Response Time: a Reference Model," *Proc. CMG 2000 International Conference*, Orlando, Florida, Dec. 2000.

[27] J. Mogul, "Network Behavior of a Busy Web Server and its Clients," *Res. Rep. 95/5*, DEC Western Research, Palo Alto, California, 1995.

[28] R. Rajamony and M. Elnozahy, "Measuring Client-Perceived Response Times on the WWW," *Proc. 3rd USENIX Symposium on Internet Technologies and Systems*, USENIX, San Francisco, California, March 2001.

[29] A. Sahai and V. Machiraju, "Enabling of the Ubiquitous e-services Vision on the Internet," Hewlett-Packard Laboratories, HPL-2001-5, January 2001.

[30] WAP Forum, www.wapforum.org.

[31] WAP Forum, "Wireless Application Protocol," White Paper, June 2000.

[32] D. Wu, Y. Hou, W. Zhu, Y. Zhang, and J. Peha, "Streaming Video Over the Internet: Approaches and Directions," *IEEE Trans. on Circuits and Systems for Video Technology*, vol. 11, no. 1, Feb. 2001.

[33] N. Yeager and R. McCrath, *Web Server Technology*, Morgan Kaufmann, San Francisco, California, 1996.

[34] G. Zipf, *Human Behavior and the Principle of Least Effort*, Addison Wesley, Cambridge, Massachusetts, 1949.

Chapter 5

Planning the Capacity of Web Services

5.1 Introduction

Planning the capacity of Web services requires that a series of steps be followed in a systematic way. This chapter starts by providing a clear definition of what adequate capacity means. It then presents a methodology that leads the capacity planner, in a step-by-step fashion, through the process of determining the most cost-effective system configuration and networking topology. Investment and personnel plans follow as a consequence. The main steps of the methodology are: understanding the environment, workload characterization, workload model validation and calibration, performance model development, performance model validation and calibration, workload forecasting, performance prediction, cost model development, cost prediction, and cost/performance analysis.

The methodology presented here requires the use of three models: a workload model, a performance model, and a cost model. The workload model captures the resource demands and workload intensity characteristics of the load brought to the system by the different types of transactions and requests. The performance model is used to predict response times, utilizations, and throughputs, as a function of the system description and workload parameters. The cost model accounts for software, hardware, telecommunications, third-party services, and personnel expenditures.

This chapter draws in part on material presented in [8] and Chapter 2 of [9]. Various steps of the methodology are discussed in further detail in subsequent chapters.

5.2   Adequate Capacity

Many organizations invest millions of dollars to build Web sites and many millions more to maintain and keep the environment up-to-date. In most cases, the overall capacity of the environment is unknown and capacity planning and procurement is done without a defined methodology. To complicate matters, the notion of what is *adequate capacity* is not well understood in many cases.

Figure 5.1 illustrates the three main elements used to define adequate capacity of a Web-based system:

- *Service-level agreements (SLA)*. Adequate capacity has to be provided so that acceptable or desirable values for performance metrics such as response time, availability, or throughput can be achieved. Examples of SLAs include: "server-side response time for search requests should not exceed 2 seconds," "end-to-end response time to download the site home page should not exceed 8 seconds for dial-up customers with a

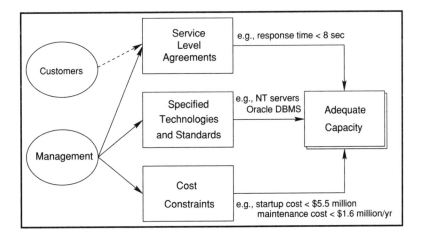

Figure 5.1. Definition of adequate capacity.

56 Kbps modem," "the ad banner third-party service should be able to deliver at least two billion ad banners per day," "the Web site must be available 99.99% of the time," and "at least 95% of the requests should have a server-side response time of 1 second."

The values of SLAs are specific to each organization and are determined by management. Even when SLAs are not formally defined, it is possible to determine a level of acceptable service when users start to complain or even abandon the site due to poor performance. SLAs are crucial to Internet data center outsourcing arrangements. In these cases, SLAs defining site uptime, network uptime, and response time, are needed to manage the various technical environments and to negotiate contracts bewteen providers and customers.

- *Specified technologies and standards.* Providing adequate capacity to meet SLAs can be done in many ways by using different types of servers, operating systems, Web servers, database management systems, and various types of networking topologies. For example, it is possible for a Windows NT-based Web server running on an Intel platform to deliver the same performance as a Unix-based Web server running on a Reduced Instruction Set Computer (RISC) machine. Some organizations may prefer to use one versus the other for reasons that are not directly related to performance (e.g., ease of system administration, familiarity with the system, cost, and number and quality of possible vendors for the underlying hardware). Users and management may also choose to adopt certain standards for network protocols and middleware, further restricting the set of solutions that can be used. Thus, users and management may specify that adequate capacity be provided with certain specified technologies and standards for reasons other than performance.

- *Cost constraints*. The problem of providing adequate capacity to meet SLAs would be somewhat easier to solve if one had unlimited monetary resources. Budget constraints are determined by management and limit the space of possible solutions. Expenditures for Web sites include startup costs and operating costs for a defined period. Startup costs include purchase expenditures for hardware and software, development costs, installation costs, personnel costs, and initial training. Operating costs include hardware and software maintenance, telecommunications costs, third-party services, and personnel costs required to maintain the system. Amortization costs may be included if they are incurred.

We say then that *a Web system has adequate capacity if the SLAs are continuously met for a specified technology and standards, and if the services are provided within cost constraints.*

5.3 A Capacity Planning Methodology for Web Services

Figure 5.2 illustrates the various steps of a capacity planning methodology for Web-based systems. While these steps are essentially the same as those for capacity planning studies of other types of environments (e.g., mainframe-

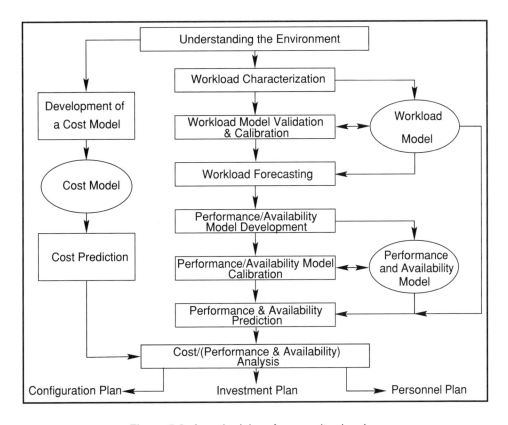

Figure 5.2. A methodology for capacity planning.

based systems), their implementation in a Web-based environment is much more complex due to the heterogeneity of hardware and software components involved and due to the nature of the workload as discussed in Chapter 4.

The capacity planning methodology relies on three models: a workload model, a performance and availability model, and a cost model. The *workload model* captures the resource demands and workload intensity characteristics for each component of a global workload within a representative time frame. The *performance and availability model* is used to predict the performance and availability of a Web-based system as a function of the system description and workload parameters. The outputs of the performance model include response times, throughputs, availability, utilizations of various system resources, and queue lengths. These performance metrics are matched against the SLAs to determine if the capacity of the system is adequate. The *cost model* accounts for software, hardware, telecommunications, and support expenditures.

The following sections discuss in greater detail what is involved in each of the steps of the methodology depicted in Fig. 5.2. We will use Fig. 5.3 to illustrate all phases of the capacity planning methodology. The picture shows the intranet of a corporation with fours LANs connected by a an FDDI ring. The company's Web site is on LAN 3, which is connected to the Internet.

5.4   Understanding the Environment

The initial phase of the methodology consists of learning what kind of hardware (clients and servers), software (operating systems, middleware, and applications), network connectivity, and network protocols, are present in

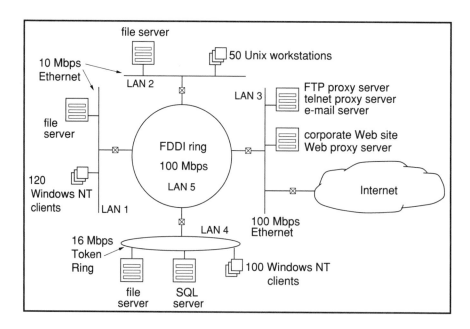

Figure 5.3. Example system for capacity planning methodology.

the environment. It also involves the identification of peak usage periods, management structures, and SLAs. This information is gathered by various means including user group meetings, audits, questionnaires, help desk records, planning documents, interviews, and other information-gathering techniques [8].

Table 5.1 summarizes the main elements that must be cataloged and understood before the remaining steps of the methodology can be taken.

An example of the outcome of the Understanding the Environment step for the example of Fig. 5.3 would be as follows.

Clients and servers. The network consists of four LAN segments (two 10-Mbps Ethernets, one 100-Mbps Ethernet, and a 16-Mbps Token Ring) interconnected through a 100-Mbps FDDI ring. LAN 3 is connected to the Internet. LAN 1 has a Windows NT-based file server and 120 Windows NT-based PC clients. LAN 2 has a RISC-type Unix file server and 50 Unix workstations. This file server uses a storage box with several RAID-5 disks and a capacity of 512 GB. LAN 3 runs an FTP proxy server, a Telnet proxy server, and the e-mail server in one box and the corporate Web server and a Web proxy server in another box. Both are Windows NT server-based, dual processor, high-end PCs. Finally, LAN 4 has a Windows NT-based file server and an SQL database server running Oracle to support enterprise-wide, mission-critical applications. This LAN has 100 Windows NT-based clients. BEA's Tuxedo [2] is used as a Transaction Processing (TP) Monitor to support C/S transaction management.

Applications. Workstations on LAN 2 are mostly used by the R&D department to run computer simulations of molecular biology experiments. Researchers store all their files in the file server in LAN 2. They use e-mail, ftp, telnet, and Web services on LAN 3. Clients on LANs 1 and 4 split their time between running office automation applications (e.g., word processing, spreadsheet, and presentation preparation packages) and running various types of C/S transactions to support sales, marketing, personnel, accounting, and financial activities. These C/S transactions use a TP monitor and the

Table 5.1. Elements in Understanding the Environment

Element	Description
Client platform	Quantity and type
Server platform	Quantity, type, configuration, and function
Middleware	Type (e.g., TP monitors)
DBMS	Type
Services/applications	Main Web services and applications supported
Network connectivity	Network connectivity diagram showing all LANs, WANs, network technologies, routers, servers, load balancers, firewalls, and number of clients per LAN segment
Network protocols	List of protocols used
Usage patterns	Peak periods (e.g., hour of day, day of week, week of month, month of year)
Service-level agreements	Existing SLAs per Web service. When formal SLAs are absent, industry standards can be used
LAN management and support	LAN management support structure, size, expertise, and responsiveness to users
Procurement procedures	Elements of the procurement process, justification mechanisms for acquisitions, expenditure limits, authorization mechanisms, and duration of the procurement cycle

SQL server on LAN 4. All users in LANs 1 and 4 read e-mail and access the Web through the proxy server on LAN 3. The company's employees use Web-based training courses hosted at the Web server on LAN 3. Most of the accesses to these online lectures come from clients on LANs 1 and 4.

Network connectivity and protocols. The network connectivity map is given in Fig. 5.3. The Internet and transport protocols used throughout all networks is TCP/IP.

Usage patterns. The C/S applications have a peak period usage between 10:00 a.m. and noon and then from 2:00 to 4:00 p.m. on weekdays. The Web-based training application has a peak period of 4:00 to 5:00 p.m. on weekdays. Most other Web services, especially the ones also available to outside customers, have equally distributed between 9:00 a.m. and 9:00 p.m. due to customers in different time zones of the US.

SLAs. The established SLAs are: i) 2 second response time on average for trivial C/S transactions against the SQL server, ii) the response time cannot exceed 5 seconds for 95% of complex C/S transactions, iii) the mail server must be able to process at least 60,000 e-mail messages during an 8-hour period and messages should take no more than 30 seconds to be processed, iv) access to the company's home page, product description pages, and Web-based search on company info and products should take no more than 4 seconds for external customers coming from 56.6-Kbps dial-up lines and no more than 1.5 seconds on average for customers coming from the company's Intranet, v) 99.9% availability for all Web services.

LAN management and support. There are 4 system administrators for the entire environment. One of the them acts as Webmaster for the Web site. There is also a Database Administrator (DBA) for the database managed by the SQL server and three network specialists that constantly monitor the performance on the FDDI ring and are responsible for overall network management functions such as assigning IP addresses to subnetworks, managing routing tables, maintaining network security, and verifying the connection to the Internet.

Procurement procedures. As an example, procurement decisions could be made by an Information Technology Committee, headed by the Chief Information Officer (CIO) of the company and composed of four user representatives and four system administrators (one from each LAN), which reviews applications for hardware and software upgrades. Decisions are made based on budget availability and on how well the requests are justified. The average procurement cycle for items over $5,000 is 2 months. Expenditures below $5,000 can be made using a much faster procedure that takes two business days on average.

5.5 Workload Characterization

Workload characterization is the process of precisely describing the systems's global workload in terms of its main components. Each workload component is further decomposed into basic components, as indicated in Fig. 5.4, which also shows specific examples of workload components and basic components. The basic components are then characterized by workload intensity (e.g., transaction arrival rates) and service demand parameters at each resource.

The parameters for a basic component are seldom directly obtained from measurements. In most cases, they must be derived from other parameters that are measured directly. Table 5.2 shows an example of three basic components, along with examples of parameters that can be measured for each. The last column indicates the type of basic component parameter—workload intensity (WI) or service demand (SD). Values must be obtained or estimated for these parameters, preferably through measurements with performance monitors and accounting systems. Measurements must be made

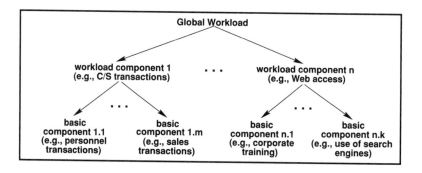

Figure 5.4. Workload characterization process.

Table 5.2. Example of Basic Component Parameters and Types (WI = workload intensity; SD = service demand)

Basic Component and Parameters	Parameter Type
Sales transaction	
Number of transactions submitted per client	WI
Number of clients	WI
Total number of I/Os to the Sales DB	SD
CPU utilization at the DB server	SD
Average message size sent/received by the DB server	SD
Web-based training	
Average number of training sessions/day	WI
Average size of video file per session	SD
Average size of HTTP documents retrieved	SD
Average number of image files retrieved/session	SD
Average number of documents retrieved/session	SD
Average CPU utilization of the Web server	SD
Mail processing	
Number of messages received per day per client	WI
Number of messages sent per day per client	WI
Number of clients	WI
Average message size	SD
CPU utilization of the mail daemon	SD

during peak workload periods and for an appropriate monitoring interval (e.g., 1 hour). For example, consider the "Mail Processing" basic component. Data would be collected relative to all messages sent during a 1 hour monitoring interval. Assume that 5,400 messages were sent during this interval. Measurements are obtained for the message size, mail server CPU time, and server I/O time for each of the 5,400 messages. The average arrival rate of send mail requests is equal to the number of messages sent (5,400) divided by the measurement interval (3,600 seconds), i.e., $5,400/3,600 = 1.5$ messages sent per second. Similar measurements must be obtained for all basic components.

Consider the case of the "Web-based training" basic component. Data was collected during several days and it was observed that an average of 11.2 videos are requested every minute. The average duration of a video is 3 minutes and videos are encoded for 300 Kbps. The average number of concurrent video deliveries, according to Little's Law, is $11.2 \times 3 = 33.6$. The average bandwidth consumed by these videos is 33.6 videos $\times$ 300 Kbps/video = 10.08 Mbps. This consumes about 10% of the bandwidth of LAN 3. A workload characterization of educational media servers can be found in [1].

5.5.1   Breaking Down the Global Workload

When workload intensity is high, large collections of workload measures can be obtained. Dealing with such collections is seldom practical, especially if workload characterization results are to be used for performance prediction through analytic models [9]. One should substitute the collection of measured values of all basic components by a more compact representation—one per basic component. This representation is called a *workload model*—the end product of the workload characterization process.

Consider a Web-based application that provides access to the corporate database, and assume that data collected during a peak period of one hour provides the CPU time and number of I/Os for each of the 20,000 transactions executed in that period in the back-end database. Some transactions are fairly simple and use very little CPU and I/O, whereas other more complex ones may require more CPU and substantially more I/O. Figure 5.5 shows a graph depicting points of the type (number of I/Os, CPU time) for all transactions executed in the measurement interval. The picture shows three natural groupings of the points in the two-dimensional space shown

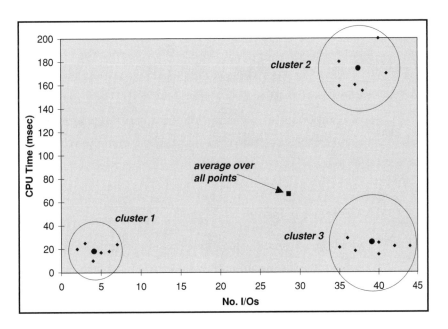

Figure 5.5. Space for workload characterization (no. of I/Os, CPU time).

in the graph. Each group is called a *cluster* and has a *centroid*—the larger circles in the figure—defined as the point whose coordinates are the average among all points in the cluster. The "distance" between any point and the centroid of its cluster is the shortest distance between the point and the centroid of all clusters. The coordinates of the centroids of clusters 1, 2, and 3, are (4.5, 19), (38, 171), and (39, 22), respectively. A more compact representation of the resource consumption of the 20,000 transactions is given by the coordinates of centroids 1, 2, and 3. For instance, transactions of class 1 perform, on the average, 4.5 I/Os and spend 19 msec of CPU time during their execution.

The graph in Fig. 5.5 also shows the point whose coordinates, (28, 68), are the average number of I/Os and the average CPU time over all points. It is clear that if we were to represent all the points by this single point—the single cluster case—we would obtain a much less meaningful representation of the global workload than the one provided by the three clusters. Thus, the number of clusters chosen to represent the workload impacts the accuracy of the workload model.

Clustering algorithms can be used to compute an optimal number of basic components of a workload model, and the parameter values that represent each component. A discussion of clustering algorithms and their use in workload characterization is presented in Chapter 6.

5.5.2   Data Collection Issues

In ideal situations, performance monitors and accounting systems are used to determine the parameter values for each basic component. In reality, the tool base required for integrated network and server data collection may not be available to the system administrators, or they may not have enough time to deploy and use a complete suite of monitoring tools. This is a chronic problem for many organizations. The problem is compounded by the fact that most monitoring tools provide aggregate measures at the resource levels (e.g., total number of packets transmitted on a LAN segment or total server CPU utilization). These measurements must be apportioned to the basic workload components. Benchmarks and rules of thumb (ROT) may be needed to apportion aggregate measures to basic components in lieu of real measurements. Figure 5.6 illustrates the range of data collection alternatives available to a capacity manager.

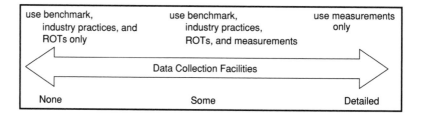

Figure 5.6. Data collection alternatives for workload characterization.

In many cases, it is possible to detect a fairly limited number of applications that account for significant portions of resource usage. Workload measurements can be made for these applications in a controlled environment such as the one depicted in Fig. 5.7.

These measurements must be made under a load submitted by clients running scripts representing typical users requesting Web services. There are many tools, called *load testers*, that capture customer requests for further replay. These measurements are aimed at obtaining service demands at the processors and storage devices at the various servers of a Web site, as well as the number of packets sent and received by the servers and packet size distributions. The results thus obtained for a specific type of server machine must be translated to other types of boxes. For this purpose, we can use specific industry standard benchmarks, such as SPEC ratings, to scale resource usage figures up or down.

Example 5.1

Assume that the CPU service demand at the server for a given application was 10 msec, obtained in a controlled environment with a server with a SPEC CINT2000 rating of 431. SPEC ratings are defined by the Standard Performance Evaluation Corporation. To find out what this service

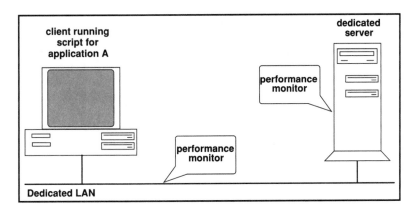

Figure 5.7. Controlled environment for workload component benchmarking.

demand would be if the server used in the actual system were faster and had a SPEC CINT2000 rating of 518, we need to scale down the 10 msec measurement by dividing it by the ratio between the two CINT2000 ratings. Thus, the service demand at the faster server would be $10/(518/431) = 8.3$ msec. Of course, the choice of which benchmark to use to scale down or up measurements taken in controlled environments depends on the type of application. If the application in question is a scientific application that does mostly number-crunching of floating-point numbers, one should use SPEC CFP2000 as opposed to SPEC CINT2000 ratings. Chapter 7 discusses the many benchmarks relevant to Web-based environments.   ■

In general, the actual service demand, ActualSvceDemand, is obtained by multiplying the measured demand, MeasuredSvceDemand, at the controlled environment by the ratio, ThroughputRatio, between ratings—such as the SPEC ratings—of the resource used in the controlled environment and the resource used in the actual environment.

$$\text{ActualSvceDemand} = \text{MeasuredSvceDemand} \times \text{ThroughputRatio} \quad (5.5.1)$$

Chapter 13 discusses in greater detail issues involved in data collection for Web-based systems.

5.5.3   Validating Workload Models

In building any model, abstractions of the reality being modeled are made for simplicity, ease of data collection and use, and the computational efficiency of the modeling process. The abstractions compromise the accuracy of the model, so the model must be validated within an acceptable margin of error, a process called *model validation*. If a model is deemed invalid, it must be calibrated to render it valid. This is called *model calibration*.

Validating workload models entails running a synthetic workload composed of workload model results and comparing the performance measures thus obtained with those obtained by running the actual workload. If the results match within a 10–30% margin of error, the workload model is considered to be valid. Otherwise, the model must be refined to more accurately represent the actual workload.

5.6   Workload Forecasting

Workload forecasting is the process of predicting how system workloads will vary in the future. Through this process one can answer questions such as: "How will the number of e-mail messages handled daily by the server vary over the next 6 months?" "How will the number of Web requests to the corporate portal vary over time?" Answering such questions involves evaluating workload trends if historical data are available and/or analyzing the business or strategic plans of the organization, and then mapping these business plans to changes in business processes (e.g., staff increases and paperwork reduction initiatives will yield 50% more e-mail and Internet usage and 80% more requests on the corporate Web server).

During workload forecasting, basic workload components are associated to business processes so that changes in the workload intensity of these components can be derived from the business process and strategic plans.

Example 5.2

Consider the corporate Web server in the example of Fig. 5.3. Assume that we plot the number of video requests from the streaming server used for online training for each of the past 6 months, as depicted in Fig. 5.8. By using linear regression, we can establish a relationship between the number of monthly video requests and the month number. In this example,

$$\text{NumberVideoRequests} = 911.94 \times \text{Month} + 16,153.$$

If we now need to forecast the number of video requests for the next month, we can use the above linear relationship to predict that 22,536 video requests will be submitted next month. The number of video requests can be associated with the required bandwidth of the streaming video server. ∎

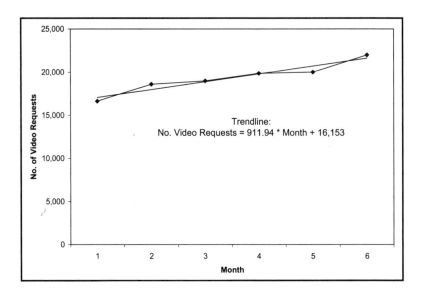

Figure 5.8. Workload forecasting.

Chapter 12 discusses workload forecasting techniques, such as moving averages, exponential smoothing, and linear regression, in detail.

5.7   Performance/Availability Modeling and Prediction

An important aspect of capacity management involves predicting whether a system will deliver performance metrics (e.g., response time, throughput, and availability) that meet desired or acceptable service levels.

5.7.1   Performance Models

Performance prediction is the process of estimating performance measures of a computer system for a given set of parameters. Typical performance measures include response time, throughput, resource utilization, and resource queue length. Examples of performance measures for the system of Fig. 5.3 include the response time for retrieving mail from the mail server, the throughput of the file server in LAN 2, the utilization of the backbone

FDDI ring, and the throughput and average number of requests queued at the Web proxy server. Parameters are divided into the following categories:

- *system parameters*: characteristics of a Web-based system that affect performance. Examples include load balancing disciplines for Web server mirroring, network protocols, maximum number of connections supported by a Web server, and maximum number of threads supported by the database management system.

- *resource parameters*: intrinsic features of a resource that affect performance. Examples include disk seek times, latency and transfer rates, network bandwidth, router latency, and CPU speed ratings.

- *workload parameters*: derived from workload characterization and divided into:

  - *workload intensity parameters*: provide a measure of the load placed on the system, indicated by the number of units of work that contend for system resources. Examples include the number of requests/day to the Web site, number of requests/sec submitted to the file server, number of sales transactions submitted per second to the database server, and the number of clients running scientific applications. Another important characteristic of the workload is the burstiness of the arrival process as discussed in Chapters 4 and 10.

  - *workload service demand parameters*: specify the total amount of service time required by each basic component at each resource. Examples include the CPU time of transactions at the database server, the total transmission time of replies from the database server in LAN 4, and the total I/O time at the Web proxy server for requests of images and video clips used in the Web-based training classes.

Performance prediction requires the use of models. Two types of models may be used: simulation models and analytical models. Both types of models have to consider contention for resources and the queues that arise at each system resource—CPUs, disks, routers, and communication lines. Queues also arise for software resources—threads, database locks, and protocol ports.

The various queues that represent a distributed system are interconnected, giving rise to a network of queues, called a queuing network (QN). The level of detail at which resources are depicted in the QN depends on the reasons to build the model and the availability of detailed information about the operation and availability of detailed parameters of specific resources.

Example 5.3

To illustrate the above concepts we will use the notation introduced in Chapter 3 to show two versions—a high level and a more detailed level—of the QN model that corresponds to LAN 3 in Fig. 5.3, its Web server, and the connections of LAN 3 to the Internet and to the FDDI ring. Figure 5.9 depicts a high-level QN model for LAN 3. The 100-Mbps LAN is depicted as a queuing resource and so are the two server boxes on LAN 3. The FDDI ring and the Internet are not explicitly modeled as this model focuses on LAN 3 only. However, traffic coming from the FDDI ring and from the Internet into LAN 3 has to be taken into account.

Note that the model of Fig. 5.9 hides many of the details of the Web server. As mentioned in Sections 5.4, both server boxes have two processors. Thus, a more detailed representation of the QN model would have to include the server processors and disks as shown in Fig. 5.10.   ∎

Chapters 8, 9, and 10 discuss, in detail, techniques used to build performance models of Web-based systems.

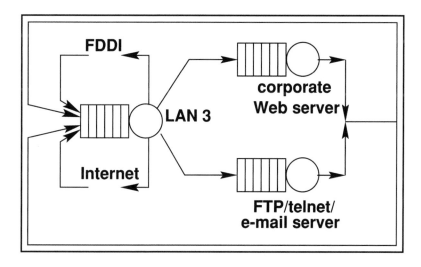

Figure 5.9. High-level QN of LAN 3.

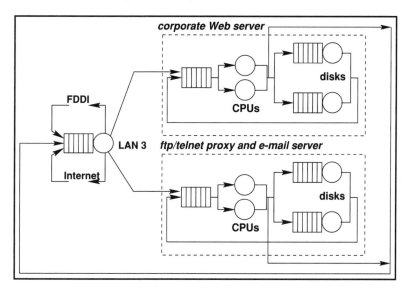

Figure 5.10. Detailed QN of LAN 3.

5.7.2   Performance Prediction Technique

To predict the performance of a Web-based system we need to be able to solve the performance model that represents the system. Analytic models [9] are based on a set of formulas and/or computational algorithms used to generate performance metrics from model parameters. Simulation models [3, 7] are computer programs that mimic the behavior of a system as transactions flow through the various simulated resources. Statistics on the time spent at each queue and each resource are accumulated by the program for all transactions so that averages, standard deviations, and even distributions of performance metrics can be reported on the performance measures.

There is a wide range of modeling alternatives. As more system elements are represented in greater detail, model accuracy increases. Data gathering requirements also increase, as shown in Fig. 5.11. It is important that a reasonable balance be made between model accuracy and ease of use to allow for the analysis of many alternatives with little effort and in very little time. Analytic models are quite appropriate for the performance prediction component of any capacity management/planning study. In this book, we explore how analytic-based QN models can be used to model Web-based systems.

Many times it is unfeasible to obtain detailed performance data. It is important to note that a detailed performance model that uses unreliable data yields non-representative results.

5.7.3   Performance Model Validation

A performance model is said to be valid if the performance metrics (e.g., response time, resource utilizations, and throughputs) calculated by the model

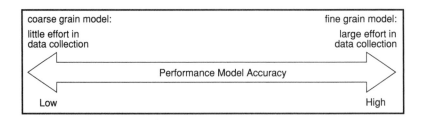

Figure 5.11. Performance model accuracy.

match the measurements of the actual system within a certain acceptable margin of error. Accuracies from 10 to 30% are acceptable in capacity planning [9].

Fig. 5.12 illustrates the various steps involved in performance model validation. During workload characterization, measurements are taken for service demands, workload intensity, and for performance metrics such as response time, throughput, and device utilization. The same measures are computed by means of the performance model. If the computed values do not match the measured values within an acceptable level, the model must be calibrated. Otherwise, the model is deemed valid and can be used for performance prediction. A detailed discussion on performance model calibration techniques is given in [9].

5.7.4   Availability Modeling

Availability models provide a way of predicting the availability of a Web service based on the configuration of the infrastructure used to support the services as well as on the intrinsic reliability of the different components used. As described in Chapter 11, by modeling the availability of a Web service one can answer questions such as How many and what type of servers should be used to build a site that will have a 99.99% availability?

5.8   Development of a Cost Model

A capacity planning methodology requires the identification of major sources of cost as well as the determination of how costs vary with system size and architecture. When evaluating the costs incurred by new Web services, one has to consider that, in some cases, the introduction of Web services may increase traffic on existing channels such as telephone-based customer support [6].

Costs are categorized into startup and operating costs. Startup costs are those incurred in setting up the system, while operating costs are the annual

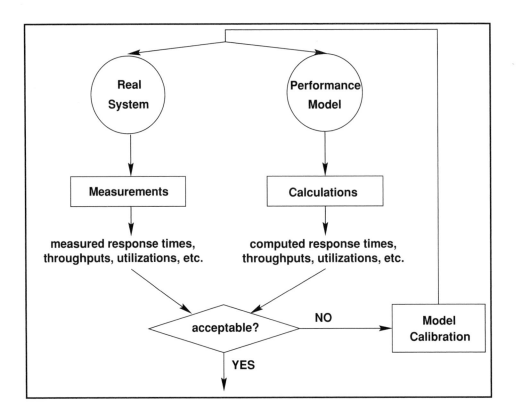

Figure 5.12. Performance model validation.

expenses incurred to maintain the system and provide upgrades in hardware and software to avoid obsolescence, performance degradation, and security vulnerabilities. Startup costs apply to hardware, software, infrastructure, content development, and initial installation charges. Operating costs are related to hardware and software maintenance and upgrades, personnel costs, training, telecommunications services, consulting fees, and other third-pary services.

The cost of the IT infrastructure needed to provide Web services is important in absolute and in relative terms as well. Relative cost metrics are usually given in dollars per some measure of system capacity. An example would be cost per throughput as illustrated in the following example.

Example 5.4

A search engine site indexes one billion Web pages and handles 50 million queries/day. The IT infrastructure is based on over 6,000 Linux-based PCs in three locations. The total startup cost of the IT infrastructure is 40 million dollars. The monthly cost to maintain this infrastructure is \$500,000. What is the average cost per query/second?

The throughput is $50 \times 10^6/(24 \times 3,600) = 579$ queries/sec. The startup cost per query/sec is then $40 \times 10^6/579 = \$69,085$/query/sec. This means that it was necessary to spend about \$69,000 for each query/sec of throughput. The monthly ongoing cost per query/sec is $5\times10^5/579 = \$864$/query/sec. So, it is necessary to spend \$864 per month for each unit of throughput (in queries/sec) provided by the search engine site. ■

In general, Web-based system costs can be divided into five major categories: hardware costs, software costs, telecommunications costs, third-party service providers, and support cost.

Hardware costs include the cost of

- client and server machines along with their disks and other peripherals, memory, and NICs
- disk storage arrays
- routers, bridges, load balancers, and intelligent switches
- backup equipment
- uninterruptable power supplies (UPS)
- cabling
- vendor maintenance and technical support

Software costs account for the cost of

- server and client network operating systems
- server and client middleware (e.g., TP monitors)

- database management systems

- database replication management software

- HTTP servers

- mail processing software

- office automation software

- business applications

- antivirus software

- security and intrusion detection software

- software development

- vendor software maintenance and upgrades

Telecommunication costs include charges for

- WAN services (e.g., Frame Relay, X.25 networks, T1, T3, ISDN)

- ISPs

Third-party service provider costs may include

- ad banner services

- Web hosting services

- content distribution networks

- application service providers

- payment authorization services

- payment services

Support and maintenance costs include

- salaries and fringe benefits of all network administrators, system administrators, and database administrators

- salaries and fringe benefits for Web site design and maintenance staff

- help desk support costs which includes salaries and fringe benefits of help desk staff, and their infrastructure (e.g., computers, servers, and phones)

- salaries and fringe benefits for technical managers

- salaries and fringe benefits for programming support staff

- salaries and fringe benefits for administrative and clerical support

- training costs for support staff (includes travel and time off for training courses)

- network management hardware and software

- performance monitoring software and services

The Microsoft Excel workbook `Cost.XLS` found in the book's Web site includes the cost categories and items presented above and can serve as a starting point to estimate the cost of Web services.

One can be as detailed as required when accounting for costs. This increases the accuracy of the cost assessment at the expense of the time and effort needed to obtain all needed information. Alternatively, one can use more aggregated cost models that account for most of the cost elements with a reasonable degree of accuracy. When some of the cost elements are not known precisely, one can use ROTs to obtain a first-cut approximation to the cost model. Examples of cost ROTs are: hardware and software upgrade is 10% of the purchase price per year, system administrator costs lie between $500 and $700 per workstation per month, training costs range from $1,500 to $3,500 per technical staff person per year, 40% of personnel costs are in the resource management category, 40% are in applications development and maintenance, and 20% in other personnel [4, 5]. Personnel costs needed to develop and operate a typical Web site have been observed to range from five to 12 times other costs, including the cost of the site's technical infrastructure [6].

5.9　Cost/Performance Analysis

Once the performance model is built and solved and a cost model developed, various analyses can be made regarding cost-performance tradeoffs. The performance model and cost models can be used to assess various scenarios and configurations. Some example scenarios are:

- "Should we mirror the Web site to balance the load, cut down on network traffic, and improve performance?"

- "Should we replace the existing Web servers with faster ones?"

- "Should we use a CDN to serve images?"

- "Should we use Web hosting services?"

For each scenario, we can predict what the performance of each basic component of the global workload will be and what the costs are for the scenario.

The comparison of the various scenarios yields a configuration plan, an investment plan, and a personnel plan. The configuration plan specifies which upgrades should be made to existing hardware and software platforms and which changes in network topology and system architecture should be undertaken. The investment plan specifies a timeline for investing in the necessary upgrades. The personnel plan determines what changes in the support personnel size and structure must be made in order to accommodate changes in the system.

5.10　Concluding Remarks

Determining the adequate capacity of complex, distributed Web-based systems systems requires careful planning so that user satisfaction is guaranteed, company goals are achieved, and investment returns are maximized.

This chapter presented the framework of a methodology for capacity planning of Web services. Chapter 6 expands on the "workload characterization" step and discusses clustering analysis techniques, data transformation, and other related issues. Chapter 7 discusses several industry standard benchmarks that can be used as an aid in the process of workload characterization in lieu of actual measurements. Techniques for measurements and data collection are discussed in Chapter 13. Chapters 8 and 9 introduce performance models. Chapter 8 looks at the issue from a systems point of view where large subsystems—a complete Web server, for example—are seen as black boxes. Chapter 9 looks at performance models that allow us to take into account the details of subsystems—the disks and processors of a Web server, for example. Chapter 10 considers performance modeling as it applies to the Web. Chapter 11 shows how to build availability models for Web services. Finally, Chapter 12 discusses various workload forecasting techniques such as linear regression, exponential smoothing, and moving averages.

Bibliography

[1] J. M. Almeida, J. Krueger, D. L. Eager, and M. K. Vernon, "Analysis of Educational Media Server Workloads," *Proc. 11th Int'l Work. Network and Operating System Support for Digital Audio and Video (NOSSDAV 2001)*, Port Jefferson, New York, June 25-26, 2001.

[2] J. M. Andrade, M. T. Carges, T. J. Dwyer and S. D. Felts, *The Tuxedo System: Software for Constructing and Managing Distributed Business Applications*, Addison Wesley, Reading, Massachusetts, 1996.

[3] J. Banks, J. S. Carson, B. L. Nelson, and D. Nicol, *Discrete Event Simulation*, Prentice Hall, Upper Saddle River, New Jersey, 2000.

[4] E. Hufnagel, "The Hidden Costs of Client/Server, Your Client/Server Survival Kit," *Network Computing*, vol. 5, 1994.

[5] Information Technology Group, "Cost of Computing, Comparative Study of Mainframe and PC/LAN Installations," Mountain View, California, 1994.

[6] K. R. T. Larsen and P. A. Bloniarz, "A Cost and Performance Model for Web Service Investment," *Comm. ACM*, vol. 43, no. 2, Feb. 2000, pp. 109–116.

[7] A. M. Law and W. D. Kelton, *Simulation Modeling and Analysis*, 2nd ed., McGraw-Hill, New York, 1991.

[8] D. A. Menascé, D. Dregits, R. Rossin, and D. Gantz, "A Federation-oriented Capacity Management Methodology for LAN Environments," *Proc. 1995 Conf. Comput. Measurement Group*, Nashville, Tennessee, Dec. 3–8, 1995, pp. 1024–1035.

[9] D. A. Menascé, V. A. F. Almeida, and L. W. Dowdy, *Capacity Planning and Performance Modeling: From Mainframes to Client-Server Systems*, Prentice Hall, Upper Saddle River, New Jersey, 1994.

Chapter 6

Understanding and Characterizing the Workload

6.1 Introduction

The performance of a distributed system with many clients, servers, and networks depends heavily on the characteristics of its load. Thus, the first step in any performance evaluation study is to understand and characterize the workload. The workload of a system can be defined as the set of all inputs that the system receives from its environment during any given period of time. For instance, if the system under study is a database server, then its workload consists of all transactions (e.g., query and update) processed by the server during an observation interval. Consider that a Web server was observed during thirty minutes and 180,000 requests were completed.

The workload of the Web server during that 30-minute period is the set of 180,000 requests. The workload characteristics are represented by a set of information (e.g., arrival and completion time, CPU time, number of I/O operations, and size of the object requested) for each of the 180,000 Web requests.

It is certainly difficult to handle real workloads with a large number of elements. Therefore, in order to work with practical problems, one needs to reduce and summarize the information needed to describe the workload. In other words, one needs to build a workload model that captures the most relevant characteristics of the real workload. Workload models exhibit several advantages over actual workloads or traces. It is possible to change model parameters to reflect changes in the system or in the actual workload. For example if one wants to increase the modeled load, one has to change just on parameter, either the interarrival time or the think time. Model parameters can be correlated in order to gain insight into the system behavior. Models can lead to improved system designs.

The choice of characteristics and parameters that will describe the workload depends on the purpose of the study. For example, if one wants to study the cost $\times$ benefit of creating a proxy caching server for a Web site, then the workload characteristics needed for the study are the frequency of document reference, concentration of references, document sizes, and interreference times. Thus, based on the percentage of documents that are responsible for the majority of requests received by the site, one can evaluate the benefits of a proxy caching server. However, if one is interested in determining the impact of a faster CPU on the response time of a Web server, a different set of information must be collected. In this case, the performance study will rely on data such as average CPU time per request, average number of I/O operations per request, and average request response time.

Although each system may require a specific approach to the analysis and characterization of its workload, there are some general guidelines that apply well to all types of systems [8, 9]. The common steps to be followed by any workload characterization project include: (1) specification of a point of view from which the workload will be analyzed, (2) choice of the set of parameters that capture the most relevant characteristics of the workload for the purpose of the study, (3) monitoring the system to obtain the raw performance data, (4) analysis and reduction of performance data, (5) construction of a workload model, and (6) verification that the characterization captures all the important performance information. This chapter describes and illustrates with examples the major steps required for the construction of workload models. The methodology presented here is based in part on the material described in Chapter 2 of [19] and Chapter 11 of [20].

6.2   Characterizing the Workload of a Corporate Portal

To help us understand the problem of workload characterization for distributed systems, consider the example of a corporate portal of a construction and engineering company. The company is planning to roll out new portal applications and to let suppliers and partners access its portal. Currently, 1,000 employeys have access to the corporate intranet. The goal is to have 3,500 users accessing the portal by the end of next year. Before starting the expansion of the portal applications, management wants to analyze the performance of the current applications. The corporate intranet offers a range of applications and services, from simple text to video and audio. The main applications are an employee directory, the human resources system, health insurance payments, quality management, and on-demand interactive training. The intranet consists of five Web servers that are accessed by employees through the corporate network, as shown in Fig. 6.1.

Users have been complaining about the response time of the human resources service. So, the starting point for the performance study is server B, which holds the service. As we mentioned earlier, the first step in any performance evaluation project is to understand and characterize the workload. Therefore, the central question is: "How do you characterize the workload of a corporate portal?"

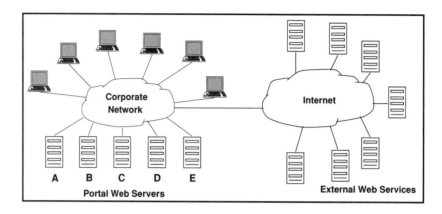

Figure 6.1. An intranet environment.

First of all, we need to define the workloads we want to characterize. There are multiple and different workloads in a distributed environment. The workload presented to a client desktop consists of commands and "clicks" given by a user and responses provided by servers to the user's requests. From the server standpoint, the workload is made up of all HTTP requests it receives during an observation period. A server may receive requests from all clients in the system. The load of a network is usually described in terms of traffic characteristics, such as packet size distribution and the interpacket arrival time.

A second question that must be answered refers to the level of the workload description. A high-level description would specify the workload from the user's point of view. For instance, one could specify the load in terms of Web transactions, such as insurance payment inquiries, document search, and interactive online training sessions. On the other hand, a low-level characterization would describe the user's requests in resource-oriented terms, such as average CPU time per request and number of packets exchanged between the client and server.

Let us start the workload characterization process by looking at the requests received by Web server B, which hosts the human resources service. To simplify the example, let us consider a very short observation period.

During a 1-second interval, the server received 10 HTTP requests from clients on the LAN. What is the workload presented to the server in the observed period of time?

The term workload designates all the processing requests submitted to a system by the user community during any given period of time [15]. Thus, the workload in question consists of the sequence of 10 requests received by the server. How could this workload be characterized? In other words, how could the workload be precisely described?

6.2.1 A First Approach

The first step in the characterization process is the identification of the basic components of the workload of a computer system. The *basic component* refers to a generic unit of work that arrives at a system from an external source. The nature of the service provided by the system determines the type of the basic component. Common types are a job, a transaction, an interactive command, a process, and an HTTP request. In C/S environments, the basic component could be a client request or a database transaction. For example, the basic component for a banking system is a transaction (e.g., savings account balance inquiry, checking account update, or loan status inquiry). The basic component of the workload presented to a file server in a distributed environment is a request for service [6]. *Read* and *write* operations to files are the most common requests made by workstations or personal computers to a file server. These file operations received by a server from the workstations and other servers during any period of time make up the server's workload.

There are many forms of workload characterization. The one to be chosen depends on the purpose of the characterization. Basically, a characterization process yields a workload model that can be used in several activities, such as selection of computer systems, performance tuning, and capacity planning. Our interest concentrates mainly on building workload models for capacity planning purposes, as illustrated by Fig. 6.2. The characterization process analyzes a workload and identifies its basic components and features that have impact on the system's performance. It also yields parameters that retain the characteristics capable of driving performance models used for capacity planning activities.

The workload of a computer system can be described at different levels, as illustrated by Fig. 6.3. At the highest level, the *business characterization* describes corporate and business plans useful in characterizing the workload in terms of features of the main applications. The business workload is a user-oriented description, with business quantities such as number of employees, transactions per user, items in the online catalog, and invoices per customer. At the next level, the *functional characterization* describes the programs, requests, or applications that make up the workload. In our example, the workload consists of a series of Web requests. This type of characterization is independent of the underlying hardware configuration but is related to the software systems (e.g., Online Transaction Processing (OLTP), HTTP services, and database systems) used to process the workload.

For performance modeling and capacity planning purposes, though, business description and pure functional models have a serious drawback: They do not capture any quantitative information about the resource consumption behavior. This complicates the accomplishment of some basic capacity planning activities such as sizing a system or predicting the performance of a new system. These activities typically require quantitative information about the workload. For example, a request for a large graphic document

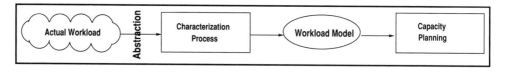

Figure 6.2. Workload characterization process.

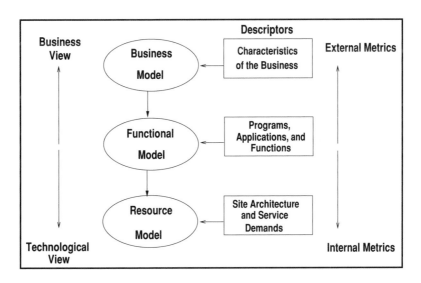

Figure 6.3. Levels of workload description.

with thousands of KB consumes much more CPU, I/O time, and network bandwidth than a request for a small HTML document does. Thus, in order to make the characterization useful, it is necessary to include in the model information about resource requirements. For instance, a request description would include information about the size of the document.

At the physical level, the *resource-oriented characterization* describes the consumption of the system resources by the workload. The resources to be included in the characterization are those whose consumption have a significant impact on performance [15]. For example, consider a Web server with enough memory and a high-bandwidth connection to the Internet. The main parameters that can be used to characterize an HTTP request would be the time spent by the request at the CPU and I/O devices. All major operating systems and HTTP servers provide facilities for determining how much CPU is being consumed by a particular process that runs on behalf of a request. Usually, operating systems include accounting logs and performance monitors that record the hardware resource usage by each process in execution. CPU time, elapsed time, total I/O operations, main memory usage, and number of page faults are examples of the type of process execution information existing in a system accounting file.

Example 6.1

Consider an online bookstore in which customers can perform the following functions: Search, Browse, Select, Register, Login, Add, and Pay. Customers interact with the site through a series of consecutive and related requests made during a session. Management has a series of questions about the workload. What is the average session length? What are the functions customers visit most? What is the percentage of images in the workload?

Because management's questions involve different views of the workload, the capacity planning analyst is thinking of a multi-layer model as the one proposed in Fig 6.3. e-business workloads are composed of sessions. During a session, a customer requests the execution of various e-business functions. A request to execute an e-business function may generate many HTTP requests to the site. For example, several images may have to be retrieved to display the page that contains the results of the execution of an e-business function. Workload characterization can be accomplished at many levels: user level, application level, and protocol level. As proposed in [21], an e-business workload can be viewed in a multi-layer hierarchical way, as shown in Fig 6.4. The characteristics of each layer can provide answers to the questions made by management. ∎

6.2.2 A Simple Example

Let us go back to the simple example of the workload seen by Web server B during the 1-second interval. If we assume that the workload presented to that Web server consists of documents of the same size, workload characterization becomes straightforward. Consider that all documents requested are 15-KB long. This implies having approximately the same CPU and I/O times for each of the 10 executions of the HTTP requests. From data avail-

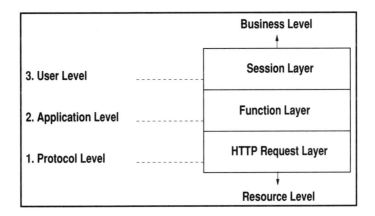

Figure 6.4. A hierarchical workload model.

able in the system accounting files and access logs, we got the following characterization: 10 requests represented by the pair (0.013, 0.09) where the two numbers represent the CPU and disks service demands of an HTTP request, in seconds, respectively. Consider now a more realistic situation. We all know that Web documents have widely varying sizes. This leads to a large variability in the values of the two parameters chosen for the characterization of the workload of this example.

Table 6.1 shows the CPU, I/O, and execution times for each of the 10 Web requests for documents of different sizes. The execution time corresponds to the elapsed time required by the server to service the request. The average execution time is 0.734 seconds. The table also shows the standard deviation and the coefficient of variation (CV) (i.e., the standard deviation divided by the average) for the CPU and I/O demands and for the execution time. The higher the CV, the higher the variability in the values. Looking at Table 6.1, we note that each execution is represented by a different pair of values of CPU and I/O times. For instance, the pair (0.0095, 0.04) is completely different, in terms of resource usage, from (0.2170, 1.20). Which pair should be chosen as a representation for the 10 executions?

A key issue in workload characterization is *representativeness*, which indicates the accuracy in representing the real workload. Bearing this in mind,

Table 6.1. Execution of HTTP Requests (sec)

Request No.	CPU Time	I/O Time	Execution Time
1	0.0095	0.04	0.071
2	0.0130	0.11	0.145
3	0.0155	0.12	0.156
4	0.0088	0.04	0.065
5	0.0111	0.09	0.114
6	0.1030	0.57	0.201
7	0.2170	1.20	4.380
8	0.0129	0.12	0.151
9	0.0091	0.05	0.063
10	0.0170	0.14	0.189
Average	0.0417	0.248	0.734
Std. Deviation	0.068	0.369	1.413
Coeff. Variation	1.63	1.49	1.92

the next step is to determine a characterization for the workload described by Table 6.1. The first idea that comes to mind is that of a *typical Web request*, averaged over all of the executions. Its characterizing parameters are the average CPU and I/O times. Table 6.2 shows the pair of parameters of a single request that now characterizes the workload displayed in Table 6.1. The real workload is now represented by a model composed of 10 requests

Table 6.2. Single-class Characterization

Type	CPU Time (sec)	I/O Time (sec)	No. of Components
Single	0.0417	0.248	10
Total	0.417	2.48	10

characterized by the pair (0.0417, 0.248), that place on the server the same CPU and I/O demands as those placed by the original requests. But how accurate is this representation?

One technique for assessing the accuracy of a workload model relies on the analysis of the effect caused on the system when a model replaces the actual workload. In a more general way, as proposed in [15], the basic tenet of the workload characterization process can be stated as: a workload model $\mathcal{W}$ is a perfect representation of the real workload $\mathcal{R}$ if the performance measures (P) obtained when running $\mathcal{W}$ and $\mathcal{R}$ on the same system are identical ($P_{\text{real}} = P_{\text{model}}$), as shown in Fig. 6.5.

Considering that the purpose of our workload characterization is to provide information to performance models, response times can be used to evaluate the accuracy of the workload model. Thus, the characterization is accurate if the response time of the server executing the workload model is close to the average response time measured during the execution of the real workload. If the response time of the execution of the request characterized

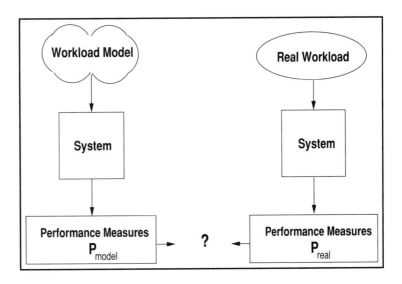

Figure 6.5. Representativeness of a workload model.

by (0.0417, 0.248) approximates 0.734 sec, then the *typical request* turned out to be a good model.

Examinations of the values displayed in Table 6.2 lead to a refinement in the characterization process. The average response time of 0.734 sec does not adequately reflect the behavior of the actual server response times. Measured response times can be grouped into three distinct classes, according to their variation range. Moreover, each class can be associated with the size of document, which is the main influence on the response time. Thus we define the following classes: small, medium, and large. Due to the heterogeneity of the components of a real workload, it is difficult to generate an accurate characterization if the workload is viewed as a single collection of requests. In an attempt to improve representativeness, the original workload is partitioned into three classes, based on resource usage, response time, and document size.

A *class* comprises components that are similar to each other concerning resource usage. The first class, named *small documents*, includes executions whose CPU and I/O times vary from 0.0001 to 0.0099 seconds and from 0 to 0.05 seconds, respectively. The second class, called *medium documents*, consists of those executions whose CPU time ranges from 0.0100 to 0.0300 seconds and I/O times vary from 0.06 to 0.14 seconds, respectively. The class of *large documents* has CPU and I/O times exceeding 0.03 and 0.14 seconds, respectively. Table 6.3 presents three pairs of average parameters that now represent the original workload. Clustering the requests into three classes preserves some important features of the real workload and emphasizes the distinction between requests that demand different amounts of resource time. It is also important to compare the coefficient of variation values in Table 6.1 and 6.3. In the case of a single class, the coefficient of variation values exceed 1.5 while in the three-class case, the values of the coefficient of variation within each class are around 0.5, illustrating the fact that each class comprises a set of more homogeneous requests than the global workload.

Table 6.3. Three-Class Characterization

Type	CPU Time (sec)	I/O Time (sec)	Components
Small (avg.)	0.0091	0.04	3
Coeff. of variation	0.0385	0.1332	
Medium (avg.)	0.0144	0.12	5
Coeff. of variation	0.1704	0.1566	
Large (avg.)	0.2170	1.20	2
Coeff. of variation	0.5038	0.5034	

Let us take a look at the following example that shows the importance of classes in the context of capacity planning. Suppose the small HTML pages, with text only, will be modified to incorporate a lot of graphics. The modification will increase the size of the pages and will transform all small documents into midsize documents. Before authorizing the modification to the pages, the system administrator wants to evaluate its effect on the server response time and the impact on network traffic. This kind of question could not be answered by a model with a single class, because the group of small documents is not explicitly represented. Breaking down the workload into classes increases the predictive power of a model.

Up until now, we have seen how to cluster a series of HTTP requests and represent them by one or more classes of requests. But, one factor is missing from completing the characterization: the rate at which requests arrive at the server. This rate depends primarily on the answers to two questions. What is the number of users that generate requests to the server? How often a user interacts with the server? When a user interacts with a system, as in our example, the average think time determines the intensity of the load. Think time, as defined in Chapter 3, is the interval of time that elapses from when the user receives the answer from the system (e.g., UNIX's prompt or the page in the browser) until he or she issues a new request. The smaller the think time, the higher the rate at which requests arrive at the server.

The workload of our previous example is simple and small: only 10 requests. In this case, if we wanted to test the performance of a faster server, it would be easier to generate the real requests for the new machine, instead of building a workload model. *Real workloads* consist of all original programs, transactions, and requests processed during a given period of time [15]. Therefore, real systems exhibit very complex workloads, composed of thousands of different programs, transactions, and requests. It would be unrealistic, even impossible, to consider the use of real workloads in capacity planning studies, where several different scenarios of hardware and software are analyzed. When a study involves comparisons of system's performance under varying scenarios, it is necessary to be able to reproduce the workload, in order to obtain the same conditions for the tests. Hence, the importance of building *workload models* that are compact, represent with accuracy the real workload, and are reproducible.

6.2.3　Workload Model

A workload model is a representation that mimics the real workload under study. It can be a set of programs written and implemented with the goal of artificially testing a system in a controlled environment. A workload model can also be a set of input data for an analytical model of a system. It would not be practical to have a model composed of thousands of basic components to mimic the real workload. Models should be compact. A compact model places on the system a demand much smaller than that generated by the actual workload.

Let us take as an example the characterization of the workload of the server we described in Table 6.1. The first model we built consists of a single typical request. Thus, instead of running 10 requests, the execution of the workload model with just one request would give us information to analyze the performance of the system under study. Thus, a model should be representative and compact. Workload models can be classified into categories, according to the way they are constructed. The two main categories of workload model are as follows.

- *Natural models* are constructed either using basic components of the real workload as building blocks or using execution traces of the real workload. A natural benchmark consists of programs extracted from the real workload of a system. The programs should be selected so that the benchmark represents the overall system load in given periods of time. Another natural model very often used in performance studies is the workload trace. It consists of a chronological sequence of data representing specific events that occurred in the system during a measurement session. For example, in the case of a Web server, the log access contains a line of information per request processed by the server. Among other information, each line specifies the name of the host making the request, the time stamp, and the name of the file requested. This type of log characterizes the real workload during a given period of time. Although traces exhibit reproducibility and representativeness features, they do have some drawbacks. Usually, traces consist of huge amounts of data that complicate their use. It is not that simple to modify a trace to represent different workload scenarios. Also, traces are suitable only for simulation models.

- *Artificial models* do not make use of any basic component of the real workload. Instead, these models are constructed out of special-purpose programs and descriptive parameters. We can also separate the artificial models into two classes: executable and non-executable models. Executable artificial models consist of a suite of programs especially written to experiment with aspects of a computer system. The class of executable models include workloads such as *instruction mixes*, *kernels*, *synthetic programs*, *artificial benchmarks*, and *drivers*. Instruction mixes are hardware demonstration programs intended to test the speed of a computer on simple computational and I/O operations. Program kernels are pieces of code drawn out of the computationally intense parts of a real program. In general, kernels concentrate on measuring the performance of processors without considering the I/O system. Synthetic programs are specifically devised codes that place demands on different resources of a computing system. Unlike benchmarks, synthetic programs do not resemble the real workload. Benchmarks, synthetic programs, and other forms of executable models are not adequate input for performance models.

When the performance of a system is analyzed through the use of analytic models, new representations for the workload are required. Because our approach to capacity planning relies on the use of analytic models for performance prediction, we will focus on workload representations suitable for this kind of model.

Non-executable workload models are described by a set of mean parameter values that reproduce the same resource usage of the real workload. Each parameter denotes an aspect of the execution behavior of the basic component on the system under study. The basic inputs to analytical models are parameters that describe the service centers (i.e., hardware and software resources) and the customers (e.g., transactions and requests). Typical parameters are:

- component (e.g., transaction and request) interarrival times

- service demands

- component sizes (e.g., document size of HTTP requests)

- execution mix (percent of each component class on the global workload)

Each type of system may be characterized by a different set of parameters. As an example, let us look at a parametric characterization of a workload on a distributed system file server, presented in [6]. The study shows the factors that have a direct influence on the performance of a file server: the system load, the device capability, and the locality of file references. From these factors, the following parameters are defined:

- frequency distribution of each type of request (e.g., read, write, create, and rename) on the total workload

- request interarrival time distribution, which indicates the intensity of the system load

- file referencing behavior, i.e., the percentage of accesses made to each file in the disk subsystem

- size of reads and writes, which has a strong influence on the time needed to service a request

The above parameters completely specify the workload model and are capable of driving synthetic programs that accurately represent real workloads. Another study [23] looks at an I/O workload from a different perspective. The workload model for a storage device (i.e., queues, caches, controllers, and disk mechanisms) is specified by three classes of parameters: access time attributes, access type (i.e., fraction of reads and writes), and spatial locality attributes. Access time attributes capture the time access pattern, which includes arrival process (i.e., deterministic, Poisson, bursty), arrival rate, burst rate, burst count, and burst fraction. Bursty workloads are discussed in Section 6.4.2. Spatial locality attributes specify the relationship between consecutive requests, such as sequential and random accesses. Due to seek delays, workloads with a larger fraction of sequential accesses may have better performance than those with random accesses (see Chapter 3). Thus, for a detailed model of an I/O device, it is important to include the spatial locality attributes of the workload.

6.2.4   Graph-Based Models

Graphs can also be used to represent workloads. The Customer Behavior Model Graph (CBMG) [20] is an example of a graph-based model that characterizes Web sessions. The CBMG can be used to capture the navigational pattern of a user through a Web site. This pattern includes two aspects: a transitional and a temporal one. The former determines how a customer moves from one state (i.e., an e-business function) to the next. This is represented by the matrix of transition probabilities. The temporal aspect has to do with the time it takes for a customer to move from one state to the next. This time is measured from the server's perspective and is called *server-perceived think time* or just think time. This is defined as the average time elapsed since the server completes a request for a customer until it receives the next request from the same customer during the same session.

Consider the CBMG of Fig. 6.6. This CBMG has seven states; the Exit state, state seven, is not explicitly represented in the figure. Let V_j be the average number of times that state j of the CBMG is visited for each visit to the e-commerce site, i.e., for each visit to the state Entry. Consider the Add to Cart state. We can see that the average number of visits (V_{Add}) to this state is equal to the average number of visits to the state Select (V_{Select}) multiplied by the probability (0.2) that a customer will go from Select to Add Cart. We can then write the relationship

$$V_{\text{Add}} = V_{\text{Select}} \times 0.2. \tag{6.2.1}$$

Consider now the Browse state. The average number of visits (V_{Browse}) to this state is equal to the average number of visits to state Search (V_{Search}) multiplied by the probability (0.2) that a customer will go from Search to Browse, plus the average number of visits to state Select (V_{Select}) multiplied by the probability (0.30) that a customer will go from Select to Browse, plus the average number of visits to the state Add to Cart (V_{Add}) multiplied by the probability (0.25) that a customer will go from Add to Cart to Browse,

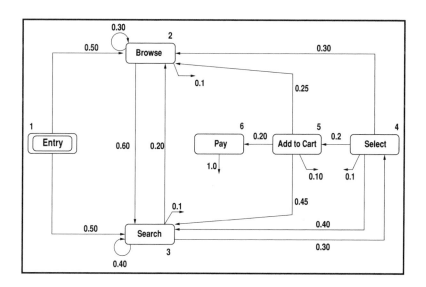

Figure 6.6. CBMG for an online bookstore.

plus the average number of visits to the state Browse (V_{Browse}) multiplied by the probability (0.30) that a customer will remain in the Browse state, plus the number of visits to the Entry state multiplied by the probability (0.5) of going from the Entry state to the Browse state. Hence,

$$V_{\text{Browse}} = V_{\text{Search}} \times 0.20 + V_{\text{Select}} \times 0.30 + V_{\text{Add}} \times 0.25 +$$
$$V_{\text{Browse}} \times 0.30 + V_{\text{Entry}} \times 0.5. \qquad (6.2.2)$$

So, in general, the average number of visits to a state j of the CBMG is equal to the sum of the number of visits to all states of the CBMG multiplied by the transition probability from each of the other states to state j. Thus, for any state j ($j = 2, \cdots, n-1$) of the CBMG, one can write the equation

$$V_j = \sum_{k=1}^{n-1} V_k \times p_{k,j}, \qquad (6.2.3)$$

where $p_{k,j}$ is the probability that a customer makes a transition from state k to state j. Note that the summation in Eq. (6.2.3) does not include state n (the Exit state) since there are no possible transitions from this state to any other state. Since $V_1 = 1$ (because state 1 is the Entry state), we can find the average number of visits V_j by solving the system of linear equations

$$V_1 = 1 \tag{6.2.4}$$

$$V_j = \sum_{k=1}^{n-1} V_k \times p_{k,j} \quad j = 2, \cdots, n - 1. \tag{6.2.5}$$

Note that $V_n = 1$ since, by definition, the Exit state is only visited once per session.

6.3   A Workload Characterization Methodology

Once we have discussed the main issues associated with workload characterization, let us describe the steps required to construct a workload model to be used as input to analytic models. Our approach focuses on resource-oriented characterization of workloads.

6.3.1   Choice of an Analysis Standpoint

As pointed out in Chapter 5, the global workload for a distributed environment is a combination of different workloads viewed by the different components of the system. Before we start to analyze and understand the workload we have to define the subsystems to be analyzed and the reference points where measurements will be taken. For example, we may decide to characterize a workload from a site point-of-view, from the point-of-view of a server within the site, or from a client point-of-view if one is interested in end-to-end response time.

6.3.2   Identification of the Basic Component

In this step, we identify the basic components that compose the workload. Transactions and requests are the most usual components. The choice of components depends both on the nature of the system and the purpose of the characterization. The product of this step is a statement such as this: The workload under study consists of transactions and requests.

6.3.3   Choice of the Characterizing Parameters

Once the basic components have been identified, the next step is to choose which parameters characterize each type of basic component. In fact, the nature of the characterizing parameters is dictated by the input information required by analytic models. The parameters can be separated into two groups. One concerns the workload intensity. The other group refers to service demands of the basic components. What is missing here is the definition of which system resources are represented in the model. Usually, the chosen resources are those that most affect the performance of the target system when executing the workload under study. In summary, each component is represented by two groups of information:

- workload intensity (e.g., arrival rate, number of clients and think time, and number of processes or threads in execution simultaneously)

- service demands, specified by the K-tuple $(D_{i1}, D_{i2}, \ldots, D_{iK})$, where K is the number of resources considered, and D_{ij} is the service demand of basic component i at resource j. In the example of Table 6.1, each request is characterized by the 2-tuple (CPU time, I/O time), such as (0.0095 sec, 0.04 sec).

6.3.4   Data Collection

This step assigns values to the parameters of each component of the model. It generates as many characterizing tuples as the number of components of the workload. Chapter 13 presents techniques and tools used for data collection in Web environments. Data collection includes the following tasks:

- Identify the *time windows* that define the measurement sessions. The time interval during which the system, the workload, and the performance indexes are observed represents the time window. Continuous observations of system behavior for days or weeks, depending on the nature of the business, allow the analyst to pick the appropriate time windows on which to base capacity planning studies.

- Monitor and measure the system activities during the defined time windows. Accounting tools available in the operating system and software monitors may be used to this end.

- From the collected data, assign values to each characterizing parameter of every component of the workload.

Many times it is not possible to obtain service demands directly from measured data. However, one can use relationships such as the ones discussed in Chapters 3 and 13 to obtain the needed service demands from the measured data. For example, assume that we are looking for the service demand of HTTP requests to image files on the Web server's disk. An analysis of the HTTP log will reveal how many image files and their sizes were read during the measurement interval. This information, combined with the disk's utilization characteristics, can be used to obtain the service demand being sought.

6.3.5 Partitioning the Workload

Real workloads can be viewed as a collection of heterogeneous components. Concerning the level of resource usage, for instance, a request for a video clip deeply differs from a request for a small HTML document. Because of this heterogeneity, many times the representation of a workload by a single class lacks accuracy. The motivation for partitioning the workload is twofold: improve representativeness of the characterization and increase the predictive power of the model. The latter stems from the fact that most forecasting methodologies rely on key indicators that are closely associated with specific classes of the workload, as shown in Chapter 12. Partitioning techniques divide the workload into a series of classes such that their populations are formed by quite homogeneous components. The aim is to group components that are somehow similar. But which attribute should be used as a basis for the measure of similarity? A description of some attributes used for partitioning a workload into classes of similar components is as follows.

6.3.5.1   Resource Usage

The resource consumption per component can be used to break the workload into classes or clusters. Table 6.4 shows an example of classes of transactions in an interactive environment. In this example, processor and I/O are considered the critical elements of the system. The attributes that divide the workload are the maximum CPU time and maximum I/O time required by a transaction. The *Light* class, for example, comprises transactions that demand more than 8 msec and at most 20 msec of CPU time and I/O time that varies between 120 and 300 msec.

6.3.5.2   Applications

A workload can have its components grouped according to the application they belong to. For instance, a workload could be partitioned into several

Table 6.4. Workload Partitioning Based on Resource Usage

Transaction	Frequency	Maximum CPU Time (msec)	Maximum I/O Time (msec)
Trivial	40%	8	120
Light	30%	20	300
Medium	20%	100	700
Heavy	10%	900	1200

classes, such as accounting, inventory, customer services, and others. Another example is based on the types of applications on the Internet. Let us consider that one wants to characterize the type of traffic that flows through the Internet connection to a company's Web site. Due to the disparity in size and duration between most current Internet transactions (e.g., WWW, FTP, email) and multimedia applications (e.g., streaming media), it is critical to break the network traffic down into different applications. The streaming media traffic stems from the transmission of meetings, workshops, and video conferences that last for long periods of time. Multimedia is a bandwidth-intensive application that has great impact on network performance. Table 6.5 shows the types of traffic and the amount of bytes transmitted during the period of observation. Part of the traffic is due to the mail server workload, composed of the requests associated with Internet protocols (i.e., SMTP and POP3). Applications which are neither significant in terms of resource consumption nor critical to the business can be grouped into a single class. In the example of Table 6.5, this class is called *Others*.

The problem with the choice of this attribute is the existence of very heterogeneous components within the same application. We can envision coexisting in the same application a very large batch job that updates a database and trivial transactions that perform a simple query to the same

Table 6.5. Workload Partitioning Based on Internet Applications

Application	Percentage of Total Traffic
HTTP	29
FTP	20
SMTP and POP3	9
Streaming	11
P2P	14
Others	17

database. These two types of components are completely different concerning resource usage. The same observation applies to the Web. While the retrieval of a small Web page may require a negligible amount of time at the server, a video can take several seconds of CPU and I/O time to be sent out by the server. Thus, if we group all components of the application into just one class, the values obtained for the parameters of the class would not be representative for components such as the very short requests and the video downloads.

6.3.5.3   Objects

One can divide a workload according to the type of objects handled by the applications. In the WWW, a workload can be partitioned by the types of documents accessed at the server. As an example, Table 6.6 exhibits a workload partitioned into categories of documents as proposed in [3, 11].

6.3.5.4   Geographical Orientation

A workload can be divided along lines of geography. Due to the inherent delays involved in WANs, it is important to make a distinction between requests or transactions that are serviced locally or remotely. As an example,

Table 6.6. Workload Partitioning Based on Document Types

Document Class	Percentage of Access (%)
HTML (e.g., html or htm)	30.0
Images (e.g., gif or jpeg)	40.0
Sound (e.g., au, mp3, or wav)	4.5
Video (e.g., mpeg, avi, or mov)	7.3
Dynamic (e.g., cgi or perl)	12.0
Formatted (e.g., ps, pdf, or doc)	5.4
Others	0.8

one can split the workload up into two classes: *local* and *remote*. The location from which the requests are submitted is also used to define classes. Let us consider the case of a study to implement a caching strategy, dedicated to reduce response time and bandwidth consumption in the Web. Based on the observation that some documents are very popular, the study aims to replicate the most popular files to cooperative servers located in areas responsible for the greatest number of requests. In this case, the workload is partitioned according to the IP address of the machine that generated the HTTP request. One class corresponds to requests that come from the East Coast, another refers to requests that originate from the West Coast, and so forth. Table 6.7 summarizes the example and indicates the percentage of requests corresponding to each geographic region.

6.3.5.5   Functional

The components of a workload may be grouped into classes according to the functions being serviced. For instance, a Unix workload can be characterized by associating process names with functions performed in the system. As an example, we may divide the workload by command names as shown in Table 6.8. As a rule of thumb, one should try to keep the number of different classes to the minimum needed by the capacity planning study. If the initial number of classes is too large, aggregation of classes should be carried out. A helpful hint for aggregation is the following: Concentrate on these classes

Table 6.7. Workload Partitioning Based on Geographical Orientation

Classes	Percentage of Total Requests
East Coast	32
West Coast	38
Midwest	20
Others	10

Table 6.8. Workload Partitioning Based on Functions

Classes	Number of Commands	Total CPU Time (sec)
Oracle	1,515	19,350
sas	58	18,020
cp	950	7,500
date	225	26
ls	90	115
find	50	60

of interest to the organization; collapse the rest into a single class. Let us assume that our interest is in analyzing the impact of predicted growth of database activities on the performance of the system. In light of this goal, the workload should be partitioned into two classes: database (e.g., Oracle) and other applications. The remaining five classes would be represented by the class *Others*.

6.3.5.6   Organizational Units

A workload can be partitioned based on the organizational units of a company. This attribute may be useful for companies that have their strategic planning and growth forecasts generated on an organizational basis. As an example, a workload can be divided into classes, taking the organizational structure as attribute of similarity, such as finance, marketing, and manufacturing.

6.3.5.7   Mode

The mode of processing or the type of interaction with the system may be used to categorize the components of a workload. The mode of processing and the parameters chosen to describe them are as follows:

- *Interactive* — an online processing class with components generated by a given number of PCs, PDAs, or workstations with a given think time. An interaction is a combination of waiting and thinking states. The user alternates between waiting for the response of the interaction and thinking before submitting the next request or clicking the mouse. An example would be a Web-based training application on a company's intranet.

- *Transaction* — an online processing class that groups components (e.g., transactions, or requests) that arrive at a computer system with a given arrival rate. An example would be the set of debit authorization requests that arrive at the Web site of an online bank.

- *Continuous* — refers to components executed continuously, such as batch jobs, and can be described by the number of active components in the system. An example would be a DNS server process that stays active all the time.

To be useful in performance evaluation, analytic models require classes of homogeneous components, concerning resource usage. It is clear that some attributes do not partition the workload into classes of homogeneous components. For instance, let us consider the case of a workload partitioned along geographical lines into two classes: West Coast and East Coast. However, the workload is composed of heterogeneous transactions that could be further divided into subclasses according to resource usage. Let us call these classes light and heavy. Therefore, it is desirable to partition a workload using multiple attributes.

Table 6.9 illustrates a partitioning based on two attributes: geographical basis and resource usage. Thus, we now have divided the workload into five classes, according to the source location of the transaction and the level of resource usage, such as "Heavy transactions from the West Coast."

Table 6.9. Workload Partitioning Based on Multiple Attributes

Number	Type	Resource Usage
1	West Coast	Light
2	West Coast	Heavy
3	East Coast	Light
4	East Coast	Heavy
5	Others	Light

6.3.6   Calculating Class Parameters

As we saw in Section 6.3.3, each component (w_i) is characterized by a K–tuple of parameters $w_i = (D_{i1}, D_{i2}, \ldots, D_{iK})$, where K is the number of resources considered and D_{ij} is the service demand requested by component i at resource j. After partitioning the workload into a number of classes, the capacity planner faces the following problem: How should one calculate the parameter values that represent a class of components? Two techniques have been widely used for this: averaging and clustering.

6.3.6.1   Averaging

When a class consists of homogeneous components concerning service demand, an average of the parameter values of all components may be used to represent the parameter values for the class. Thus, for a class composed of p components, the arithmetic mean of each parameter of the K–tuple $(D_{i1}, D_{i2}, \ldots, D_{iK})$ is given by:

$$\overline{D}_j \;=\; \frac{1}{p}\sum_{l=1}^{p} D_{lj}, \qquad j = 1, 2, \ldots, K \tag{6.3.6}$$

where $\overline{D}_j$ is the mean service demand of this class at resource j. The K-tuple $(\overline{D}_1, \overline{D}_2, \ldots, \overline{D}_K)$ then represents a given class. To evaluate the homogeneity of a class, a capacity planner may use some statistical measures of variability, such as variance, coefficient of variation, and the relative difference between the maximum and minimum values observed in the class.

6.3.6.2 Clustering

Figure 6.7 shows a graph of the two parameters that define a given workload composed of transactions. Each point (x, y) in the graph corresponds to an execution of a transaction. The x-axis represents the CPU time demanded by an execution, whereas the y-axis depicts the I/O time.

Suppose that we want to partition the workload of Fig. 6.7 into classes of similar transactions. The question is, How should one determine groups of components of similar resource requirements? The answer lies in *clustering analysis*. Basically, clustering of workloads is a process in which a large number of components are grouped into clusters of similar components. Although

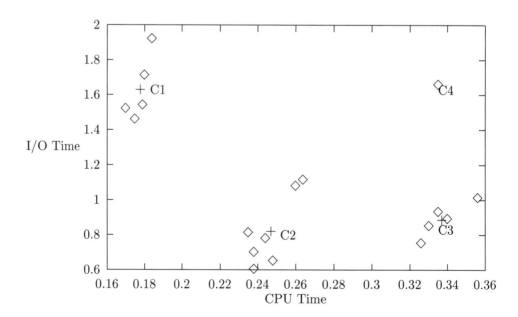

Figure 6.7. Service demands of a C/S transaction.

clustering analysis can be automatically performed by specific functions of some software packages, it is important to be aware of the fundamentals of this technique.

Before discussing the technique in detail, let us first state the problem more precisely. Let a workload $\mathcal{W}$ be represented by a set of p points $w_i = (D_{i1}, D_{i2}, \ldots, D_{iK})$ in a K-dimensional space, where each point w_i represents a component of $\mathcal{W}$, and K is the number of service demand parameters. To make the notation clear, let us revisit the example of Table 6.1 in Section 6.2.2. In that example, each request represents a point in the workload model. Thus, $p = 10$ and $K = 2$, because we are using just two resources (i.e., CPU and I/O) to characterize each request. For instance, using the notation proposed here, we have $w_1 = (0.0095, 0.04)$ and $w_8 = (0.0129, 012)$.

A clustering algorithm attempts to find natural groups of components based on similar resource requirements. Let the *centroid* of a cluster be the point whose parameter values are the means of the parameter values of all points in the cluster. To determine cluster membership, most algorithms evaluate the distance between a point w_i and the cluster centroids in the K-dimensional space. The point w_i is then included in the cluster that has the nearest centroid in the parameter space. As noted from Fig. 6.7, the components of the workload are naturally grouped into three clusters C_1, C_2, and C_3, whose centroids are indicated by a cross symbol. The component represented by point C_4 is called an *outlier* because it does not fit into any of the clusters within a reasonable distance.

The output of a clustering algorithm is basically a statistical description of the cluster centroids with the number of components in each cluster. For performance modeling purposes, each cluster defines a class of similar components. The characterization parameters of a class coincide with those of the cluster's centroid. The cluster analysis partitions a workload $\mathcal{W}$ into a set of R classes. If we apply a clustering method to the points of Table 6.1, we would get three clusters representing the classes displayed in Table 6.3.

The centroids of the classes are the pairs of values (CPU time, I/O time) displayed in the Table 6.3. For instance, the centroid of the small documents class is the pair (0.0091, 0.04). Let us now describe the steps required to perform a clustering analysis of a given workload.

6.3.6.2.1 Data Analysis The first step prepares the raw data that characterizes a workload. The input to this step consists of a set of K-tuples $(D_{i1}, D_{12}, \ldots, D_{iK})$ corresponding to the workload components. The input data analysis involves the following activities:

- sampling drawing

- parameter transformation

- outlier removal

The number of components that make up a workload is a function of the length of measurement sessions. If this number is very large, a sample should be drawn from the measured workload. The purpose is to keep the time required to perform the clustering analysis within acceptable limits. Random sampling yields representative subsets of a workload. Special situations, however, may require other sampling criteria. For example, if the Webmaster of a site is interested in knowing the effect of large video retrievals on network traffic, then the sample must include these requests.

The distribution of each parameter of a tuple should undergo an analysis to eliminate values that may distort the mean parameter value. From a frequency distribution of a parameter, one may observe very few large values that correspond to a small percentage of the components (e.g., 1% or 2%). If a histogram is unable to exhibit useful information because of a highly skewed format of a distribution, a *logarithmic* or another transformation may be required to obtain a more clear representation of the data.

Parameter values that range several orders of magnitude may lead to outliers. When examining the raw data, you should be very cautious about discarding a point considered as an outlier. The reason stems from the fact that measurements of several distributed systems (e.g., Internet, WWW, Ethernet traffic) show numbers that exhibit a pattern known as "heavy-tailed." This means that very large numbers could be present in samples of measurements, such as number of bytes transmitted, file sizes, and CPU times. These extremely large numbers do affect the performance of a system and should not be ignored. However, there are cases when you do not need to consider these very large numbers as part of the data. That is the case with some special tasks. Once in a while, a company runs a large job that reorganizes databases and disk space. Usually, these jobs take a very long time to run. Thus, depending on the time window you are analyzing, you may discard the points that correspond to these jobs, because you have control over their execution and you are able to move them out of your period of analysis. Depending on how often they run, these jobs may be classified as outliers, or they may form a special class in the workload characterization. Outlier analysis should be done carefully to avoid the elimination of a very few components that have great impact on system performance. For a complete treatment of this subject see [17].

To prevent the extreme values of a parameter from distorting the distribution, one should use some kind of transformation or scaling. One technique consists of trimming the distribution and use the 95th or 98th percentile value as the maximum value in a linear transformation such as the following:

$$D_i{}^t = \frac{\text{measured } D_i - \text{minimum of } \{D_i\}}{\text{maximum of } \{D_i\} - \text{minimum of } \{D_i\}} \qquad (6.3.7)$$

where D_i is the original service demand parameter, $D_i{}^t$ is the transformed parameter, and $\{D_i\}$ represents the set of all measured values of D_i. The above transformation maps the parameter values onto the interval from 0 to 1.

6.3.6.2.2   Distance Measures   The distance between two points is the most common metric used by clustering techniques to assess similarity among components of a workload. A popular distance measure is the *Euclidean Metric*, which defines the distance d between two points $w_i = (D_{i1}, D_{i2}, \ldots, D_{iK})$ and $w_j = (D_{j1}, D_{j2}, \ldots, D_{jK})$ as

$$d = \sqrt{\sum_{n=1}^{K} (D_{in} - D_{jn})^2}. \tag{6.3.8}$$

The use of raw data in the computation of Euclidean distances may lead to distorted results. For example, let us consider a three-tier C/S application that performs claim processing for a health insurance company. The user site is located in LAN A, and the application server and the DB server are both located in LAN B, which is connected to LAN A via WAN links. Users are complaining about poor performance. The analyst identified that the long response times occur with two types of transactions during the peak hour of the prime shift time. Using network monitors and tools from the operating system, the analyst traced the execution of the transactions. It was found out that most of the transaction execution time was spent in the WAN and in the DB server. For the purpose of the study, the analyst decided to characterize the workload using two attributes: CPU time at the database server and the size of the reply message from the DB server to the client. The reply size is used to estimate the transmission delays. Table 6.10 presents the information concerning the execution of the three most popular transactions, labeled Tr1, Tr2, and Tr3, which are inquiry, update, and retrieve transactions. The sample transactions are characterized in terms of CPU time (in msec) and reply size (in bytes).

The Euclidean distances calculated according to Eq. (6.3.8) are

$$d_{Tr1Tr2} = \sqrt{(90 - 500)^2 + (13,000 - 4,000)^2} = 9{,}009.3$$

$$d_{Tr1Tr3} = \sqrt{(90 - 700)^2 + (13,000 - 25,000)^2} = 12{,}015.5$$

$$d_{Tr2Tr3} = \sqrt{(500 - 700)^2 + (4,000 - 25,000)^2} = 21{,}001.0.$$

We can note from the above results that point Tr1 is closer to Tr2 than to Tr3. Let us now change the unit of the parameter that represents the

Table 6.10. Transaction Execution Profile

Transaction	Server CPU Time (msec)	Reply Size (bytes)
Tr1	90	13,000
Tr2	500	4,000
Tr3	700	25,000
Mean	430	14,000
Standard Deviation	310.96	10,535.65

reply size from bytes to KB (1,024 bytes). The new values of reply size for transactions Tr1, Tr2, and Tr3 are 12.7, 3.9, and 24.4 KB, respectively. Thus, the Euclidean distances among the same points become

$$d_{Tr1Tr2} = \sqrt{(90 - 500)^2 + (12.7 - 3.9)^2} = 410.1$$

$$d_{Tr1Tr3} = \sqrt{(90 - 700)^2 + (12.7 - 24.4)^2} = 610.1$$

$$d_{Tr2Tr3} = \sqrt{(500 - 700)^2 + (3.9 - 24.4)^2} = 201.1.$$

Changing the units used to represent the parameters implied in the modification of the relative distances among points Tr1, Tr2, and Tr3. Now, point Tr2 is closer to Tr3 than to Tr1. When CPU time was specified in msec and reply size in bytes, the second parameter dominated the computation of the Euclidean distance, making the effect of the first parameter on the results negligible. Scaling techniques should be used to minimize problems that arise from the choice of units and from the different ranges of values of the parameters.

6.3.6.2.3   Scaling Techniques   These are used to avoid problems that accrue from parameters with very different relative values and ranges. As we saw in the example of the computation of Euclidean distances, there are cases where it is desirable to work with unit-free parameters. Thus, a transformation is needed. The z score is a transformation that makes use of the mean and the standard deviation of each parameter over the values measured. The z score of a given parameter is calculated as

$$\text{z score} = \frac{\text{measured value} - \text{mean value}}{\text{standard deviation}}. \tag{6.3.9}$$

Let us now calculate the z score of the reply size parameter of Table 6.10. Both units (bytes and KB) are used to show that the z score is unit-free. The mean and standard deviation for the reply size (RS) in bytes are 14,000 and 10,535.65, respectively.

$$z_{RS_{Tr1}} = \frac{13,000 - 14,000}{10,535.65} = -0.095$$

$$z_{RS_{Tr2}} = \frac{4,000 - 14,000}{10,535.65} = -0.949$$

$$z_{RS_{Tr3}} = \frac{25,000 - 14,000}{10,535.65} = 1.044.$$

The mean and standard deviation for the reply size in KB are 13.67 and 10.29, respectively. So, the new z-scores are

$$z_{RS_{Tr1}} = \frac{12.7 - 13.67}{10.29} = -0.095$$

$$z_{RS_{Tr2}} = \frac{3.91 - 13.67}{10.29} = -0.949$$

$$z_{RS_{Tr3}} = \frac{24.41 - 13.67}{10.29} = 1.044$$

which are the same as before.

6.3.6.2.4 Clustering Algorithms The goal of a clustering algorithm is to identify natural groups of components, based on similar resource requirements. There are various clustering algorithms available in the literature. References [4, 13] present a thorough review of clustering techniques. They can be grouped into two broad categories: hierarchical and non-hierarchical. The former includes those techniques where the input data are not partitioned into the desired number of classes in a single step. Instead, a series of successive fusions of data are performed until the final number of clusters

is obtained. Non-hierarchical techniques start from an initial partition corresponding to the desired number of clusters. Points are reallocated among
clusters so that a particular clustering criterion is optimized. A possible criterion is the minimization of the variability within clusters, as measured by
the sum of the variance of each parameter that characterizes a point. Two
widely known clustering algorithms are discussed in detail.

The minimal spanning tree (MST) method is a hierarchical algorithm
that begins by considering each component of a workload to be a cluster.
Next, the two clusters with the minimum distance are fused to form a single
cluster. The process continues until either all points are grouped into a single
cluster or the final number of desired clusters is reached. The definition of the
desired number of clusters may be obtained with the help of a measure called
linkage distance, which represents the farthest distance between a component
in one cluster to a component in another cluster [7]. The linkage distance
increases as a function of how different the components being combined are.
If the linkage distance exceeds a given limit, the algorithm stops with the
current number of clusters. Considering a workload represented by p tuples
of the form $(D_{i1}, D_{i2}, \ldots, D_{iK})$, the steps required by the MST algorithm [17]
are shown in Fig. 6.8.

A *k-means algorithm* is a non-hierarchical clustering technique that begins by finding k points in the workload, which act as an initial estimate
of the centroids of the k clusters. The remaining points are then allocated
to the cluster with the nearest centroid. The allocation procedure iterates
several times over the input points until no point switches cluster assignment or a maximum number of iterations is performed. Figure 6.9 shows
the steps required by the k-means algorithm to perform a clustering analysis
on a workload represented by p points of the form $w_i = (D_{i1}, D_{i2}, \ldots, D_{iK})$,
$i = 1, \cdots, p$.

A common question when dealing with clustering algorithms is how many
clusters accurately represent the workload. For practical purposes in capacity planning studies, it is desirable to keep this number small. The value

---

1. Set the initial number of clusters equal to the number of components of the workload (i.e., $j = p$).

2. Repeat the following steps until the desired number of clusters is obtained.

3. Determine the parameter values of centroid C_j of each of the j clusters. Their parameter values are the means of the parameter values of all points in the cluster.

4. Calculate the $j \times j$ intercluster distance matrix, where each element (m, n) represents the distance between the centroids of clusters m and n.

5. Determine the minimum non-zero element (q, r) of the distance matrix. It indicates that clusters q and r are to be merged. Then, decrease the number of clusters ($j \leftarrow j - 1$).

Figure 6.8. Minimal spanning tree algorithm.

depends on factors such as the goals of the study, the number of critical applications, the types of objects, and the modes of processing (e.g., transaction, interactive, or batch). However, this question can be answered by examining the variation of two metrics: the average distance between points of a cluster and its centroid—the intracluster distance—and the average distance between centroids—the intercluster distance. This variation can be characterized by the coefficient of variation (CV). In general, the purpose of clustering is to minimize the intracluster CV while maximizing the intercluster CV. It is clear that if the number of clusters is made equal to the number of points, we will have achieved this goal. On the other hand, we want a compact representation of the workload. So, we need to select a relatively small number of clusters such that the intracluster variance is small and the

1. Set the number of clusters to k.

2. Choose k starting points, to be used as initial estimates of cluster centroids. For example, one can select either the first k points of the sample or the k points mutually farthest apart. In this case, the distance matrix is required.

3. Examine each point of the workload and allocate it to the cluster whose centroid is nearest. The centroid's position is recalculated each time a new point is added to the cluster.

4. Repeat step 3 until no point changes its cluster assignment during a complete pass or a maximum number of passes is performed.

Figure 6.9. k-means algorithm.

intercluster variance is large. The ratio between the intracluster and inter-cluster CVs, denoted by β_{CV}, is a useful guide in determining the quality of a clustering process. The smaller the value of β_{CV}, the better.

Example 6.2

To illustrate the use of clustering techniques, let us consider the example of a Web server composed of a fast processor and a large disk subsystem. The server is dedicated to deliver HTML documents on request. During a specific time window, the access logs of the Web server recorded the execution behavior of all requests. With the purpose of keeping the example small, a random sample of the workload was drawn and seven requests were selected. The performance study aims at analyzing the cost $\times$ benefit of caching the most popular documents in main memory. For that purpose, we need to study the relationship between document size and popularity, in order to have an idea of the size of the main memory required by the document cache. Table 6.11 shows the parameters that characterize the workload for the purpose of this study. As can be noted from the table, the components

Table 6.11. Workload Sample

Document	Size (KB)	Number of Accesses
1	12	281
2	150	28
3	5	293
4	25	123
5	7	259
6	4	241
7	35	75

of this workload are not homogeneous. Therefore, we want to find out classes of similar components. A step-by-step description of the clustering process is now presented.

1. Because of the difference in magnitude in the values of document size and frequency of access, a change of scale is required. Table 6.12 shows the parameter values transformed by a $\log_{10}$ function. For instance, the value 150 in Table 6.11 is transformed to $2.18 = \log_{10} 150$ in Table 6.12.

2. Let us consider that our goal is to obtain three clusters. In the general case, we would repeat the clustering process for several number of clusters and pick the one that represents the smaller value of β_{CV}. We use the Euclidean distance as the metric to evaluate distances between clusters. The MST algorithm is selected.

3. The initial number of clusters is set to seven, which is the number of components.

4. The parameter values of the centroids of each cluster coincide with the parameter values of the components, as shown in Table 6.13. In this case, each cluster has a single component.

Table 6.12. Logarithmic Transformation of Parameters

Document	Size (KB)	Number of Accesses
1	1.08	2.45
2	2.18	1.45
3	0.70	2.47
4	1.40	2.09
5	0.85	2.41
6	0.60	2.38
7	1.54	1.88

5. Let us now calculate the intercluster distance matrix, using Eq. (6.3.8). For instance, we note from Table 6.14 that the distance between clusters C5 and C6 is 0.25.

6. The minimum distance among the clusters of Table 6.14 is that between C3 and C6, i.e., 0.13. These clusters are merged to form a larger cluster

Table 6.13. Centroids of the Initial Clusters

Document	Size (KB)	Number of Accesses
C1	1.08	2.45
C2	2.18	1.45
C3	0.70	2.47
C4	1.40	2.09
C5	0.85	2.41
C6	0.60	2.38
C7	1.54	1.88

Table 6.14. Intercluster Distance Matrix

Cluster	C1	C2	C3	C4	C5	C6	C7
C1	0	1.49	0.38	0.48	0.24	0.48	0.74
C2		0	1.79	1.01	1.64	1.83	0.76
C3			0	0.79	0.16	**0.13**	1.03
C4				0	0.64	0.85	0.26
C5					0	0.25	0.88
C6						0	1.07
C7							0

C36. The coordinates of its centroid are $(0.70 + 0.60)/2 = 0.65$ and $(2.47 + 2.38)/2 = 2.43$.

7. Now, we have six clusters. We recompute the distance matrix for the new number of clusters, as shown in Table 6.15.

8. The smallest element of Table 6.15 corresponds to the distance between clusters C36 and C5 which are therefore merged. The coordinates of the centroid of cluster C356 are $(0.65 + 0.85)/2 = 0.75$ and $(2.43 + 2.41)/2 = 2.42$.

Table 6.15. Intercluster Distance Matrix

Cluster	C1	C2	C36	C4	C5	C7
C1	0	1.49	0.43	0.48	0.24	0.74
C2		0	1.81	1.01	1.64	0.76
C36			0	0.82	**0.19**	1.05
C4				0	0.64	0.26
C5					0	0.88
C7						0

9. We now have five clusters; the distance matrix for the new cluster configuration is given in Table 6.16.

10. The smallest element of Table 6.16 corresponds to the distance between clusters C4 and C7 which are therefore merged. The coordinates of the centroid of C47 are $(1.40+1.54)/2 = 1.47$ and $(2.09+1.88)/2 = 1.99$.

11. The number of clusters is now four, and the distance matrix for the new cluster configuration is given in Table 6.17.

12. The smallest element of Table 6.17 corresponds to the distance between clusters C1 and C365 which are therefore merged. The parameter values of the centroid of C1365 are $(1.08+0.75)/2 = 0.92$ and $(2.45+2.42)/2 = 2.44$.

13. The number of clusters is now three, and the distance matrix for the new cluster configuration is given in Table 6.18.

14. The original workload given in Table 6.11 has been partitioned into three classes of similar requests. Each class is represented by parameter values that are equal to the average of the parameter values of all components of the class. Table 6.19 presents the output of the clustering process. It contains the description of the centroids that represent

Table 6.16. Intercluster Distance Matrix

Cluster	C1	C2	C365	C4	C7
C1	0	1.49	0.33	0.48	0.74
C2		0	1.73	1.01	0.76
C365			0	0.73	0.96
C4				0	**0.26**
C7					0

Table 6.17. Intercluster Distance Matrix

Cluster	C1	C2	C365	C47
C1	0	1.49	**0.33**	0.61
C2		0	1.73	0.89
C365			0	0.84
C47				0

each cluster and its number of components. Each cluster corresponds to one class in the workload. In the example, classes are named according to their document size. For instance, the class of small documents corresponds to an average document size of 8.19 KB and an average number of accesses equal to 271.51. This class has four documents. Note that the values in Table 6.19 were scaled back to the original scale. ∎

6.4 Web Workloads

There is a significant body of work on workload characterization of Web traffic. Some of the characteristics considered deal with file size distributions, file popularity distribution, self-similarity in Web traffic, reference locality,

Table 6.18. Intercluster Distance Matrix

Cluster	C1365	C2	C47
C1356	0	1.60	0.72
C2		0	0.89
C47			0

Table 6.19. Output of the Clustering Process

Type	Class	Document Size (KB)	No. of Accesses	No. of Components
Small	C1356	8.19	271.51	4
Medium	C47	29.58	96.05	2
Large	C2	150.00	28.00	1

and user request patterns. A number of studies of different Web sites found file sizes to exhibit *heavy-tailed* distributions and object popularity to be Zipf-like. Other studies of different Web site environments demonstrated long-range dependencies in the user request process, in other words, strong correlations in the user requests. In particular, Arlitt and Williamson [3] identified 10 workload properties, called *invariants*, across six different data sets, which included different types of information provider Web sites. Some of the most relevant invariants are: i) images and HTML files account for 90-100% of the files transferred; ii) 10% of the documents account for 90% of all requests and bytes transferred; iii) file sizes follow the Pareto distribution, and iv) the file inter-reference times are independent and exponentially distributed. Shortly after, Almeida et. al. [2] discovered that the popularity of documents served by Web sites dedicated to information dissemination follows Zipf's Law. Crovella and Bestavros pointed to the self-similar nature of Web server traffic [10]. A very helpful survey can be found in a paper by Pitkow [22]. Even though the focus of this chapter is on workload characterization methodologies, it is important to review some basic properties found in the analysis of actual Web traffic, namely the presence of power law distributions and the bursty nature of the traffic.

6.4.1   Power-Laws

Power-laws are expressions of the form $y \propto x^{\alpha}$, where α is a constant and x and y are the measures of interest. It has been shown that power-laws can be used to describe Internet topology properties, such as the number of neighbors within h hops [14]. Self-similarity and heavy tails have been found in many descriptions of Web traffic [10, 22]. A variable X follows a heavy-tailed distribution if

$$P[X > x] = kx^{-\alpha}L(x)$$

where $L(x)$ is a slowing varying function. A Pareto distribution is a special case of heavy-tailed distribution where the number of events larger than x is an inverse power of x. The tail (i.e., 1 - the cumulative distribution function) of a Pareto distribution is

$$P[X > x] = kx^{-\alpha}$$

. In a log-log plot, $x^{-\alpha}$ is a straight line with slope $-\alpha$. Among other implications, a heavy-tailed distribution presents a great degree of variability, and a non-negligible probability of high sample values. When α is less than 2, the variance is infinite, and when α is less than 1, the mean is infinite. Common distributions, such as the exponential distribution decay much faster than the Pareto distribution.

Another power-law is Zipf's Law [24], which is a relationship between the frequency of occurrence of an event and its rank, when the events are ranked with respect to the frequency of occurrence. Zipf's Law was originally applied to the relationship between words in a text and their frequency of use. It states that if one ranks the popularity of words used in a given text (denoted by r) by their frequency of use (denoted by $f(r)$) then

$$f(r) \sim 1/r. \tag{6.4.10}$$

This expression can be generalized as

$$f(r) = C/r^{\alpha}, \tag{6.4.11}$$

where C is a constant and α a positive parameter equal to one. This law describes phenomena where large events are rare, but small ones are quite common.

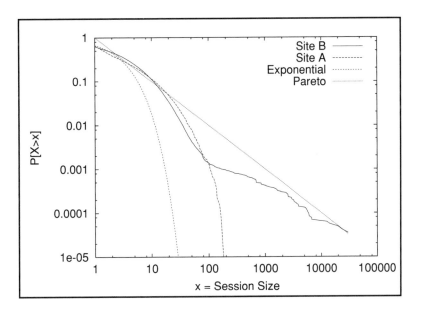

Figure 6.10. Session size distribution (reprinted from [21]).

Power law distributions have been observed in various aspects of the Web and can be used to characterize user behavior. Prior studies of Web traffic have found that distribution of Web requests follow Zipf's Law. In particular, the popularity of static pages (i.e., documents) served by information provider Web sites follows Zipf's Law [2, 3]. Surfing patterns on the Web have been shown to display strong statistical regularities, which can be described by universal laws [16]. Zipf's Law has been extensively used to explain the patterns of access to Web servers and proxies. Patterns of keywords used by customers during their interaction with an e-business site are described by Zipf's Law [21]. Relationships such as Zipf's Law can be used to facilitate both cache resource planning and strategies for distributing Web contents and functions.

As an example of the use of Zipf's Law, let us look at the distribution of the session sizes obtained from logs of two actual e-business sites [21]. Figure 6.10 plots the distribution of session sizes for both sites. The graph shows the empirical probability that X is greater than x. We can distinguish two regions in the plot. The first one comprises session sizes up to 100, in which the curves for both sites are similar. In particular, in the region from about 5 to 100, they are fit by a straight line (not shown for clarity) with inclination ~ -2.05. For sessions longer that 100, the behavior changes. We can see that for site A, the probability for longer sessions falls abruptly, whereas for site B it remains close to the straight-line plot, which is for a Pareto-like distribution with $\alpha = 1$. This "very" heavy tail is most likely due to the accesses by robots, which tend to exhibit long sessions. Site A was not accessed by any robot and does not exhibit very large sessions in the logs.

6.4.2 Bursty Workloads

New phenomena have been observed in large distributed systems such as the Internet, intranets, and WWW. Several studies [3, 10, 18] have revealed new properties of network traffic, such as *self-similarity*. Intuitively, a self-similar process looks bursty across several time scales. A study [18] shows that total traffic (measured in bytes per second or packets per second) on Ethernet LANs and on WANs is self-similar. In another study [10], it is shown that Web traffic contains bursts observable over four orders of magnitude. A visual inspection of the number of requests arriving at a Web site on different time scales, i.e., in time intervals of varying length (see Fig. 6.11) reveals "burstiness" or high variability, which may degrade performance and throughput if not accounted for. What is important for us in this book is that self-similarity of network traffic (i.e., Internet, WWW, Ethernet) implies burstiness at several time scales. And burstiness has a strong impact on the performance of networked systems.

As pointed out in [5], HTTP request traffic is bursty with the burstiness being observable over different time-interval scales. Peak rates during bursts

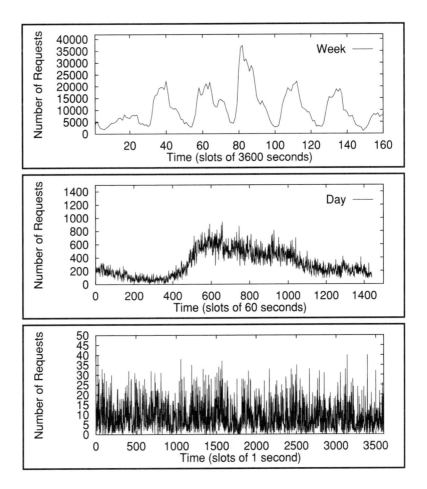

Figure 6.11. WWW traffic burst (reprinted from [21]).

exceed the average rate by factors of five to ten and can easily surpass the capacity of the server. It is also shown in [5] that even a small amount of burstiness degrades the throughput of a Web server. So, we need to include burst effects in our models. The question that arises naturally is: How can we represent burstiness in the workload characterization?

Burstiness in a given observation period can be represented by a pair of parameters, (a, b). Parameter a is the ratio between the maximum observed request rate and the average request rate during the monitoring period. Parameter b is the fraction of time during which the instantaneous arrival rate exceeds the average arrival rate. In [5], it is shown that even a small amount of burstiness ($a = 6$, $b = 5\%$) can degrade the throughput of a Web server by 12–20%.

Chapter 10 presents simple analytical models that incorporate the effects of burstiness. It is important to keep in mind that the representativeness of workload models for analytic models is limited. Very often, simplifying assumptions are introduced in the workload representation so that the solution of the analytical model remains simple and efficient. To illustrate the problem, let us examine the case of modeling Ethernet environments. The workload of an Ethernet network consists of the packets transmitted by workstations on the network and can be characterized by packet length and interarrival time statistics. With the purpose of simplifying the model, many studies on workload characterization of Ethernet environments assume homogeneous arrivals of packets. However, measurement experiments described in [6] show that the packet arrival process in Ethernet environments is bursty. The packet arrival pattern follows a train model, where the network traffic consists of a collection of packet streams flowing between various pairs of workstations [17]. One of the sources of this arrival pattern stems from the fact that messages transmitted are often much larger than the maximum packet size on the Ethernet and must be partitioned into smaller units that are consecutively transmitted. This operational behavior of Ethernet networks clearly contrasts with the homogeneous arrival assumption. Although the simplifications imply loss of accuracy, they do not invalidate the use of simple models; they are still capable of capturing some fundamental performance properties of computer systems. Simple performance models are valuable tools for practitioners.

6.4.3   Streaming Media Workloads

Digital audio and video is becoming an important component of Internet traffic and therefore it is important to understand this type of workload.

Compared to HTTP traffic, streaming media consumes much more bandwidth and requires higher data rates. Two studies [1, 12] present extensive analysis of streaming media workloads. Reference [12] presents a client-based streaming media workload generated by a large organization. During a one-week period, 4,786 clients accessed 23,738 objects from 866 servers, transferring 56 GB of streaming media. A number of properties were derived from the collected data: (1) multimedia exhibits a strong temporal locality during peak hours, (2) 20-40% of the active sessions shared streams concurrently, (3) most of the streams accessed had a short duration (i.e., less than 10 seconds) and a modest size (i.e., less than 1 MB), (4) the distribution of client requests to objects is Zipf-like ($\alpha = 0.47$). Peak bandwidth consumed by clients over a 5-minute period was 2.8 Mbps.

While reference [12] looked at the workload from a client standpoint, reference [1] characterizes the traffic from the server viewpoint. It analyzes log data for two media servers in use at major universities in the U.S. The media server used records one log entry per client session. In this context, a session is defined as a sequence of client requests for a given media. In both servers, it was observed a significant fraction of requests of short duration, i.e., less than 3 minutes. The study examines file access frequency distributions and the distribution of accesses to each 10-second segment within a media file. The study also found a high degree of interactivity in one of the logs, represented by the fact that 90% of the requests are for fewer than three minutes of video. The initial steps to characterize media server workloads are similar to those used in characterization of HTTP workloads. In other words, the characterization process starts by looking at information such as: distribution of request interarrival times, measurement of media segment access frequencies, session length distributions, file size distribution, and percentage of accesses to infrequently requested files and segments. The major findings of the characterization of the two media server workloads are: (1) there is a high degree of similarity in the measures obtained from the two servers; (2) the client session arrival process is approximately Poisson, whereas the time between interactive requests is heavy-tailed; (3) for the most popular files, all 10-second segments of the media have about the same fraction of accesses.

6.5   Concluding Remarks

Understanding and characterizing a workload are key issues in any performance study. This process represents the first step for capacity planning, performance tuning, system procurement and selection, and for the design of new systems. The better one understands the workload of a system, the more chances one has to obtain the best possible level of performance, given the system's workload. Although each system may require a specific approach to the analysis of its workload, there are some common guidelines that apply well to most systems. The basic steps to perform a workload characterization are summarized as:

- selection of a point-of-view from which the workload will be analyzed
- identification of the basic components of the workload
- selection of the set of parameters that capture the most relevant characteristics of the workload for the purpose of the study
- monitoring the system to collect raw performance data
- partitioning of the workload into classes of similar components
- calculation of the values of the parameters that characterize each class
- construction and validation of a workload model

Bibliography

[1] J. M. Almeida, J. Krueger, D. Eager, and M. K. Vernon, "Analysis of Educational Media Server Workloads," *Proc. 11th Int'l. Workshop on Network and Operating System Support for Digital Audio and Video (NOSSDAV 2001)*, Port Jefferson, New York, June 25-26, 2001.

[2] V. A. F. Almeida, M. Crovella, A. Bestavros, and A. Oliveira, "Characterizing Reference Locality in the WWW," *Proc. IEEE/ACM International Conference on Parallel and Distributed System (PDIS)*, Miami Beach, Florida, Dec. 1996, pp. 92–103.

[3] M. Arlitt and C. Williamson, "Web Server Workload Characterization: The Search for Invariants," *Proc. ACM 1996 SIGMETRICS Conf. Measurement Comput. Syst.*, Philadelphia, Pennsylvania, May 1996, pp. 126–137.

[4] M. R. Anderberg, *Cluster Analysis for Applications*, Academic Press, New York, 1973.

[5] G. Banga and P. Druschel, "Measuring the Capacity of a Web Server," *Proc. USENIX Symp. Internet Technol. Syst.*, Monterey, California, Dec. 1997.

[6] R. Bodnarchuk and R. Bunt, "A Synthetic Workload Model for a Distributed File System," *Proc. 1991 ACM SIGMETRICS Conf. Measurement Comput. Syst.*, May 1991.

[7] J. Cady and B. Howarth, *Computer System Performance Management and Capacity Planning*, Prentice Hall, Upper Saddle River, New Jersey, 1990.

[8] M. Calzarossa, L. Massari, and D. Tessera, "Workload Characterization Issues and Methodologies," in *Performance Evaluation: Origins and Directions*, G. Haring, C. Lindemann, and M. Reiser, eds., Springer-Verlag, Berlin, Germany, Lecture Notes in Computer Science, 2000.

[9] M. Calzarossa and G. Serazzi, "Workload Characterization," *Proc. IEEE*, vol. 81, no. 8, Aug. 1993.

[10] M. Crovella and A. Bestavros, "Self-Similarity in World Wide Web Traffic: Evidence and Possible Causes," *IEEE/ACM Transactions on Networking*, 5(6):835–846, Dec. 1997.

[11] C. Cunha, A. Bestavros, and M. Crovella, "Characteristics of WWW Client-Based Traces," *Tech. Rep. BU-CS-95-010*, Comput. Sci. Department, Boston University, Boston, Massachusetts, Nov. 1995.

[12] M. Chesire, A. Wolman, G. Voelker, and A. Levy, "Measurement and Analysis of a Streaming-Media Workload," *Proc. 3rd USENIX Symposium on Internet Technologies and Systems*, San Francisco, California, March 2001.

[13] B. Everitt, *Cluster Analysis*, 4th ed., Oxford University Press, 2001.

[14] C. Faloutsos, M. Faloutsos, and P. Faloutsos, "On Power-Law Relationships of the Internet Topology," *Proc. of ACM SIGCOMM*, Aug. 1999.

[15] D. Ferrari, G. Serazzi, and A. Zeigner, *Measurement and Tuning of Computer Systems*, Prentice Hall, Upper Saddle River, New Jersey, 1983.

[16] B. Huberman, P. Pirolli, J. E. Pitkow, and R. Lukose, "Strong Regularities in World Wide Web Surfing," *Science*, vol. 280, April, 1998.

[17] R. Jain, *The Art of Computer System Performance: Analysis, Techniques for Experimental Design, Measurement, Simulation, and Modeling*, John Wiley and Sons, New York, 1991.

[18] W. Leland, M. Taqqu, W. Willinger, and D. Wilson, "On the Self-Similar Nature of Ethernet Traffic (Extended Version)," *IEEE/ACM Trans. Commun. Techno.*, Feb. 1994.

[19] D. A. Menascé, V. A. F. Almeida, and L. W. Dowdy, *Capacity Planning and Performance Modeling: From Mainframes to Client-Server Systems*, Prentice Hall, Upper Saddle River, New Jersey, 1994.

[20] D. A. Menascé and V. A. F. Almeida, *Scaling for E-Business: Technologies, Models, Performance, and Capacity Planning*, Prentice Hall, Upper Saddle River, New Jersey, 2000.

[21] D. A. Menascé, V. A. F. Almeida, R. Riedi, F. P. Ribeiro, R. Fonseca, and W. Meira Jr., "In Search of Invariants for E-Business Workloads," *Proc. 2000 ACM Conf. in E-commerce*, Minneapolis, Minnesota, Oct. 17-20, 2000.

[22] J. E. Pitkow, "Summary of WWW Characterization," *Proc. World Wide Web Conf.*, 2 (1), Jan. 1999, pp. 3–13.

[23] E. Shriver, *Performance Modeling for Realistic Storage Devices,* Ph.D. Dissertation, Dept. Computer Science, New York University, New York, May 1997.

[24] G. Zipf, *Human Behavior and the Principle of Least Effort*, Addison Wesley, Cambridge, Massachusetts, 1949.

Chapter 7

Benchmarks and Performance Tests

7.1 Introduction

It's common sense—everyone agrees that the best way to study the performance of a given system is to run the actual workload on the hardware platform and measure the results. However, many times this approach is not feasible.

Here are two situations where one needs to take alternate approaches to study the performance of a system. The first case is that of a company that is planning to roll out a new Web-based order system. Management has already specified the software architecture and is about to start the procurement process to select the server systems. The performance analyst understands that it is not either viable or cost-effective to set up configurations of Web servers to run pieces of the actual workload and measure their performance. Therefore, the analyst decided to use standard benchmark results. *Benchmarking* is the primary method for measuring the performance of an actual physical machine [7]. Benchmarking refers to running a set of representative programs on different computers and networks and measuring the results. Benchmark results are used to evaluate the performance of a given system on a well-defined workload. Much of the popularity of standard benchmarks comes from the fact that they have performance objectives and workloads that are measurable and repeatable. Usually, computer system procurement studies and comparative analyses of products rely on benchmarks. They are also used as monitoring and diagnostic tools. Vendors, developers, and users run benchmarks to pinpoint performance problems of new systems.

Consider now an online brokerage's trading site that is planning a major change in the services it provides on the Internet. The application is ready for deployment and the engineers are prepared to put the code on the live site. But management is cautious about this procedure and wants to make sure its customers will not face unpleasant surprises when accessing the new site. Management is concerned about scalability problems and is not sure if the site can handle heavy traffic loads. In other words, management wants to do predictive testing rather than reacting to failures. The most commonly used approach to obtain performance results of a given Web service is *performance testing*, which means to run tests to determine the performance of the service under specific application and workload conditions. In the Web environment, companies cannot afford to deploy services and applications before ensuring that they run really well. It is crucial to predict how a particular Web service will respond to a specific workload. Benchmarks are not able to provide accurate answers to questions about specific scenarios of workload and applications. Therefore, one has too look for specific performance tests. Based on a particular workload and application scenario, performance testing should provide information on how the service will respond to realistic loads before it goes into production.

This chapter presents several different standard industry benchmarks and discusses them in the context of performance modeling and capacity planning. It also shows a methodology for performance testing, that follows the various steps of the capacity planning methodology introduced in Chapter 5.

7.2   The Nature of Benchmarks

Time and rate are the basic measures of system performance. From the user's viewpoint, program or application execution time is the best indicator of system performance. Users do not want to know if the service is executed next to the desktop computer on the LAN or if it is processed thousands of miles away from her/his location, connected through various networks. Users always want fast response time. From management's viewpoint, the performance of a system is defined by the rate at which it can perform work. For example, system managers are interested in questions such as: How many transactions can the system execute per minute, or how many requests is the Web site able to service per second? In addition, both users and managers are always concerned with cost, reflected in questions such as: What is the system's operational cost? And what is the server purchase cost? As a consequence of all these different viewpoints, the basic problem remains: What is a good standard measure of system performance?

Computer makers usually refer to the speed of a processor by its cycle time, which can be expressed by its length (e.g., 1 nanosecond) or by its rate (e.g., 1 GHz). However, one common misperception is the use of the clock speed (i.e., in gigahertz or nanoseconds) to compare processor performance. The overall performance of a processor is directly affected by other architectural traits, such as caching, pipelining, functional units and compiler technology [5]. In the past, a popular way of rating processor performance was MIPS (millions of instructions per second). Although MIPS had been largely employed as a basis for comparisons of processors, it is important to remind the reader about the problems with its use. MIPS is dependent on the instruction set, which makes it difficult to compare computers with different repertoires of instructions. For instance, using MIPS to compare the performance of a Reduced Instruction Set Computer (RISC) with that of a Complex Instruction Set Computer (CISC) has little significance. As MIPS is not defined in a domain of any specific application, its use may be misleading. Different programs running on the same computer may reach different levels of MIPS.

System performance is complex; it is the result of the interplay of many hardware and software components. Compounding the problem is the fact that every Web service architecture is unique in its configuration, applications, operating systems, and workload. Furthermore, Web services exhibit a large variation in performance when running different workloads. No single number can represent the performance of a Web system on all applications. In a quest to find a good performance measure, standard programs, known as *benchmarks*, have been used to evaluate the performance of systems.

Benchmark results can both inform and confuse users about the real capability of systems to execute their actual production workloads. The source of confusion lies on how one interprets benchmark results. Before using benchmark results, one must understand the workload, the system under study, the tests, the measurements, and the results. Otherwise, one will not be able to interpret the benchmark results properly. Therefore, the first step is to answer the following questions.

- What is a particular benchmark actually testing?

- How close does the benchmark resemble the user environment workload?

- What is the benchmark really measuring?

Once benchmark results are well understood, one can use them to increase one's knowledge about the performance of the system under study. For example, benchmark results can be used to estimate input parameters for performance models of Web service environments. Or they can give an idea about the performance of a system when processing heavy workloads. However, it is important to note that most benchmarks are good tools for comparing systems, rather than accurate tools for sizing or capacity planning for a given Web service.

7.2.1   Benchmark Hierarchy

Benchmarks can be viewed as grouped into two categories: coarse-grain benchmarks and fine-grain benchmarks [7]. The granularity of the benchmark is determined by the granularity of the property that can be measured by the benchmark. For example, a benchmark measuring the performance of an e-commerce system is considered coarse-grain, while a benchmark measuring the CPU speed is considered fine-grain. A series of complex tests, of different granularities, has been designed to investigate the performance of computer systems. The plethora of existing benchmark programs can be thought of as a hierarchy, where different levels are characterized by the complexity and granularity of their tests as well as by their ability to predict actual performance.

At the innermost level of the hierarchy, as shown in Fig. 7.1, are synthetic benchmarks that perform only *basic operations*, such as addition and multiplication. Dhrystone is an example of this type of program: It is a synthetic benchmark aimed at measuring the speed of a system when executing fixed-point computations. This type of program does not compute any real task and its utility to the comprehension of performance of practical systems is very limited.

At the second level of the benchmark hierarchy are the so-called *toy benchmarks*. They are very small programs that implement some classical puzzles, such as Sieve of Eratosthenes and Towers of Hanoi [5]. These types

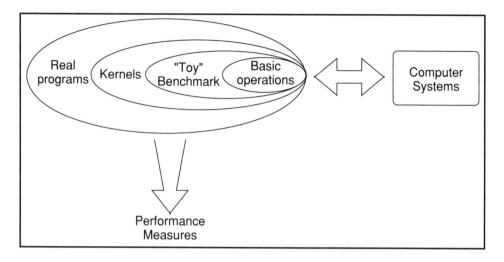

Figure 7.1. Benchmark hierarchy.

of benchmark are not helpful in predicting the performance of real workloads and have no use in the analysis of practical problems.

Kernels, the third level, are portions of code extracted from real programs. These pieces of code represent the essence of the computation, i.e., where most of the time is spent. Livermore Loops and Linpack are good examples of program kernels. In general, this type of benchmark concentrates on the system's capability to execute some numeric computation and therefore measures only the processor performance. Because they are not real programs, they provide little information about the performance perceived by end users. At the outermost level of the hierarchy is the workload composed of full-scale, real programs used to solve real problems. These programs make up benchmark suites, such as SPEC, and TPC. As an example, there are some domain-oriented benchmarks that use programs such as components of the C programming language compiler, word processing, and debit and credit bank transactions. They offer useful information about the performance of a given system when running some given applications.

7.2.2   Avoiding Pitfalls

As in any performance study, the first step to safely interpret the benchmark results is to understand the environment (see Chapter 5). In other words, one needs to know where and how the benchmark tests were carried out. Basically, one needs information such as processor specification (e.g., model, cache, and number of processors), memory, I/O subsystem (e.g., disks, models, and speed), network (e.g., LAN, WAN, and operational conditions), and software (e.g., operating system, compilers, transaction processing monitor, and database management system). Once you understand the benchmark environment, then you should consider several other factors before making use of the benchmark numbers. To avoid pitfalls, you should ask yourself some key questions to find out how relevant the benchmark results are to your particular system or application. Examples of these key questions are:

- Does the SUT have a configuration similar to the actual system? Examine the configuration description and compare the hardware, the network environment (topology, routers, protocols, and servers), the software, the operating system parameters, and the workload. Does the testing environment look like my system environment? Is the number of processors in your system the same as that described in the benchmark environment? What version of the OS was used in the tests? What were the memory and cache sizes of the server? These are typical questions you should answer before drawing conclusions about the benchmark results.

- How representative of the actual workload are the benchmark tests? For example, if your system is dedicated to order processing, then a transaction processing benchmark can give you some insight about the performance of your application. However, if you are planning a new graphical application, transaction processing benchmark results are useless, because the two workloads are very dissimilar.

As systems evolve, so must the benchmarks that are used to compare them. All standard benchmarks release new versions periodically. Therefore, when examining benchmark results, pay attention to the version used and look for new features included in the latest releases.

7.2.3   Common Benchmarks

Many benchmark tests are used to evaluate a wide variety of systems, subsystems, and components under different types of workloads and applications. Users groups and searches on the Web are good sources of updated information about several types of benchmarks. However, to be useful, a benchmark should have the following attributes [4]:

- Relevance: It must provide meaningful performance measures within a specific problem domain.

- Understandable: The benchmark results should be simple and easy to understand.

- Scalable: The benchmark tests must be applicable to a wide range of systems, in terms of cost, performance, and configuration.

- Acceptable: The benchmarks should present unbiased results that are recognized by users and vendors.

Two consortia offer benchmarks that are common yardsticks for comparing different computer systems. The System Performance Evaluation Corporation (SPEC) [11] is an organization of computer industry vendors that develops standardized performance tests, i.e., benchmarks, and publishes reviewed results. SPEC publishes benchmark performance results of CPU, multiprocessor systems, file server, mail server, Web server, and graphics [11]. The Transaction Processing Performance Council (TPC) [15] is a nonprofit organization that defines transaction processing, database, and e-commerce benchmarks. TPC-C, TPC-H, TPC-R are commonly used industry benchmarks that measure throughput and price/performance of OLTP environments and decision support systems [4] and TPC-W measures the performance of systems that deliver e-commerce service. The next sections discuss characteristics of various standard benchmarks.

7.3   Processor Benchmarks

SPEC CPU benchmark is designed to provide measures of performance for comparing compute-intensive workloads on different computer systems. SPEC CPU benchmarks are designated as SPECxxxx, where *xxxx* specifies the generation of the benchmark. SPEC2000 [6] contains two suites of benchmarks: *int* and *fp*. The former is designed for measuring and comparing compute-intensive integer performance. The latter focuses on floating-point performance. Because these benchmarks are compute-intensive, they concentrate on the performance of the computer's processor, the memory architecture, and the compiler.

7.3.1   Workload

The SPEC benchmark suite consists of programs selected from various sources, primarily academic and scientific. Some are reasonably full implementations and other programs are adaptations to fulfill the benchmark goal of measuring CPU. The *fp* suite for measuring floating-point compute performance contains fourteen applications written in the FORTRAN and C languages. The benchmark suite (CINT2000) that measures integer compute performance comprises twelve applications written in C and C++. In addition to the short description of the benchmarks, Table 7.1 also shows the SPECint performance for a given machine. Performance is stated relative to a reference machine, a 300-MHz Sun Ultra5_10, which gets a score of 100. Each benchmark program is run and measured on this machine to establish a reference time for that benchmark. These times are used to calculate the SPEC results described in the next section.

Table 7.1. SPECint Benchmarks

Number	Benchmark	Score	Application Area
1	164.gzip	237	compression
2	175.vpr	266	FPGA circuit placement and routing
3	176.gcc	337	C programming language compiler
4	181.mcf	238	combinatorial optimization
5	186.crafty	369	game playing: chess
6	197.parser	206	word processing
7	252.eon	365	computer visualization
8	253.perlbmk	312	Perl programming language
9	254.gap	251	group theory, interpreter
10	255.vortex	400	object-oriented database
11	256.bzip2	328	compression
12	300.twolf	371	place and route simulator

7.3.2   Results

SPEC CPU2000 provides performance measurements for system speed and throughput. The speed metric measures how fast a machine completes running all of the CPU benchmarks. The throughput metric indicates how many tasks a computer can complete in a given amount of time. The SPEC CPU benchmark results are organized along three dimensions of the compute-intensive performance domain: integer versus floating point, speed versus throughput, and aggressive versus conservative. The conservative or base results are aggregate performance statistics with minimal compiler optimizations. Aggressive or non-base numbers are obtained with heavy optimizations. For the purpose of measuring speed, each benchmark test, denoted by nnn, has its own ratio, defined as:

$$\text{SPECratio for } nnn.\text{benchmark} = \frac{nnn.\text{benchmark reference time}}{nnn.\text{benchmark run time}}.$$

SPECint is the geometric mean of 12 normalized ratios, one for each benchmark program in Table 7.1. This metric refers to the benchmark results compiled with aggressive (i.e., non-base) optimizations. SPECint_base is the geometric mean of 12 normalized ratios when compiled with conservative optimization for each benchmark. For each benchmark of the CINT suite, a throughput measure is calculated. SPECint_rate is the geometric mean of twelve normalized throughput ratios. SPECint_rate_base is the geometric mean of twelve normalized throughput ratios when compiled with conservative optimization for each benchmark. Similar measures are calculated for the CFP suite using the individual results obtained for each of the fourteen programs that make up the benchmark. Table 7.2 shows the SPEC CPU performance results for system $\mathcal{X}$. Benchmark results can be used to provide information to performance models to answer some typical *what if* questions, as shown in Ex. 7.1.

Example 7.1

Suppose that a vendor is announcing a machine to be used as an advanced Web server with a faster processor and a larger on-chip cache memory. The

Table 7.2. SPEC CPU Benchmark Results for System $\mathcal{X}$

Measure	Result
SPECint	543
SPECint_base	526
SPECint_rate	6.07
SPECint_rate_base	5.94
SPECfp	564
SPECfp_base	549
SPECfp_rate	6.53
SPECfp_rate_base	6.34

vendor says that the new technology improves performance by 60%. Before deciding on the upgrade, you want an answer to the classic question: "What if we use the new Web server?" Although the vendor does not provide specific information about the performance of Web services, it points to the SPECint results. In this case, SPECint is relevant because the technology upgrade reflects directly on the CPU speed. To estimate the new server impact on the response time of HTTP requests, we can use the models described in Chapter 10. However, we need to feed the model with input data that reflect the speed of the new server. Note that the new technology basically improves the CPU performance. The SPECint for the old and new servers are 363 and 489, respectively. Therefore, we should change the CPU service demands to reflect the server upgrade. Let α denote the ratio between the SPECint of the two servers:

$$\alpha = \frac{\text{SPECint}^{\text{new}}}{\text{SPECint}^{\text{old}}} = \frac{489}{363} = 1.35.$$

The new CPU service demand, denoted by $D_{\text{cpu}}^{\text{new}}$, is

$$D_{\text{cpu}}^{\text{new}} = \frac{D_{\text{cpu}}^{\text{old}}}{\alpha} = \frac{D_{\text{cpu}}^{\text{old}}}{1.35}. \qquad (7.3.1)$$

What Eq. (7.3.1) says is that the CPU service time of the HTTP requests will be smaller in the new processor. In other words, the CPU time dedicated to service the requests should be divided by $\alpha = 1.35$ to reflect the faster processor. Although CPU is a key component of a system, the overall system performance depends on many factors, such as I/O and networking. Performance models, such as those described in Chapters 9 and 10, are able to calculate the effect of upgrading the CPU on the overall performance of the system using the new CPU demands.   ■

7.4   Web Server Benchmarks

A set of tests and workloads are specified to measure Web servers. The most commonly used Web server benchmarks are detailed next. This sec-

tion describes three Web server benchmarks: Webstone, SPECweb [11], and
Scalable URL Reference Generator (SURGE) [3]. Those programs simulate
Web clients. They generate requests to a server, according to some specified workload characteristics, receive the responses returned by the server
and collect the measurements. It is important to note that Web server
benchmarks are usually carried out in small, isolated LANs, with almost no
transmission errors. On the contrary, Web services, offered in *real world*,
are accessed through the Internet or large intranets, which involve WAN
connections, gateways, routers, bridges, and hubs that make the network
environment noisy and error-prone. Moreover, latencies are much higher
in real-world environments than in the LANs used in benchmarking efforts.
Thus, the analysis of Web benchmark results should take this observation
into account.

7.4.1   SPECweb

SPECweb is a software benchmark product developed by SPEC [11], designed to measure a system's ability to act as a Web server. SPECwebxx
specifies the generation (xx) of the Web server benchmark. SPECweb99
measures the maximum number of simultaneous connections that a Web
server is able to support while still meeting specific throughput and error
rate requirements. The standard benchmark workload includes both static
and dynamically generated HTML and support for HTTP 1.1. It can be
used to evaluate the performance of Web server software running on Posix-
compliant UNIX or Windows NT systems. SPECweb99 uses one or more
client systems to generate the HTTP workload for the server. Each client
sends HTTP requests to the server and then validates the response received.
At the end of the benchmark run, the data from all the clients is collected
by the prime client. The *prime* client process coordinates the test execution
of the client processes on the client machines. This client uses this data
to calculate aggregate bit rate for the test and determine the number of
simultaneous connections that conform to the specified bit rate limits.

7.4.1.1   Workload

The workload characteristics for SPECweb99 were drawn from the logs of several popular Internet servers and some smaller Web sites. Thus, SPECweb tries to mimic the access patterns to the documents of a server of a typical Web service provider that supports home pages for various companies and organizations. Each home page is a collection of files ranging in size from small icons to large documents or images. The different types of requests that comprise the overall workload mix are summarized in Table 7.3.

The SPECweb workload mixes four classes of files, according to their file sizes and access percentages, as displayed in Table 7.4. The workload file set consists of a number of directories. Each directory contains nine files per class, 36 files in total. Within each class, access distributions reflect the fact that certain files are more popular than others. Accesses are generated using the Zipf's Law distribution. The resulting overall distribution is very close to actual measured distributions on real servers [11]. It is worth noting that the relationship established for file sizes and frequency in this workload follows the heavy-tailed distribution concepts discussed in Chapter 4. The total size of the file set of SPECweb scales with the expected throughput. The rationale for that stems from the fact that expectations for a high-end server, in terms of the variety and size of the documents available, are much

Table 7.3. Percentage of Requests in the SPECweb99 Workload

Request	Percentage
Static GET	70.00
Standard Dynamic GET	12.45
Standard Dynamic GET (CGI)	0.15
Customized Dynamic GET	12.60
Dynamic POST	4.80

Table 7.4. File Sizes Per Class and Access Frequency for SPECweb

Class	File sizes (KB)	Access percentage
0	0 – 1	35
1	1 – 10	50
2	10 – 100	14
3	100 – 1,000	1

greater than for a smaller server. Fileset sizes vary from 1.4 GB to 2.7 GB depending on load.

7.4.1.2 Results

The SPECweb99 metric represents the actual number of simultaneous connections that a server can support. In the benchmark, a number of simultaneous connections are requested. For each simultaneous connection, there is a process or thread created to generate workload for the benchmark. Each of these processes/threads sends HTTP requests to the SUT in a continuous manner. The SPECweb99 metric is implemented by measuring the maximum number of load generating threads of execution that are retrieving URLs between a maximum of 400,000 bps and a minimum of 320,000 bps. A simultaneous connection is considered conforming to the required bit rate if its aggregate bit rate is more than 320,000 bps. Table 7.5 illustrates an example of results obtained with SPECweb99.

Example 7.2

A media company is planning to revamp its portal, with new applications and services to its customers. The system administrator considers that the SPECweb workload could be used as an approximation for the initial workload of the company Web site. The business analyst estimates that the number of concurrent customers, N, during the peak period will be 10,000.

Table 7.5. Results for SPECweb 99

System	Conforming Connections	Throughput operations/sec	Response msec	Kbps
A	1890	5190.1	351.9	341.1
B	3222	9020.4	358.5	335.9
C	8710	24,334.1	359.6	340.2

For the purpose of planning the capacity of the service, a customer is an active Web browser that periodically sends requests from a client machine to the service. A customer is considered to be *concurrent* with other customers as long as he or she is on the system submitting requests, receiving results of requests, viewing the results, and submitting new requests. So, a concurrent customer alternates between two states: viewing results (i.e., thinking) and waiting for the response of the request (i.e., the service is busy executing the request).

IT management agreed on defining an upper limit of 4 seconds for the average user-perceived response time, R. In order to have a first idea about the type and size of system needed, the capacity planning analyst used a simple model to estimate the throughput, X_0, that will be required from the system. The business analyst estimates that the average think time, Z, for a concurrent customer is 3 seconds. Using the Response Time Law, we have:

$$X_0 \geq \frac{N}{R+Z} = \frac{10,000}{4+3} = 1429 \text{ requests/sec.}$$

Now, the analyst wants to know what is the average number of simultaneous connections generated by the 10,000 concurrent customers. In order to estimate this number, the analyst considered that the user-perceived response time is composed of two components: network time and Web site time. The analyst estimates that the network time is around 1.2 sec. Therefore, the Web site time, R_{site}, should not exceed 2.8 $(= 4.0 - 1.2)$ seconds.

Using Little's Law, we are able to estimate the average number of simultaneous connections, N_{conn}, as

$$N_{\text{conn}} = X_0 \times R_{\text{site}} = 1429 \times 2.8 = 4,001.$$

By examining the SPECweb benchmark results, the analyst found a system that meets the load requirements, i.e., the number of conforming connections is greater than 4,001 and the throughput is greater than 1429 requests/sec. ■

7.4.2   Webstone

Webstone is a configurable C/S benchmark for HTTP servers that uses workload characterization parameters and client processes to generate HTTP traffic to stress a server in different ways [14]. It was designed to measure maximum server throughput and average response time for connecting to the server. It makes a number of GET requests for specific documents on the Web server under study and collects performance data. The first version of the benchmark did not include CGI loads or the effects of encryption or authentication in the tests. Webstone is a distributed, multiprocess benchmark, composed of master and client processes. The master process, local or remote, spawns a predefined number of client processes that start generating HTTP requests to the server. After all client processes finish running, the master process gathers the performance summary report. The user can either specify the duration of the test or the total number of iterations.

7.4.2.1   Workload

There are four different synthetic page mixes that attempt to model real workloads. The characteristics of each page mix, i.e., file sizes and access frequencies, were derived from the access patterns to pages available in some popular Web sites. Webstone allows one to model user environment workloads, via synthetic loads generated according to some input parameters, specified by the user. The specification parameters are:

- Number of clients that request pages. Clients request pages as fast as the server can send them back. User think times cannot be represented in the Webstone workload.

- Type of page, defined by file size and access frequency. Each page in the mix has a weight that indicates its probability of being accessed.

- The number of pages available on the server under test.

- The number of client machines, where the client processes execute on.

Webstone 2.x offers new workloads for dynamic pages. It allows one to test Web servers using three different types of pages: HTML, CGI and API. In the case of API workload, Webstone comes with support for both NSAPI and ISAPI.

7.4.2.2   Results

The main results produced by Webstone are throughput and latency. The former, measured in bytes per second, represents the total number of bytes received from the server divided by the test duration. Two types of latency are reported: connection latency and request latency. For each metric, the mean time is provided, as well as the standard deviation of all data, plus the minimum and maximum times. Connection latency reflects the time taken to establish a connection, while request latency reflects the time to complete the data transfer once the connection has been established. User-perceived latency will include the sum of connection and request latencies, plus any network latency due to WAN connections, routers, or modems. Table 7.6 displays a summary of Webstone results for a test run of 10 minutes [14]. The Webstone number corresponds to the throughput measured in pages per minute. The total amount of data moved is the product of the total number of pages retrieved and the page sizes. The page size is the sum of all files associated with the page plus the HTTP overhead in bytes. The other results are self-explanatory.

Table 7.6. Typical Webstone Results

Metric	Value
Webstone number	456
Total number of clients	24
Total number of pages retrieved from the server	4,567
Total number of errors	0
Total number of connects to server	12,099
Average time per connect (sec)	0.0039
Maximum time per connect (sec)	0.0370
Total amount of bytes moved	129,108,600
Average throughput (bytes/sec)	215,181
Average response time (sec)	1.181
Maximum response time (sec)	18.488

Webstone also presents a metric called Little's Load Factor (LLF), derived from Little's Law [9]. It indicates the degree of concurrency on the request execution, that is, the average number of connections open at the Web server at any particular instant during the test. It is also an indication of how much time is spent by the server on request processing, rather than on overhead and errors. Ideally, LLF should be equal to the number of clients. A lower value indicates that the server is overloaded, and some requests are not being serviced before they time out. From Chapter 3, we know that the total number of customers in a box is equal to the throughput of the box multiplied by the average time each customer spends in the box. Thinking of the Web server as a box, we have that

$$\text{AvgNumberOfConnections} = \text{ConnectionRate} \times \text{AvgResidenceTime}.$$

$$(7.4.2)$$

The average residence time is the average response time plus the connection time. Plugging numbers from Table 7.6 into Eq. (7.4.2), we have that

$$\text{AvgNumberOfConnections} = 12,099/(10 \times 60) \times (1.181 + 0.0039) = 23.89.$$

In this example, the average number of connections (23.89) is very close to the number of clients (24).

Example 7.3

Assume that the results displayed in Table 7.6 correspond to a Webstone run with parameters configured to represent the workload forecast for the Web site of a hotel company. The capacity planner wants to size the bandwidth of the link that connects the site to the ISP. The bandwidth of the link should support incoming and outgoing traffic. Let us consider that the average size of an HTTP request is 100 bytes. During the 10-minute test, the server received 4,567 page requests. Thus, the total amount of incoming bits in the period was $(4,567 \times 100 \times 8)/(10 \times 60) = 6,089.3$ bps. The outgoing traffic is given by the server throughput, $215,181 \times 8 = 1,721,448$ bps. Considering a full-duplex link, the minimum required bandwidth is given by

$$\text{LinkBandwidth} \geq \max\{6,089.3; 1,721,448\} = 1.72 \text{ Mbps.}$$

Therefore, in order to support the estimated demand for pages, the company's Web site should be connected to the Internet through two T1 links $(2 \times 1.544 \text{ Mbps})$. Because Webstone allows one to tailor the workload to represent a specific user environment, Webstone can be used as a monitoring tool. In this example, we used the performance measurements collected by Webstone during the test to size the network bandwidth.   ∎

7.4.3 Analytically-Based Generators

A key component of a benchmark is the workload generator. Two approaches are commonly used to generate the workload. The trace-based approach uses traces from actual workloads and either samples or replays traces to generate workloads [3]. The other approach is to use mathematical models to represent characteristics of the workload and then generate requests that follow the models. Reference [3] describes a tool for generating analytically-based Web workloads. The tool, called SURGE, consists of two concepts: user equivalents and distributional models.

A user equivalent is defined as a single process in an endless loop that alternates between making HTTP requests and remaining idle. Load intensity can then be measured in terms of user equivalents. Many studies [1, 2, 3] point out that Web distributions exhibit heavy tails, that can be described by a power law:

$$P[X > x] \sim x^{-\alpha} \qquad 0 < \alpha \leq 2.$$

SURGE identified the following characteristics of Web workloads and found statistical distributions to represent them. The distributions are specified by their probability density functions (pdf), which are characterized by location and scale parameters. The parameters are typically used for modeling purposes. The effect of a scale parameter is to strech or compress the pdf. Th location parameter simply shifts the graph left or right on the horizontal axis. Many probability distributions represent a family of distributions. Shape parameters allow a distribution to take on different forms. Thus, one can use different parameter values to model a variety of data sets.

- *File Sizes:* Size distributions of the collection of files stored on a Web server can be modeled by a combination of two distributions: lognormal for the body of the curve and Pareto for the tail. The probability density functions, $p(x)$, for the two distributions are:

  - Lognormal Distribution

  $$p(x) = \frac{1}{x\sigma\sqrt{2\pi}} e^{-(\ln x - \mu)^2/2\sigma^2}$$

  where σ is the shape parameter and μ the location parameter.

- Pareto Distribution

$$p(x) = \alpha k^{\alpha} x^{-(\alpha+1)}$$

- *Request Sizes:* The files transferred from the server are called requests. The size distributions of requests can be different from the distribution of file sizes at the Web server because of the different popularity of the various files. Request sizes are modeled by a Pareto distribution.

- *Popularity:* Popularity measures the distribution of requests on a per-file basis. Several researchers [1, 2] have observed that the relative frequency with which Web pages are requested follows Zipf's Law. Thus, the number of of references to a Web page $\mathcal{P}$, $N(\mathcal{P})$, tends to be inversely proportional to its rank $r(\mathcal{P})$.

$$N(\mathcal{P}) = kr(\mathcal{P})^{-1}$$

- *Embedded References:* A Web object (e.g., HTML page) is actually composed of multiple objects on the server and requires multiple requests. Thus, in order to capture the structure of Web objects, it is necessary to characterize the distribution of the number of embedded files in a object. Data reported in [3] indicates that Pareto can be used to represent the distribution of embedded references.

- *Temporal Locality:* Temporal locality refers to the property that a Web object frequently accessed in the past is likely to be accessed in the future. One way to measure temporal locality is by using the notion of *stack distance* [1]. The distribution of distance probability is an indication of temporal locality because it measures the number of intervening references to unique objects between two references to the same Web object. Small stack distances result from frequent references to a Web object. Stack distance data were found to be best fit by a lognormal distribution.

- *OFF Times:* OFF times represent idle times of the processes (i.e., user equivalents) that generate requests. Two types of OFF times were identified in Web workloads. One corresponds to the user think time. Pareto has been used to model this type of OFF time. The other type of OFF time corresponds to the time between transfer of components of a single Web object, due to the parsing and formatting activities carried out by the browser. These OFF times can be modeled by the Weibull Distribution, with the probability density function $p(x)$:

$$p(x) = \frac{bx^{b-1}}{a^b} e^{(x/a)^b}$$

where b is the shape parameter and a the scale parameter.

SURGE meets the requirements of the distributions found for the six characteristics of Web workloads and combines these distributions to generate a single output stream of requests. The traffic of requests generated by SURGE is *self-similar*, i.e., it exhibits significant variability over various time scales.

7.5   System Benchmarks

System benchmarks measure the entire system. They measure the processor, the I/O subsystem, the network, the database, the compilers, and the operating system. TPC benchmarks measure the processor, I/O subsystem, network, operating system, database management system, and transaction monitor. They assess the performance of applications such as debit/credit transactions, wholesale parts supplier, and ad hoc business questions (e.g., sales trends and financial analysis). TPC runs four benchmarks: C, H, R, and W. TPC-C simulates an order-entry environment. The purpose of TPC-H and TPC-R are to evaluate the price/performance ratio of a given system executing decision support applications. These applications support the formulation of business questions solved through long and complex queries against large databases. The performance metric reported by

TPC-H is called the TPC-H Composite Query-per-Hour Performance Metric (QphH@Size), and reflects multiple aspects of the capability of the system to process queries.

7.5.1 TPC-C

TCP-C is an industry standard benchmark for moderately complex online transaction processing systems. It models an application that manages orders for a wholesale supplier. TPC-C provides a conceptual framework for order-entry applications with underlying components that are typical of other transaction processing systems.

7.5.1.1 Workload

The workload for TPC-C consists of five transactions: *New-order, Payment, Delivery, Order-Status*, and *Stock-level*, which update, insert, and delete. The five transactions have different percentages of execution time in the benchmark. *New-order* and *Payment* represent 45% and 43%, respectively, of the total transactions in the mix. Each of the other three transactions account for 4% of the load. The TPC-C workload is database-intensive, with substantial I/O and cache load. It meets Atomicity, Consistency, Isolation, and Durability (ACID) requirements and includes full-screen presentation services.

7.5.1.2 Results

TPC-C yields a performance measure known as tpmC (i.e., transactions per minute). In the TPC-C terminology, throughput is the maximum number of *New-order* transactions per minute that a system services while executing the four other transaction types. TPC-C is satisfied with 90% of the *New-order* transactions responding in less than 5 seconds during the test. Other transactions have different response time requirements. This property assures the service level for the *New-order* transactions, which indicates repeatable response times. For example, a 39,000-tpmC system is able to service 39,000 *New-order* transactions per minute while satisfying the rest of the TPC-C mix workload. Table 7.7 shows some of the typical results provided by TPC-C. As we can observe from Table 7.7, a price/performance measure is provided by TPC-C. The pricing methodology covers all components and dimensions of a transaction processing system. Thus, the following factors are included in the total system cost: computer system, terminals, communication devices, software (e.g., database management system and transaction monitor), and a five-year maintenance cost. Suppose that the total cost of system $\mathcal{X}$ is \$445,747 and the throughput is 34,600 tpmC. Then, the price/performance ratio for system $\mathcal{X}$ equals \$12.89 per tpmC.

Example 7.4

The IT manager of an insurance company wants to replace its database management software. The manager is considering a new software that is said to be 30% faster than the one in use. How can the manager assess the

Table 7.7. TPC-C Results

System Information	
Company	$\mathcal{X}$
System	$\mathcal{Z}$
Processors	4
Total Storage	2.61 Terabytes
DBMS	Microsoft SQL
Operating System	Windows NT
Transaction Monitor	Microsoft COM+
Total system cost	\$445,747
TPC-C throughput (tpmC)	34,600
Price/performance	\$12,89

impact of the new software on the system's order-processing application?

The TPC-C benchmark can be used to evaluate the relative performance of two different software systems on the same hardware. By examining the TPC-C results we learned that the performance measures of the current and new software are 30,000 and 36,000 tpmC, respectively. The throughput ratio of the two software systems is

$$P_x = \frac{\text{throughput of the new software}}{\text{throughput of the current software}} = \frac{36,000}{30,000} = 1.2.$$

Using the performance models of Chapters 8 and 9, we can calculate the transaction response time, after adjusting the DB server throughputs by P_x. To represent the new software, the throughputs of the model are related by the relationship

$$X_{\text{server}}^{\text{new}} = P_x \times X_{\text{server}}^{\text{old}}.$$

Another way of looking at the TPC-C results is to look at the cost issue. The price/performance numbers of the system with the two different DBMS software packages are $10.03 and $12.29 for the current and new DB software. The price/performance ratio for the new software is 22.5% higher than the current software. The question is whether the throughput and response time improvements are worth the cost for the new system and whether users want to pay more for the additional speed.   ■

Example 7.5

A transaction server is planned to be part of the infrastructure of a Web service. It is estimated that the service should support 800 (N) concurrent users. The average think time (Z) is 20 seconds, which means that after receiving a reply from the Web service, each user waits on average 20 seconds to submit a new request. Every service request accesses the transaction server 15 times. The average request response time should be 4 seconds. In order to have fast request response time, the system designers have specified that 90% of the accesses to the transaction server should not take longer than 1 second. Management wants to size the transaction server system. We have learned in this section that TPC-C benchmark results includes the ninetieth percentile for the response time for various transaction servers. Before using the TPC-C results, the capacity-planning analyst realizes that the TPC-C workload could be used as an approximation for the application workload. Therefore, the first step is to determine the minimum throughput required from the transaction server. The Forced Flow Law, discussed in Chapter 3, establishes a relationship between component and system throughput. It states that

$$X_{\text{ts}} = V_{\text{ts}} \times X_0 \qquad (7.5.3)$$

where X_{ts} is the transaction server throughput, X_0 denotes the total system throughput and V_{ts} is the average number of visits per service request to the transaction server, also called visit ratio. Let us first calculate the system throughput in requests/sec. From the Response Time Law, we have:

$$X_0 = N/(R + Z) = 800/(4 + 20) = 33.3 \text{ request/sec.}$$

Considering that the minimum system throughput is 33.3 requests/sec and each request accesses the transaction server 15 times, we have that the minimum transaction server throughput, measured in tps, is

$$X_{\text{ts}} > 15 \times 33.3 = 499.5 \text{ tps} = 29,970 \text{ tpmC.}$$

By examining the TPC-C results, management found out that system $\mathcal{XXX}$ is able to handle 32,000 tpmC with response time equal to 0.92 sec for 90% of the *new order* transactions. Also, transaction server $\mathcal{ZZZ}$ executes 35,450 tpmC with 0.84 sec of response time for 90% of the transactions. Once both transaction servers meet the system performance specifications, other factors such as cost, reliability, and vendor reputation should be used to select the server.   ■

7.5.2   TPC-W

The TPC-W benchmark aims at evaluating sites that support e-business activities. This section provides a brief description of this benchmark and refer the reader to the TPC-W specification for more details [15]. The business model of TPC-W is that of a retail store that sells products and services over the Internet. The site provides e-business functions that let customers browse through selected products (e.g., best-sellers or new products), search information on existing products, see product detail, place an order, or check the status of a previous order. Interactions related to placing an order are encrypted using Secure Sockets Layer (SSL) connections. Customers need to register with the site before they are allowed to buy.

The site maintains a catalog of items that can be searched by a customer. Each item has a description and a 5KB thumbnail image associated with it. TPC-W specifies that the site maintains a database with information about customers, items in the catalog, orders, and credit card transactions. All database updates must have the ACID property [4]. The size of the catalog is the major scalability parameter for TPC-W. The number of items in the catalog may be one of the following: 1,000, 10,000, 100,000, 1,000,000, or 10,000,000.

7.5.2.1   Workload

TPC-W specifies that the activity with the site being benchmarked is driven by *emulated browsers (EB)*. These EBs generate *Web interactions*, which represent a complete cycle that starts when the EB selects a navigation option from the previously displayed page and ends when the requested page has been completely received by the EB. User sessions are defined as sequences of Web interactions that start with an interaction to the home page. TPC-W classifies Web interactions into two broad categories:

- *Browse* interactions involve browsing and searching but no product ordering activity. Typical interactions that fall in this category are Home, Browse, Select, Product Detail, and Search.

- *Order* interactions involve product ordering activities only and include the following interaction: Shopping Cart, Login, Buy Request, Buy Confirm, Order Inquiry, and Order Display.

TPC-W specifies three different types of session profiles, according to the percentage of Browse and Order Web interactions found in each session.

- *Browsing mix*: 95% of Browse Web interactions and 5% of Order Web interaction. These sessions are characterized by a 0.69% buy/visit ratio.

- *Shopping mix*: 80% of Browse Web interactions and 20% of Order Web interaction. The buy/visit ratio in these sessions is 1.2%.

- *Ordering mix*: 50% of Browse Web interactions and 50% of Order Web interaction. These sessions have a buy/visit ratio of 10.18%.

7.5.2.2   Results

TPC-W has two types of performance metrics: a throughput metric and a cost/throughput metric as explained in what follows. There are three throughput metrics depending on the type of session. The main throughput metric for TPC-W is called WIPS (Web Interactions Per Second) and measures the average number of Web Interactions completed per second during an interval in which all the sessions are of the shopping type. Throughput is expressed in WIPS at a tested scale factor (i.e., WISP@scale_factor), where scale factor is the number of items in the catalog. There are two secondary throughput metrics. One, called WIPSb, measures the average number of Web Interactions Per Second completed during an interval in which all sessions are of the browsing type. The other, called WIPSo, measures the average number of Web Interactions Per Second completed during an interval in which all sessions are of the ordering type. The cost related metric specified by TPC-W is $/WIPS and indicates the ratio between the total cost of the system under test and the number of WIPS measured during a shopping interval. Total cost includes purchase and maintenance costs for all hardware and software components for the system under test. Table 7.8 shows some of the typical results provided by TPC-W.

Table 7.8. TPC-W Results

System Information	
Company	$\mathcal{X}$
System	$\mathcal{Z}$
Scaling	10,000
Processors	4
DBMS	Microsoft SQL
Operating System	Windows NT
HTTP Server	Microsoft IIS
Load Balancer	Microsoft Windows DNS Server
Search Engine	Microsoft SQL Server FT Search
Total system cost	$211,214
TPC-W Performance	3,130
Price/performance	$67.50

7.6   Performance Testing

One way to determine how users will experience the performance of a Web service is to carry out performance testing. The main purpose of running performance tests is to understand the performance of the service under specific workload conditions. Performance tests can be used in all stages of Web service development and deployment process. Performance testing can generate a system activity that mimics the behavior of actual users and can help management identify problems with Web services before they go live [12]. Performance testing is a joint effort, which requires participation of development, production and capacity planning teams. The tests should be planned in advance, so that enough time is left to fix problems discovered during the tests. The key to performance testing is to simulate the production environment and workload scenarios so as to obtain the most accurate real-world results possible.

7.6.1   Types of Performance Tests

Performance testing should include situations that represent steady-state activity as well as peak-load activity, so that one can determine Web service behavior under both conditions. To test that a Web service can support a certain demand, a known load must be generated. There are basically three types of performance tests, characterized by the intensity of the generated load.

- *Load testing:* One goal of testing is to determine whether a Web service fulfills the performance requirements defined for it. More specifically, how will the Web service respond to the load of requests to be created by its community of users? This is called load testing. To test the Web service, a simulated load is created that mimics the regular regimen of operation.

- *Stress testing:* It is also important to make sure that a Web service works as it should, even under extreme conditions. This is called stress testing. It focuses on worst-case scenarios and uses a load heavier than expected.

- *Spike testing:* In the case of spike testing, the Web service is tested under very specific conditions, when the load is several times larger than the average. Usually, this type of test occurs for a short period of time that resembles load spikes which occur in the Web.

There are also various modes of running Web performance tests. In component monitoring mode, a locally generated load is used to evaluate performance of the components of the Web service infrastructure. Web servers, application servers, and database servers are the focus of this type of performance testing. In simulated network mode, agents are deployed at several locations on the network backbone. Most monitoring services apply scripted robot systems to simulate user activity with Web sites. These agents generate load to the Web service and collect performance data. This type of service simulates end-user-generated traffic. In distributed peer-to-peer mode [10], the load is generated by lightweight client software installed on actual end user machines that are part of a peer-to-peer network. This type of test provides performance data that represents the end-user perception of performance, because it includes all components of networking delays, including the so-called last mile. It gathers performance metrics from the user's point-of-view.

7.6.2   A Methodology for Performance Testing

Following the capacity planning model discussed in Chapter 5, we define a performance testing methodology, with its main steps illustrated in Fig. 7.2.

7.6.2.1   Defining the Testing Objectives

The purpose of this step is to define the goals of the performance tests. These goals have a strong influence on cost and effort involved in the testing project. Examples of testing goals are as follows:

- Determine the Web server capacity.

- Find out the maximum number of concurrent users a Web service supports within the limits of the SLAs.

- Determine the capacity of the application layer.

- Identify the bottlenecks in the Web service infrastructure.

- Identify network impact on the end-user perceived response time.

- Find out the capacity of the DB server.

- Identify the most expensive Web functions.

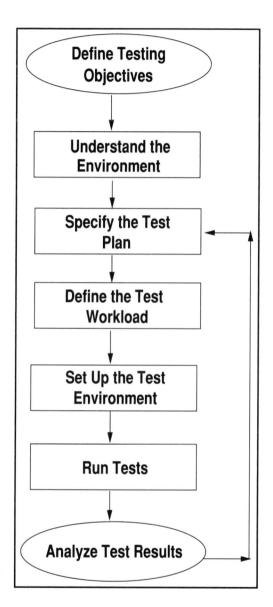

Figure 7.2. A methodology for performance testing.

7.6.2.2   Understanding the Environment

This phase of the methodology consists of learning what kind of infrastructure (i.e., servers and third party services), software (i.e., operating systems, middleware, and applications), network connectivity, and network protocols, are present in the environment. It also involves the identification of steady-state and peak periods, and SLAs. The goal of this step is to understand as accurately as possible the nature of the workload and services provided by the system under test (SUT).

7.6.2.3   Specifying the Test Plan

Tests plans should provide a detailed audit trail for the testing process. The plan is specifically designed to identify which Web services and functions are to be tested, how to request a service, the order in which functions and services should be tested and what the testing team should expect. The plan should also include workload scenarios (e.g., optimistic and pessimistic) and the SLAs that will be verified. In this step, one has to plan on running tests that represent the application activity on the Web service, using the same infrastructure as the production environment. All steps of the performance testing process and their corresponding schedule should be prepared at this stage, including the design of experiments [8]. Typical questions to be answered at this stage are: "How input variables are controlled or changed?" "What is the desired degree of confidence in the measurements?"

7.6.2.4   Specifying the Test Workload

In this step, one has to devise an application scenario that includes requests and activity that are typical of the Web service. Basically, one has to characterize the user behavior, generate scripts that represent the user behavior, and create scenarios that combine different group of users. Some workload characterization techniques discussed in Chapter 6 can be used in this step. For example, user sessions can be represented by a Customer Behavior Model Graph (CBMG) resulting from the workload characterization process. These graphs can be used to create the scripts that will generate the load. Different types of profiles may be characterized by different CBMGs in terms of the transition probabilities. Consider, for instance, two customer profiles: occasional and heavy buyers. The first category is composed of customers who use the Web store to find out about existing products, such as new books or best fares and itineraries for travel, but end up not buying, most of the time, at the Web store. The second category is composed of customers who have a higher probability of buying if they see a product that interests them at a suitable price.

7.6.2.5   Setting Up the Test Environment

Setting up the environment is the process of installing measurement and testing tools. Two methods for implementing Web load testing can be used: manual and automatic testing. Because testing is often a labor-intensive undertaking, manual testing is not a practical option. Thus, automated load testing tools are a key resource for performance testing. A typical automated testing tool consists of two basic components: controller and virtual users. The controller subsystem organizes, drives and manages the load. Virtual users emulate real users accessing services by delivering a workload of user activity to the Web service. Automated test tools can evaluate performance and response times. They measure the application quality and response time that will be achieved in the actual environment. Automated test tools emulate real scenarios in order to truly test Web service performance. Every component of the SUT should be monitored: Web servers, application servers, database systems, clients, and the network.

7.6.2.6   Running the Tests

The execution of the tests should follow the plans developed for performance testing of the Web service. The tests should be conducted by a team under the supervision of the project manager. For each service or application, the analyst should document results and any discrepancy between the expected and actual results. A detailed description of the test should be prepared so that the test can be reproduced.

7.6.2.7   Analyzing the Results

This is the most important step of the methodology. Based on the data collected, the analysts should be able to determine the location of the bottlenecks that cause performance problems or represent obstacles to the growth in the number of concurrent users. At this point of the testing process, the analysts should be able to provide a diagnosis of the SUT or specify new testing requirements. One of the goals of any performance testing is to recommend actions to fix problems found during the tests. The assumption that adding extra hardware can solve any performance problem is common. This is not always true for Web services. In a case study reported in [13], the author showed that 50% of the performance gains of the site came from application and database engineering. Through extensive performance tests, analysts are able to understand the reasons of poor performance and remove a number of bottlenecks. Another important issue when analyzing the results is to make sure that the reported measurements are coherent. In other words, one should look for the possibility of errors in the measurement process. Using the operational laws described in Chapter 3 is a good way of checking the consistency of the measurement data.

Example 7.6

One of X Corporation's primary business goals is to provide a broad range of services that meet the diversifying demands of the modern financial marketplace. These services range from traditional commercial and retail banking to financial consulting, investment counseling, and brokerage. To meet the critical needs of its key businesses, X Corp. is planning to implement a diverse mix of services on the Web. In preparation for new services, X Corp. adopted a testing strategy that follows the steps of the methodology described in Section 7.6.2. The goal of the testing project is to locate and correct performance shortfalls before going into production with the services on the Web site.

Define Testing Objectives. The project consists of testing and measuring the capacity and performance of the application servers. The team also wants to certify that the response times of the application will be below critical thresholds at the anticipated live load level.

Understand the Environment. The SUT is a Web-based loan service system aimed at an audience of 100,000 users, who will be able to perform basic account activities: view account status, make personal information changes, submit loan application, etc. The load on the system is specified by the number of concurrent users. Business analysts estimate the average number of concurrent users to be around 1% of the total base of customers. The architecture of the Web service consists of six Web servers, installed on Windows systems and two application servers running Linux with an off-the-shelf application system acquired from an external vendor. A large and powerful DB server, running Oracle, is also part of the infrastructure.

Specify the Test Plan. The technique used is stress testing, which means a repeatable method for high volume simulation of real world workload. Some of the key activities that should be part of the test plan are: (1) design the test environment, (2) define load scenarios, (3) design and build the test scripts, (4) populate tables and databases, (5) install the monitoring software, and (6) define the team and develop the test schedule. The plan is to validate that the application server will support up to 1,000 concurrent users within acceptable timings.

Define the Test Workload. When analyzing the workload, the system analyst identified the *view account status* as the most frequent and resource-intensive user action. The test workload is generated by virtual users created by the automated testing tool. In the stress test mode, as soon as a virtual user receives a response, it immediately submits the next request. In other words, the virtual user think time equals zero ($Z = 0$). In defining the test workload, one has to specify the number of concurrent virtual users. This number can be estimated as follows: Let R denote the average application server response time, X_0 the server throughput, N_r the number of simultaneous real customers, and N_v the number of virtual users. Considering that the throughput and the response time should be the same during the tests and the live operation, one can write the following:

$$X_0 = N_r/(R + Z)$$

$$X_0 = N_v/(R + 0).$$

From the two above equations, we have

$$N_v/N_r = R/(R + Z).$$

Let us assume that we have set $R = 2$ seconds as the average response time goal and $Z = 20$ seconds for actual users. Then,

$$N_v = N_r \times 2/(2 + 20) = 1,000 \times 1/11 = 90.9 \sim 91.$$

So, the tests should use up to 91 virtual users to generate the requests.

Set up the Environment. A test facility was built to provide a safe environment in which Web services could be tested prior to deployment. An automated stress testing tool was selected because it could run a large number of virtual users in a controlled lab environment, while closely emulating real-life activity to identify system performance problems. Among the requirements for testing the system, one needs to check the following: (1) license from the load test vendor for the number of concurrent users to be tested; (2) performance monitoring tools for Web servers, application servers, database system, and network.

Run Tests. Once the tests were assembled, initial test iterations indicated serious performance issues at low levels of users. Subsequent test iterations indicated that the application server software was not configured properly. The test plan was used to change the system configuration. These are typical situations faced when running tests. In order to get statistical stability, tests will be repeated 100 times for each level of concurrency. Confidence intervals on the averages of the 100 measurements should be computed.

Analyze Results. The main activities in this step are examining trends versus test objectives, correlating performance measurements and developing recommendations for management. Through the use of the load testing tool, the analysts were able to evaluate response times for all iterations with the SUT and isolate the specific performance issue. Table 7.9 shows the response time and CPU utilization measured for a varying number of virtual users.

At first glance, we observe that as new users are added to the system, the response time increases. We also observe that the CPU utilization levels off at 60%, which indicates the system has reached a bottleneck. Let us use some simple models to understand the performance data. For each value of N, the system can be represented by a closed model and we can use Little's Law to calculate the system throughput $X_0 = N/R$. So, dividing the first column by the second one of Table 7.9, we get the throughput, that is shown in the fourth column of the same table. We also know that $X_0 = U_i/D_i$, for each component i of the system. Considering that the maximum value for U_i is 100%, we have that $X_0 \leq 1/D_i$. The maximum system throughput observed is around 12.5 and indicates that some component of the system, rather than the CPU, has reached 100% utilization and is limiting the system throughput. Because the response time has exceeded the limit of 2 seconds, the main recommendation at this point is to get the application vendor involved in the testing process to find out the origins of the performance bottleneck. ■

7.7   Concluding Remarks

This chapter presented several industry standard benchmarks. They provide a standard yardstick for comparing performance across different systems. As pointed out in the introduction, benchmark results can both inform and confuse users about the real capacity of systems to execute their actual pro-

Table 7.9. Key Performance Results

Number of Virtual Users	Resp. Time (sec)	CPU utilization (%)	X_0 (req/sec)
5	1.5	12	3.3
10	1.8	15	5.6
15	1.9	18	7.9
20	2.0	22	10.0
25	2.1	28	11.9
30	2.9	33	10.3
35	3.5	40	10.0
40	3.8	48	10.5
45	3.9	50	11.5
50	4.3	51	11.6
55	4.5	54	12.2
60	4.8	52	12.5
65	5.1	55	12.7
70	5.6	58	12.5
75	6.1	60	12.3
80	6.4	61	12.5
85	6.8	61	12.5
90	7.3	62	12.3
95	7.6	61	12.5
100	7.9	62	12.6

duction workloads. It depends on how one interprets the results. Before using benchmark results, one must understand the workload, the system under study, the tests, the measurements, and the results. Standard benchmarks can be used in a variety of ways provided one understands them. For instance, benchmark results can be used for comparing different hardware systems running the same software or different software products on one system. They can also be used to compare different models of systems in a compatible family. Standard benchmarks, though, are not adequate tools for capacity planning for a system with a customized workload. However, benchmark results can be used in conjunction with performance models for capacity planning purposes.

This chapter also examined performance testing issues. Performance testing is a commonly used method to determine how users will experience the performance of a Web service. The main purpose of running performance tests is to understand the performance of the service under specific workload conditions. Here we define a performance testing methodology based on the use of automatic load testing tools. As we saw in the various examples of this chapter, benchmark results can provide useful input information for performance models. Also, simple analytic models can help in the understanding of the meaning of results provided by benchmarking and performance testing. Next chapters show how to construct performance model of Web services.

Bibliography

[1] V. A. F. Almeida, M. Crovella, A. Bestavros, and A. Oliveira, "Characterizing Reference Locality in the WWW," *Proc. IEEE/ACM International Conference on Parallel and Distributed System (PDIS)*, Miami Beach, Florida, Dec. 1996, pp. 92–103.

[2] M. Arlitt and C. Williamson, "Web Server Workload Characterization: The Search for Invariants," *Proc. 1996 ACM SIGMETRICS Conf. Measurement Comput. Syst.*, ACM, Philadelphia, Pennsylvania, May 1996, pp. 126–137.

[3] P. Barford and M. Crovella, "Generating Representative Web Workloads for Network and Server Performance Evaluation," *Proc. 1998 ACM SIG-*

METRICS Int. Conf. Measurement and Modeling of Computer Systems, Madison, Wisconsin, June 22-26, 1998, pp. 151–160.

[4] J. Gray, ed., *The Benchmark Handbook for Database and Transaction Processing Systems*, 2nd ed., Morgan Kaufmann, San Mateo, California, 1993.

[5] J. Hennessy and D. Patterson, *Computer Architecture: A Quantitative Approach*, Morgan Kaufmann, San Francisco, California, 1996.

[6] J. Henning, "SPEC CPU2000: Measuring CPU Performance in the New Millennium," *Computer*, IEEE, July 2000.

[7] U. Krishnaswamy and I. Scherson, "A Framework for Computer Performance Evaluation Using Benchmark Sets," *IEEE Trans. Computers*, vol. 49, no. 12, Dec. 2000.

[8] D. Lilja, *Measuring Computer Performance*, Cambridge University Press, Cambridge, United Kingdom, 2000.

[9] D. A. Menascé, V. A. F. Almeida, and L. W. Dowdy, *Capacity Planning and Performance Modeling: From Mainframes to Client-Server Systems*, Prentice Hall, Upper Saddle River, New Jersey, 1994.

[10] D. Lipshultz, "Letting the World Plug into Your PC, for a Profit," *The New York Times*, June 3, 2001.

[11] System Performance Evaluation Corporation, www.spec.org

[12] J. Shaw, "Web Application Performance Testing - a Case Study of an On-line Learning Application," *BT Technology Journal*, vol. 18, no. 2, April 2000.

[13] M. Schwartz, "Test Case," *Computerworld*, Aug. 14, 2000.

[14] G. Trent and M. Sake, "WebSTONE: the First Generation in HTTP Benchmarking, *MTS Silicon Graphics*, Feb. 1995.

[15] Transaction Processing Performance Council, www.tpc.org

[16] N. Yeager and R. McCrath, *Web Server Technology*, Morgan Kaufmann, San Francisco, California, 1996.

Chapter 8

System-Level Performance Models

8.1 Introduction

As pointed out in Chapter 5, a performance model can be developed at different levels of detail. In this chapter, we look at performance models from a system-level point of view as opposed to a component-level point of view. A *system-level* performance model views the system being modeled as a "black box." In this case, the internal details of the box are not modeled explicitly; only the throughput function of the box is considered. The throughput function, $X_0(k)$, gives the average throughput of the box as a function of the number, k, of requests present in the box. Figure 8.1a depicts a black box view of a Web server. A system-level performance model is represented

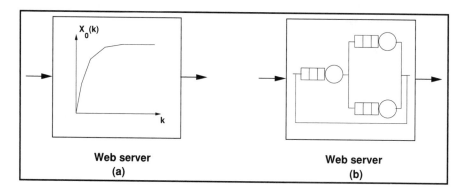

Figure 8.1. (a) System-level view. (b) Component-level view.

by a state transition diagram (STD) that illustrates the states that a system can be found in as well as how it transitions from state to state. A detailed discussion of STDs and their use in system-level performance modeling is given in this chapter.

A *component-level* model takes into account the different resources of the system and the way they are used by different requests. Processors, disks, and networks are explicitly considered by the model. Figure 8.1b shows a component-level view of the same Web server shown in Fig. 8.1a. Component models use queuing networks and are the topic of Chapter 9.

This chapter starts by introducing very simple models so that the reader can understand the approach. Complexity is progressively introduced and the solution to each model is presented using first principles and intuitive concepts. After a few models are presented, the approach is generalized. A few more examples are discussed under the more general framework.

8.2   Simple Server Model I—Infinite Queue

Consider a Web server accessible to a very large population. One could imagine that this is one of the Web servers of an online bookstore or of a news organization. Typically, these sites have many Web servers, but for the sake of simplicity, let us concentrate on one of them and assume that a load balancer distributes the overall load seen by the site to all its Web servers. The number of people in the user population is unknown and very large. By "very large" we mean that the arrival rate of Web requests is not influenced by the number of requests that arrived already and are being processed. From now on, we will refer to this as the *infinite population* case. The arrival process to the Web server is then characterized by requests arriving at an average arrival rate of λ requests/sec. We also assume that all requests are statistically indistinguishable. This implies that the requests present in the Web server are not important, only the number of requests that are present counts. This is the single class or *homogeneous workload* assumption [3].

Since this is our first and simplest example, we assume that the average throughput function is very simple. It is a constant, that is, it does not depend on the number of requests in the system. What could be simpler? So, the average throughput of the Web server is given by $X_0(k) = \mu$ requests/sec. It should be noted that the server's service rate is not just a function of its physical characteristics (e.g., processor and disk speeds and number of processors), but also of the demands of the workload (e.g., service demands of a Web request at the processors and disks).

We also assume, in this example, that the Web server does not refuse any requests. All arriving requests are queued for service. This assumption is known as *infinite queue*. We will see in the next subsections that we can as easily model finite queue situations to illustrate the case where a server can only handle a maximum number of requests—the *finite queue* case.

The analyses presented in this section and in all chapters of this book assume that the systems being analyzed are in *operational equilibrium* [1]. This means that the number of requests present in the system at the start of an observation interval is equal to the number of requests present at the end of the interval. The number of requests in the system may vary between the start and end of the interval. For reasonably large intervals, the number of departures tends to approach the number of arrivals and therefore the operational equilibrium assumption holds with negligible error.

Requests arrive at the Web server at a rate of λ requests/sec, queue for service, get served at a rate of μ request/sec, and depart. We want to compute the fraction of time, p_k, that there are k $(k = 0, 1, \cdots)$ requests in the Web server, the average number of requests present, the average response time of a request at the Web server, and the server's utilization and throughput.

We start by deciding how to describe the *state* of the Web server. Given the assumptions presented thus far, the state description for our Web server is a *single* parameter, the number of requests present in the server—waiting or receiving service. It turns out that by choosing such a simple state description we are implicitly making the additional assumption that old story is irrelevant. This means that it does not matter how the system arrived at a certain state k nor does it matter for how long the system has been in this state. The only thing that matters is that the system is at state k. This is also known as the *memoryless* or *Markovian* assumption.

The possible states are then given by the integers $0, 1, 2, \cdots, k, \cdots$. Due to the infinite population and infinite queue length assumptions used in this example, we have an infinite, but enumerable, number of states. We then draw an STD, where each state is represented by a circle (see Fig. 8.2). Transitions between states correspond to physical events in the system and are represented by arrows between states. For example, an arrival of a new request when the server has k requests will take the server to state $k+1$. This type of transition happens upon request arrivals, and therefore the rate at which these transitions occur is λ transitions/sec, the arrival rate. Similarly, if the Web server has k requests and one of them completes, the new state is $k - 1$. These transitions occur at rate μ, the request completion rate.

We start by obtaining the values of p_k $(k = 0, 1, \cdots)$. Since we are assuming operational equilibrium, the flow of transitions going into a state k has to be equal to the flow of transitions going out of that state. For a more

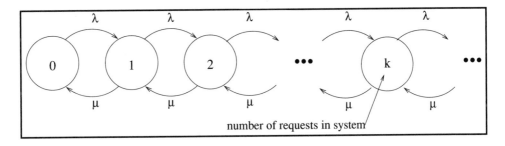

Figure 8.2. State transition diagram—infinite population/infinite queue.

formal discussion on this, see [1]. This is called *flow equilibrium equation* or *flow-in = flow-out* principle and can in fact be applied to any set of states. Consider Fig. 8.3 that shows a sequence of boundaries (dashed lines) around states. Each boundary contains one more state than the previous. The first boundary contains state 0 only. The next includes states 0 and 1. The next boundary includes states 0, 1, and 2, and so on. The flow-in = flow-out principle applies to any of these boundaries.

The flow out of a boundary is computed by considering all transitions that go from a state within the boundary to a state outside the boundary. The flow into a boundary includes all transitions that come from a state outside the boundary to a state inside the boundary. The following is the

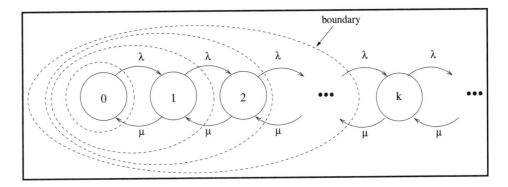

Figure 8.3. State transition diagram with boundaries.

set of flow-in = flow-out equations for Fig. 8.3:

$$\text{flow} - \text{in} = \text{flow} - \text{out}$$

$$\mu \, p_1 = \lambda \, p_0 \tag{8.2.1}$$

$$\mu \, p_2 = \lambda \, p_1 \tag{8.2.2}$$

$$\cdot$$

$$\cdot$$

$$\cdot$$

$$\mu \, p_k = \lambda \, p_{k-1} \tag{8.2.3}$$

$$\cdot$$

$$\cdot$$

$$\cdot$$

Note that if we combine Eqs. (8.2.1) through (8.2.3), we get

$$p_k = \frac{\lambda}{\mu} \, p_{k-1} = \frac{\lambda}{\mu} \left(\frac{\lambda}{\mu} \, p_{k-2} \right) = \cdots = p_0 \left(\frac{\lambda}{\mu} \right)^k, \quad k = 1, 2, \cdots \tag{8.2.4}$$

We now have p_k as a function of p_0 for all values of $k = 1, 2, \cdots$. We just need to find p_0. Our Web server has to be in one of the possible states at any time. So, the sum of the fractions of time that the server is at any possible state, from 0 to ∞, equals one. Hence,

$$p_0 + p_1 + p_2 + \cdots + p_k + \cdots = \sum_{k=0}^{\infty} p_k = \sum_{k=0}^{\infty} p_0 \left(\frac{\lambda}{\mu} \right)^k = 1. \tag{8.2.5}$$

This leads to

$$p_0 = \left[\sum_{k=0}^{\infty} \left(\frac{\lambda}{\mu} \right)^k \right]^{-1} = 1 - \frac{\lambda}{\mu}. \tag{8.2.6}$$

Note that the infinite sum in Eq. (8.2.6) is the sum of a geometric series. This series only converges (i.e., has a finite sum) if $\lambda/\mu < 1$. This means that an equilibrium solution to the system can only be found if the average arrival rate of requests is smaller than the service rate. This makes a lot of sense!

Example 8.1

Requests arrive to the Web server at a rate of 30 requests/sec. Each request takes 0.02 seconds on the average to be processed. What is the fraction of time that k $(k = 0, 1, \cdots)$ requests are found in the Web server?

If the server can process μ requests in 1 second, one request takes an average of $1/\mu$ seconds to complete. Then, the average service rate μ is the inverse of the average service time per request. So, $\mu = 1/0.02 = 50$ requests/sec. The average arrival rate is $\lambda = 30$ requests/sec. So, the fraction of time that the Web server is idle, i.e., p_0, is $1 - (\lambda/\mu) = 1 - (30/50) = 1 - 0.6 = 40\%$. Then, the server is utilized $1 - p_0 = \lambda/\mu = 60\%$ of the time. The fraction of time that there are k requests at the server is given by

$$p_k = (1 - \lambda/\mu)(\lambda/\mu)^k = 0.4 \times 0.6^k \quad k = 0, 1, \cdots. \tag{8.2.7}$$

Figure 8.4 shows how p_k decays rapidly with k. This is a geometric distribution. ∎

So, from what we saw in Ex. 8.1, the utilization U of the server is

$$U = 1 - p_0 = \lambda/\mu \tag{8.2.8}$$

This means that $p_k = (1 - U) U^k$ for $k = 0, 1, \cdots$. The state distribution depends only on the ratio between the arrival and service rates, i.e., the utilization, and not on their individual values!

Now that we know p_k, we can easily find the average number $\overline{N}$ of requests at the server by using the definition of average. Thus,

$$\overline{N} = \sum_{k=0}^{\infty} k \times p_k = \sum_{k=0}^{\infty} k \times (1 - U) U^k = (1 - U) \sum_{k=0}^{\infty} k \times U^k. \tag{8.2.9}$$

But, the summation $\sum_{k=0}^{\infty} k \times U^k = U/(1 - U)^2$ for $U < 1$. Making the proper substitutions we get

$$\overline{N} = U/(1 - U). \tag{8.2.10}$$

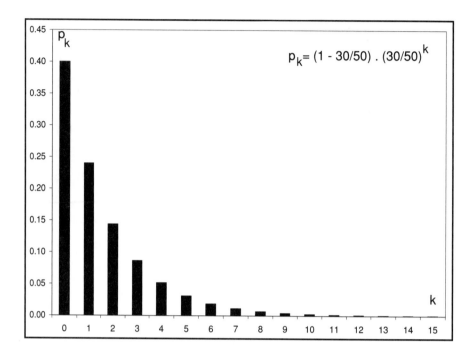

Figure 8.4. Fraction of time (p_k) vs. k for Ex. 8.1.

So, using the parameters of Ex. 8.1 in Eq. (8.2.10), we get that the average number of requests at the server is $0.6/(1 - 0.6) = 1.5$.

The throughput of the server is μ when there is at least one request being processed—this occurs during a fraction of time equal to U. The throughput equals zero when the server is idle. So, the average throughput, X, of the server is

$$X = U \times \mu + 0 \times (1 - U) = (\lambda/\mu)\, \mu = \lambda. \tag{8.2.11}$$

This is an expected result since no requests are being lost at the server. So, in equilibrium, the average arrival rate will be equal to the average departure rate.

We now compute the average response time, R, at the server by using Little's Law (see Chapter 3). The black box in this case is the server. So, given the throughput X, computed in Eq. (8.2.11), and the average number of requests $\overline{N}$, given by Eq. (8.2.10), we get that

$$R = \overline{N}/X = (U/\lambda)/(1 - U) = (1/\mu)/(1 - U) = S/(1 - U) \qquad (8.2.12)$$

where $S = 1/\mu$ is the average service time of a request at the server. Let us understand what Eq. (8.2.12) is telling us. First, when the utilization of the server is very low, i.e., U is close to zero, the average response time is equal to the average service time. This is expected since no time is spent queuing due to the presence of other requests. When the utilization is very high, i.e., U is close to 1, the denominator of Eq. (8.2.12) goes to zero and R goes to infinity! In fact, R goes to infinity quickly as U gets close to 100%. Figure 8.5 shows the ratio of the average response time over the average service time as a function of the utilization.

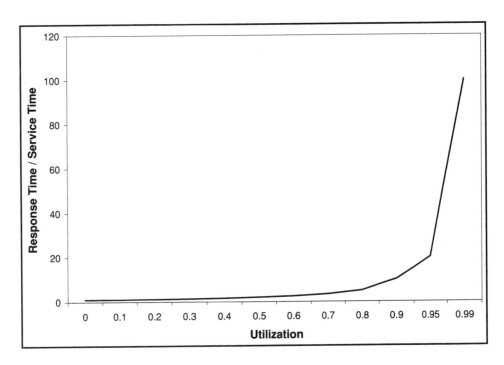

Figure 8.5. Response time/service time for infinite population-infinite queue server.

Example 8.2

Consider again the parameters for Ex. 8.1. What is the average response time at the server? What is the average response time if the server is replaced with a server twice as fast? What would the response time be if the arrival rate doubles when the server becomes twice as fast?

Using Eq. (8.2.12), the average response time is $R = (1/50)/(1 - 0.6) = 0.05$ sec. If the server is twice as fast, $\mu = 100$ requests/second, and the server utilization becomes $U = 30/100 = 0.3$. So, $R = (1/100)/(1 - 0.3) = 0.014$ sec. So, by using a server that is twice as fast, the response time is reduced to about 28% of its original value. If both the arrival rate and the service rate are doubled, the utilization remains the same, $U = 0.6$. Using Eq. (8.2.12), we get that $R = (1 / 100)/(1 - 0.6) = 0.025$ sec.   ■

Example 8.3

The designers of the Web site for a search engine are considering how many and what type of Web servers they should use for the site. They ran a benchmark on various types of servers and obtained the throughput of each one in search requests/sec. They want to know what is the minimum number of servers they should buy of each type to guarantee that the average response time will not exceed a threshold $R_{\max}$.

Let X be the throughput of each server, N be the number of servers, and λ the arrival rate of search requests to the site. Assuming perfect load balancing, each Web server receives search requests at a rate of λ/N requests/sec. The average service time of a request at each server is $1/X$. Then, using Eq. (8.2.12), we have that

$$R = \frac{1/X}{1 - (\lambda/N)/X}. \tag{8.2.13}$$

From Eq. (8.2.13) we can obtain N as a function of R, λ and X as

$$N = \frac{\lambda \times R}{X \times R - 1}. \tag{8.2.14}$$

Replacing R by R_{max} in Eq. (8.2.14) we get the minimum, N_{min} as

$$N_{min} = \left\lceil \frac{\lambda \times R_{max}}{X \times R_{max} - 1} \right\rceil. \qquad (8.2.15)$$

Table 8.1 shows the values of the minimum number of servers for two values of R_{max}, 0.4 sec and 1 second, and for a global arrival rate of 500 requests/sec. The table indicates that if the search engine site uses low-end servers, i.e., the ones that can process 10 requests/sec, they will need 11 more servers to reduce their response time SLA from 1 second to 0.4 sec. Another interesting observation from this example is that an SLA of 0.4 sec for the response time can obtained with 67 low-end servers or with 12 high-end ones. The question is which configuration is cheaper. Another consideration is availability, which will be addressed in Chapter 11.   ■

The expressions for the infinite population/infinite queue server are summarized in Fig. 8.6. They are also implemented in the Microsoft Excel workbook `SysMod.XLS` that can be found on the book's Web site.

Before we consider other situations, let us briefly summarize the steps we took in solving this problem. We will be following exactly the same steps in the rest of this chapter.

Table 8.1. Minimum Number of Web Servers for Ex. 8.3

Throughput	N_{min}	
(req/sec)	$R_{max} = 0.4$ sec	$R_{max} = 1$ sec
10	67	56
15	40	36
20	29	27
25	23	21
30	19	18
35	16	15
40	14	13
45	12	12

Fraction of time server has k requests:

$$p_k = (1 - \lambda/\mu)\,(\lambda/\mu)^k \quad k = 0, 1, \cdots$$

Server utilization:
$$U = \lambda/\mu$$

Average server throughput:

$$X = \lambda$$

Average number of requests in the server:

$$\overline{N} = U/(1 - U)$$

Average response time:

$$R = (1/\mu)/(1 - U) = S/(1 - U)$$

Figure 8.6. Infinite population/infinite queue server equations.

1. Determine a proper representation for the state of the system being modeled.

2. Determine the set of feasible states.

3. Determine the possible transitions between states by considering the possible events that can happen in the system being modeled. Examples of events are arrival of a request and completion of a request.

4. For each possible transition between states, determine the transition rate by looking at the event that caused the transition. For example, if the event that caused the transition from state k to state $k+1$ is an arrival of a request, the transition rate is the rate at which requests arrive when the system is at state k.

5. Use the *flow equilibrium principle* (flow-in = flow-out) to write down equations that relate the values of p_k—the fraction of time the system is at state k. Remember that the sum of all p_ks has to be equal to one.

6. Solve for the p_ks and use them to compute performance metrics such as utilizations, throughput, average number of requests, and average response time.

8.3   Simple Server Model II—Finite Queue

Consider now that the server considered in Section 8.2 cannot queue all incoming requests. Arriving requests that find W requests in the server—queued or being processed—are rejected. Some servers set limits on the number of requests that can be handled to guarantee a good performance for those requests in the system. Another reason for limiting the number of requests is that each request consumes system resources such as space in various system tables.

Let us now use the steps we outlined at the end of the previous section to find $p_k, U, \overline{N}$, and R for this case. Since the server refuses any additional requests when there are W requests in the system, the possible states are $0, 1, \cdots, W$. An arriving request that finds k $(k < W)$ requests in the system causes a transition to state $k + 1$ at rate λ. A completing request at state k $(k = 1, \cdots, W)$ causes a transition to state $k - 1$ with rate μ. Figure 8.7 shows the state transition diagram for this case.

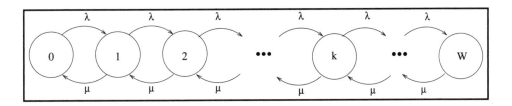

Figure 8.7. State transition diagram—infinite population/finite queue.

If we draw the same type of boundaries as we did in Fig. 8.3, we get that

$$p_k = p_0 \ (\lambda/\mu)^k \quad k = 1, \cdots, W. \tag{8.3.16}$$

The difference now comes in the computation of p_0. We now have a finite number of states as opposed to an infinite number of states, as in the previous case. So,

$$p_0 + p_1 + \cdots + p_W = p_0 \sum_{k=0}^{W}(\lambda/\mu)^k = p_0 \left[\frac{1 - (\lambda/\mu)^{W+1}}{1 - \lambda/\mu} \right] = 1 \tag{8.3.17}$$

which implies that

$$p_0 = \frac{1 - \lambda/\mu}{1 - (\lambda/\mu)^{W+1}}. \tag{8.3.18}$$

We will assume for the moment that $\lambda \neq \mu$. We will revisit this issue at the end of this sub-section.

Example 8.4

Consider again the Web server of Ex. 8.1, but now assume that at most four requests can be queued at the server—including requests being processed. What is the fraction of time that k $(k = 0, \cdots, 4)$ requests are found in the DB server?

Using the values $\lambda = 30$ requests/sec, $\mu = 50$ requests/sec, and W = 4, in Eq. (8.3.18), we get that

$$p_0 = \frac{1 - (30/50)}{1 - (30/50)^5} = 0.43 \tag{8.3.19}$$

and $p_k = 0.43 \times 0.6^k$ for $k = 1, \cdots, 4$. ∎

The utilization of the server is the fraction of time the server is not idle. So, as before, $U = 1 - p_0$ where p_0 is given by Eq. (8.3.18). Making the proper substitutions, we get

$$U = \frac{(\lambda/\mu) \ [1 - (\lambda/\mu)^W]}{1 - (\lambda/\mu)^{W+1}}. \tag{8.3.20}$$

In a server with a finite queue, an important performance metric is the fraction of requests that are lost because the queue is full. This is given by p_W since requests are only lost when the system is in state W. So, $p_{loss} = p_W$.

The average number of requests at the server is computed in a way similar to the previous section. Thus,

$$\overline{N} = \sum_{k=0}^{W} k \times p_k = p_0 \sum_{k=0}^{W} k \, (\lambda/\mu)^k. \qquad (8.3.21)$$

But, using the fact that $\sum_{k=0}^{W} k \times a^k = [W \times a^{W+2} - (W+1) \, a^{W+1} + a]/(1-a)^2$, combined with the value for p_0 given in Eq. (8.3.18) and making the proper algebraic manipulations, we get that

$$\overline{N} = \frac{(\lambda/\mu)[W(\lambda/\mu)^{W+1} - (W+1) \, (\lambda/\mu)^{W} + 1]}{[1 - (\lambda/\mu)^{W+1}](1 - \lambda/\mu)}. \qquad (8.3.22)$$

The throughput X of the server is μ when the server is busy and zero otherwise. The fraction of time the server is busy is its utilization. So,

$$X = U \times \mu + 0 \times (1 - U) = \frac{\lambda \, [1 - (\lambda/\mu)^{W}]}{1 - (\lambda/\mu)^{W+1}}. \qquad (8.3.23)$$

Once more, we use Little's Law to compute the average response time R as $\overline{N}/X$, where $\overline{N}$ and X are given by Eqs. (8.3.22) and (8.3.23), respectively. So, making the proper substitutions we get that

$$R = \overline{N}/X = \frac{S \, [W(\lambda/\mu)^{W+1} - (W+1) \, (\lambda/\mu)^{W} + 1]}{[1 - (\lambda/\mu)^{W}](1 - \lambda/\mu)}. \qquad (8.3.24)$$

Example 8.5

Consider the same parameters for arrival rate and service rate used in Ex. 8.1. What should the minimum value for the maximum number of accepted requests be so that less than 1% of the requests are rejected?

We want to compute the value of W such that $p_W = p_0 \, (\lambda/\mu)^{W} < 0.01$. Using the values of $\lambda = 30$ requests/sec and $\mu = 50$ requests/sec, we get that $p_0 = 0.4/(1 - 0.6^{W+1})$ according to Eq. (8.3.18). We want the value of W such that

$$0.4 \times 0.6^W/(1 - 0.6^{W+1}) < 0.01.$$

After some algebraic manipulations and applying logarithms we find that $W \geq 8$. Alternatively, one can use the workbook SysMod.XLS and look at the table that shows the fraction of lost requests versus W and pick the correct value of W. Figure 8.8 shows how the fraction of lost requests decreases with W. As it can be seen, the drop is more substantial for smaller values of W.   ∎

Let us now define $\rho = \lambda/\mu$ and let us turn our attention to the case of $\lambda = \mu$ or equivalently, $\rho = 1$. In this case, the equations just derived for p_k, U, X have a term of the form zero divided by zero when $\rho = 1$. This problem can be taken care of by using the well-known L'Hospital's Theorem to find the limit of p_k, U and X when $\rho \to 1$. All equations for the case of

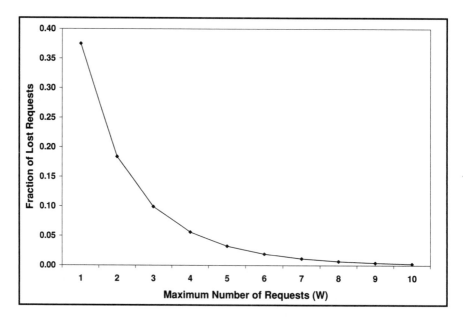

Figure 8.8. Fraction of lost requests vs. maximum number of requests (W).

fixed service server, infinite population, and finite queue are summarized in Fig. 8.9. These results include the case of $\rho = 1$.

Example 8.6

A search engine site with N servers receives 500 requests/sec. Assume that the load is equally distributed among the N servers. Thus the arrival rate to each server is $500/N$ requests/sec. The servers were benchmarked

---

Fraction of time server has k requests:

$$
p_k = \begin{cases} \frac{1-\lambda/\mu}{1-(\lambda/\mu)^{W+1}} \left(\frac{\lambda}{\mu}\right)^k & k = 0,\cdots,W \quad \lambda \neq \mu \\[2em] 1/(W+1) & k = 0,\cdots,W \quad \lambda = \mu \end{cases}
$$

Server utilization:

$$
U = \begin{cases} \frac{(\lambda/\mu)\,[1-(\lambda/\mu)^W]}{1-(\lambda/\mu)^{W+1}} & \lambda \neq \mu \\[2em] W/(W+1) & \lambda = \mu \end{cases}
$$

Average server throughput:

$$
X = U \times \mu
$$

Average number of requests in the server:

$$
\overline{N} = \begin{cases} \frac{(\lambda/\mu)[W(\lambda/\mu)^{W+1}-(W+1)\,(\lambda/\mu)^W+1]}{[1-(\lambda/\mu)^{W+1}](1-\lambda/\mu)} & \lambda \neq \mu \\[2em] W/2 & \lambda = \mu \end{cases}
$$

Average response time:

$$
R = \overline{N}/X
$$

Figure 8.9. Infinite population/finite queue server equations.

and were shown to be able to process 20 requests/sec on average. Each server can process up to 200 connections simultaneously. After that point, connections are rejected. The site planners want to know how many servers they should use to provide an average response time not exceeding 2 seconds and a probability of rejection below 5%.

Using the equations in Fig. 8.9, with $\lambda = 500/N$ requests/sec, $\mu = 20$ requests/sec, and $W = 200$ requests, we can plot the response time versus N (see Fig. 8.10). The average response time for 26 servers is 1.3 sec. The fraction of losts requests in this case can be computed as 0.002%. For 25 servers, the average response time jumps to 5.0 sec and the fraction of lost requests to 0.498%. Thus, given the requirements, we need to use at least 26 servers. This implies that the site will be able to handle 5,200 (=26 × 200) simultaneous connections.

The shape of the response-time curve of Fig. 8.10 is quite typical of

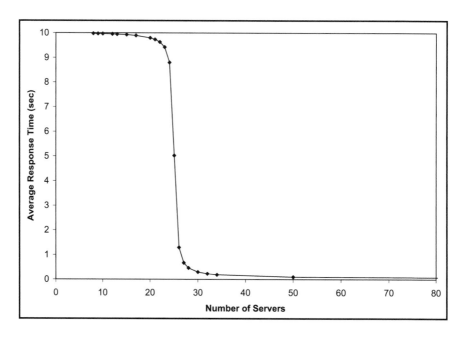

Figure 8.10. Response time vs. number of servers for Ex. 8.6.

systems with finite queues. The abrupt change occurs as the utilization reaches 100%. At this point, the throughput of each server reaches its maximum throughput, μ, and the site throughput becomes constant and equal to $N \times \mu$.   ∎

Example 8.7

A search engine has to keep its database of Web pages or Web page summaries current. For that purpose, it must send robots that bring new pages to be indexed or changed/updated for re-indexing [4]. See Fig. 8.11 for an illustration of the indexing service. The indexing service is capable of indexing 1 page/sec and has a finite buffer that can store at most 15 pages: one is being indexed and the others are waiting to be indexed. The number of robots is fixed and each robot brings a new page to be indexed at a rate of 0.1 pages/sec. We want to determine a good value for the number of robots used by the indexing service. As the number of robots increases, more Web pages brought by them are lost due to buffer overflow resulting in wasted resources such as network bandwidth. For a decreasing number of robots, the indexing service will be idle waiting for pages to index, reducing the indexing rate and the quality of the search engine.

This situation can be modeled using a fixed arrival rate (typical of infinite population models), a fixed service rate, and a finite queue system-level model as explained in what follows. If the number of robots is N and each generates pages to be indexed at a rate of 0.1 pages/sec, the overall arrival rate λ to the indexing service is $0.1 \times N$ pages/sec. The service rate of the indexing service is constant and equal to $\mu = 1$ pages/sec and the finite queue is limited at $W = 15$ pages.

We now use the infinite population, fixed service rate, and finite queue worksheet of the SysMod.XLS workbook for various values of the number of robots N to obtain a plot of p_0 and p_W, the probability that the indexing service is idle and the probability that an arriving page is lost, respectively,

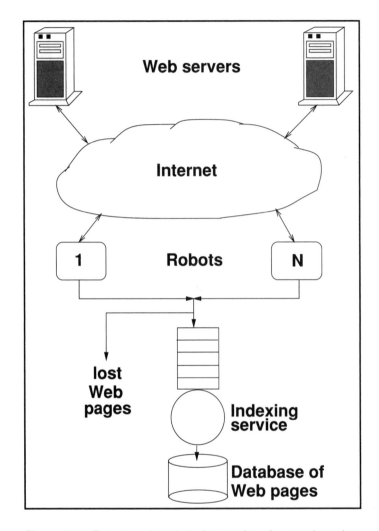

Figure 8.11. Robots and the indexing service of a search engine.

versus N. Note that p_0 is simply $1 - U$. As Fig. 8.12 indicates, p_0 and p_W go in opposite directions as the number of robots increases. As we can see, $N = 10$ is a crossover point. After that point, the decrease in p_0 is less pronounced than before that point. Also, after $N = 10$, the fraction of lost pages increases faster than before. So, by looking at the graph, we should pick $N = 10$ as the number of robots to be used in this case. The fraction of lost pages for ten robots is 6.25% and the fraction of time the

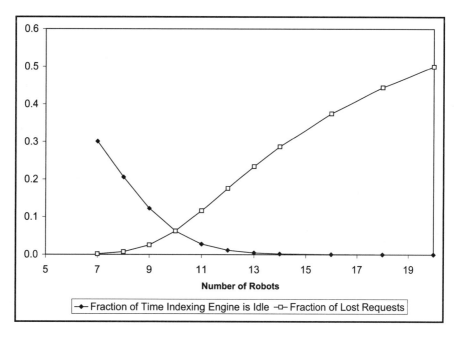

Figure 8.12. Fraction of time that the service engine is idle (p_0) and fraction of lost pages (p_W) vs. number of robots.

indexing service is idle is 0.0625. This translates into an effective indexing rate of 0.9375 ($10 \times 0.1 \times (1 - 0.0625)$) pages/sec. Note that the maximum indexing rate is 1 page/sec and this is achieved when the indexing service is continuously busy. Thus, with 10 robots one can achieve 93.75% of the maximum indexing rate with a relatively small waste of resources. The work in [4] studies the case of dynamically controlling the number of robots.   ■

8.4   Generalized System-Level Models

The examples of Sections 8.2 and 8.3 can be generalized to allow us to model other situations. We follow here the same basic approach outlined at the end of Section 8.2, except that we will allow the arrival and service rates to be a function of the state. This means that the arrival rate, λ_k, and the service rate, μ_k, may depend on the state k. In general, we may have infinite states. An STD for this generalized system-level model is given in Fig. 8.13.

Using the same kind of boundaries we used in the STD of Fig. 8.3 and applying the flow-in = flow-out principle, we get that

$$\lambda_{k-1} \, p_{k-1} = \mu_k \, p_k \quad k = 1, 2, \cdots \tag{8.4.25}$$

We can then write, by applying Eq. (8.4.25) recursively, that

$$p_1 = \frac{\lambda_0}{\mu_1} \, p_0 \tag{8.4.26}$$

$$p_2 = \frac{\lambda_1}{\mu_2} \, p_1 = \frac{\lambda_1}{\mu_2} \frac{\lambda_0}{\mu_1} \, p_0 \tag{8.4.27}$$

$$\cdot$$
$$\cdot$$
$$\cdot$$

$$p_k = \frac{\lambda_{k-1}}{\mu_k} \, p_{k-1} = \frac{\lambda_{k-1}}{\mu_k} \, \cdots \, \frac{\lambda_1}{\mu_2} \frac{\lambda_0}{\mu_1} \, p_0 \tag{8.4.28}$$

$$\cdot$$
$$\cdot$$
$$\cdot$$

Using a more compact notation we get that

$$p_k = p_0 \prod_{i=0}^{k-1} \frac{\lambda_i}{\mu_{i+1}}. \tag{8.4.29}$$

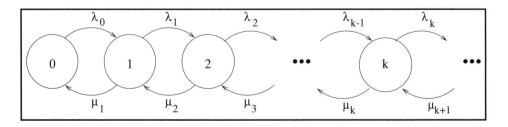

Figure 8.13. State transition diagram for generalized system-level model.

But, as before, the sum of all p_k equals to one. Thus,

$$\sum_{k=0}^{\infty} p_0 \prod_{i=0}^{k-1} \frac{\lambda_i}{\mu_{i+1}} = 1. \tag{8.4.30}$$

This implies that

$$p_0 = \left[\sum_{k=0}^{\infty} \prod_{i=0}^{k-1} \frac{\lambda_i}{\mu_{i+1}} \right]^{-1}. \tag{8.4.31}$$

Equations (8.4.29) and (8.4.31) can be specialized to many different situations by chosing the proper expressions for λ_k and μ_k. We will use these results in the following sections to analyze several other Web-based systems. Figure 8.14 summarizes all equations for the generalized system-level model.

8.5   Other System-Level Models

Given the generalized framework discussed in the previous section, we can consider many possible alternatives when modeling Web-based systems. We consider here three dimensions to the problem:

- *Population size*: We consider the infinite population case and the finite population case with M clients.

- *Server service rate*: We consider fixed service rate servers, $X(k) = \mu$, and variable service rate servers, $X(k) = \mu_k$.

- *Maximum queue size*: The two cases considered here are infinite queue size and maximum queue size limited to W requests. Note that for the finite population case with M clients, a maximum queue size of M is equivalent to an infinite queue since a maximum of M requests can be in the system.

Fraction of time server has k requests:

$$p_k = p_0 \prod_{i=0}^{k-1} \frac{\lambda_i}{\mu_i + 1}$$

where

$$p_0 = \left[\sum_{k=0}^{\infty} \prod_{i=0}^{k-1} \frac{\lambda_i}{\mu_i + 1} \right]^{-1}$$

Server utilization:

$$U = 1 - p_0$$

Average server throughput:

$$X = \sum_{k=1}^{\infty} \mu_k \, p_k$$

Average number of requests in the server:

$$\overline{N} = \sum_{k=1}^{\infty} k \times p_k$$

Average response time:

$$R = \frac{\overline{N}}{X} = \frac{\sum_{k=1}^{\infty} k \times p_k}{\sum_{k=1}^{\infty} \mu_k \, p_k}$$

Figure 8.14. Generalized system-level model equations.

8.5.1   Infinite Population Models

Infinite population models are adequate to represent WWW environments, where the number of users is potentially very large. Sections 8.2 and 8.3 considered two cases of infinite population models. Infinite population models are also known as *open models* and can be depicted as in Fig. 8.15.

Besides the open models considered in Sections 8.2 and 8.3, we consider here the cases of variable service rate with limited and infinite queue size.

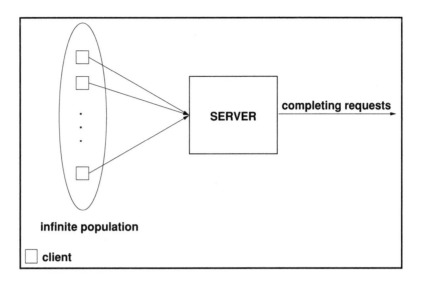

Figure 8.15. Open model.

8.5.1.1   Variable Service Rate and Infinite Queue

The throughput of the server is usually a function of the number of requests present in the system. A typical throughput curve $X(k)$ is shown in Fig. 8.16. The figure shows that as the number of requests in the system increases from zero, the throughput increases almost linearly with the number of requests. This reflects the fact that at light loads, requests face very little congestion at the system internal queues. After some point, congestion starts to build up and throughput increases at a much lower rate until it saturates, reaching its maximum value. This maximum value is determined by the bottleneck device at the server.

We will use the generalized expressions for p_k and p_0 given by Eqs. (8.4.29) and (8.4.31). The expressions for λ_k and μ_k used in this case are $\lambda_k = \lambda$ for $k = 0, 1, \cdots$ and $\mu_k = X(k)$ for $k = 1, 2, \cdots$. Thus, making the proper substitutions, we get

$$p_k = \left[1 + \sum_{j=1}^{\infty} \frac{\lambda^j}{\prod_{i=1}^{j} X(i)}\right]^{-1} \frac{\lambda^k}{\prod_{i=1}^{k} X(i)}. \qquad (8.5.32)$$

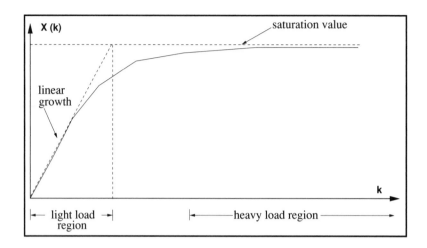

Figure 8.16. Typical throughput curve.

The summation in Eq. (8.5.32) has an infinite number of terms and cannot be computed for the general case where all values of the throughput are different. Fortunately, as we pointed out before, the throughput saturates after a certain value of k. Let J be the value of k after which the value of the throughput no longer changes. Now, the expression for μ_k becomes

$$\mu_k = \begin{cases} X(k) & k \leq J \\ X(J) & k > J \end{cases}. \tag{8.5.33}$$

Using the expression of μ_k given in Eq. (8.5.33) in Eq. (8.5.32) and doing some manipulations, we get that

$$p_0 = \left[1 + \sum_{k=1}^{J} \frac{\lambda^k}{\beta(k)} + \frac{\lambda^J}{\beta(J)} \frac{\rho}{1-\rho} \right]^{-1} \tag{8.5.34}$$

and

$$p_k = \begin{cases} p_0\, \lambda^k/\beta(k) & k \leq J \\ \\ p_0\, X(J)^J\, \rho^k/\beta(J) & k > J \end{cases} \tag{8.5.35}$$

where $\beta(k) \stackrel{\text{def}}{=} X(1) \times X(2) \times \cdots \times X(k)$ and $\rho \stackrel{\text{def}}{=} \lambda/X(J)$. Equations (8.5.34) and (8.5.35) are only valid if $\lambda < X(J)$, that is, if the arrival rate is less than the maximum service rate.

A closed form expression for the average number of requests in the server can be found using Eqs. (8.5.34) and (8.5.35) and the fact that $\overline{N}$ is computed as $\overline{N} = \sum_{k=0}^{\infty} k \times p_k$. After some manipulations, we get

$$\overline{N} = p_0 \left[\sum_{k=1}^{J} \frac{k \times \lambda^k}{\beta(k)} + \frac{\rho\,\lambda^J\,[\rho + (J+1)\,(1-\rho)]}{(1-\rho)^2\,\beta(J)} \right]. \qquad (8.5.36)$$

The average throughput in open models with unbounded queue sizes is equal to the average arrival rate. So, $X = \lambda$. Finally, the response time R is obtained from Little's Law as $R = \overline{N}/X$. Note that Eqs. (8.5.34)–(8.5.36) become, as expected, the equations for the infinite population, fixed service rate, and infinite queue size case when $J = 1$.

Example 8.8

A Web server receives requests at a rate of 30 requests/sec. The throughput of the server when there is one request present is 18 requests/sec, for two requests it is 35 requests/sec, and for three or more requests is 50 requests/sec. What are the server utilization, average throughput, average number of requests in the system, and average response time?

Note that $\lambda = 30$ requests/sec, $J = 3$, $X(1) = 18$ requests/sec, $X(2) = 35$ requests/sec, and $X(J) = 50$ requests/sec. Using these values, we get that $\rho = 30/50 = 0.6$, $\beta(1) = 18$, $\beta(2) = 18 \times 35 = 630$, and $\beta(3) = 18 \times 35 \times 50 = 31,500$. Using these values in Eq. (8.5.34), we get that $p_0 = 0.16$ and, therefore, the server utilization is $U = 1 - p_0 = 0.84 = 84\%$. From Eq. (8.5.36), we get that $\overline{N} = 2.27$ requests. Since the throughput X is equal to $\lambda = 30$ requests/sec, we get that the response time is $R = \overline{N}/X = 2.77/30 = 0.076$ sec. ∎

8.5.1.2 Variable Service Rate and Limited Queue Size

The difference between this case and the previous one is that now requests can be lost if W requests are already at the server upon arrival of a new request. The expressions for λ_k and μ_k are $\lambda_k = \lambda$ for $k = 0, \cdots, W - 1$ and

$$
\mu_k = \begin{cases} X(k) & k = 1, \cdots, J \\ X(J) & k = J + 1, \cdots, W \end{cases} \tag{8.5.37}
$$

if $W \geq J$. If $W < J$, then $\mu_k = X(k), k = 1, \cdots, W$.

The expression for p_k now becomes

$$
p_k = \begin{cases} p_0 \times \lambda^k/\beta(k) & k = 1, \cdots, J \\ p_0 \times \rho^k \times X(J)^J/\beta(J) & k = J + 1, \cdots, W \end{cases} \tag{8.5.38}
$$

if $W \geq J$ and $p_k = p_0\, \lambda^k/\beta(k)$ if $W < J$. The expression for p_0 is given by

$$
p_0 = \left[1 + \sum_{k=1}^{J} \frac{\lambda^k}{\beta(k)} + \frac{\rho \times \lambda^J \, (1 - \rho^{W-J})}{\beta(J)\,(1 - \rho)} \right]^{-1}. \tag{8.5.39}
$$

for $W \geq J$ and

$$
p_0 = \left[1 + \sum_{k=1}^{W} \frac{\lambda^k}{\beta(k)} \right]^{-1}. \tag{8.5.40}
$$

for $W < J$. Note that the last term within the brackets of Eq. (8.5.39) becomes zero divided by zero when $\rho = 1$. As before, we can use L'Hospital's Theorem to find the limit of that term when $\rho \to 1$. This gives us

$$
\lim_{\rho \to 1} \frac{\rho \times \lambda^J \, (1 - \rho^{W-J})}{\beta(J)\,(1 - \rho)} = \frac{\lambda^J \times (W - J)}{\beta(J)}. \tag{8.5.41}
$$

The fraction of lost requests is simply $p_W = p_0 \times \rho^W \times X(J)^J/\beta(J)$ for $W \geq J$ and $p_W = p_0 \times \lambda^W/\beta(W)$ for $W < J$. The average number of requests in the server can be computed as $\overline{N} = \sum_{k=1}^{W} k \times p_k$. The average throughput X is given by $X = \sum_{k=1}^{W} X(k) \times p_k$, which in the case of $W \geq J$ becomes

$$
X = \sum_{k=1}^{W} X(k) \times p_k = \sum_{k=1}^{J} X(k)\, p_k + X(J) \sum_{k=J+1}^{W} p_k. \tag{8.5.42}
$$

Finally, the response time is computed from Little's Law as $R = \overline{N}/X$.

Special care has to be taken when implementing the formulas above, since it is very easy to cause overflows or underflows when computing terms of the form $\lambda^k/\beta(k)$. We recommend that this type of computation be implemented as

$$\frac{\lambda}{X(1)} \times \frac{\lambda}{X(2)} \times \cdots \times \frac{\lambda}{X(k)}. \tag{8.5.43}$$

While this approach does not totally eliminate overflows or underflows, it significantly reduces the likelihood they will occur. This is the approach used in the workbook SysMod.XLS.

Example 8.9

Consider the same Web server of Ex. 8.7 except that now the server's queue is limited to five requests. What are the new values for the the server utilization, average throughput, average number of requests in the system, average response time, and the fraction of lost requests?

Using the expressions derived in this subsection as implemented in the Microsoft Excel workbook SysMod.XLS, we get that the server utilization is $U = 82.7\%$, the average number of requests at the server is $\overline{N} = 1.85$ requests, the average throughput is equal to 28.4 requests/sec, and from Little's Law, the average response time is $1.85/28.4 = 0.065$ sec. The fraction of lost requests is $0.053 = 5.3\%$.   ∎

8.5.2   Finite Population Models

Consider now the case of a Web server of a corporate portal that is accessed only by client workstations in the same company. We now have a *finite population* of, say, M clients in what is also called a *closed model* (see Fig. 8.17). Each of these clients submits a request, waits for the response of that request, analyzes the response, and composes a new request to be submitted to the server. As defined in Chapter 3, the time spent by the client from the time a response to a request is received and the next request is submitted is called *think time*. Let Z be the average think time, in seconds, at each

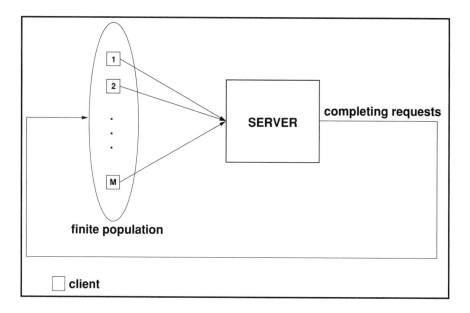

Figure 8.17. Closed model.

client. When a client is in the think state, it submits one request at each Z time units. Thus, the average rate at which each client in the think state submits requests to the server is $1/Z$. Assume as before that the state of the server can be characterized by the number k of requests in the server. The STD for a finite population model has only $M+1$ states (from 0 to M), where M is the number of clients.

If the system is in state k, that is, requests submitted by k of the M clients are in the server, $M - k$ clients are in the think state. Since each of these $M - k$ clients generates requests at a rate of $1/Z$ requests/sec, the average rate at which requests arrive at the server when it is at state k is $\lambda_k = (M - k)/Z$ for $k = 0, \cdots, M$. Figure 8.18 shows the state transition diagram for the finite population case.

The next subsections consider the finite population case with a fixed service rate and with a variable service rate.

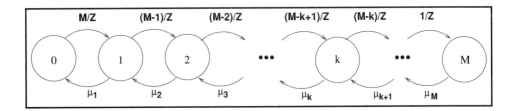

Figure 8.18. State transition diagram—finite population.

8.5.2.1   Fixed Service Rate and Unlimited Queue

Consider, as before, that the server's service rate is fixed, that is, it is not state-dependent. So, $\mu_k = \mu$ for $k = 1, \cdots, M$. Using the proper definitions of λ_k and μ_k in Eq. (8.4.29) and (8.4.31) we get that

$$p_k = p_0 \; \frac{M!}{(M-k)! \, (\mu \, Z)^k} \quad k = 1, \cdots, M \tag{8.5.44}$$

where

$$p_0 = \left[\sum_{k=0}^{M} \frac{M!}{(M-k)! \, (\mu \, Z)^k} \right]^{-1}. \tag{8.5.45}$$

A few words about the computations in Eqs. (8.5.44) and (8.5.45) are in order. Even though there is no closed form expression for the summation in Eq. (8.5.45), it is a finite summation and therefore can always be computed. Some numerical problems may arise in the computation of p_k and p_0 for very large values of M due to the factorials that appear in the numerator and the denominator. Imagine, for example, a client server system with 200 clients. If we used the naive approach of first computing $200! = 200 \times 199 \times \cdots 2 \times 1$, we could easily exceed the limit of the largest number that can be stored in the computer we are using to do the computation. An alternative way is to expand the factorials in the numerator and denominator and rearrange the terms as follows

$$p_k = p_0 \; \overbrace{\frac{M}{\mu \, Z} \cdot \frac{M-1}{\mu \, Z} \cdot \frac{M-2}{\mu \, Z} \cdot \cdots \cdot \frac{M-(k-1)}{\mu \, Z}}^{k \text{ terms}} \quad k = 1, \cdots, M \tag{8.5.46}$$

and

$$p_0 = \left[\sum_{k=0}^{M} \overbrace{\frac{M}{\mu\,Z} \cdot \frac{M-1}{\mu\,Z} \cdot \frac{M-2}{\mu\,Z} \cdots \cdots \frac{M-(k-1)}{\mu\,Z}}^{k\ \text{terms}} \right]^{-1}. \qquad (8.5.47)$$

Note that once we obtain the value of p_k for $k = 0, \cdots, M$, we can compute all performance metrics of interest.

Example 8.10

A C/S application is used by 50 clients. The software that runs at the client workstation runs a local computation that lasts for 2 seconds, on average, before submitting a new request to the server. The server can process requests at a rate of 80 requests/sec. What are the average response time, average server throughput, average number of requests at the server, and the server utilization?

The number of clients is $M = 50$, the average think time is $Z = 2$ seconds, and the service rate is $\mu = 80$ requests/sec. Using Eq. (8.5.47), we can compute the value of p_0 as 0.69 with the help of the spreadsheet in the Microsoft Excel workbook SysMod.XLS. The server utilization is $U = 1 - p_0 = 0.31 = 31\%$. The average number of requests is computed as $\sum_{k=1}^{50} k \times p_k$. Again, using the same spreadsheet, we get $\overline{N} = 0.443$ requests. The server throughput is

$$X = \sum_{k=1}^{50} \mu \times p_k = \mu \sum_{k=1}^{50} p_k = \mu\,(1 - p_0) = 80 \times 0.31 = 24.8 \text{ tps.} \quad (8.5.48)$$

Using Little's Law, we can compute the average response time as $R = \overline{N}/X = 0.443/24.8 = 0.018$ sec. ∎

8.5.2.2   Fixed Service Rate and Limited Queue Size

The difference between this case and the previous is that the maximum number of requests in the system is limited to W ($W < M$). The expressions for p_k and p_0 become

$$p_k = p_0 \, \frac{M!}{(M-k)! \, (\mu \, Z)^k} \quad k = 1, \cdots, W \qquad (8.5.49)$$

and

$$p_0 = \left[\sum_{k=0}^{W} \frac{M!}{(M-k)! \, (\mu \, Z)^k} \right]^{-1}. \qquad (8.5.50)$$

The fraction of lost requests is given by p_W. The main differences between Eqs. (8.5.49) and (8.5.50) and their equivalent (8.5.44) and (8.5.45) for the unlimited queue size is that the number of states is limited to $W+1$ and that the upper limit on the summation of p_0 is W instead of M.

8.5.2.3   Variable Service Rate

The difference between this case and the previous is that the service rate of the server is variable and given by

$$\mu_k = \begin{cases} X(k) & k = 1, \cdots, J \\ \\ X(J) & k > J \end{cases} \qquad (8.5.51)$$

The arrival rate λ_k is given by $\lambda_k = (M-k)/Z$ for $k = 0, \cdots, M$ as before. The expression for p_k becomes

$$p_k = \begin{cases} p_0 \, \frac{M!}{(M-k)! \, Z^k \beta(k)} & k = 1, \cdots, J \\ \\ p_0 \, \frac{M! \, X(J)^J}{(M-k)! \, [Z \, X(J)]^k \, \beta(J)} & k = J+1, \cdots, M \end{cases} \qquad (8.5.52)$$

and p_0 is given by

$$p_0 = \left[1 + \sum_{k=1}^{J} \frac{M!}{(M-k)! \, Z^k \, \beta(k)} + \frac{X(J)^J}{\beta(J)} \sum_{k=J+1}^{M} \frac{M!}{(M-k)! \, [Z \, X(J)]^k} \right]^{-1} \qquad (8.5.53)$$

where $\beta(k)$ was defined in Section 8.5.1. The average number of requests at the server is given by $\overline{N} = \sum_{k=1}^{M} k \times p_k$ and the average throughput as

$$X = \sum_{k=1}^{M} X(k) \, p_k = \sum_{k=1}^{J} X(k) \, p_k + X(J) \sum_{k=J+1}^{M} p_k. \qquad (8.5.54)$$

Finally, the response time is computed from Little's Law as $R = \overline{N}/X$.

Example 8.11

Consider the same parameters as in the client/server of the previous example, except that now the service rate is no longer constant but is given by $X(1) = 18$ requests/sec, $X(2) = 35$ requests/sec, and $X(k) = 50$ requests/sec for $k = 3, \cdots, M$. What are the server utilization, average throughput, average number of requests in the system, and average response time?

Using the above equations, we get that server utilization is $U = 76.3\%$, the average number of requests at the server is $\overline{N} = 1.57$ requests, the average throughput is equal to 24.21 requests/sec, and from Little's Law, the average response time is $1.57/24.21 = 0.065$ sec.   ■

8.6   Concluding Remarks

The performance of servers in a Web environment can be analyzed at a high level, from a system's point of view, or at a low level, where the various components of the system are modeled explicitly. This chapter covered the high-level view and discussed system-level models. These types of models are based on state transition diagrams that represent the states a system can be found in. State transition rates are associated with the rates at which events occur at the underlying system being modeled. By equating the flow into a state or set of states with the flow out of that set, we are able to derive a set of equations that relate the fraction of time that the system is at each state. From these fractions of time, we can obtain performance metrics of interest, such as the server utilization, average number of requests in the system, average response times, and fraction of requests rejected.

This chapter presented a general set of equations for state transition diagrams that have state-dependent arrival and departure rates. These equations were specialized to cover various cases including: infinite population/fixed server rate/infinite queue, infinite population/fixed server rate/finite queue, infinite population/variable server rate/infinite queue, infinite population/variable server rate/finite queue, finite population/fixed server rate/unlimited queue, finite population/fixed server rate/limited queue, and finite population/variable server rate. All equations derived in this chapter are implemented in the Microsoft Excel workbook `SysMod.XLS` that can be found in the book's Web site. A more formal treatment—based on the theory of stochastic processes—of the models discussed in this chapter can be found in [2].

The next chapter discusses the lower-level models, called component models, and also shows how system-level models can be combined with component-level models.

Bibliography

[1] J. P. Buzen, "Operational Analysis: An Alternative to Stochastic Modeling," *Performance of Computer Installations*, North Holland, June 1978, pp. 175–194.

[2] L. Kleinrock, *Queueing Systems, Vol. I: Theory*, John Wiley and Sons, New York, 1975.

[3] D. A. Menascé, V. A. F. Almeida, and L. W. Dowdy, *Capacity Planning and Performance Modeling: From Mainframes to Client-Server Systems*, Prentice Hall, Upper Saddle River, New Jersey, 1994.

[4] J. Talim, Z. Liu, Ph. Nain, and E. G. Coffman, Jr., "Controlling the Robots of Web Search Engines," *Proc. Joint Int'l. Conf. Measurement and Modeling of Comp. Systems*, ACM Sigmetrics and IFIP WG 7.3, Cambridge, Massachusetts, June 16-20, 2001, pp. 236–244.

Chapter 9

Component- Level Performance Models

9.1 Introduction

In Chapter 8 we looked at computer systems characterized by their through-put function $X(n)$, where n represents the load of the system in terms of the number of requests present at the system. In this chapter, we look at the components that make up a networked system and examine how we can build models that take into consideration the interaction of these compo-nents. These models are called queuing networks (QN). We discuss solution methods for both open and closed QNs with multiple classes of customers. The Microsoft Excel workbooks `OpenQN.XLS` and `ClosedQN.XLS`, which can be found on the book's Web site, implement the algorithms and solution

341

methods discussed here. We also present bounds on performance and provide models for dealing with multiple resource queues to model multiprocessor servers and other such situations. The chapter concludes with an example of a model of an intranet.

9.2   Queuing Networks

Chapter 5 introduced the notion of a QN, as a network of interconnected queues that represents a computer system (see Section 5.7.1). A *queue* in a QN stands for a resource (e.g., CPU, disk, network) and the queue of requests waiting to use the resource. A queue is characterized by a function $S(n)$ that represents the average service time per request when there are n requests at the queue. Remember that the term queue stands for the waiting queue plus the resource itself; the number of requests, n, at the queue is called the *queue length*. There are three categories of resources in a QN and they vary according to whether there is queuing or not and whether the average service time, $S(n)$, depends on the queue length n or not. The resource types are described below. The graphical notation used to represent them as well as an example of the curve $S(n)$ is given in Fig. 9.1.

- Load-independent resources: represent resources where there is queuing but the average service time does not depend on the load; that is, $S(n) = S$ for all values of n (Fig. 9.1a).

- Load-dependent resources: used to represent resources where there is queuing and the average service time depends on the load; that is, $S(n)$ is an arbitrary function of n (Fig. 9.1b).

- Delay resources: indicate situations where there is no queuing. Thus, the total time spent by a request at a delay resource is the request's service time. The average service time function does not depend on the number of requests present at the resource; that is, $S(n) = S$ for all values of n (Fig. 9.1c).

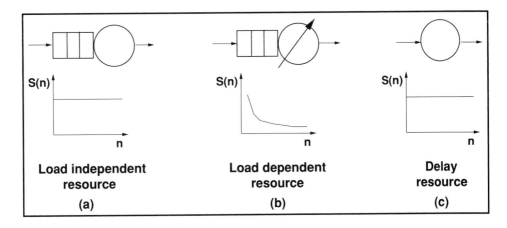

Figure 9.1. Types of resources in a queuing network.

Not all requests that flow through the resources of a QN are similar in terms of the resources used and the time spent at each resource. As pointed out in Chapter 6, the total workload submitted to a computer system may be broken down into several workload components, which are represented in a QN model by a *class* of requests. Different classes may have different service demand parameters and different workload intensity parameters. Classes of requests may be classified as *open* or *closed* depending on whether the number of requests in the QN is unbounded or fixed, respectively. Open classes allow requests to arrive, go through the various resources, and leave the system. Closed classes are characterized by having a fixed number of requests in the QN. A QN in which all classes are open is called an open QN. A QN in which all classes are closed is called a closed QN. A QN in which some classes are open and others are closed is called a *mixed* QN.

Figure 9.2a shows an example of an open QN that represents a DB server with a multiprocessor with four CPUs and two disks. The set of four CPUs is represented in the QN as a single queue that acts as a load-dependent resource. The service time function is of the form

$$S(n) = \begin{cases} 1/(n \times \alpha) & n \leq 4 \\ 1/(4 \times \alpha) & n > 4 \end{cases} \tag{9.2.1}$$

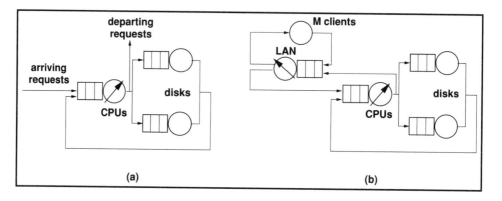

Figure 9.2. (a) Example of an open QN. (b) Example of a closed QN.

to indicate that the average service time decreases with the number of requests as more processors are used until all four processors are busy. Figure 9.2b illustrates the same DB server receiving requests from a fixed number, M, of clients that send their requests through an Ethernet LAN. The set of clients is represented in the QN as a delay resource because a request that returns to a client does not have to queue for access to the client. The service demand at that resource is the average time spent at the client before submitting a new request to the database—the think time. The LAN is represented by a load-dependent resource to indicate that, as the load on the network increases, the throughput on the LAN decreases due to the increase in the number of collisions for access to the network medium.

In the following sections of this chapter we will be studying both open and closed QNs. We will show how to determine performance metrics such as throughput, response time, resource utilization, and bottlenecks.

9.3 Open Systems

We consider first the case of single-class open QNs and then generalize for the case where multiple classes are considered.

9.3.1   Single-Class Open Queuing Networks

Let us examine first the case of a single-class open QN where all resources are either delay- or load-independent resources. Consider the following notation.

- λ: average arrival rate of requests to the QN

- K: number of queues

- X_0: average throughput of the QN. In the case of open systems with operational equilibrium, the average throughput is the same as the average arrival rate. So, $X_0 = \lambda$

- V_i: average number of visits to queue i by a request

- S_i: average service time of a request at queue i per visit to the queue

- W_i: average waiting time of a request at queue i per visit to the queue

- X_i: average throughput of queue i

- R_i: average response time of a request at queue i, defined as the sum of the average waiting time plus average service time per visit to the queue.   So, $R_i = W_i + S_i$

- R'_i: average residence time of a request at queue i.   This is the total waiting time (i.e., the queuing time) plus the total service time (i.e., the service demand), over all visits to queue i. So, $R'_i = Q_i + D_i = V_i \times R_i$

- R_0: average response time; equal to the sum of the residence times over all queues. So, $R_0 = \sum_{i=1}^{K} R'_i$

- n_i: average number of requests at queue i waiting or receiving service from any resource at queue i

- N: average number of requests in the QN

We start by obtaining the average response time R_i at queue i. We note that the average response time is equal to the average service time S_i plus the average waiting time of a request. The average waiting time is equal to the average number of requests *seen* at queue i by an arriving request to the queue multiplied by the average service time S_i per request. An important result, known as the Arrival Theorem [8, 12], applied to open QNs, says that the average number of requests seen upon arrival to queue i is equal to the average number, n_i, of requests in the queue. Thus,

$$R_i = S_i + n_i \times S_i. \tag{9.3.2}$$

But, from Little's Law, $n_i = X_i \times R_i$. Combining this result with Eq. (9.3.2) and noting from the Utilization Law that $U_i = X_i \times S_i$, we get that

$$R_i = S_i/(1 - U_i). \tag{9.3.3}$$

From Eq. (9.3.3), we can get the residence time at queue i as

$$R_i' = V_i \times R_i = \frac{V_i \times S_i}{1 - U_i} = \frac{D_i}{1 - U_i}. \tag{9.3.4}$$

Using Little's Law, Eq. (9.3.3), and the Utilization Law again we can obtain the average number of requests at queue i as

$$n_i = U_i/(1 - U_i). \tag{9.3.5}$$

One common question in the analysis of C/S systems is "what is the maximum theoretical value of the arrival rate λ?" This question has an easy answer that depends solely on the service demands of all resources. Note that the service demand, the utilization, and the arrival rate are related by $\lambda = U_i/D_i$ for all resources i. Because the utilization of any resource cannot exceed 100%, we have that $\lambda \leq 1/D_i$ for all i's. The maximum value of λ is limited by the resource with the highest value of the service demand, called the bottleneck resource. Thus,

$$\lambda \leq \frac{1}{\max_{i=1}^{K} D_i}. \tag{9.3.6}$$

Example 9.1

A DB server has one CPU and two disks and receives requests at a rate of 10,800 requests per hour. Each request needs 200 msec of CPU and performs five I/Os on disk 1 and three I/Os on disk 2 on the average. Each I/O takes an average of 15 msec. What are the average response time per request, average throughput of the server, utilization of the CPU and disks, and the average number of requests at the server? What is the maximum theoretical arrival rate of requests sustained by this server?

The throughput, X_0, equal to the average arrival rate λ, is $10,800/3,600$ = 3 requests/sec. The service demand at the CPU, D_{CPU} is 0.2 sec. The service demands at disks 1 and 2 are computed as $D_{disk1} = V_1 \times S_{disk} = 5 \times 0.015 = 0.075$ sec, and $D_{disk2} = V_2 \times S_{disk} = 3 \times 0.015 = 0.045$ sec, respectively. From the Service Demand Law (see Section 3.5.3), $U_i = D_i \times X_0$. So, the utilization of the CPU and disks is given by $U_{CPU} = D_{CPU} \times X_0 = 0.2 \times 3 = 60\%$, $U_{disk1} = D_{disk1} \times X_0 = 0.075 \times 3 = 22.5\%$, and $U_{disk2} = D_{disk2} \times X_0 = 0.045 \times 3 = 13.5\%$, respectively. The residence times can now be computed as

$$R'_{CPU} = D_{CPU}/(1 - U_{CPU}) = 0.2/(1 - 0.60) = 0.50 \text{ sec}$$
$$R'_{disk1} = D_{disk1}/(1 - U_{disk1}) = 0.075/(1 - 0.225) = 0.097 \text{ sec}$$
$$R'_{disk\ 2} = D_{disk2}/(1 - U_{disk2}) = 0.045/(1 - 0.135) = 0.052 \text{ sec.}$$

The total response time is just the sum of all residence times. So, $R_0 = R'_{CPU} + R'_{disk1} + R'_{disk2} = 0.50 + 0.097 + 0.052 = 0.649$ sec. The average number of requests at each queue is given by

$$n_{CPU} = U_{CPU}/(1 - U_{CPU}) = 0.60/(1 - 0.60) = 1.5$$
$$n_{disk1} = U_{disk1}/(1 - U_{disk1}) = 0.225/(1 - 0.225) = 0.29$$
$$n_{disk2} = U_{disk2}/(1 - U_{disk2}) = 0.135/(1 - 0.135) = 0.16.$$

The total number of requests at the server is given by $N = n_{CPU} + n_{disk1} + n_{disk2} = 1.5 + 0.29 + 0.16 = 1.95$ requests.

The maximum arrival rate is $1/\max\{0.2, 0.075, 0.045\} = 5$ requests/sec. Figure 9.3 shows how the average response time varies as the average arrival rate of requests increases. The curve shows the dramatic increase seen when the arrival rate approaches its maximum possible value.   ■

9.3.2   Multiple-Class Open Queuing Networks

The expressions we derived for the single-class case can be generalized for the case where there are multiple classes of requests. The generalization on the notation used so far is quite obvious. We use the subscripts i, r to indicate variables associated with queue i and class r. For example, $R'_{i,r}$ stands for the residence time of class r requests at queue i. We use R for the number of classes. Different classes may have different values of the arrival rate λ_r. The set of all arrival rates $\lambda_1, \cdots, \lambda_r, \cdots, \lambda_R$ is denoted for convenience as the vector $\vec{\lambda} = (\lambda_1, \cdots, \lambda_r, \cdots, \lambda_R)$. Since all performance metrics depend

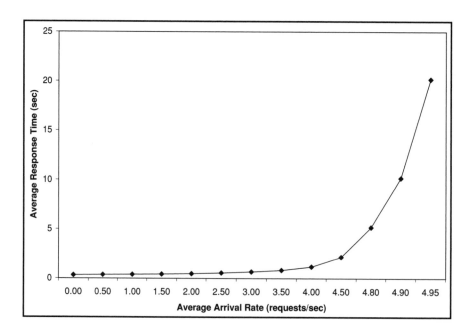

Figure 9.3. Response time vs. arrival rate for Ex. 9.1.

on the values of the arrival rates, we extend our notation $R'_{i,r}$ to $R'_{i,r}(\vec{\lambda})$ to indicate that $R'_{i,r}$ is a function of the values of the arrival rates.

Figure 9.4 summarizes all equations for the multiple-class case of open QNs with no load-dependent resources. Readers interested in the detailed derivations of these formulas should refer to [6]. The equations for multi-class open QN models are implemented in the Microsoft Excel workbook OpenQN.XLS that can be found on the book's Web site.

Example 9.2

A database server is subject to two types of transactions: query and update. The arrival rate of query transactions is 5 tps and that of update transactions is 2 tps. The service demands for the CPU, disks 1 and 2, are given in the top part of Table 9.1. What are the response times, residence times, and utilizations?

Using the equations in Fig. 9.4 we obtain the utilizations per resource per class and the overall resource utilization. The residence times per resource per class depend on the service demands and on the overall resource utilizations. For example, the residence time of query transactions at the CPU is 0.50 sec. This number is obtained by dividing the CPU service demand for query transactions, 0.10 sec, by $(1 - U_{\text{CPU}}) = (1 - 0.8) = 0.2$. The residence time is the time spent by a transaction at a resource, waiting or receiving service, over all visits to the resource. The sum of the residence times for all resources is the response time. So, the response time for query transactions is $0.50 + 0.40 + 0.16 = 1.06$ sec.   ∎

9.4   Closed Models

The open-queuing network models we studied in the previous section do not place any limits on the maximum number of requests present in the system. There are situations where we want to model computer systems with a fixed and finite number of requests in the system. These situations arise when we want to model a system with a maximum degree of multiprogramming

Input Parameters: $D_{i,r}$ and λ_r

Utilization:

$$U_{i,r}(\vec{\lambda}) = \lambda_r \times V_{i,r} \times S_{i,r} = \lambda_r \times D_{i,r} \qquad (9.3.7)$$

$$U_i(\vec{\lambda}) = \sum_{r=1}^{R} U_{i,r}(\vec{\lambda}) \qquad (9.3.8)$$

Average number of class r requests at resource i:

$$n_{i,r}(\vec{\lambda}) = \frac{U_{i,r}(\vec{\lambda})}{1 - U_i(\vec{\lambda})} \qquad (9.3.9)$$

Average residence time of class r requests at resource i:

$$R'_{i,r}(\vec{\lambda}) = \begin{cases} D_{i,r} & \text{delay resource} \\[2mm] \dfrac{D_{i,r}}{1 - U_i(\vec{\lambda})} & \text{queuing resource} \end{cases} \qquad (9.3.10)$$

Average class r request response time:

$$R_{0,r}(\vec{\lambda}) = \sum_{i=1}^{K} R'_{i,r}(\vec{\lambda}) \qquad (9.3.11)$$

Average number of requests at resource i:

$$n_i(\vec{\lambda}) = \sum_{r=1}^{R} n_{i,r}(\vec{\lambda}) \qquad (9.3.12)$$

Figure 9.4. Formulas for multiclass open QNs with no load-dependent resources.

under heavy load, a C/S system with a known number of clients sending requests to a server, or a multithreaded server.

Models that have a fixed number of requests per class are called *closed models*. The technique we present here to solve closed queuing networks is called Mean Value Analysis (MVA) [8]. It is rather elegant and intuitive. The first efficient technique to solve closed queuing network models is the

Table 9.1. Service Demands, Arrival Rates, and Performance Metrics for Ex. 9.2

	Queries	Updates
Arrival Rate (tps)	5	2
Service Demands (sec)		
CPU	0.10	0.15
Disk 1	0.08	0.20
Disk 2	0.07	0.10
Utilizations (%)		
CPU	50	30
Disk 1	40	40
Disk 2	35	20
Residence times (sec)		
CPU	0.50	0.75
Disk 1	0.40	1.00
Disk 2	0.16	0.22
Response times (sec)	1.06	1.97

convolution algorithm due to Buzen [4]. We first discuss MVA for single-class QNs and consider next the multiple-class case. The notation used for closed QN models is similar to the one used for open models with the exception that instead of denoting our variables as a function of the arrival rate, we denote them as a function of the number of requests, n, in the system. So, for instance, $R'_i(n)$ stands for the residence time at queue i when there are n requests in the system.

9.4.1   Single-Class Closed Models

MVA is based on recursively using three equations: the residence time equation, the throughput equation, and the queue length equation. We derive here these equations from first principles.

Consider a closed queuing network with n requests. Let us start by computing the response time, $R_i(n)$, per visit to resource i. As we know, the response time is the sum of the service time S_i, plus the waiting time $W_i(n)$. The waiting time is equal to the time to serve all requests found in the queue by an arriving request. This is equal to the average number, $n_i^a(n)$, of requests found in the queue by an arriving request multiplied by the average service time per request. So,

$$R_i(n) = S_i + W_i(n) = S_i + n_i^a(n) \times S_i = S_i \left[1 + n_i^a(n)\right]. \qquad (9.4.13)$$

An important result, the Arrival Theorem [8, 12], applied to closed QNs, says that the average number of requests seen upon arrival to queue i when there are n requests in the QN is equal to the average number of requests in queue i in a QN with $n - 1$ requests, i.e., with the arriving request to queue i removed from the queuing network. After all, the arriving request cannot find itself in the queue! Thus, from the Arrival Theorem we have that,

$$n_i^a(n) = n_i(n - 1). \qquad (9.4.14)$$

Combining Eqs. (9.4.13) and (9.4.14), we get that

$$R_i(n) = S_i \left[1 + n_i(n - 1)\right]. \qquad (9.4.15)$$

Multiplying both sides of Eq. (9.4.15) by V_i, we get the first equation of MVA:

$$R_i'(n) = D_i \left[1 + n_i(n - 1)\right]. \qquad (9.4.16)$$

If we add the residence time $R_i'(n)$ for all queues i we get the response time $R_0(n)$. Applying Little's Law to the entire QN we obtain MVA's throughput equation:

$$X_0(n) = \frac{n}{R_0(n)} = \frac{n}{\sum_{i=1}^{K} R_i'(n)} \qquad (9.4.17)$$

To obtain the third equation of MVA, the queue length equation, we apply Little's Law and the Forced Flow Law to queue i. Hence,

$$n_i(n) = X_i(n) \times R_i(n) = X_0(n) \times V_i \times R_i(n) = X_0(n) \times R_i'(n). \qquad (9.4.18)$$

We repeat the three equations for single-class MVA in Fig. 9.5.

The residence time for n requests in the QN, $R_i'(n)$, requires that we know the value of the queue length for a QN with one less request, $n_i(n-1)$. But, $n_i(n-1)$ depends on $R_i'(n-1)$, which depends on $n_i(n-2)$, which depends on $R_i'(n-2)$, and so on. This indicates that we need to start with $n = 0$ and work our way up to the value of n we are interested in. Fortunately, the results for $n = 0$ are trivial because when there are no requests in the QN, the queue lengths are zero at all queues. So, $n_i(0) = 0$ for all i's. This allows us to compute $R_i'(1)$ for all i's. With the residence times for $n = 1$ we can use the throughput equation to obtain the throughput for $n = 1$. From the queue length equation we can obtain $n_i(1)$ since we now have $R_i'(1)$ and $X_0(1)$, and so on. This computation is illustrated in Fig. 9.6.

The MVA algorithm is very well suited for an implementation in a spreadsheet. The following example illustrates this.

Residence time equation:

$$R_i'(n) = \begin{cases} D_i & \text{delay resource} \\ \\ D_i \left[1 + n_i(n-1)\right] & \text{queuing resource} \end{cases} \tag{9.4.19}$$

Throughput equation:

$$X_0(n) = \frac{n}{\sum_{i=1}^{K} R_i'(n)} \tag{9.4.20}$$

Queue length equation:

$$n_i(n) = X_0(n) \times R_i'(n) \tag{9.4.21}$$

Figure 9.5. Formulas for single-class MVA with no load-dependent resources.

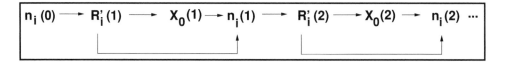

Figure 9.6. Sequence of computations for Mean Value Analysis.

Example 9.3

A DB server receives requests from 50 clients. Each request to the DB server requires that five records be read on average from the server's single disk. The average read time per record is 9 msec. Each database request requires 15 msec of CPU to be processed. What is the throughput of the server, average time spent at the CPU and the disk by each request, average number of requests at the CPU and disk, and the average response time of requests as a function of the number of requests concurrently being executed at the server?

The service demand at the CPU is 15 msec and at the disk is $V_{\text{disk}} \times S_{\text{disk}} = 5 \times 9 = 45$ msec. Using the MVA equations, we obtain the values shown in Table 9.2 for the value n of concurrent requests from zero to seven. Note that the fourth column, the average response time R_0, is obtained by adding the two previous columns. For example, for $n = 3$, $R = 20.77 + 117.69 = 138.46$ msec. Column 5, the throughput, is obtained by dividing the value in column 1 by the value in column 4, the response time. For example, for $n = 3$, $X_0 = 3/138.46 = 0.0217$ requests/msec. The residence time for the CPU, R'_{cpu}, for $n = 3$ is computed as $D_{\text{cpu}} [1 + n_{\text{cpu}}(2)] = 15 [1 + 0.385] = 20.77$ msec. As we can see, as the number of requests increases, the throughput saturates at a value of 0.0222 transactions/msec, or 22.2 tps. Figure 9.7 shows how the throughput in transactions per second varies as a function of the number of concurrent requests in the DB server.■

Table 9.2. MVA Results for Ex. 9.3

n	R'_{cpu}	R'_{disk}	R_0	X_0	n_{cpu}	n_{disk}
0	0.00	0.00	0.00	0.0000	0.000	0.000
1	15.00	45.00	60.00	0.0167	0.250	0.750
2	18.75	78.75	97.50	0.0205	0.385	1.615
3	20.77	117.69	138.46	0.0217	0.450	2.550
4	21.75	159.75	181.50	0.0220	0.479	3.521
5	22.19	203.43	225.62	0.0222	0.492	4.508
6	22.38	247.87	270.25	0.0222	0.497	5.503
7	22.45	292.64	315.10	0.0222	0.499	6.501

9.4.1.1   Bounds for Closed QNs

Example 9.3 showed that the maximum achievable throughput is 22.2 requests/sec. This value happens to be equal to the inverse of the service demand at the disk ($22.2 = 1/0.045$). The disk is the resource with the largest service demand and therefore is the bottleneck. So, the maximum throughput of the server is limited by the device that is the bottleneck! Let us examine the bound on throughput in closer detail. Consider first the arguments we made to derive Eq. (9.3.6), which established a bound on the arrival rate of an open system. If we replace the arrival rate λ by the throughput $X_0(n)$, we get

$$X_0(n) \leq \frac{1}{\max_{i=1}^K D_i}. \tag{9.4.22}$$

Consider now the throughput equation of MVA and note that $R'_i(n) \geq D_i$ for all queues i. Thus,

$$X_0(n) = \frac{n}{\sum_{i=1}^K R'_i(n)} \leq \frac{n}{\sum_{i=1}^K D_i}. \tag{9.4.23}$$

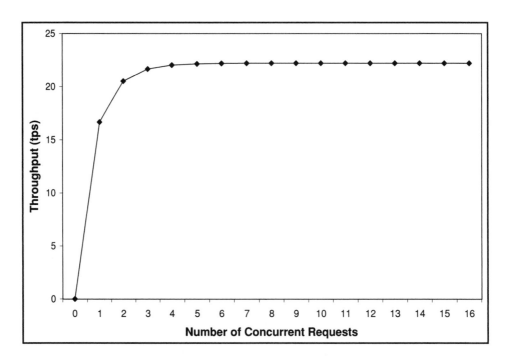

Figure 9.7. Throughput vs. number of request for Ex. 9.3.

Combining Eqs. (9.4.22) and (9.4.23), we get the following bound on the throughput of a closed QN:

$$X_0(n) \leq \min \left[\frac{n}{\sum_{i=1}^{K} D_i}, \ \frac{1}{\max_{i=1}^{K} D_i} \right]. \qquad (9.4.24)$$

The bound given by Eq. (9.4.24) tells us that at the beginning, under light load, the throughput grows linearly at a rate equal to $1/\sum_{i=1}^{K} D_i$ and then flattens at a value equal to $1/\max_{i=1}^{K} D_i$. When the throughput reaches its maximum value, the response time becomes

$$R_0(n) \approx \frac{n}{\text{maximum throughput}} \quad \text{for large } n. \qquad (9.4.25)$$

So, the response time grows linearly with n at a rate of $1/$maximum throughput $= \max_{i=1}^{K} D_i$. Thus,

$$R_0(n) \approx n \max_{i=1}^{K} D_i \quad \text{for large } n. \qquad (9.4.26)$$

For very small values of n ($n = 1$), the response time is equal to the sum of the service demands for all resources, since there is no queuing. So, a lower bound for the response time is

$$R_0(n) \geq \max \left[\sum_{i=1}^{K} D_i, n \max_{i=1}^{K} D_i \right]. \tag{9.4.27}$$

Example 9.4

Consider the same DB server of Ex. 9.3. Imagine the following scenarios: a) More indexes were built into the database to reduce the average number of reads per access from five to 2.5 b) The disk was replaced by a disk 60% faster, i.e., the average service time dropped to 5.63 msec c) The CPU was replaced by a CPU twice as fast, i.e., the service demand at the CPU dropped to 7.5 msec. What are the bounds on throughput for the following combinations of scenarios: a, b, c, a+b, and a+c?

We show on Table 9.3 the service demands at the CPU, disk, the sum of the service demands ($\sum D_i$), and the inverse of the maximum service demand ($1/\max D_i$). As shown in Table 9.3, the maximum throughput, 0.067 requests/msec or 67 requests/sec, is achieved for configuration "a+b". In that configuration, the CPU is the bottleneck, but its service demand is very close to that of the disk. Note that configurations "a" and "a+c" have the same maximum throughput even though configuration "a+c" uses a CPU that is twice as fast. Since the bottleneck in configuration "a" is not the CPU, upgrading the CPU contributes very little to improve performance. In fact, the maximum throughput remains unchanged. The only difference is that in the case of configuration "a+c", the throughput increases slightly faster with n than in configuration "a" ($1/30 = 0.0333$ for configuration "a+c" as opposed to $1/37.50 = 0.0267$ for configuration "a"). ∎

Table 9.3. Table for Ex. 9.4

Case	D_{cpu} (msec)	D_{disk} (msec)	$\sum D_i$ (msec)	$1/\max D_i$ (req/msec)	Bottleneck
a	15	$2.5 \times 9 = 22.5$	37.50	0.044	disk
b	15	$5 \times 5.63 = 28.15$	43.15	0.036	disk
c	$15/2 = 7.5$	45	52.50	0.022	disk
a+b	15	$2.5 \times 5.63 = 14.08$	29.08	0.067	CPU
a+c	$15/2 = 7.5$	$2.5 \times 9 = 22.5$	30.00	0.044	disk

9.4.2   Multiple-Class Closed Models

The equations for multiclass closed models of QNs are very similar to those for single-class. There are some differences in notation though. As in the case of multiclass open QNs, we use the subscript i, r to indicate variables related to queue i and class r. In the case of multiclass QNs, there is a fixed number of requests, N_r, in the system for each class, which we represent conveniently by the load intensity vector $\vec{N} = (N_1, \cdots, N_r, \cdots, N_R)$. We use $\vec{1}_r$ as a notation to indicate a vector where all components are zero except for the rth component, which is equal to one. So, if the number of classes is three, $\vec{1}_2 = (0, 1, 0)$. Thus, $R'_{i,r}(\vec{N})$ stands for the residence time of class r requests at queue i when the number of class 1 requests in the system is N_1, the number of class 2 requests is N_2, $\cdots$, and the number of class R requests is N_R.

Figure 9.8 shows the MVA equations for multiclass QNs. The residence time equation for queuing resources shows a much more complex dependency on queue lengths for different load intensity values than in the single-class case. For example, consider a QN with two classes and assume that $\vec{N} = (2, 4)$. The computation of the residence time at queue i for class 1 for $\vec{N} = (2, 4)$ requires the queue length at queue i for $\vec{N} = (1, 4)$. The computation of the residence time for the same queue for class 2 and for

---

Residence time equation for class r at queue i:

$$R'_{i,r}(\vec{N}) = \begin{cases} D_{i,r} & \text{delay resource} \\ D_{i,r}[1 + n_i(\vec{N} - \vec{1}_r)] & \text{queuing resource} \end{cases} \qquad (9.4.28)$$

Throughput equation for class r:

$$X_{0,r}(\vec{N}) = \frac{N_r}{\displaystyle\sum_{i=1}^{K} R'_{i,r}(\vec{N})} \qquad (9.4.29)$$

Queue length equation for class r at queue i:

$$n_{i,r}(\vec{N}) = X_{0,r}(\vec{N}) \times R'_{i,r}(\vec{N}) \qquad (9.4.30)$$

Queue length equation for queue i:

$$n_i(\vec{N}) = \sum_{r=1}^{R} n_{i,r}(\vec{N}) \qquad (9.4.31)$$

Figure 9.8. Formulas for multiclass MVA with no load-dependent resources.

the same load intensity vector $\vec{N} = (2,4)$ requires the queue length for $\vec{N} = (2,3)$. So, to compute the residence time values for a load intensity vector $\vec{N} = (2,4)$, we need the queue length for $\vec{N} = (1,4)$ and $\vec{N} = (2,3)$. In general, to compute the residence time values for a load intensity vector $\vec{N} = (N_1, \cdots, N_r, \cdots, N_R)$, we need the queue lengths for the load intensity vectors $\vec{N} - \vec{1}_1$, $\vec{N} - \vec{1}_2$, $\cdots$, $\vec{N} - \vec{1}_r$, $\cdots$, $\vec{N} - \vec{1}_R$. Because of these dependencies, the number of computations for multiclass MVA grows very fast with the number of queues and classes.

To avoid this problem, Schweitzer [10] came up with a very nice approximation technique for the term $n_{i,r}(\vec{N} - \vec{1}_r)$ needed to compute $n_i(\vec{N} - \vec{1}_r)$ that appears in the residence time equation. It is based on the assumption that the number of class r requests in each queue increases proportionally with the number of class r customers in the QN. From this observation, it follows that

$$\frac{n_{i,r}(\vec{N} - \vec{1}_r)}{n_{i,r}(\vec{N})} = \frac{N_r - 1}{N_r} \tag{9.4.32}$$

$$n_{i,r}(\vec{N} - \vec{1}_r) = \frac{N_r - 1}{N_r}\, n_{i,r}(\vec{N}). \tag{9.4.33}$$

So, using this approximation in the example just mentioned, we would get that

$$n_{i,2}((2,3)) = \frac{3}{4}\, n_{i,2}((2,4)). \tag{9.4.34}$$

This method avoids the computational complexity of the exact solution but requires an iterative approach to compute the performance measures. The reason is that $n_{i,r}(\vec{N} - \vec{1}_r)$ depends on $n_{i,r}(\vec{N})$. An easy way to solve this problem is to start with some (guessed) values for the queue lengths and refine these values in an iterative way. A good way to initialize the queue lengths is by equally distributing the number of requests per class over all queues visited by the class. So, if class r visits only K_r of the K queues, the initial value for $n_{i,r}$ would be N_r/K_r. We can now use the residence time equations, the throughput equation, and the queue length equations to obtain better estimates of the queue lengths. These estimates are used to obtain better values of the queue lengths. These iterations continue until the maximum relative error in the queue lengths between successive iterations is less than a tolerance specified by the user.

Figure 9.9 shows the algorithm used to implement approximate MVA for multiple classes. The Microsoft Excel workbook `ClosedQN.XLS` that can be found on this book's Web site implements these equations and provides an easy way to model multiclass closed systems.

Example 9.5

Consider a DB server subject to two types of workloads: query and update. The number of concurrent query transactions is five and the number

---

Input Parameters: $D_{i,r}$, N_r, and ϵ

Initialization

$\vec{N} = (N_1, N_2, \cdots, N_R)$

For $r := 1$ to R do For $i := 1$ to K do If $D_{i,r} > 0$ then $n_{i,r}^e(\vec{N}) = N_r/K_r$

Repeat

    Queue length estimates become current queue lengths

    For $r := 1$ to R do For $i := 1$ to K do $n_{i,r}(\vec{N}) = n_{i,r}^e(\vec{N})$

    For $r := 1$ to R do

        Begin

          For $i := 1$ to K do

            Begin

               Use Schweitzer's approx. to compute queue i's queue length with one less class r request

$$n_i(\vec{N} - \vec{1}_r) = \frac{N_r - 1}{N_r} n_{i,r}(\vec{N}) + \sum_{t=1 \ \& \ t \neq r}^{R} n_{i,t}(\vec{N})$$

               Compute class r residence time at queue i.

$$R'_{i,r}(\vec{N}) = \begin{cases} D_{i,r} & \text{delay} \\ D_{i,r}\left[1 + n_i(\vec{N} - \vec{1}_r)\right] & \text{queuing} \end{cases}$$

          End;

        Compute the throughput for class r.

        $X_{0,r}(\vec{N}) = N_r/\sum_{i=1}^{K} R'_{i,r}(\vec{N})$

    End;

    Compute new estimates for queue lengths.

    For $r := 1$ to R do For $i := 1$ to K do $n_{i,r}^e(\vec{N}) = X_{0,r}(\vec{N}) \times R'_{i,r}(\vec{N})$

Until $\max_{i,r} |[n_{i,r}^e(\vec{N}) - n_{i,r}(\vec{N})] / n_{i,r}^e(\vec{N})| < \epsilon$

Figure 9.9. Approximate MVA algorithm for multiple classes.

of concurrent updates is two. The server has one CPU and two disks. The service demands at the CPU, disk 1, and disk 2 for queries and updates are given in Table 9.4. What are the response times and throughputs for query

Table 9.4. Service Demands in msec for Ex. 9.5 (msec)

	Query	Update
CPU	20	40
Disk 1	80	160
Disk 2	32	48

and updates? How would these numbers change if the number of concurrent query requests were to increase?

Table 9.5 shows the results obtained by applying the approximate MVA algorithm to this example. It shows that after 11 iterations, the maximum absolute relative error in the queue length values is less than 0.05%. The throughput in transactions per second for both query and update transactions is shown in the last two columns of the table. Note that the initial values of the queue lengths at the CPU, disk 1, and disk 2, are initialized as $5/3 = 1.6667$ for query and $2/3 = 0.6667$ for update transactions (see iteration 1). Table 9.6 shows the response times and throughput values for different values of the number of concurrent query transactions maintaining the number of update transactions fixed at two. These values are also shown as a graph in Fig. 9.10 illustrating that the throughput for query transactions increases at the expense of a decreased throughput of update transactions. Both throughput curves show that the value of the throughput saturates at a maximum and minimum value for query and update transactions, respectively. Figure 9.10 also shows the increase in response time for both types of transactions. Both query and update transactions experience an increase in response time as the number of query transactions increases. However, the rate of increase for update transactions is higher than that for query transactions. ∎

Table 9.5. Approximate MVA Computations for Ex. 9.5

Ite-ration	Query				Update			
	Queue Length			TPUT	Queue Length			TPUT
	CPU	Disk 1	Disk 2	(tps)	CPU	Disk 1	Disk 2	(tps)
1	1.6667	1.6667	1.6667	12.63	0.6667	0.6667	0.6667	2.69
2	0.7576	3.0303	1.2121	10.18	0.3226	1.2903	0.3871	2.13
3	0.3927	3.8396	0.7678	9.22	0.1633	1.5911	0.2456	1.90
4	0.2725	4.1785	0.5489	8.88	0.1122	1.7152	0.1726	1.82
5	0.2363	4.3055	0.4582	8.77	0.0969	1.7601	0.1430	1.79
6	0.2255	4.3511	0.4235	8.73	0.0922	1.7760	0.1318	1.78
7	0.2221	4.3674	0.4106	8.71	0.0908	1.7816	0.1276	1.78
8	0.2210	4.3732	0.4059	8.71	0.0903	1.7836	0.1261	1.78
9	0.2206	4.3752	0.4042	8.70	0.0902	1.7843	0.1255	1.78
10	0.2205	4.3760	0.4035	8.70	0.0901	1.7846	0.1253	1.78
11	0.2205	4.3762	0.4033	8.70	0.0901	1.7847	0.1252	1.78

9.5   Modeling Multiprocessors

The open and closed models described in the previous sections did not account for queues with multiple resources (see Fig. 9.11a). These types of

Table 9.6. Response Times (sec) and Throughput (tps) for Ex. 9.5

No. Query	R_{query}	R_{update}	X_{query}	X_{update}
5	0.6	1.1	8.70	1.78
10	1.0	1.9	10.32	1.05
15	1.4	2.7	10.98	0.74
20	1.8	3.5	11.33	0.57
25	2.2	4.3	11.55	0.47
30	2.6	5.1	11.70	0.39
35	3.0	5.9	11.81	0.34

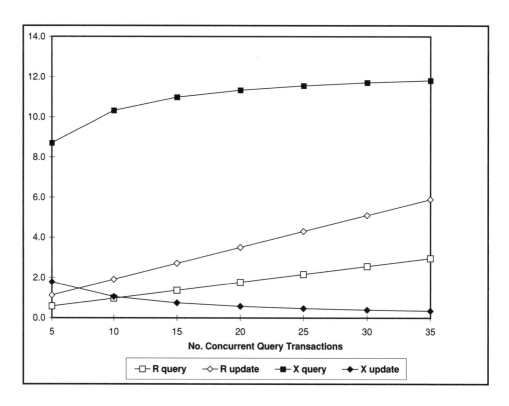

Figure 9.10. Throughput and response time curves for Ex. 9.5.

queues are needed to model servers with multiple processors. As we discussed, one way to deal with this problem is to use load-dependent resources. Dealing with load-dependent resources in closed multiclass models may pose some convergence problems to the iterative MVA solution method we described earlier. We offer here an approximation proposed by Seidmann et al. [11] that avoids convergence problems.

The basic idea is as follows. A queue with m resources and service demand D at each resource (see Fig. 9.11a) should be replaced in the QN model (open or closed) by two queues in tandem (see Fig. 9.11b). The first is a single resource queue with service demand D/m, that is, with a resource that works m times faster than any of the resources in the original multiple resource queue. The second is a delay resource, that is, no queuing takes

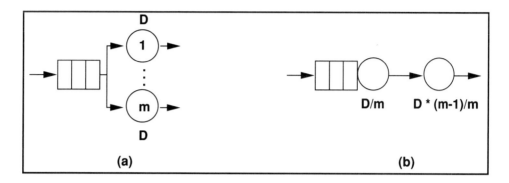

Figure 9.11. Approximation for multiple resource queues.

place. The service demand for the delay resource is equal to $D\,(m-1)/m$.

Under light load, there is virtually no queuing at the first queue and requests spend D/m seconds at this queue and $D\,(m-1)/m$ at the delay queue. So, the total time spent by a request at these two queues is $D/m + D\,(m-1)/m = D$, which is the expected time spent in the original multiple resource queue under light load. Under heavy load, all resources will be busy most of the time and the multiple resource queue behaves as if it had a single resource that works m times faster. In this case, the time spent at the queue in the single resource queue dominates the time spent at the delay server. Thus, the approximation behaves well at both light and heavy loads.

Experiments show that at intermediary loads, the error introduced by this approximation is small and increases as the service demand at the multiple resource queue increases with respect to the service demands at other queues. In these experiments, the error is smaller than 5% when the multiple resource queue has a service demand five times bigger than the other queues. The error approaches 11% when the service demand at the multiple resource queue is ten times bigger than that of any other queue.

The generalization of this approximation for the multiple-class case is straightforward: Replace the m-resource queue i with service demands $D_{i,r}$ for class r by two queues in tandem—a single resource queue with service demand $D_{i,r}/m$ and a delay resource with service demand $D_{i,r}\,(m-1)/m$. One advantage of this approximation is that we can use the methods already presented to deal with multiple resource queues. This approach is implemented in both Microsoft Excel workbooks `OpenQN.XLS` and `ClosedQN.XLS`.

Example 9.6

Consider again Ex. 9.2 where a single processor database server is modeled as an open QN. Consider now that we want to investigate the impact on response time of increasing the number of processors to 2, 3, and 4.

We use the approximation just described and the Microsoft Excel workbook `OpenQN.XLS` to obtain the values of the response time for 2, 3, and 4 processors. As shown in Table 9.7, there is a significant improvement in response time when the number of processors increases from one to two. After that point, the improvement is negligible since the bottleneck shifts to disk 1 for both classes.   ■

9.6   Combining System- and Component-Level Models

In Chapter 8 we learned how to solve system level models with variable service rate and finite queue. The service rate, or throughput, can be obtained by using a component level model, which can be solved using the MVA techniques presented in this chapter. The following example illustrates the approach.

Table 9.7. Response times for Ex. 9.6 as a Function of Number of Processors

Number of	Response Time (sec)	
Processors	Query	Update
1	1.056	1.972
2	0.689	1.422
3	0.668	1.390
4	0.662	1.382

Example 9.7

A Web site receives requests at a rate of 900 requests/sec. These requests are served by a Web server cluster composed of 60 identical servers. A load balancer distributes the load equally among all servers in the cluster. Each request takes 48 msec of CPU and requires six I/O operations on average. Each I/O operation takes 10 msec on average. Each server can be configured to limit the number of requests that can be processed concurrently in accordance to its capacity. So, if an arriving request finds the server processing a number of requests equal to its limit, W, the arriving request is rejected. We want to know what is the minimum number of requests that should be handled by each server so that no more than 1% of the requests are rejected. We also want to know what is the average response time and the site throughput at that point.

To answer these questions we combine a system-level model for each server in the cluster with a component-level model that takes into account the components, i.e., CPU and disks, of each server. The system-level model sees the server as a black box. The type of system-level model used in this case is an infinite population, limited queue, and variable service rate model. The service rate is the throughput of the server obtained by solving a component-level model, using MVA, for the server. This combined model is depicted in Fig. 9.12.

To solve the component-level model we need the CPU and disk service demands. They are $D_{\text{CPU}} = 0.048$ sec and $D_{\text{disk}} = 6 \times 0.010 = 0.060$ sec. As a first observation, the maximum throughput is $1/0.060 = 16.7$ requests/sec. The throughput values are $X(1) = 9.3$, $X(2) = 12.3$, $X(3) = 13.8$, $X(4) = 14.6$, $X(5) = 15.2$, $X(6) = 15.6$, $X(7) = 15.8$, $X(8) = 16.0$, $X(9) = 16.2$, $X(10) = 16.3$, $X(11) = 16.4$, $X(12) = 16.4$, $X(13) = 16.5$, $X(14) = 16.5$, $X(15) = 16.5$, $X(16) = 16.6$, $X(17) = 16.6$, $X(18) = 16.6$, $X(19) = 16.6$, $X(20) = 16.6$, $X(21) = 16.6$, $X(22) = 16.6$, $X(23) = 16.6$, and $X(24) = 16.7$.

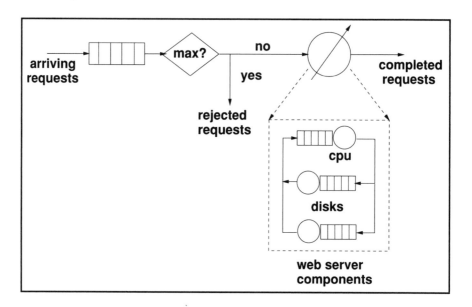

Figure 9.12. Combined system- and component- level models.

We can now solve the system-level model for various values of W, the maximum number of requests per server, using the workbook SysMod.XLS. We use $J = 24$ since the throughput does not increase significantly after this point. The arrival rate at each server is 15 ($= 900 \div 60$) requests/sec. The results are shown in Table 9.8. The table shows that as W increases the response time increases because more requests will be contending for the server resources (CPU and disk). At the same time, the probability that requests are rejected decreases as W increases. So, if we want to guarantee that the site will reject at most 1.0% of the requests, each server in the cluster has to be able to process at least 26 requests simultaneously. The average response time is then 0.633 sec. With this configuration, the site can handle $1,560$ ($= 60 \times 26$) simultaenous requests with an average throughput of 891 ($= 900 \times 0.99$) requests/sec since 1% of the incoming requests are rejected.   ∎

The following example shows how the technique of combining system- and component-level models can be used to model contention for both software and physical resources. As we saw in Chapter 4, a Web server is gen-

Table 9.8. Response Time and Percent Rejected Requests vs. W for Example 9.7

W	Response Time (sec)	Rejected Requests (%)
1	0.108	61.8
3	0.174	31.9
5	0.236	19.6
8	0.320	10.9
10	0.371	7.8
15	0.478	3.8
17	0.514	2.9
20	0.561	2.0
25	0.623	1.1
26	0.633	1.0
28	0.652	0.8
29	0.661	0.7
30	0.669	0.6
40	0.724	0.2

erally implemented as a multithreaded process. As indicated in Fig. 9.13, arriving requests join the queue for threads if the maximum number of requests W at the Web server (in the queue for threads plus requests being processed) has not been reached. Otherwise, requests are lost. When a thread is busy processing a request, it uses the server physical resources (e.g., CPU and disks).

We can model a situation like this by using an infinite queue/variable service rate/finite queue system level model. The variable service rate $X_0(k)$ is obtained by solving MVA for the component-level model that represents the physical resources. The value of k has to vary from 0 to J, the number of threads.

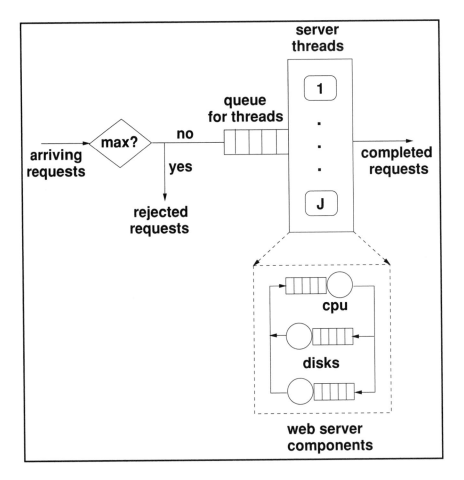

Figure 9.13. Software and hardware contentions at a Web server.

Example 9.8

Consider the Web server of the previous example with the same service demands for the CPU and disks. Assume that there are 128 threads and that the maximum number of Web requests at the server is also 128. How does the response time vary with the arrival rate of requests.

Using `ClosedQN.XLS` and `SysMod.XLS` we can solve this problem and obtain the graph of Fig. 9.14. The graph shows that when the arrival rate approaches the maximum throughput of the physical subsystem, given

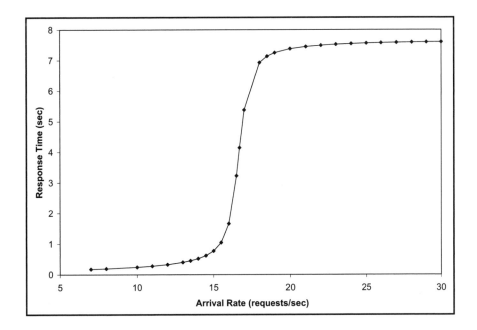

Figure 9.14. Response time vs. arrival rate for Web server.

by $16.7 = 1/\max (0.060, 0.048)$ requests/sec, the response time increases abruptly. At very high arrival rates, the response time saturates since all threads will tend to be busy all the time, and the queue for threads will tend to be always full. All other arriving requests will be lost. This behavior was also observed in another study of Web server performance [7]. ■

9.7   An Intranet Model

This section shows how the models presented in the previous sections can be used to model the performance of an intranet. Consider the intranet illustrated in Fig. 9.15 composed of three Ethernet LANs, one 16 Mbps Token Ring LAN, and a 100 Mbps FDDI ring backbone. A Web server that only serves clients within the intranet is located on LAN 3. The only Web-based application considered in this example is corporate training.

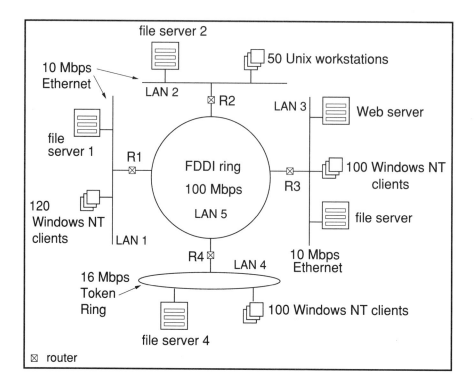

Figure 9.15. Example of an intranet.

The training application is multimedia-rich. A typical training session can be characterized by a user visiting an average of 20 text pages. Each page has an average of 2,000 bytes of text and five inline images averaging 50,000 bytes each. Links to higher resolution images, video clips, and audio files are also available. A user would typically request an average of 15 of these objects whose average size is 2,000,000 bytes. Users spend an average of 45 seconds looking at the object retrieved before clicking on the next link.

Each LAN has a local NFS file server. Each client generates an average of 0.1 NFS requests/sec. Each request generates a transfer of 8,192 bytes on average through the LAN. We assume, for the sake of this example, that all file servers and the Web server have a single CPU and a single disk. We need to map the intranet depicted in Fig. 9.15 to a queuing network model. For that purpose, we need to take the following steps:

1. decide the goal of the performance modeling effort (e.g., are we interested in predicting the performance of a specific application, the response time of the Web server, or the network utilization?);

2. decide what kind of model, that is, open or closed, will be used;

3. determine the number of classes of the model and what they represent;

4. decide how the system components will be mapped into queues and decide on the type of queues (load-independent, delay, multiple resource queue) are used to represent each component;

5. compute the service demands for each queue and each class;

6. determine the number of requests per class for closed models and the average arrival rate of requests for open models.

For our specific example, we will use a closed model, given that we know the number of clients that generate load to the various servers. The model will be a multiclass model where a class is associated to the tuple (client group, application, server). For example, access to File Server 1 from clients in LAN 1 would be mapped to a class in the QN model. The client groups in LANs 1 through 4 are denoted by CL1, CL2, CL3, CL4, according to the LANs they are in. The applications considered in this example are FS for file server access and TR for training. The four NFS servers are denoted by FS1 through FS4 and the Web server is denoted as WebS. So, there are eight workloads labeled as (CL1, FS, FS1), (CL2, FS, FS2), (CL3, FS, FS3), (CL4, FS, FS4), (CL1, TR, WebS), (CL2, TR, WebS), (CL3, TR, WebS), and (CL4, TR, WebS). We assume that 85% of the users are doing non-Web related work at any time. During this time their applications need to access the file server in their local area network. So, for example, the number of customers for class (CL1, FS, FS1) is 102 (= 120 × 0.85) and the number of customers in class (CL1, TR, WebS) is 18 (= 120 × 0.15).

We will use delay resources for the clients to represent the time spent by a request at the client before a new request to the server is made—the think time. Routers and the FDDI ring will also be modeled as delay resources due to the very low latency per packet at the routers and the very high bandwidth of the backbone. All other components, CPUs, disks, and LANS, are modeled as load-independent queues.

The computation of service demands is essentially done by using the $D_{i,r} = V_{i,r} \times S_{i,r}$ relationship for each class and queue. More specifically, we use the formulas developed in Chapter 3 for disk service times and network service times to compute the service demands at the disks and different networks. In fact, we used the Microsoft Excel workbook `ServTime.XLS` that can be found on this book's Web site, which implements these service time formulas.

Some explanations are in order. For the Web server access, we computed an average request size by considering that a typical training session generates 20 requests for text documents, 100 requests to inline images ($= 20$ text pages $\times$ 5 inlines/text page), and 15 requests to other multimedia objects. So, the total number of requests per training session is 135, distributed as 15% ($= 20 \div 135$) for text documents, 74% ($= 100 \div 135$) for inlines, and 11% ($= 15 \div 135$) for multimedia objects. The average size of a document retrieved per HTTP request is calculated as a function of the types of documents, their size, and frequency. Therefore, the average document size is $0.15 \times 2,000 + 0.74 \times 50,000 + 0.11 \times 2,000,000 = 257,300$ bytes.

To compute disk service demands we assumed that accesses to text pages are random requests and access to larger objects are sequential requests. The run length for each sequential request is equal to the number of blocks to be read. In this numerical example, we assumed all disks to be identical, with the following characteristics: 9-msec average seek time, disk speed of 7,200 RPM, transfer rate of 20 MB/sec, disk controller time of 0.1 msec, and block size of 2,048 bytes. Other assumptions include 1 msec latency per packet at the routers, and 1-msec processing time per HTTP request and per NFS request.

With these parameters and with the help of the ServTime.XLS workbook, we obtained the service demands for each of the 23 queues (five networks, four client groups, five CPUs, five disks, and four routers) and eight classes. Using the ClosedQN.XLS Microsoft Excel workbook, we solve the closed QN network and obtain the results shown in Table 9.9.

If we add the throughput of all Web-based related classes, we get the throughput of the Web server as 1.04 HTTP requests/sec. If we analyze in more detail the outputs of the solver in the ClosedQN.XLS workbook, we see that the bottleneck for the FS workloads is the disk at the file server. The residence time at that device accounts for 86 to 92% of the response time for these four workloads. For the Web-based training workloads, the Web server disk is responsible for the bulk of the response time—from 89 to 96%—for all four such workloads. This indicates that if we need to improve the Web server to reduce the response time for Web server applications, we need to upgrade the I/O subsystem of the Web server.

Table 9.9. Response Times and Throughputs for Intranet Model

Class	Throughput (req/sec)	Response Time (sec)
(CL1, FS, FS1)	10.12	0.08
(CL2, FS, FS2)	4.23	0.06
(CL3, FS, FS3)	8.44	0.08
(CL4, FS, FS4)	8.44	0.07
(CL1, TR, WebS)	0.34	8.58
(CL2, TR, WebS)	0.14	8.55
(CL3, TR, WebS)	0.28	7.96
(CL4, TR, WebS)	0.28	8.35

9.8   Concluding Remarks

This chapter introduced powerful techniques to analyze the performance of Web-based systems and intranets. These techniques are based on open and queuing network models. Some of the important results in the theory of queuing networks are worth noting here. One of them is the BCMP theorem [2], developed by Baskett, Chandy, Muntz, and Palacios, that specifies the combination of service time distributions and scheduling disciplines that yield multiclass product-form queuing networks with any combination of open and closed classes. Buzen developed the Convolution Algorithm—the first computationally efficient method to solve QNs [4]. Sevcik and Mitrani [12] developed the Arrival Theorem and Reiser and Lavenberg [8] developed Mean Value Analysis, which is based on the Arrival Theorem. An interesting account of how the MVA algorithm was developed is given by Reiser [9]. Several approximations to QNs for the non product-form case were developed (see [1] and [5]).

The algorithms discussed in this chapter are backed by the Microsoft Excel `OpenQN.XLS` and `ClosedQN.XLS` workbooks that can be found on the book's Web site. They solve open and closed queuing networks, respectively, and provide results, such as utilization, residence times, queue lengths, per class and per device, as well as response times and throughputs per class. The next chapter discusses specific issues of Web performance modeling, such as modeling of burstiness, heavy-tailed distributions, and sizing aspects from the client and server sides.

Bibliography

[1] S. Agrawal, *Metamodeling: A Study of Approximations in Queuing Models*, MIT Press, Cambridge, Massachusetts, 1985.

[2] F. Baskett, K. Chandy, R. Muntz, and F. Palacios, "Open, Closed, and Mixed Networks of Queues with Different Classes of Customers," *J. ACM*, vol. 22, no. 2, April 1975.

[3] J. P. Buzen, "Operational Analysis: An Alternative to Stochastic Modeling," *Performance of Computer Installations*, North Holland, June 1978, pp. 175–194.

[4] J. P. Buzen, "Computational Algorithms for Closed Queuing Networks with Exponential Servers, *Commun. ACM*, vol. 16, no. 9, Sept. 1973.

[5] E. Lazowska, J. Zahorjan, S. Graham, and K. Sevcik, *Quantitative System Performance: Computer System Analysis Using Queueing Network Models*, Prentice Hall, Upper Saddle River, New Jersey, 1984.

[6] D. A. Menascé, V. A. F. Almeida, and L. W. Dowdy, *Capacity Planning and Performance Modeling: From Mainframes to Client-Server Systems*, Prentice Hall, Upper Saddle River, New Jersey, 1994.

[7] P. Reeser and R. Hariharan, "Analytic Model of Web Servers in Distributed Environments," *Proc. Second International Workshop on Software and Performance*, ACM, Ottawa, Canada, Sept. 17-20, 2000.

[8] M. Reiser and S. Lavenberg, "Mean-value Analysis of Closed Multi-Chain Queuing Networks," *J. ACM*, vol. 27, no. 2, 1980.

[9] M. Reiser, "Mean Value Analysis: A Personal Account," *Performance Evaluation: Origins and Directions*, G. Haring, C. Lindemann, and M. Reiser, eds., Springer, Berlin, LNCS State-of-the-Art Survey, no. 1769, 2000.

[10] P. Schweitzer, "Approximate Analysis of Multiclass Closed Networks of Queues," *Proc. Int. Conf. Stochastic Cont. Optimization*, Amsterdam, 1979.

[11] A. Seidmann, P. Schweitzer, and S. Shalev-Oren, "Computerized Closed Queueing Network Models of Flexible Manufacturing Systems," *Large Scale Syst. J.*, North Holland, vol. 12, pp. 91–107, 1987.

[12] K. Sevcik and I. Mitrani, "The Distribution of Queuing Network States at Input and Output Instants," *J. ACM*, vol. 28, no. 2, April 1981.

Chapter 10

Web
Performance
Modeling

10.1 Introduction

In Chapters 8 and 9 we discussed performance models that can be applied in general to distributed computing systems. Web services are a special case with very interesting characteristic aspects such as the burstiness of Web traffic and heavy-tail distributions of file sizes as discussed in Chapters 4 and 6. This chapter shows how these elements can be accounted for in performance models for the Web. It also shows how the performance models discussed in the two previous chapters can be specialized to take care of Web performance modeling.

10.2   Incorporating New Phenomena

Web workloads exhibit two special features: *burstiness* and *heavy tails*, introduced in Chapter 4. In this section, we show how to represent these features in the workload specification. In other words, we illustrate how we can modify the model input parameters to reflect these features. In particular, we show how to inflate service demands to account for burstiness and how classes of requests in QN models can be used to represent heavy tails.

10.2.1   Burstiness Modeling

In this section we offer an operational treatment [3] of the burstiness phenomenon and show how it can be reflected into a performance model. A characteristic of this approach is that all quantities are based on measured or known data. Our starting point is the HTTP log that records information about every access to a Web server.

As pointed out in [2], bursts of traffic cause increased congestion on system resources. To account for this increase in congestion we modify the service demand at the bottleneck component using a *burstiness factor* that can be derived by analyzing the HTTP log as explained in what follows.

10.2.1.1   Defining a Burstiness Factor

Consider an HTTP log composed of L requests to a Web server. Let

- T: time interval during which the requests of the HTTP log arrive at the Web server

- λ: average arrival rate of requests observed in the HTTP log, given by

$$\lambda = \frac{L}{T}. \tag{10.2.1}$$

Consider now that the time interval T is divided into n equal subintervals of duration T/n called *epochs*. Let

- Arr (k): number of HTTP requests that arrive in epoch k
- λ_k: arrival rate of requests during epoch k given by

$$\lambda_k = \frac{\text{Arr } (k)}{(T/n)} = \frac{n \times \text{Arr } (k)}{T} \qquad (10.2.2)$$

- Arr$^+$: total number of HTTP requests that arrive in epochs in which the epoch arrival rate λ_k exceeds the average arrival rate λ observed in the HTTP log. So,

$$\text{Arr}^+ = \sum_{\forall \ k \ \text{s.t.} \ \lambda_k > \lambda} \text{Arr } (k) \qquad (10.2.3)$$

- Arr$^-$: total number of HTTP requests that arrive in epochs where the epoch arrival rate λ_k does not exceed the average arrival rate λ observed in the HTTP log. So,

$$\text{Arr}^- = \sum_{\forall \ k \ \text{s.t.} \ \lambda_k \leq \lambda} \text{Arr } (k) \qquad (10.2.4)$$

Clearly, the number of requests in the HTTP log is equal to the number of requests in epochs with arrival rates exceeding the log average arrival rate plus the number of requests in epochs with arrival rates below or equal to the HTTP log average arrival rate. Thus,

$$L = \text{Arr}^+ + \text{Arr}^-. \qquad (10.2.5)$$

We now review the definition of the burstiness parameter b given in Chapter 6 in light of the above operational definitions. The *burstiness parameter b* is defined as the fraction of time during which the epoch arrival rate exceeds the average arrival rate of the log. Hence,

$$b = \frac{\text{Number of epochs for which } \lambda_k > \lambda}{n}. \qquad (10.2.6)$$

Note that if traffic is not bursty, i.e., is uniformly distributed over all epochs, $Arr(k) = L/n$, $\lambda_k = (L/n)/(T/n) = L/T = \lambda$ for all $k = 1, \cdots, n$. So, there are no epochs in which $\lambda_k > \lambda$. Thus, $b = 0$. We can now define the *above-average* arrival rate, λ^+, for the HTTP log as

$$\lambda^+ = \frac{\text{Arr}^+}{b \times \mathcal{T}}. \tag{10.2.7}$$

We now redefine parameter a defined in Chapter 6 in light of the operational definitions above as the ratio between the above-average arrival rate and the average arrival rate computed from the log over the entire period $\mathcal{T}$. Thus,

$$a = \lambda^+/\lambda = [\text{Arr}^+/(b \times \mathcal{T})]/(L/\mathcal{T}) = \text{Arr}^+/(b \times L). \tag{10.2.8}$$

Since a and b are related through Eq. (10.2.8), we will use only b as an indicator of burstiness. The C program `burst.c` that can be found in the book's Web site can be used to compute the burstiness parameters a and b of an HTTP log (see Appendix B for a description of the program).

Example 10.1

Consider that 19 get requests are logged at a Web server at instants 1, 3, 3.5, 3.8, 6, 6.3, 6.8, 7.0, 10, 12, 12.2, 12.3, 12.5, 12.8, 15, 20, 30, 30.2, and 30.7 during an interval $\mathcal{T}$ of duration equal to 31 seconds. Compute the burstiness parameter b for the log, considering that the interval $\mathcal{T}$ is divided into n subintervals, for values of n ranging from 21 to 30.

We show the computations for $n = 21$ and then show a plot illustrating the values of b for all values of n. Each epoch has duration equal to $\mathcal{T}/n = 31/21 = 1.48$ sec. The average arrival rate for the entire log is $\lambda = 19/31 = 0.613$ requests/sec. The number of arrivals in each of the 21 epochs are 1, 0, 3, 0, 4, 0, 1, 0, 4, 0, 1, 0, 0, 1, 0, 0, 0, 0, 0, 0, and 4. The arrival rate in the first epoch, $\lambda_1 = 1/1.48 = 0.676$ requests/sec, exceeds the average arrival rate of 0.613 requests/sec for the log. In eight of the 21 epochs, the epoch arrival rate λ_k exceeds the HTTP log arrival rate λ. So, the burstiness factor is $b = 8/21 = 0.381$. Figure 10.1 shows a graph of the burstiness factor for values of n ranging from 21 to 30. As it can be seen in the figure, the value

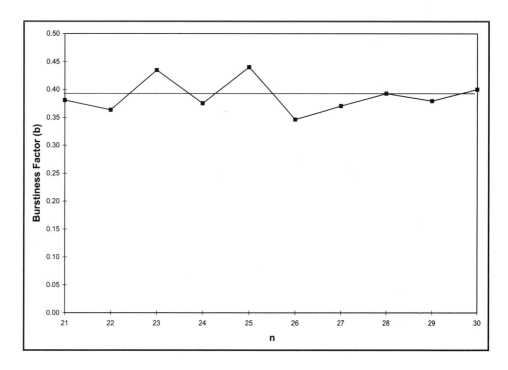

Figure 10.1. Burstiness factor vs. number of epochs.

of b oscillates around an average value of 0.39 with a maximum deviation around the mean equal to 13%. This is an expected behavior if the value of n is such that the epoch duration is close to the duration of the bursts. In this example, all requests arrive during epochs in which $\lambda_k > \lambda$. So, $\text{Arr}^+ = L$ and $a = 1/b = 1/0.381 = 2.625$.   ∎

10.2.1.2   Adjusting Service Demands to Burstiness

We present in this section an approximation that allows one to capture the effect of burstiness on the performance of Web servers. As shown in [2], the maximum throughput of a Web server decreases as the burstiness factor increases. We know from Chapter 9 that the maximum throughput is equal to the inverse of the maximum service demand or the service demand of the bottleneck resource. So, to account for the burstiness effect, we will write the service demand, D, of the bottleneck resource as

$$D = D_f + \alpha \times b \tag{10.2.9}$$

where D_f is the portion of the service demand that does not depend on burstiness and $\alpha \times b$, for $\alpha > 0$ is a term proportional to the burstiness factor b, used to inflate the service demand of the bottleneck component according to the burstiness of the arrival stream. The constant α can be determined using the procedure given below.

1. Consider a measurement interval $\mathcal{T}$ and let $\mathcal{L}$ be the HTTP log collected during this interval. Divide the interval into two subintervals of duration $\mathcal{T}/2$ each and let $\mathcal{L}_1$ and $\mathcal{L}_2$ be the HTTP logs corresponding to these two intervals.

2. During the interval $\mathcal{T}$, measure the utilization of all resources (e.g., CPU, disks, and communication links) of the Web server, the throughput, and the burstiness factor for each of the subintervals. Let U_1 and U_2 be the utilization of the resource that is the bottleneck throughout both subintervals, respectively. The throughputs, X_0^1 and X_0^2 of subintervals 1 and 2, are computed from the two sub-logs $\mathcal{L}_1$ and $\mathcal{L}_2$ by dividing the number of successful requests in each sub-log by $\mathcal{T}/2$, the duration of each subinterval. Let b_1 and b_2 be the values of the burstiness factors computed for sub-logs $\mathcal{L}_1$ and $\mathcal{L}_2$ using the aforementioned approach.

3. For each of the two subintervals, we can use the Service Demand Law to write the service demand at the bottleneck resource as the ratio between its utilization and the system throughput during each subinterval. Thus,

$$U_1/X_0^1 = D_f + \alpha \times b_1 \tag{10.2.10}$$

and

$$U_2/X_0^2 = D_f + \alpha \times b_2. \tag{10.2.11}$$

We are assuming that the fixed service demand D_f is a function of the characteristics of the requests that arrive at the Web server and that the nature of the requests is fairly homogeneous during the entire period $\mathcal{T}$. The value of the constant α can be easily obtained by subtracting Eq. (10.2.11) from Eq. (10.2.10) and solving for α. Hence,

$$\alpha = \frac{U_1/X_0^1 - U_2/X_2^0}{b_1 - b_2}. \tag{10.2.12}$$

Example 10.2

Consider the HTTP log of Ex. 10.1. During the 31 seconds in which the 19 HTTP requests arrived, the CPU was found to be the bottleneck component. What is the burstiness adjustment that should be applied to the CPU service demand to account for the effect of burstiness on the performance of the Web server?

The number of HTTP requests during each of the 15.5-sec subintervals is 14 and 5, respectively. Thus, the throughputs in each subinterval are $X_0^1 = 14/15.5 = 0.903$ requests/sec and $X_0^2 = 5/15.5 = 0.323$ requests/sec. The measured utilization of the CPU in each subinterval was 0.18 and 0.06, respectively. If we apply the procedure described in Section 10.2.1.1 to the two subintervals, we obtain $b_1 = 0.273$ and $b_2 = 0.182$, respectively. Thus,

$$\alpha = \frac{0.18/0.903 - 0.06/0.323}{0.273 - 0.182} = 0.149. \tag{10.2.13}$$

So, if we consider the entire HTTP log, the adjustment factor to the CPU service demand would be $\alpha \times b = 0.149 \times 0.381 = 0.057$ sec.   ■

Figure 10.2 shows how the maximum system throughput varies with the burstiness factor. The figure assumes that the CPU is the bottleneck, that its fixed service demand D_f is 0.02 sec, and α has the value computed in Ex. 10.2, i.e., 0.149. Remember that the maximum system throughput is

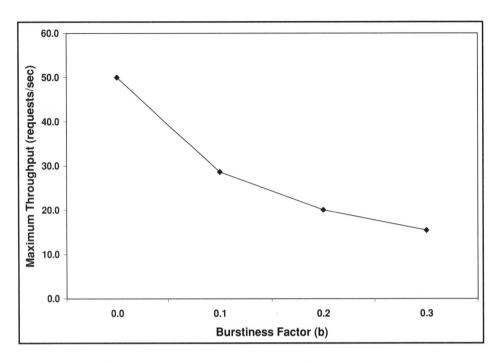

Figure 10.2. Maximum throughput vs. burstiness factor.

the inverse of the maximum service demand. As shown in the figure, the maximum throughput falls from 50 HTTP requests/sec to 15.5 requests/sec as we go from a nonbursty workload to a workload with a burstiness factor of 0.3.

10.2.2   Accounting for Heavy Tails in the Model

As discussed in Chapters 4 and 6, Web traffic exhibits file-size distributions that decrease with a power tail [5]. In practical terms, this implies that we should expect to see a large percentage of HTTP requests for small documents and a small percentage of requests to documents that are one or two orders of magnitude larger than the small documents. Due to the large variability of the size of documents, average results for the whole population of requests would have very little statistical meaning. Categorizing the requests into a number of classes, defined by ranges of document sizes, improves the accuracy and significance of the performance metrics.

The models we offer to address this situation are the multiclass queuing network models we discussed in Chapter 9. Different classes are associated with requests for documents of different sizes. The workload intensity parameters (e.g., arrival rates) per class reflect the percentage of requests for each file size.

Example 10.3

The HTTP log of a Web server was analyzed during 1 hour. A total of 21,600 requests were successfully processed during this interval. Table 10.1 shows the distribution of document sizes and the percent of requests in each category.

One can then build a multiclass QN model to represent the Web server. There are five classes in the model, each corresponding to the five file size ranges. The arrival rate for each class r is a fraction of the overall arrival rate $\lambda = 21,600/3,600 = 6$ requests/sec. So, $\lambda_1 = 6 \times 0.25 = 1.5$ requests/sec, $\lambda_2 = 6 \times 0.40 = 2.4$ requests/sec, $\lambda_3 = 6 \times 0.20 = 1.2$ requests/sec, $\lambda_4 = 6 \times 0.10 = 0.6$ requests/sec, and $\lambda_5 = 6 \times 0.05 = 0.3$ requests/sec. ■

Table 10.1. File Size Distributions for Ex. 10.3

Class	File Size Range	Percent of Requests
1	size < 5 KB	25
2	5 KB ≤ size < 50 KB	40
3	50 KB ≤ size < 100 KB	20
4	100 KB ≤ size < 500 KB	10
5	size ≥ 500 KB	5

10.3   Client-Side Models

We consider here the performance perceived by a client browser and discuss models that can be used to answer some of the most important capacity and performance questions from the client's viewpoint, such as:

1. What should be the bandwidth of the link to the ISP to support Web traffic with acceptable performance?

2. What should be the bandwidth of the LAN to support Web traffic with acceptable performance?

3. Should I use a cache proxy server?

10.3.1   No Cache Proxy Server Case

The first environment discussed consists of a collection of M client workstations running Web browsers. These client workstations are connected to a LAN, which is connected through a router to the Internet through an Internet Service Provider (ISP) (see Fig. 10.3a).

The performance of a remote Web server, as perceived by a user, depends on various factors including:

- performance characteristics of the client platform
- bandwidth of the LAN that connects the clients to the router
- bandwidth of the link that connects the router to the ISP
- router performance characteristics
- delays imposed by the Internet
- delays to retrieve the desired documents from the remote Web server
- delays at the ISP to which the client is connected

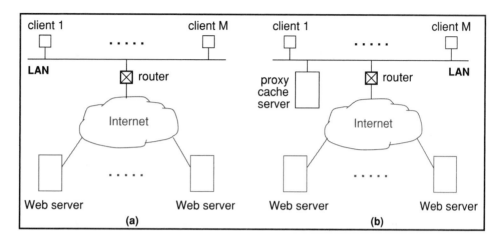

Figure 10.3. (a) Client access to Web servers without cache proxy server. (b) Client access to Web servers with cache proxy server.

- workload characteristics of the requests generated by the clients

10.3.1.1   The Performance Model

Figure 10.4a shows the QN model that corresponds to Fig. 10.3a. It is a closed QN model with the following six queues: Queue 1 is a delay queue that represents the set of clients. The time spent at this queue is the client think time which represents the time spent by a client between when it starts to receive a document until it requests a new document. Queue 2 is a load-independent queue that represents the LAN. The router is represented by a delay queue due to its relatively small latency when compared with the other delays involved. The link that connects the router to the ISP is a full-duplex link. This means that it can receive and transmit at the same time at the same bandwidth. Thus, we need to model the outgoing and incoming links separately as two separate load-independent queues—queues 4 and 6, respectively. Finally, the delays at the ISP, its link to the Internet, the Internet itself, and the remote servers, are represented by delay queue 5. The entities that flow through the QN model are HTTP requests.

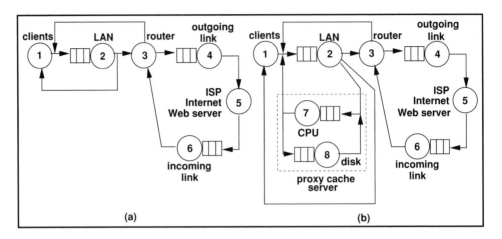

Figure 10.4. (a) Client-side QN model without cache proxy server. (b) Client-side QN model with cache proxy server.

We give now the general parameters to be considered and show how the service demands for the QN model can be computed.

- LANBandwidth: LAN bandwidth in megabits per second

- MaxPDU: maximum Protocol Data Unit (PDU) size for the LAN's network layer protocol in bytes

- FrameOvhd: frame overhead of the LAN's link layer protocol, in bytes

- RouterLatency: router latency in microseconds per packet

- LinkBandwidth: bandwidth, in megabits per second, of the connection to the ISP

- InternetDelayRTT: Internet average RTT, in milliseconds

- InternetDataRate: Internet data transfer rate, in Kbps

- BrowserRate: rate, in HTTP operations/sec, at which a browser requests a new document when the user is in think mode; the inverse of the user's think time

- NumberClients: number of client workstations

- PercentActive: percent of client workstations actively using the Web

- AvgSizeHTTPRequest: average size of the HTTP request sent by the browser to the server, in bytes

Besides the parameters listed above, we need to know the distribution of the sizes of the documents requested by the browsers. Let the document sizes be divided into R categories and consider the two following additional parameters:

- DocumentSize$_r$: average document size, in KB, of category r ($r = 1, \cdots, R$) documents

- PercentSize$_r$: percent of documents requested that are in category r ($r = 1, \cdots, R$)

The average document size, in KB, over all requests issued by a client is given by

$$\text{DocumentSize} = \sum_{r=1}^{R} \text{DocumentSize}_r \times \text{PercentSize}_r. \qquad (10.3.14)$$

10.3.1.2   Computing Service Demands

We now compute all service demands, in seconds, based on the parameters given above. The service demand, D_{cl}, at queue 1 per HTTP request is given by

$$D_{\text{cl}} = 1/\text{BrowserRate}. \qquad (10.3.15)$$

To compute the service demand per request at the LAN, D_{LAN}, we need to remember that HTTP requests use TCP, and therefore we need to account for the overhead incurred by TCP and the underlying protocols, IP and the LAN link-level protocol, on top of which TCP is located. We use the service times equations given in Section 3.3.2, which we adapt to our case. Let NetworkTime (m, B) denote the service time for a message m bytes long over a network with bandwidth B megabits per second. Using the equations in Section 3.3.2, we have that

$$\text{NetworkTime}\,(m, B) = \frac{8 \times [m + \text{Overhead}\,(m)]}{10^6 \times B} \qquad (10.3.16)$$

where the TCP plus IP overhead due to sending an m-bytes long message is

$$\text{Overhead}\,(m) = \text{NDatagrams}\,(m) \times (\text{TCPOvhd} + \text{IPOvhd} + \text{FrameOvhd}) \qquad (10.3.17)$$

and the number of datagrams needed to send an m-bytes long message is

$$\text{NDatagrams}\,(m) = \left\lceil \frac{m}{\text{MSS}} \right\rceil \qquad (10.3.18)$$

where MSS is the maximum TCP segment size. Thus, the LAN service demand can be computed by adding the LAN service time for the request from the browser to the server plus the service time from the server to the browser:

$$
\begin{aligned}
D_{\text{LAN}} = {} & \text{NetworkTime}\,(\text{AvgSizeHTTPRequest}, \text{LANBandwidth}) + \\
& \text{NetworkTime}\,(1{,}024 \times \text{DocumentSize}, \text{LANBandwidth})
\end{aligned}
$$
$$(10.3.19)$$

The service demand at the router, D_{router}, is

$$D_{\text{router}} = [\text{NDatagrams}\,(1{,}024 \times \text{DocumentSize}) + 6] \times \text{RouterLatency} \times 10^{-6}. \qquad (10.3.20)$$

The term "6" in Eq. (10.3.20) accounts for two synchronization segments needed to establish a TCP connection (the third is piggy-baked in the HTTP request), one TCP data segment to carry the HTTP request, and three TCP synchronization segments to close the connection [4]. The service demand per request, D_{OutL}, at the outgoing link is

$$
\begin{aligned}
D_{\text{OutL}} = {} & \text{NetworkTime}\,(\text{AvgSizeHTTPRequest}, \text{LinkBandwidth}) + \\
& 3 \times \text{NetworkTime}\,(0.0001, \text{LinkBandwidth}).
\end{aligned}
$$
$$(10.3.21)$$

The second term in Eq. (10.3.21) accounts for the fact that the outgoing link carries one TCP synchronization segment to open a TCP connection and two to close it. We use the value of 0.0001 instead of zero in Eq. (10.3.21) to force the number of datagrams for each TCP segment to be computed as 1 instead of zero by the function NDatagrams. Note that the effect of using $m = 0.001$ in Eq. (10.3.16) gives a negligible error.

The service demand D_{Int} at the Internet is the sum of the RTT to establish the TCP connection with the server, plus another round trip time for the first byte of the document to arrive at the client, plus the data transfer delay to send the document from the server to the client. So,

$$D_{\text{Int}} = \frac{2 \times \text{InternetDelayRTT}}{1,000} + \frac{\text{DocumentSize}}{\text{InternetDataRate}}. \qquad (10.3.22)$$

Finally, the service demand per request, D_{InL}, at the incoming link is computed as

$$D_{\text{InL}} = \text{NetworkTime (DocumentSize, LinkBandwidth)} +$$
$$2 \times \text{NetworkTime (0.0001, LinkBandwidth)}. \qquad (10.3.23)$$

The second term in Eq. (10.3.23) accounts for the two TCP segments that cross the incoming link: one when the connection is being opened, and the other when it is being closed.

We now have all service demands for the QN model. The number of requests in the system is equal to NumberClients × PercentActive.

The following example shows how this model can be used to answer some useful capacity planning questions from the client side.

Example 10.4

A site has 150 PCs connected to an Ethernet LAN, which is connected to the Internet through a router that has a latency of 50 μsec/packet. The connection to the Internet is a 56-Kbps link. Ten percent of the clients are actively browsing the Web at any given time, and each user generates requests to external Web servers at an average rate of 0.3 requests/sec when they are in the thinking state. This includes requests to inline documents. The documents requested from clients were classified into four categories with average size and frequency of occurrence given by: 0.8 KB (35%), 5.5 KB (50%), 80 KB (14%), and 800 KB (1%). The average Internet RTT to the sites most used by the clients in the site was measured to be 100 msec using the ping command (typical values for this parameter range from 89 to 161 msec [9]). The effective Internet transfer rate from these same remote servers was observed to be 20 KB/sec on average (typical values for this parameter range from 0.1 to 1 Mbps [9]). The average size of the HTTP requests sent by a browser to the remote servers is 100 bytes. What is the throughput in requests/sec for all clients, what is the bottleneck, and what is the average response time seen by each user?

The values of the input parameters are:

- LANBandwidth = 10 Mbps

- FrameOvhd = 18 bytes

- MSS = 1,460 bytes

- RouterLatency = 50 μsec/packet

- LinkBandwidth = 56 Kbps

- InternetDelayRTT = 100 msec

- InternetDataRate = 20 KB/sec

- BrowserRate = 0.3 requests/sec

- NumberClients = 150

- PercentActive = 0.1

- AvgSizeHTTPRequest = 290 bytes

The average document size is given by

$$DocumentSize = 0.8 \times 0.35 + 5.5 \times 0.5 + 80 \times 0.14 + 800 \times 0.01 = 22.23 \text{ KB.}$$

We can now compute the service demands for the QN model of Fig. 10.4a using the equations derived in this section:

$$D_{\text{cl}} = 1/\text{BrowserRate} = 1/0.3 = 3.333 \text{ sec}$$

$$D_{\text{LAN}} = \text{NetworkTime} (290, 10) +$$
$$\text{NetworkTime} (22.23 \times 1,024, 10) = 0.0192 \text{ sec}$$

$$D_{\text{router}} = [\text{NDatagrams} (22.23 \times 1,024) + 6] \times 50 \times 10^{-6} = 0.0011 \text{ sec}$$

$$D_{\text{OutL}} = \text{NetworkTime} (290, 0.056) +$$
$$3 \times \text{NetworkTime} (0.0001, 0.056) = 0.0746 \text{ sec}$$

$$D_{\text{Int}} = 2 \ \times \ 100/1,000 + 22.23/20 = 1.3115 \text{ sec}$$

$$D_{\text{InL}} = \text{NetworkTime} (22.23 \times 1,024, 0.056) +$$
$$2 \times \text{NetworkTime} (0.0001, 0.056) = 3.4011 \text{ sec.}$$

We now use the Microsoft Excel `ClosedQN.XLS` workbook, which implements the performance model of Chapter 9, to solve the resulting QN model, using $150 \times 0.1 = 15$ requests as the effective number of clients. The results are shown in Table 10.2.

As shown in Table 10.2, the bottleneck is the link to the Internet. This resource is almost 100% utilized and limits the throughput. Most of the

Table 10.2. Results for Ex. 10.4

	Residence Times (sec)	Utilizations (%)
LAN	0.019	0.56
Router	0.001	0.03
Outgoing Link	0.076	2.18
Incoming Link	46.620	99.33
Throughput: 0.2920 requests/sec		
Throughput: 51.9 Kbps		
Response Time: 48.0 sec		

response time, $46.62/48 = 97\%$, is spent in the incoming link. If we want to improve performance, i.e., increase the throughput and decrease the response time, we have two alternatives: use a faster connection to the Internet, which is more expensive, or decrease the demand on the incoming link by using a cache proxy server as discussed in the next subsection. ■

The Microsoft Excel workbook `WebModels.XLS` implements the equations to compute the service demands for the client-side under the no-proxy and proxy case.

10.3.2 Using a Cache Proxy Server

Figure 10.4b shows an environment similar to the one we analyzed in the previous section with the addition of a cache proxy server (see Chapter 4). Requests from clients go first to the cache proxy server, which holds copies of the most sought-after documents. If the requested document is in the cache, a *cache hit* is said to occur. In this case, the document is returned to the client; otherwise, the proxy server acts as a client, makes a connection to the originating Web server, requests the document, stores it into its cache, and then returns it to the client that requested it in the first place. Accessing documents that are found in the proxy server is generally much faster than accessing them from their originating servers. However, a document not found on the proxy server takes longer to retrieve because of the proxy server overhead. According to [15], a proxy server can speed up document access between two and ten times on cache hits and slow down document retrieval time by a factor of two on cache misses.

A QN model corresponding to the environment depicted in Fig. 10.3b is shown in Fig. 10.4b. The cache proxy server is modeled as having one CPU (queue 7) and one disk (queue 8). Extending the model to a multiprocessor cache server with multiple disks would be straightforward.

To model this situation, we need to add a few more parameters besides the ones discussed in Section 10.3.1.

- p_{hit}: fraction of requests that can be served from the proxy server's cache (typical values for p_{hit} range from 0.2 to 0.5 [13, 15])

- HitCPUTime: CPU time, in seconds, needed to process the request at the cache proxy server and return the document to the server when the document is found in the cache

- MissCPUTime: CPU time, in seconds, needed to process a request at the cache proxy server, request the document from the originating server, store it into the cache, run a cache replacement algorithm, if needed, and send the document to the client that originally requested it

- DiskTime: disk time per kilobyte at the cache proxy server, in milliseconds

The expressions for service demands derived in Section 10.3.1 have to be revised for the LAN, router, Internet, and outgoing and incoming links. We use the superscript p to indicate service demands in the proxy server case.

The service demand at the LAN, D_{LAN}^p, is equal to the value computed in the no-proxy case, D_{LAN}, when the document is found in the proxy server. However, if there is a cache miss, the request has to flow through the LAN again to the router to be sent to the originating server. The document coming from the originating server will traverse the LAN twice: one from the router to the cache proxy server and the other from the cache proxy server to the client. Thus,

$$D_{\text{LAN}}^p = p_{\text{hit}} \times D_{\text{LAN}} + (1 - p_{\text{hit}}) \times 2 \times D_{\text{LAN}} = (2 - p_{\text{hit}}) \times D_{\text{LAN}}. \quad (10.3.24)$$

Traffic will only go through the router, outgoing link, Internet, and incoming link when the document is not found in the cache proxy server. In this case, the service demand at these various queues is the same as in the no-proxy case. So,

$$D_{\text{router}}^p = (1 - p_{\text{hit}}) \times D_{\text{router}} \quad (10.3.25)$$

$$D_{\text{OutL}}^p = (1 - p_{\text{hit}}) \times D_{\text{OutL}} \quad (10.3.26)$$

$$D^p_{\text{Int}} = (1 - p_{\text{hit}}) \times D_{\text{Int}} \qquad (10.3.27)$$

$$D^p_{\text{InL}} = (1 - p_{\text{hit}}) \times D_{\text{InL}} \qquad (10.3.28)$$

The service demand at the CPU is given by

$$D^p_{\text{CPU}} = p_{\text{hit}} \times \text{HitCPUTime} + (1 - p_{\text{hit}}) \times \text{MissCPUTime}. \qquad (10.3.29)$$

The disk is used both in the case of cache hits and misses. In the first case, to retrieve the document from the cache and in the second, to store the document retrieved from a remote Web server into the cache. The average service demand, in seconds, at the disk is then

$$D^p_{\text{disk}} = \text{DiskTime} \times \text{DocumentSize}/1{,}000. \qquad (10.3.30)$$

Example 10.5

Consider adding a cache proxy server to the environment of Ex. 10.4. Consider that the CPU time per request at the cache proxy server is 0.25 msec in the case of a hit and 0.50 msec in the case of a miss. Consider also that the disk service time at the cache proxy server is 6 msec per kilobyte read. How do the throughput and response time vary as a function of the hit ratio?

Using the equations derived in this section and implemented in the enclosed Microsoft Excel workbook `WebModels.XLS`, we compute the service demands for values of p_{hit} equal to 0.2, 0.3, 0.4, and 0.5. We then use the Microsoft Excel workbook `ClosedQN.XLS` to solve the model for each set of values of the service demands. The results are summarized in Table 10.3. The throughput with a 50% hit ratio is 160% higher than the throughput obtained without a proxy server (see Table 10.2). The response time for the same value of the hit ratio drops to 60% of the value it had without the proxy cache. The link to the Internet continues to be the bottleneck and its utilization varies between 98.7% and 99.2%. ∎

Table 10.3. Results for Ex. 10.5

p_{hit}	Throughput (requests/sec)	Response Time (sec)
0.20	0.364	37.82
0.30	0.416	32.72
0.40	0.485	27.61
0.50	0.581	22.50

Example 10.6

Consider the parameters of Ex. 10.5 but assume that the link to the Internet is replaced by a T1 link (1.544 Mbps). Assume that the cache hit ratio is 40%. What is the throughput and the average response time, and which resource is the bottleneck?

Using the workbooks `WebModels.XLS` and `ClosedQN.XLS`, we obtain a throughput of 3.347 HTTP requests/sec, i.e., 357.1 ($= 3.347 \times (1 - 0.4) \times 22.23 \times 8$) Kbps over the T1 Link (the incoming link), which is now 23% utilized and is not the bottleneck any longer. The new bottleneck is the disk at the cache proxy server with a 45% utilization; the response time now dropped to 1.149 sec.   ∎

10.4   Server-Side Models

We now turn our attention to the server side and show the performance models that can be used to answer questions such as:

- What should be the bandwidth of the link that connects the Web server to the Internet so that acceptable service levels are provided?

- Should the company install mirror sites? How many?

- What is the best alternative: a cluster of many low-end and inexpensive servers or a cluster with a few high-end servers?

- How do we assess the impact of using CDN services on the servers of the company's site?

- How do we assess the impact of adding much more multimedia contents to a Web site?

- How do I assess new strategies for server operation, including replicating popular documents on separate disks?

- What if I store my files on a RAID-5 disk rather than on regular disks? Should the HTTP log be on a non-RAID volume?

- What is the maximum throughput of my Web site?

- What is the impact of using compression on large multimedia objects?

- What is the impact of replacing CGI scripts with Java servlets?

- What is the impact of using compiled CGI scripts versus interpreted CGI scripts?

- What are the performance impacts of using a multithreaded Web server versus using one that forks a new kernel level process per HTTP request?

This list is not exhaustive, but gives an idea of the kind of concerns that a Web server administrator is faced with.

10.4.1   Single Web Server

Figure 10.5a shows a typical environment with a single Web server at the site. The Web server is connected to a LAN, which is connected to a router that connects the site to the ISP and then to the Internet. The document tree (set of documents served by the Web server) is stored at the same machine where the Web server runs.

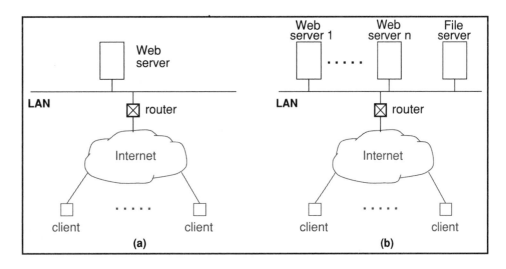

Figure 10.5. (a) Single Web server. (b) Mirrored Web servers with a shared file system.

10.4.1.1   The Performance Model

The queuing network model corresponding to Fig. 10.5a is shown in Fig. 10.6a. We are assuming here that we are dealing with a Web server that is publicly available on the Internet. Thus, there is a very large population of unknown size of clients that will access the Web server. Thus, we can only characterize the arrival rate of requests for various document sizes. Therefore, we will model the Web server as an open multiclass QN model. Different classes in the model correspond to HTTP requests of different size as discussed in Ex. 10.3. Let R be the number of classes and λ_r $(r = 1, \cdots, R)$ be the arrival rate of class r requests. As explained in Ex. 10.3, the average arrival rate is computed as

$$\lambda_r = \lambda \times \text{PercentSize}_r \qquad (10.4.31)$$

where λ is the overall arrival rate of HTTP requests to the Web server.

As in Section 10.3, the incoming and outgoing links and the LAN are represented by load-independent queues and the router as a delay queue. The Web server is represented by two load-independent queues: one for the CPU and another for the disk. One could have many more disks and a multiprocessor CPU as well.

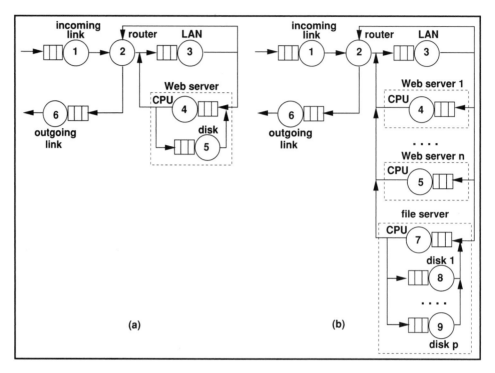

Figure 10.6. (a) QN model for a single Web server. (b) QN model for mirrored Web servers and a shared file system.

We consider some of the parameters defined in Section 10.3, such as LANBandwidth, MaxPDU, FrameOvhd, RouterLatency, DocumentSize$_r$, AvgSizeHTTPRequest, and PercentSize$_r$, as well as the following additional parameters:

- CPUTimePerHTTPRequest$_r$: total CPU time, in seconds, to process one HTTP request of class r

- DiskTime: disk time per KB transferred, in milliseconds

10.4.1.2   Computing Service Demands

We now compute the service demands, in seconds, based on the parameters given above. The service demand, $D_{\mathrm{InL},r}$, at the incoming link is the same for all classes and has the same expression as the service demand for the outgoing link for the client side given in Eq. (10.3.21). Thus,

$$D_{\text{InL},r} = = \text{NetworkTime (AvgSizeHTTPRequest, LinkBandwidth)} +$$
$$3 \times \text{NetworkTime (0.0001, LinkBandwidth)}. \qquad (10.4.32)$$

The router service demand for class r, $D_{\text{router},r}$, is similar to Eq. (10.3.20) derived in Section 10.3, except that we now use the document size value for each class as opposed to the average document size. Thus,

$$D_{\text{router},r} = [\text{NDatagrams}(1{,}024 \times \text{DocumentSize}_r) + 6] \times \text{RouterLatency} \times 10^{-6}.$$
$$(10.4.33)$$

The LAN service demand, $D_{\text{LAN},r}$, is also very similar to Eq. (10.3.19) since in the client side and server side cases, the LAN is used to carry the HTTP requests and the documents retrieved as a result of the requests. Hence,

$$D_{\text{LAN},r} = \text{NetworkTime (AvgSizeHTTPRequest, LANBandwidth)} +$$
$$\text{NetworkTime (1,024} \times \text{DocumentSize}_r, \text{LANBandwidth)}.$$
$$(10.4.34)$$

The service demand at the outgoing link, $D_{\text{OutL},r}$, has the same expression as the service demand for the incoming link at the client side (see Eq. [10.3.23]), except that now we specialize them per class as

$$D_{\text{OutL},r} = \text{NetworkTime (DocumentSize}_r, \text{LinkBandwidth)} +$$
$$2 \times \text{NetworkTime (0.0001, LinkBandwidth)}. \qquad (10.4.35)$$

The service demand at the CPU, $D_{\text{CPU},r}$, for class r is given by

$$D_{\text{CPU},r} = \text{CPUTimePerHTTPRequest}_r + f(\overline{n}) \times \text{CPUOvhd} \qquad (10.4.36)$$

where $f(\overline{n})$ is a function f of the average number $\overline{n}$ of requests being processed at the server and CPUOvhd is the CPU overhead factor per request.

The average number of requests $\bar{n}$ at the Web server is the sum of all requests of all classes at the CPU and disk. So,

$$\bar{n} = \sum_{r=1}^{R} (n_{\mathrm{CPU},r} + n_{\mathrm{disk},r}). \tag{10.4.37}$$

The first term in Eq. (10.4.36) is called the *intrinsic* service demand and the second is called the *load-dependent* service demand. Processing overhead in networked environments depends on several factors, such as protocol, message sizes, number of simultaneous connections, and workload characteristics. There are several categories of overhead in network software. In [10], the authors propose seven categories: network buffer management, operating system functions, protocol-specific processing, checksum computation, data structure manipulations, data movement, and error checking. The same study shows that the categories of overhead for TCP/IP vary with message sizes. In [1, 11], measurement results show that more clients and larger files stress the Web server and operating system in different ways. For example, as the server load increases, the size of the system tables used to keep track of the processes and their TCP states grows larger. These tables consume CPU cycles to be searched on each packet arrival and to match the corresponding TCP state information.

Finally, the disk service demand, $D_{\mathrm{disk},r}$, for class r is computed as

$$D_{\mathrm{disk},r} = \mathrm{DocumentSize}_r \times \mathrm{DiskTime}/1,000. \tag{10.4.38}$$

We are now ready to solve our open multiclass QN model since we have all the parameters. We can use the algorithms presented in Chapter 9 and the Microsoft Excel workbook `OpenQN.XLS`. There is only one problem: The service demand at the CPU depends on the average number of requests at the Web server for all classes. But, this number can only be obtained once we solve the model. We can solve this problem by using an iterative procedure as explained later. Before we discuss how this should be done, we give an example of service demand computations.

Example 10.7

A Web server is connected to a 10-Mbps Ethernet, which is connected to an ISP through a router. The router has a latency of 50 μsec/packet and connects the LAN to the ISP through a T1 line. No file server is used and the site has only one Web server. Consider the following parameters: FrameOvhd = 18 bytes, AvgSizeHTTPRequest = 290 bytes, MSS = 1,460 bytes, DiskTime = 6 msec. There are four different types of workloads submitted to the Web server. Table 10.4 shows the main characteristics of the workload. The total arrival rate of HTTP requests is 6 requests/sec. Compute the service demands and arrival rates per class.

Table 10.4. Workload Parameters for Ex. 10.7

Class	Average File Size (KB)	% of Requests	CPU time per HTTP request (sec)
1	5.0	35	0.00645
2	10.0	50	0.00816
3	38.5	14	0.01955
4	350.0	1	0.14262

The arrival rates per class are $\lambda_1 = 6 \times 0.35 = 2.1$ requests/sec, $\lambda_2 = 6 \times 0.50 = 3.0$ requests/sec, $\lambda_3 = 6 \times 0.14 = 0.84$ requests/sec, and $\lambda_4 = 6 \times 0.01 = 0.06$ requests/sec . If we use the expressions given in this section and implemented by the Microsoft Excel workbook `WebModels.XLS`, we obtain the service demands shown in Table 10.5. The CPU service demands shown in this table are the intrinsic service demands.   ∎

We consider now the problem of computing the load-dependent service demands. If the overhead factor, CPUOvhd, in Eq. (10.4.36) is zero, then we can use an open multiclass QN models and the Microsoft Excel workbook `OpenQN.XLS` to solve the model. But, if CPUOvhd is not zero, we can use the following iterative procedure:

Table 10.5. Service Demands for Ex. 10.7 (sec)

Component	1	2	3	4
LAN	0.0046	0.0088	0.0331	0.2984
Router	0.0005	0.0007	0.0017	0.0126
Outgoing link	0.0277	0.0555	0.2127	1.9309
Incoming link	0.0027	0.0027	0.0027	0.0027
Web server CPU	0.0064	0.0082	0.0196	0.1426
Web server Disk	0.0300	0.0600	0.2310	2.1000

1. Solve the open multiclass QN model, assuming CPUOvhd $= 0$, and obtain $\overline{n}$, the average number of requests at the server using Eq. (10.4.37).

2. Compute the new value of $D_{\text{CPU},r}$ as

$$D_{\text{CPU},r} = \text{CPUTimePerHTTPRequest}_r + f(\overline{n}) \times \text{CPUOvhd}. \quad (10.4.39)$$

3. Solve the model using the new value of $D_{\text{CPU},r}$ and obtain a new value of $\overline{n}$.

4. If the absolute value of the relative error between the current and previous values of $\overline{n}$ exceeds a certain tolerance (say 10^{-3}), then go to step 2, else stop.

The following example illustrates this procedure.

Example 10.8

Consider that a fifth workload was added to the Web server of Ex. 10.7. This workload consists of requests to execute CGI scripts. The intrinsic service demand at the Web server's CPU for the new CGI workload is 0.35 sec. The new distribution of file sizes, percent of each type of request, and CPU time per class are given in Table 10.6. Assume that, according to measurements taken, the operating system and protocol management overhead at

Table 10.6. Workload Parameters for Ex. 10.8

Class	Average File Size (KB)	% of Requests	CPU time per HTTP request (sec)
1	5.0	25	0.00645
2	10.0	30	0.00816
3	38.5	19	0.01955
4	350.0	1	0.14262
5	1.0	25	0.35000

the CPU are linear with the number of requests being executed, and that the load-dependent portion of the service demand at the CPU can be characterized as $0.003 \times \bar{n}$ for all classes. This kind of behavior could be explained by the fact that many TCP implementations do sequential lookups on Protocol Control Block (PCB) tables [11]. So, the more TCP connections are open, the longer it takes to establish a new connection. What are the response times for each class?

Using the iterative procedure described in this section, we obtain the results shown in Table 10.7. Five iterations were needed to converge to an error of 0.02%. Column two of Table 10.7 shows the value of the average number of requests at the Web server. The response times per class are obtained in the last iteration.   ∎

10.4.2   Mirrored Web Servers

Let us start by considering the case where the environment of Fig. 10.5a is generalized in such a way that the Web server is mirrored (see Chapter 4) into n Web servers, that is, the document tree of the Web site is replicated into n identical Web servers. Let us examine how the model parameters need to be changed to reflect this situation. The arrival rates per class are clearly the same. The incoming link, router, LAN, and outgoing link demands are

Table 10.7. Results for Ex. 10.8

Iteration	$\overline{n}$	% Error	Response Times (sec) per class				
			1	2	3	4	5
1	2.6110	–	0.147	0.279	1.034	9.286	0.863
2	2.9113	10.32	0.170	0.302	1.061	9.350	0.989
3	2.9508	1.34	0.173	0.306	1.065	9.358	1.006
4	2.9560	0.18	0.173	0.306	1.065	9.359	1.008
5	2.9567	0.02	0.173	0.306	1.065	9.359	1.008

unchanged. However, the service demands at the CPU and disks of the Web server have to be divided by n, assuming the load will be equally split among all servers.

To understand why this is the case, remember that the service demand at a queue is the product of the average number of visits made by a request to the queue, multiplied by the average service time per visit. The service demand measured at any of the components (e.g., CPU, disks) of a server does not change by the addition of mirrored servers. But, the average number of visits to the queues that represent these components change due to the load balancing between the n mirrored servers. Consider a single class of requests, to simplify the notation, and let V_{server}^j be the average number of visits to Web server j $(j = 1, \cdots, n)$. Let i be a component (e.g., CPU or disk) or Web server j, and let V_i^j be the average number of visits to queue i, given that a request is sent to Web server j. Note that V_i^j does not change because mirror servers are added. The average number of visits, V_i, to the queue that represents component i in the QN model is

$$V_i = V_{\text{server}}^j \times V_i^j \tag{10.4.40}$$

since for every visit to the Web server, a request makes V_i^j visits, on the average, to component i. But since $V_{\text{server}}^j = 1/n$ for all Web servers,

$$V_i = V_i^j / n. \tag{10.4.41}$$

Let S_i be the average service time of a request at component i. This value does not change with the number of Web servers. If we multiply both sides of Eq. (10.4.41) by S_i, we get that

$$V_i \times S_i = (V_i^j \times S_i)/n. \tag{10.4.42}$$

But $V_i \times S_i$ is D_i, the service demand of component i in the QN that represents the mirrored server case, and $V_i^j \times S_i$ is the service demand of a request measured at the Web server, that is, the service demand for the single Web server case.

So, using the superscript m to indicate service demands in the mirrored case, we have that

$$D_{CPU,r}^m = D_{CPU,r}/n \tag{10.4.43}$$

and

$$D_{\text{disk},r}^m = D_{\text{disk},r}/n. \tag{10.4.44}$$

Example 10.9

Consider the parameters of Ex. 10.8. Assume that the arrival rate of requests is expected to increase from 6 to 8 requests/sec. The Web site administrator wants to know if two Web servers sharing the overall load would provide the same service levels as the ones currently offered.

To answer this question, we add two more queues to our QN model: the CPU and disk for the new server. Assume that the overall load will be equally split between the two servers. Therefore, the service demand at the CPU and disk of the original Web server has to be divided by two and assigned to the CPU and disk of each of the two servers as indicated in Eq. (10.4.44). If we solve the model again, we obtain the following response time for classes 1–5, respectively: 0.159 sec, 0.300 sec, 1.105 sec, 9.903 sec, and 0.623 sec.

These numbers are very similar to the ones obtained in the previous example as seen in Table 10.7. This indicates that the two Web servers will be able to handle the increase in workload intensity while maintaining the same quality of service.   ■

Consider now the environment of Fig. 10.5b in which the document tree, instead of being replicated in all Web servers, is stored in a shared file system with P disks. This arrangement alleviates the problem of maintaining the mirrored copies' consistency. There is a penalty, though: The LAN and the file server are now shared among all Web servers and could potentially become a bottleneck if not adequately sized. Figure 10.6b shows the QN model that corresponds to Fig. 10.5b. We need an additional parameter CPUTimePerFSRequest that stands for the total CPU time in seconds per KB accessed. Let us analyze how the service demands have to modified to account for the shared file server.

Each HTTP request uses the LAN to reach one of the n Web servers. The document specified in the URL is requested from the file server. The document uses the LAN to go to the requesting Web server and uses the LAN again to go to the router on its way to the outgoing link. So, if we neglect the short requests to the file server and consider the typically bulkier replies from the file server to the Web server, we have that

$$D_{\text{LAN},r}^{m} = \text{NetworkTime}\,(\text{AvgSizeHTTPRequest}, \text{LANBandwidth}) +$$
$$2 \times \text{NetworkTime}\,(1{,}024 \times \text{DocumentSize}_r, \text{LANBandwidth}).$$
$$(10.4.45)$$

The service demand, $D_{\text{FSCpu},r}$, at the file server's CPU for class r, is given by

$$D_{\text{FSCpu},r} = \text{DocumentSize}_r \times \text{CPUTimePerFSRequest}. \qquad (10.4.46)$$

The service demand, $D_{\text{FSdisk},r}$, at each of the P disks of the file server, is

$$D_{\text{FSdisk},r} = (\text{DocumentSize}_r \times \text{DiskTime}/1{,}000)/P. \qquad (10.4.47)$$

All equations for computing the service demands for Web servers with or without mirroring are in the Microsoft Excel workbook WebModels.XLS.

Example 10.10

Consider the same parameters as in Ex. 10.9 with the difference that, instead of each of the two Web servers maintaining a replica of the document tree each, they use a shared file server with two disks. The arrival rate of requests is still 8 requests/sec. The Web site administrator wants to know what will be the impact on performance of using a shared file server.

The QN model has nine queues now: the incoming link, the router, the LAN, the two Web server CPUs, the file server CPU, the two file server disks, and the outgoing link. If we use the workbook WebModels.XLS, we obtain the service demands for this model. We can now use the workbook OpenQN.XLS to solve the model and answer the capacity planning question posed by the Web site administrator. Table 10.8 compares the response times for the nonshared file server case (Ex. 10.9) and the shared file server case considered in this example. The last row of the table shows the percent variation of the results. The first four classes—retrieval of HTTP documents—show an increasing percent variation on the response time. The maximum increase is 8.2% and is observed for class 4, the one with the largest average document size. The main reason for the increase is increased congestion at the LAN. The last column of the table shows that the LAN utilization doubled because of the use of a shared file server. Class 5, the CGI script workload, exhibits a 1.3% decrease in response time. The reason is that the CPU processing associated with the file system has been moved from the Web server CPU to the CPU of the file server. Thus, the CGI scripts execute faster now.

By looking at the results of the QN model, one can see that in this case, the bottleneck is the outgoing link for classes 1–4 and the Web server CPU for class 5. The Web site administrator examined Table 10.8 and decided that using a shared file server would be advisable, despite the relatively small increase in the response time of some of the classes, since it would eliminate the problem of keeping the various copies of the document tree consistent.■

Table 10.8. Results for Ex. 10.10

	Response Times (sec) per Class					Lan Utilization
	1	2	3	4	5	(%)
No FS	0.159	0.300	1.105	9.903	0.623	10.7
Shared FS	0.167	0.320	1.192	10.718	0.615	21.1
% variation	5.0	6.7	7.9	8.2	-1.3	97.2

10.5   Concluding Remarks

The performance models presented in this chapter specialize and extend the models presented in Chapters 8 and 9 to deal with specific aspects of the Web, from the client and server sides. The chapter showed that the effects of burstiness of Web traffic can be incorporated into the models by inflating the service demands of the bottleneck resource by a factor proportional to a burstiness factor that can be obtained by analyzing the HTTP log. Heavy tails of file size distributions are handled by the performance models through the use of multiple classes that account for the different ranges of file sizes.

The client-side models presented here are closed QN models and allow for the proper sizing of the bandwidth of the connection to the Internet, among other things. The server-side models are open multiclass QN models and can be used to analyze Web sites with many different configurations, including mirroring with and without shared file servers.

The examples given in the chapter are illustrative of scenarios that can be analyzed with these models. They are not in any way all encompassing. Many other situations can be analyzed by following the approach presented here.

To support the computation of service demands for the client and server sides, we developed Microsoft Excel workbook `WebModels.XLS` which computes the matrix of service demands from the values of the parameters. This matrix can be cut and pasted into the workbooks `ClosedQN.XLS` and

`OpenQN.XLS` to conveniently solve the client- and server-side models, respectively.

A study of the performance impact of Web browsers on CPU and memory resources at the client side is given in [6]. Measurements of Web server resource CPU, disk, and memory, consumption are presented in [8]. Other modeling techniques, such as Layered Queuing Models [12, 14], have been used to model Web servers [7].

Bibliography

[1] J. M. Almeida, V. A. F. Almeida, and D. Yates, "Measuring the Behavior of a World Wide Web Server," *Proc. Seventh Conf. High Perform. Networking (HPN'97)*, IFIP, New York, April 1997.

[2] G. Banga and P. Druschel, "Measuring the Capacity of a Web Server," *Usenix Symp. Internet Technol. Syst.*, Dec. 1997.

[3] J. P. Buzen, "Operational Analysis: an Alternative to Stochastic Modeling," *Performance of Computer Installations*, North Holland, June 1978, pp. 175–194.

[4] D. E. Comer, *Computer Networks and Internets*, Prentice Hall, Upper Saddle River, New Jersey, 1997.

[5] M. Crovella and A. Bestavros, "Self-Similarity in World-Wide Web Traffic: Evidence and Possible Causes," *Proc. 1996 SIGMETRICS Conf. Measurement Comput. Syst.*, ACM, Philadelphia, Pennsylvania, May 1996.

[6] Y. Ding and S. Agrawal, "The Performance Impact of Web Servers," *Proc. 1996 Comput. Measurement Group Conf.*, San Diego, California, Dec. 8–13, 1996, pp. 62–73.

[7] J. A. Dilley, R. J. Friedrich, T. Y. Jin, and J. Rolia, "Measurement Tools and Modeling Techniques for Evaluating Web Server Performance," *Tech. Rep. HPL-96-161*, Hewlett Packard Labs, Dec. 1996.

[8] A. A. Hafez and Y. Ding, "Measuring Web Server Resource Consumption," *Proc. 1997 Comput. Measurement Group Conf.*, Orlando, Florida, Dec. 9–12, 1997.

[9] J. Heidmann, K. Obraczka, and J. Touch, "Modeling the Performance of HTTP Over Several Transport Protocols," *IEEE/ACM Trans. Networking*, vol. 5, no. 5, pp. 616–630, Oct. 1997.

[10] J. Kay and J. Pasquale, "Profiling and Reducing Processing Overheads in TCP/IP," *IEEE/ACM Trans. Networking*, vol. 4, no. 6, Dec. 1996.

[11] J. Mogul, "Network Behavior of a Busy Web Server and its Clients," *Res. Rep. 95/5*, DEC Western Res. Lab., 1995.

[12] J. Rolia and K. Sevcik, "The Method of Layers," *IEEE Trans. Software Eng.*, vol. 21, no. 8, pp. 689–700, Aug. 1995.

[13] M. R. Stadelman, "UNIX Web Server Performance Analysis," *Proc. 1996 Comput. Measurement Group Conf.*, San Diego, California, Dec. 8–13, 1996, pp. 1026–1033.

[14] C. M. Woodside, J. E. Neilson, D. C. Petriu, and S. Majumdar, "The Stochastic Rendezvous Network Model for Performance of Synchronous Client-Server-Like Distributed Software," *IEEE Trans. Comput.*, vol. 44, no. 1, Jan. 1995, pp. 20–34.

[15] N. Yeager and R. McCrath, *Web Server Technology*, Morgan Kaufmann, San Francisco, California, 1996.

Chapter 11

Availability of Web Services

11.1 Introduction

Before the Internet era, computer and telephone networks made much progress in terms of increased dependability, i.e., a combination of integrity/reliability, security, and availability [2]. According to Jim Gray, things got worse as a result of the significant complexity of Internet sites, the speed with which Web sites are developed and deployed, and the increased exposure to attacks by hackers [2]. It is not uncommon for large sites to be built out of thousands of elements including servers, firewalls, communication links, storage boxes, and all sorts of software systems. It is also the case that many Web site projects are carried out in three to four months at most because of the need to beat competitors and quickly establish a Web presence. This rush to become visible online often comes at the expense of lack of careful design and testing, leading to site performance, security, and availability vulnerabilities. Finally, because Web sites can be accessed from anywhere in the world and by anyone, it is a never-ending challenge to build sites that can withstand attacks by hackers.

In previous chapters we discussed how we can compute and measure several important performance metrics such as response time, throughput, and fraction of rejected requests. However, these metrics are only relevant if users can get to the site, i.e., if the Web services are available. There are many reasons why a Web service may become unavailable, including hardware failures, network connectivity problems, software failures, and even Denial of Service attacks. Software failures, as we discuss in this chapter, are not necessarily independent from site overload.

In this chapter, we provide a quantitative approach to understand and compute availability and reliability metrics for Web sites. Many sites achieve higher degrees of availability by using redundant components such as clusters of servers. As servers in a cluster fail, the original load has to be processed by fewer servers, resulting in degraded performance. Thus, performance and availability have to be considered simultaneously. We provide in this chapter an integrated analysis of performance and availability, as well as a discussion on the issue of software aging and rejuvenation.

11.2   A Motivating Availability Example

In this section we consider a simple example of an online brokerage which is in the process of designing its site and selecting the components that will be used in its design. The main consideration here is the site availability, which has to be at least 99.99% ("four-9's") according to management decision. The site is used by users to get quotes on stocks and mutual funds, manage portfolios, conduct portfolio risk analysis, and to place orders to trade stocks and mutual funds. In the security trading business, Web service availability is a key QoS metric. If customers are denied access to the trading services, they may incur financial losses and the trading company may be liable for these losses.

Figure 11.1 shows the architecture of the trading site. It is composed of a load balancer that distributes the incoming requests to one of n_{WS} Web servers. The Web servers are all implemented using the same type of hardware and software. At the back-end, n_{DS} database servers are used to store all the persistent data needed to support customer trading transactions. The database is fully replicated at each of the n_{DS} database servers to increase availability and distribute the load. It is worth mentioning that providing highly available servers is not sufficient for guaranteeing highly available Web services. Other elements in the end-to-end path may cause service outages. A good example is Internet connectivity failure.

The company is considering two types of boxes: highly reliable, expensive, high-end servers with hot-swappable CPU boards and disks, as well as less expensive, less reliable, low-end servers. Management wants to answer the following questions: What is the least expensive configuration that meets the 99.99% availability requirement? All low-end servers, all high-end servers, or a mix of low-end and high-end servers?

To answer this question, we will introduce several concepts in the following sections and we will then revisit this example.

11.3   Why and How Systems Fail

There are many reasons why a computer system may fail. To discuss the causes of failures, it is important to categorize the different types of failures. We use a taxonomy composed of the following three dimensions: duration, effect, and scope. The first dimension is related to the *duration* of the failure and comprises the following cases:

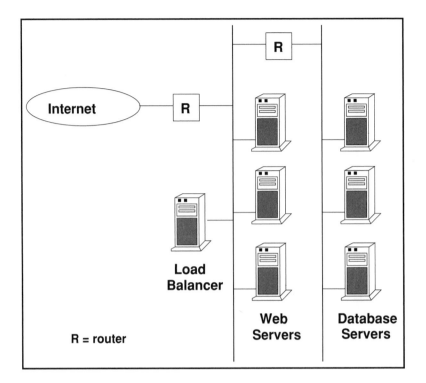

Figure 11.1. Trading site architecture.

- *Permanent failures:* A system stops working and there is no possibility of repairing or replacing it. This could happen in systems deployed in unmanned space ships.

- *Recoverable failures:* In this case, the system is placed back in operation after a fault is recovered. For example, a Web site may become inaccessible because its connection to the Internet goes down. After network connectivity is restored, the site is said to have recovered from the failure.

- *Transient failures:* These failures are characterized by having a very short duration and may not require major recovery actions. Examples of these failures include problems that are solved by resetting network routers or rebooting servers.

The second dimension is related to the *effect* of the failure. We consider two possibilities here:

- *Functional failures:* This is the case in which a system does not operate according to its functional specifications. For example, an online bookstore fails to display information about a book even though it is in the catalog.

- *Performance failures:* Here, even though the system may be executing the requested functions correctly, they are not executed in a timely fashion. In other words, the performance specifications or SLAs are not being met. Consider the case of a search engine that presents very accurate results to requests for search but takes more than a minute on average to process each request. It is clear that users would see the site as a failure in terms of performance.

Finally, the third dimension is the *scope* of the failure. We consider the following two cases:

- *Partial:* In this case, some of the services provided by the computer system become unavailable, while others can still be used. For example, the services that allow customers to bid in an online auction site may become unavailable due to the failure of the servers that process these types of requests, while customers may still be able to see existing bids.

- *Total:* These failures are characterized by a complete disruption of all services offered by the computer system. Power outages could cause a Web site to go down completely.

11.4   Reliability and Availability Basics

The *reliability* of a system or component is the probability that it is functioning properly and constantly over a fixed time period [5]. A related concept, *availability*, is based on the notion that a component (or system) alternates through periods in which it is operational—the up periods—and periods in which it is down—the down periods. This is illustrated in Fig. 11.2. Suppose that once a system becomes operational, it will take a certain time to fail again. The average time it takes for the system to fail is called MTTF (Mean Time to Failure). Once the system fails, it will take a certain time to recover from the failure and return to an operational state. The average time it takes for the system to recover is called MTTR (Mean Time to Recover). The average time between failures is called MTBF (Mean Time Between Failures) and can be written as

$$MTBF = MTTF + MTTR \qquad (11.4.1)$$

as shown in Fig. 11.2. Availability is then defined as the fraction of time that a component (or system) is operational.

Computer systems tend to be labeled by the number of "9"s in the availability. For example a "five-9's" system has an availability of 99.999%. Table 11.1 classifies computer systems according to how good their availability is and shows the number of minutes of down time per year for each [3]. So, if a Web site has one hour of scheduled down time per week, can it have a "five-9" availability? Well, since there are 52 weeks/year, the site has a scheduled down time of 52 hours per year. By looking at Table 11.1, we see that the site availability will be at most 99.99%. It could be less than that due to unscheduled down times.

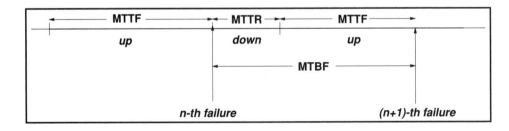

Figure 11.2. Relationship between MTTF, MTTR, and MTBF.

Table 11.1. Classes of Systems According to Availability

Availability Class	Availability	Unavailable (min/year)	System Type
1	90.0%	52,560	Unmanaged
2	99.0%	5,256	Managed
3	99.9%	526	Well-Managed
4	99.99%	52.6	Fault-Tolerant
5	99.999%	5.3	Highly Available
6	99.9999%	0.53	Very Highly Available
7	99.99999%	0.0053	Ultra Available

Let us use the state transition diagrams discussed in Chapter 8 to obtain an expression for the availability of a system. The simple diagram depicted in Fig. 11.3 shows that the system can be in one of two states: up and down.

The system fails, i.e., goes from up to down, with a rate λ and gets repaired, i.e., goes from down to up, with a rate μ. These rates can be

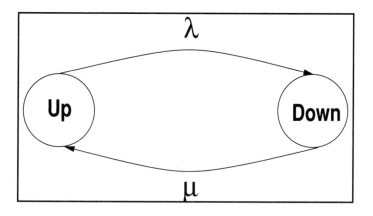

Figure 11.3. State transition diagram for availability computation.

written in terms of the MTTF and MTTR as

$$\lambda = \frac{1}{\text{MTTF}} \quad \text{and} \quad \mu = \frac{1}{\text{MTTR}}. \qquad (11.4.2)$$

Using the *flow-in-flow-out* principle introduced in Chapter 8, we can write that

$$\lambda \times p_{\text{up}} = \mu \times p_{\text{down}} \qquad (11.4.3)$$

where p_{up} and p_{down} are the probability that the system is up and down, respectively. Note that the availability A is simply p_{up} and that

$$p_{\text{up}} + p_{\text{down}} = 1. \qquad (11.4.4)$$

Combining Eqs. (11.4.3) and (11.4.4), we get that

$$A = p_{\text{up}} = \frac{\mu}{\mu + \lambda} = \frac{1/\text{MTTR}}{1/\text{MTTR} + 1/\text{MTTF}} = \frac{\text{MTTF}}{\text{MTTF} + \text{MTTR}} \qquad (11.4.5)$$

and

$$U = p_{\text{down}} = \frac{\lambda}{\mu + \lambda} = \frac{\text{MTTR}}{\text{MTTF} + \text{MTTR}} = \frac{\text{MTTR}}{\text{MTBF}} \qquad (11.4.6)$$

where U is the system *un-availability*. In most systems of interest, MTTF $\gg$ MTTR, i.e., it takes significantly longer for the system to fail than to be repaired. Then, the unavailability can be approximated as

$$U \sim \frac{\text{MTTR}}{\text{MTTF}}. \qquad (11.4.7)$$

It can be shown (see [7] for example) that the availability expression given in Eq. (11.4.5) does not depend on the probability distribution of the time to fail nor on the probability distribution of the time to recover.

There are two ways to improve availability: reduce the frequency of failures or reduce the time to recover from them [1]. The time to recovery can be decomposed into four main components: (1) time to detect the failure, (2) time to diagnose the cause of the failure, (3) time to determine possible solutions to the problem, and (4) time to correct the problem. In order to reduce MTTR, one has to choose which components to analyze first. To reduce problem solution time, one can log previous errors and their solutions to help identify the solution of future problems. It is generally easier to reduce the MTTR than to increase the MTTF in large and evolving systems [1].

Example 11.1

Consider a Web site composed of two Web servers, one application server, and one database server. Suppose that historical data shows that the application server machine is rebooted every twenty days on average. Assuming that the system administrator takes 10 minutes to reboot the machine, what is the application server availability?

We can then say that the MTTF is 20 days ($= 20 \times 24 \times 60 = 28,800$ minutes) and the MTTR is 10 minutes. Therefore, the availability is given by

$$A = \text{MTTF}/(\text{MTTF} + \text{MTTR}) = 28,800/(28,800 + 10) = 99.965\%$$

It is interesting to note the importance of reducing the time to recovery. If the system administrator were able to cut the reboot time in 20%, the availability would be $A = 28,800/(28,800 + 8) = 99.972\%$. To achieve the same availability of 99.972% with the original MTTR of 10 minutes, the MTTF would have to be increased to 35,704 minutes, i.e., a 24% increase.■

Example 11.2

The distinction between reliability and availability can be better understood in this example. Consider an online brokerage that goes down for one minute every four hours, i.e., every 240 ($= 4 \times 60$) minutes. The site's availability can be computed as

$$A = \frac{240 - 1}{240} = \frac{239}{240} = 99.583\%. \qquad (11.4.8)$$

While this may be regarded as a reasonably high availability, the site reliability is low if the down times occur at a critical time during which the market is going through very volatile periods in the day and customers want to trade their stocks.   ■

So, as we said before, reliability is the probability that a system is continuously operating correctly during a fixed time period T. When the time period T becomes very large, i.e., goes to infinity, the reliability becomes the availability [7].

11.5　The Reliability of Systems of Components

Suppose we know the reliability r of a component which is then used along with other components to build a system. An important question is "What is the reliability of the system as a function of the reliability of the components?"

Let us start with a simple example of components connected in series, as in Fig. 11.4. An example of this situation could occur when a Web site has a Web server connected to an application server which is then connected to a database server, each on its own dedicated machine.

Inside each box in the diagrams of Fig. 11.4 are the reliabilities $r_1, \cdots, r_n$ of the n components. Let us compute the reliability, R_s, of the series system of Fig. 11.4. In other words, we want to know what is the probability that the entire system shown inside the dashed box of Fig. 11.4 is operational when needed. So, all n components must be operational for the system to be operational. We will assume that the n components fail in an independent way. In other words, failure of one component does not affect any other component. In this case, we can use a well-known result of probability theory that says that the probability of an event expressed as the intersection of independent events (in our case, "all n components are operational") is the product of the probabilities of the independent events (each event being "component i is working") [7]. This observation leads to

$$R_s = r_1 \times r_2 \cdots r_n = \prod_{i=1}^{n} r_i \qquad (11.5.9)$$

Let us examine the implications of Eq. (11.5.9). Each reliability value, r_i, is a probability and therefore, $r_i \leq 1$. So, as we add more components in

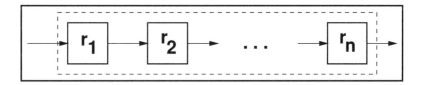

Figure 11.4. Reliability block diagram for a serial system.

series we decrease the system reliability, unless the added component has a reliabilility of 1, which is highly unlikely.

Example 11.3

A Web site has a Web server (WS), an application server (AS), and a database server (DS) in series. Let $r_{\text{WS}}, r_{\text{AS}}$, and r_{DB} be the reliabilities of these components and assume that their values are $r_{\text{WS}} = 0.9$, $r_{\text{AS}} = 0.95$, and $r_{\text{DB}} = 0.99$. Management wants to replace the database server with a highly reliable and expensive model that is advertised as having a 0.999 reliability. Is this a wise decision?

The reliability of the site with the current database server is

$$R_{\text{site}} = r_{\text{WS}} \times r_{\text{AS}} \times r_{\text{DS}}$$
$$= 0.9 \times 0.95 \times 0.99 = 0.84645. \qquad (11.5.10)$$

The reliability of the site with the new database server is

$$R_{\text{site}}^{\text{newDS}} = r_{\text{WS}} \times r_{\text{AS}} \times r_{\text{DS}}^{\text{new}}$$
$$= 0.9 \times 0.95 \times 0.999 = 0.85415. \qquad (11.5.11)$$

Let us now examine what would happen if we kept the database server but replaced the Web server, the most unreliable component, with a Web server that has a reliability of 0.95. The site reliability now becomes

$$R_{\text{site}}^{\text{newWS}} = r_{\text{WS}}^{\text{new}} \times r_{\text{AS}} \times r_{\text{DS}}$$
$$= 0.95 \times 0.95 \times 0.99 = 0.89348. \qquad (11.5.12)$$

The above computations show that replacing the most unreliable component has a more pronounced effect in terms of improving overall system reliability. Of course, cost issues must also be taken into consideration when comparing alternatives.   ■

Consider now the special case of Eq. (11.5.9) in which all components have the same reliability r. Then, the system reliability is given by $R_s = r^n$ and decreases very fast as more components are added. Figure 11.5 shows the reliability of a system comprised of n components with identical reliability r versus n for three value of r: 90%, 95%, and 99%. We can see how the reliability decreases quite fast with n. Also, the lower the reliability of each component, the faster the decay in system reliability.

We now turn our attention to the parallel system of Fig. 11.6. Using components in parallel is one of the most common ways to use redundancy to improve reliability. The reliability of the parallel system, R_p, is the probability that it is in operation when needed. This probability is equal to

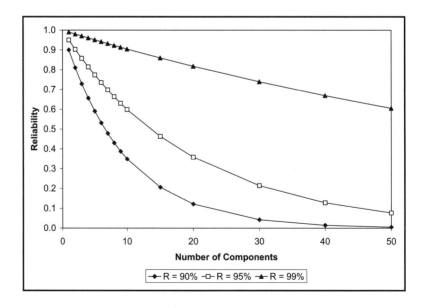

Figure 11.5. Reliability of a series of identical components.

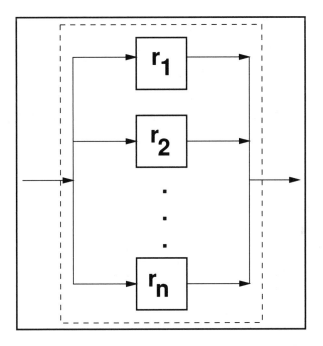

Figure 11.6. Reliability block diagram for a parallel system.

one minus the probability that the system is not in operation. For this to happen, all n components must be down. The probability that component i is down is simply $(1 - r_i)$. So, assuming independence of failures between components, we get

$$
\begin{aligned}
R_p &= 1 - \Pr\,[\text{all components are down}] \\
&= 1 - [(1 - r_1) \times (1 - r_2) \times \cdots (1 - r_n)] \\
&= 1 - \prod_{i=1}^{n}(1 - r_i).
\end{aligned}
\tag{11.5.13}
$$

Consider now the special case of Eq. (11.5.13) when all components have the same reliability r. In this case, we get

$$
R_p = 1 - (1 - r)^n.
\tag{11.5.14}
$$

This equation is illustrated in Fig. 11.7 for three values of r. As we can see, as we increase the number of components, system reliability grows very fast.

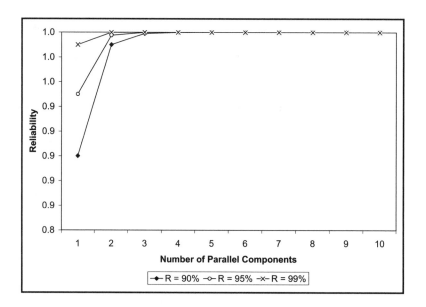

Figure 11.7. Reliability of identical components in parallel.

In fact, a small number of components is usually enough to provide a very high level of system reliability.

Example 11.4

A search engine site wants to achieve a site reliability of 99.999% using a cluster of very cheap and unreliable Web servers. A cluster is a parallel combination of a number of servers. Each one has a reliability of 85%. How many servers should be used in the cluster?

From Eq. (11.5.14), we know that

$$0.99999 = 1 - (1 - 0.85)^n = 1 - 0.15^n. \tag{11.5.15}$$

So,

$$0.15^n = 1 - 0.99999 = 0.00001. \tag{11.5.16}$$

If we apply logarithms to both sides of the above equation and we take into consideration that n must be an integer, we get that

$$n = \left\lceil \frac{\ln 0.00001}{\ln 0.15} \right\rceil = \lceil 6.069 \rceil = 7 \qquad (11.5.17)$$

So, seven unreliable Web servers can provide a high-level of reliability when used in parallel. ∎

We can generalize the results of the previous example, and provide an expression for the minimum number, n_{min}, of servers with reliability r that are needed to build a cluster of servers with reliability R_p.

$$n_{min} = \left\lceil \frac{\ln(1 - R_p)}{\ln(1 - r)} \right\rceil \qquad (11.5.18)$$

Example 11.5

A Web site has a three-tier architecture composed of a layer of Web servers, a layer of application servers, and a layer of database servers. Their respective reliabilities are 0.99, 0.999, and 0.9999, respectively. Sixty percent of the requests only use services from the Web server layer. The remaining 40% use the application server layer. Eighty-four percent of these requests need services from the database server layer. What is the site availability?

For the 60% of the requests that only use the Web servers, the site availability is 99%. For the 6.4% $(= (1 - 0.6) \times (1 - 0.84))$ of the requests that only need Web and application server layer services, the availability is 0.98901 $(= 0.99 \times 0.999)$. Finally, for the 33.6% $((1 - 0.6) \times 0.84)$ of requests that need to use all three layers, the site availability is 0.9889111. So, the average site availability is

$$0.6 \times 0.99 + 0.064 \times 0.98901 + 0.336 \times 0.9889111 = 0.98957077 \quad (11.5.19)$$

which is very close to the reliability of the Web server layer even though the back-end database is quite reliable and probably quite expensive. ∎

We summarize in Fig. 11.8 the main formulas derived in this section. The Microsoft Excel workbook `Availability.XLS` that can be found in the book's Web site contains most the data and graphs discussed in this section.

Availability (A):

$$A = \frac{\text{MTTF}}{\text{MTTF} + \text{MTTR}} \qquad (11.5.20)$$

Unavailability (U):

$$U = \frac{\text{MTTR}}{\text{MTTF} + \text{MTTR}} = \frac{\text{MTTR}}{\text{MTBF}} \qquad (11.5.21)$$

Mean Time Between Failures (MTBF):

$$\text{MTBF} = \text{MTTF} + \text{MTTR} \qquad (11.5.22)$$

Reliability (R_s) of n components with reliability r_i in series:

$$R_s = \prod_{i=1}^{n} r_i \qquad (11.5.23)$$

Reliability (R_p) of n components with reliability r_i in parallel:

$$R_p = 1 - \prod_{i=1}^{n} (1 - r_i) \qquad (11.5.24)$$

Minimum number ($n_{\min}$) of servers with reliability r needed to build a parallel system with reliability R_p:

$$n_{\min} = \left\lceil \frac{\ln(1 - R_p)}{\ln(1 - r)} \right\rceil \qquad (11.5.25)$$

Figure 11.8. Summary of availability/reliability equations.

11.6   Revisiting the Online Broker Example

We now return to the motivating example of Section 11.2. Let r_{LB}, r_{WS}, and r_{DS} be the reliability of the load balancer, Web servers, and database servers, respectively. The reliability block diagram for the system of Fig. 11.1 is shown in Fig. 11.9.

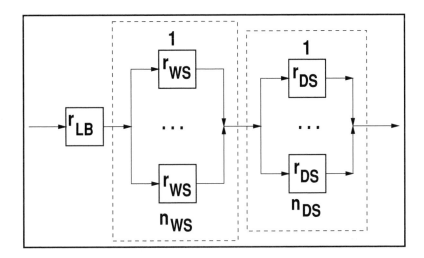

Figure 11.9. Reliability block diagram for the trading site example.

We can now use the formulas we learned in the previous section to compute the reliability of the Web site. Note that we can consider the site as composed of a series of three systems: the load balancer, the set of Web servers, and the set of application servers. The reliability of the set of Web servers, R_{WS}, can be computed as a function of the reliability of the the individual Web servers. It is the same case for the database servers. So, the Web site reliability, R_{site}, can be written as

$$R_{\mathrm{site}} = r_{\mathrm{LB}} \times R_{\mathrm{WS}} \times R_{\mathrm{DB}}$$
$$= r_{\mathrm{LB}} \times [1 - (1 - r_{\mathrm{WS}})^{n_{\mathrm{WS}}}] \times [1 - (1 - r_{\mathrm{DS}})^{n_{\mathrm{DS}}}]. \quad (11.6.26)$$

As a design goal, we want R_{site} to be 0.9999. Let us assume that the reliability of the load balancer is very high and equal to 99.999%. If we plug in these values in Eq. (11.6.26), we get

$$0.99991 = [1 - (1 - r_{\mathrm{WS}})^{n_{\mathrm{WS}}}] \times [1 - (1 - r_{\mathrm{DS}})^{n_{\mathrm{DS}}}]. \quad (11.6.27)$$

which after some algebraic manipulation leads to

$$n_{\mathrm{WS}} = \left\lceil \frac{\ln\left(1 - 0.99991/[1 - (1 - r_{\mathrm{DS}})^{n_{\mathrm{DS}}}]\right)}{\ln(1 - r_{\mathrm{WS}})} \right\rceil. \quad (11.6.28)$$

Equation (11.6.28) provides a relationship between the number of Web servers and the number and reliability of database servers. We can then use this relationship to explore some possible configurations for the site. It should be noted that, to achieve the desired level of site availability, there are some constraints besides those implied by Eq. (11.6.27). For example, if the Web servers have maximum reliability, i.e., $r_{WS} = 1$, then Eq. (11.6.27) leads to

$$(1 - r_{DS})^{n_{DS}} < 0.00009. \tag{11.6.29}$$

Similarly, if we assume that the database servers have maximum reliability, i.e., $r_{DS} = 1$, then Eq. (11.6.27) requires that

$$(1 - r_{WS})^{n_{WS}} < 0.00009. \tag{11.6.30}$$

Let us assume that the reliability of the low-end servers is 0.85 and that the reliability of the high-end servers is 0.999. If we use these values in Eq. (11.6.28) and take into account the constraints of Eqs. (11.6.29) and (11.6.30) we obtain the three configurations shown in Table 11.2. The table shows for each configuration whether low-end or high-end servers are used for the Web and database servers and what is the minimum number of each that satisfies the SLA constraint for site reliability of 99.99%. The last column provides the resulting site reliability for each configuration. For example, if we adopt the last configuration, which uses only high-end servers, the site reliability is 99.999%. Under this type of configuration, it is not possible to use less than two high-end servers at each level without violating the SLA. To evaluate which configuration must be selected, cost must be taken into account. Remember that cost includes not only the purchase cost of the hardware and software but also maintenance cost.

11.7　Performance and Availability

Performance, measured as response time for example, is highly correlated to availability in systems that use redundancy to improve availability. Consider

Table 11.2. Configuration Options for Online Trading Site

Configuration	r_{WS}	r_{DB}	n_{WS}	n_{DS}	R_{site}
Low End WS/Low End DS	0.850	0.850	6	5	99.990%
Low End WS/High End DS	0.850	0.999	5	2	99.991%
High End WS/High EndDS	0.999	0.999	2	2	99.999%

for example the case of an Internet Data Center (IDC) that uses n identical Web servers to distribute the load of processing incoming requests. Each Web server is composed of a CPU and a disk. The total arrival rate of requests to the site is λ requests/sec and is assumed to be equally distributed among all servers that are up. So, if k $(k = 1, ..., n)$ servers are up, the load seen by each server is λ/k.

We now proceed to analyze this system in three steps. First, we analyze the availability aspects only. Then, we consider performance issues only. Finally, we combine both analyses into what is called *performability* analysis.

11.7.1   Availability Analysis

We will use the state transition diagram (STD) technique introduced in Chapter 8 to derive the probability p_k that k servers are down. Our failure and recovery model makes the following assumptions:

- Each server fails at a rate of 1/MTTF, the inverse of its time to fail.

- Up to m servers may be in the process of being repaired at any given time. The rate at which each failed server is put back into operation, once it it being repaired, is 1/MTTR, the inverse of the recovery time.

Figure 11.10 illustrates how servers move from being up to going to the repair pool, where they either wait to be repaired if all m repair stations

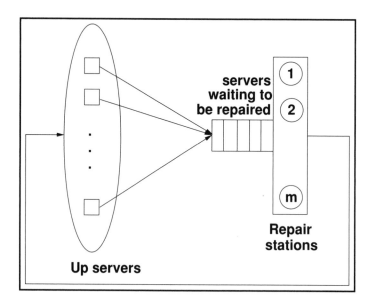

Figure 11.10. Flow of servers from up to down.

are taken or start to be repaired immediately. Once repaired, a server goes back to the set of up servers. The astute reader will recognize the similarity between this situation and the one shown on Fig. 8.16.

We will build an STD in which the state k $(k = 0, \cdots, n)$ represents the number of down servers. Transitions from state $(k-1)$ to k indicate a failure of a server and transitions from state k to $(k-1)$ represent a repaired server being placed back in operation. Let α_k, $k = 0, \cdots, n-1$, be the transition rate from state k to $(k+1)$ and μ_k, $k = 1, \cdots, n$, the transition rate from state k to $(k-1)$.

The overall failure rate, when k servers are down, i.e., $n-k$ are up, is $\alpha_k = (n-k)/\text{MTTF}$ since each of the $n-k$ up servers fail at a rate of $1/\text{MTTF}$. This is similar to our discussion of finite-population systems in Chapter 8 in which each customer stayed at the population for an average time equal to Z, the think time before arriving. Here, each server stays on average MTTF time units before "arriving" to the pool of servers to be repaired.

When $k, k \le m$, servers are down, each is repaired at a rate of $1/\text{MTTR}$, so the overall repair rate is $\mu_k = k/\text{MTTR}$. When there are more than k down servers, the overall repair rate is limited at m/MTTF. So, in summary,

$$\alpha_k = (n - k)/\text{MTTF}$$

$$\mu_k = \begin{cases} k/\text{MTTR} & k = 1, \cdots, m \\ m/\text{MTTR} & k = m + 1, \cdots, n. \end{cases} \tag{11.7.31}$$

We can think of this system as a case of finite population with variable service rate. The STD for this model is shown in Fig. 11.11.

Using the generalized system-level model presented in Section 8.5, we can compute the probability p_k that k servers are down. This results in

$$p_k = \begin{cases} p_0 \; \rho^k \begin{pmatrix} n \\ k \end{pmatrix} & k = 1, \cdots, m \\ \\ p_0 \; \rho^k \; n!/[m! \; (n - k)! \; m^{k-m}] & k = m + 1, \cdots, n \end{cases} \tag{11.7.32}$$

where ρ is defined as MTTR / MTTF and

$$p_0 = \left[\sum_{k=0}^{m} \rho^k \begin{pmatrix} n \\ k \end{pmatrix} + \frac{n!}{m!} \sum_{k=m+1}^{n} \frac{\rho^k}{(n - k)! \; m^{k-m}} \right]^{-1}. \tag{11.7.33}$$

The availability, A, of the site is the probability that at least one server is up, or in other words, one minus the probability that all of them are down. So,

$$A = 1 - p_n. \tag{11.7.34}$$

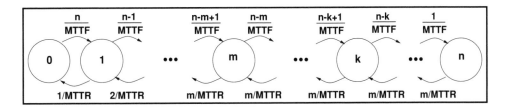

Figure 11.11. STD for number of down servers.

The average number of up nodes, $\overline{N}_{\text{up}}$, can be computed as

$$\overline{N}_{\text{up}} = \sum_{k=0}^{n-1} (n - k) \times p_k \qquad (11.7.35)$$

The equations for cluster failure and recovery are summarized in Fig 11.12 and are implemented as Visual Basic^{TM} modules in the Microsoft Excel workbook `Performability.XLS` that can be found at the book's Web site.

Definitions: $\rho = \text{MTTR}/\text{MTTF}$ and $m = $ maximum number of servers being repaired

Probability k servers are down:

$$p_k = \begin{cases} p_0 \, \rho^k \begin{pmatrix} n \\ k \end{pmatrix} & k = 1, \cdots, m \\[2em] p_0 \, \rho^k \, n!/[m! \, (n-k)! \, m^{k-m}] & k = m+1, \cdots, n \end{cases} \qquad (11.7.36)$$

$$p_0 = \left[\sum_{k=0}^{m} \rho^k \begin{pmatrix} n \\ k \end{pmatrix} + \frac{n!}{m!} \sum_{k=m+1}^{n} \frac{\rho^k}{(n-k)! \, m^{k-m}} \right]^{-1}. \qquad (11.7.37)$$

Site Availability:

$$A = 1 - p_n. \qquad (11.7.38)$$

Average Number of Up Servers:

$$\overline{N}_{\text{up}} = \sum_{k=0}^{n-1} (n - k) \times p_k \qquad (11.7.39)$$

Probability of more than k servers down:

$$\Pr\left[\text{more than } k \text{ servers are down}\right] = \sum_{j=k+1}^{n} p_j \qquad (11.7.40)$$

Figure 11.12. Formulas for server cluster failure and recovery.

Example 11.6

The designer of a Web site wants to build the site using 10 servers, but she has the choice of many different server platforms. Before making a decision, she wants to understand the impact of MTTF and MTTR on the site availability. She will only be able to repair one server at a time in case a server fails.

As we saw in the equations above, the values of the probabilities p_k depend only on the ratio ρ between MTTR and MTTF. Using the equations derived in this section with $n = 10$ and $m = 1$, we can experiment with the following values of ρ: 0.01, 0.05, 0.1, 0.2, and 0.3. Figure 11.13 shows how the probability that k nodes are down varies with k for the various values of ρ. As the value of ρ increases, the shape of the curve changes and the average number of down servers increases. Another useful way of looking at the probability distribution is to consider the *tail* of the distribution, namely

$$\Pr\left[\text{more than } k \text{ servers are down}\right] = \sum_{j=k+1}^{n} p_j \qquad (11.7.41)$$

as illustrated in Fig. 11.14. As we can see, for $\rho = 0.05$, the probability that more than two servers are down is 8% and for $\rho = 0.1$ it reaches 23%. So, a significant number of servers may be down when needed. Management has to trade the cost of a server platform, usually reflected in its MTTF, with the cost of the repair infrastructure, reflected in the MTTR.   ∎

11.7.2   Performance Analysis

We now use the results of Chapter 9 to model the site. We use a combined system- and component-level model as described in Section 9.6. This is illustrated in Fig. 11.15. The figure only shows the $n - k$ servers that are up. The arrival rate of requests to each of them is $\lambda/(n-k)$ requests/sec. If the maximum number of connections is reached, then requests are rejected.

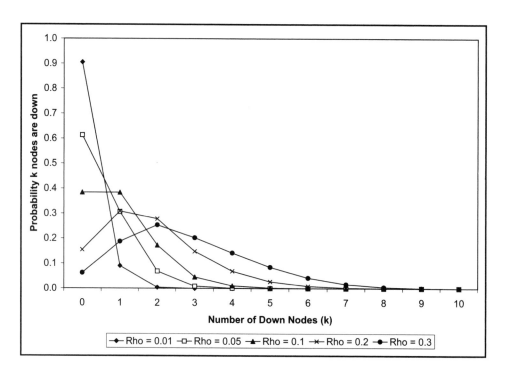

Figure 11.13. Probability that k servers are down for Ex. 11.5.

Each Web server is further decomposed into its components: the CPU and the disk. Let D_{CPU} and D_{IO} be the CPU and I/O service demands for a request at any of the Web servers. Using Mean Value Analysis (MVA) we can compute the throughput $X_0(n)$ for various values of the number of requests at each Web server. We assume that $D_{CPU} = 0.1$ sec and $D_{IO} = 0.25$ sec and obtain the following throughput values: $X_0(1) = 2.857$ req/sec, $X_0(2) = 3.590$ req/sec, $X_0(3) = 3.842$ req/sec, $X_0(4) = 3.938$ req/sec, $X_0(5) = 3.975$ req/sec, $X_0(6) = 3.990$ req/sec, $X_0(7) = 3.996$ req/sec, $X_0(8) = 3.998$ req/sec, $X_0(9) = 3.999$ req/sec, and $X_0(10) = 4.000$ req/sec.

We now use an infinite population, variable service rate, finite queue model (see Chapter 8) to compute the average response time, fraction of lost requests, and throughput of each Web server for each value of the number k of down servers using $\lambda/(n - k)$ requests/sec as the arrival rate to each

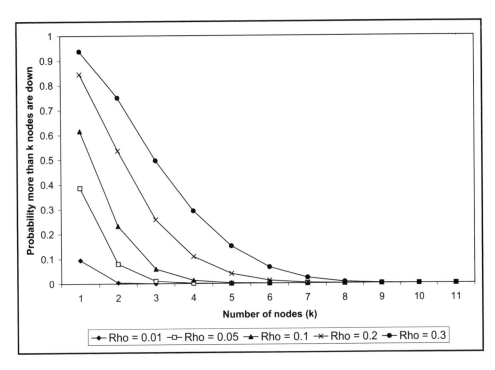

Figure 11.14. Probability that more than k servers are down for Ex. 11.5.

server. Assume that the total number of servers, n, is 10, the overall site arrival rate is $\lambda = 30$ req/sec, and that at most 10 requests can be handled simultaneously by each Web server. Table 11.3 shows the values of the arrival rate, λ_s, per server, the throughput, X_0^s, of each server, the site average response time, and the fraction of lost requests.

As we can see, performance degrades significantly as servers go down. For example, when all servers are up, only 1.7% of the requests are rejected and the average response time is below 1 second. When only one server is up ($k = 9$), then 86.7% of the requests are rejected. Those that are accepted see a response time 2.5 ($= 2.462/0.977$) higher than when all servers are up. The site throughput is equal to the overall arrival rate λ multiplied by one minus the fraction of lost requests. So, for example, when two servers are down, the site throughput is 27.9 $[= 30 \times (1 - 0.07)]$ requests/sec.

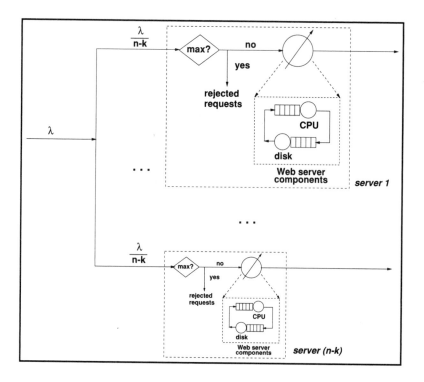

Figure 11.15. Performance model for performability example.

11.7.3 Performability Analysis

In this section we combine the results of sections 11.7.1 and 11.7.2 to compute the average response time R_{up}, fraction of lost requests F_{up}, and site throughput X_{up}, given that the site is up, i.e., given that there is at least one server up. These metrics are obtained by multplying the value of each metric for each value of k (see Table 11.3) by the probability p_k and summing these products for the values of k from 0 to $n-1$. Note that $k = n$ is not included since in this case, all servers are down. Hence,

$$R_{up} = \sum_{k=0}^{n-1} p_k \times R(k)$$

$$F_{up} = \sum_{k=0}^{n-1} p_k \times F(k)$$

Table 11.3. Performance Metrics vs. Number of Down Servers

No. Down Servers	λ_s (req/sec)	X_0^s (req/sec)	Avg. Response Time (sec)	Fraction of Lost Requests
0	3.0	2.948	0.977	1.7%
1	3.3	3.216	1.136	3.5%
2	3.8	3.488	1.342	7.0%
3	4.3	3.724	1.587	13.1%
4	5.0	3.885	1.840	22.3%
5	6.0	3.965	2.060	33.9%
6	7.5	3.992	2.224	46.8%
7	10.0	3.998	2.335	60.0%
8	15.0	3.999	2.409	73.3%
9	30.0	4.000	2.462	86.7%

$$X_{\text{up}} = \sum_{k=0}^{n-1} p_k \times (n-k) \times X_s(k) \qquad (11.7.42)$$

where $R(k), F(k)$, and $X_s(k)$ are the response time, fraction of lost requests, and server throughput for a given value of k.

Using MTTF = 200 hours and MTTR = 8 hours (i.e., a value of $\rho = 8/200 = 0.04$) for the 10 servers, we obtain the following values of p_k according to Eqs. (11.7.32) and (11.7.33): $p_0 = 0.6224$, $p_1 = 0.2489$, $p_2 = 0.0896$, $p_3 = 0.0287$, $p_4 = 0.0080$, $p_5 = 0.0019$, $p_6 = 0.0004$, $p_7 = 6.2 \times 10^{-5}$, $p_8 = 7.4 \times 10^{-6}$, $p_9 = 5.9 \times 10^{-7}$, and $p_{10} = 2.4 \times 10^{-8}$.

We can now combine performance and availability as in Eq. (11.7.42) and obtain the following results: $R_{\text{up}} = 1.08$ sec, $F_{\text{up}} = 3.2\%$, and $X_{\text{up}} = 29.03$ requests/sec.

11.8   Software Aging and Rejuvenation

It has been reported recently that software systems degrade with time due to many different causes such as memory bloating and leaking, unterminated processes or threads, unreleased file or database locks, data corruption, storage space fragmentation, and accumulation of round-off errors [4, 8]. This phenomenon is called *software aging*. Software aging tends to be more pronounced at higher load levels and may lead to software system performance degradation and, ultimately, to software crashes.

To counter this effect, a technique called *software rejuvenation* has been proposed [8]. This technique involves stopping the software regularly to restore its initial state after some "clean-up." Cleaning-up may involve doing garbage collection, flushing buffers to disk, and reinitializing internal data structures [4]. A more radical approach of software rejuvenation is a system reboot. Software rejuvenation can be thought as preventive maintenance and is quite useful to increase the availability of server clusters in which servers in the cluster can be rejuvenated one at a time [8].

Let us use the state transition diagrams of Chapter 8 to study the effect of software aging and rejuvenation on the availability of server clusters. Let us first consider one of the servers of a server cluster. Assume that the software system of the server may be in one of three states:

- Robust (r): In this state, the software is functioning at its best possible performance.

- Degraded (d): Here, the software has accumulated enough problems over time that it is functioning at a much less than optimal performance.

- Down (w): In this state, the software stopped working entirely.

Figure 11.16 shows the STD for the software system of a server. The system can go from the robust state into the degraded state through software

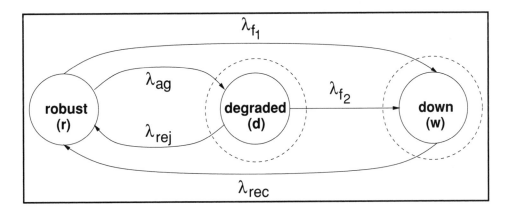

Figure 11.16. STD for software aging and rejuvenation.

aging at a rate of λ_{ag}. Once in the degraded mode, the system may be rejuvenated and return to the robust state at the rate of λ_{rej} or it may fail, i.e., go to the down state at a rate of λ_{f_2}. Once in the down state, the system may recover and go to the robust state at the rate of λ_{rec}. Finally, the system may also fail when in the robust state at a rate of λ_{f_1}.

We want to obtain the probabilities p_r, p_d and p_w that the system is at the states robust, degraded, and down, respectively. We use our well-known *flow-in-flow-out* principle at the boundaries indicated by the dashed lines in Fig. 11.16 along with the fact that the sum of all three probabilities is equal to one to obtain the following equations.

$$\lambda_{ag} \times p_r = (\lambda_{f_2} + \lambda_{rej}) \times p_d \qquad (11.8.43)$$

$$\lambda_{f_1} \times p_r + \lambda_{f_2} \times p_d = \lambda_{rec} \times p_w \qquad (11.8.44)$$

$$p_r + p_d + p_w = 1 \qquad (11.8.45)$$

Equation (11.8.43) gives us

$$p_r = \frac{\lambda_{f_2} + \lambda_{rej}}{\lambda_{ag}} \times p_d. \qquad (11.8.46)$$

Combining Eqs. (11.8.44) and (11.8.46) we obtain

$$p_w = \frac{1}{\lambda_{rec}} \left[\lambda_{f_2} + \frac{\lambda_{f_1} (\lambda_{f_2} + \lambda_{rej})}{\lambda_{ag}} \right] \times p_d. \qquad (11.8.47)$$

Using Eqs. (11.8.45), (11.8.46), and (11.8.47), we obtain the value for p_d as

$$p_d = \left[1 + \frac{\lambda_{f_2} + \lambda_{rej}}{\lambda_{ag}} + \frac{1}{\lambda_{rec}} \left[\lambda_{f_2} + \frac{\lambda_{f_1} (\lambda_{f_2} + \lambda_{rej})}{\lambda_{ag}} \right] \right]^{-1} \qquad (11.8.48)$$

Since p_r and p_w are given in terms of p_d in Eqs. (11.8.46) and (11.8.47), we have the three probabilities that we were looking for. The availability of each server, A_s can be given as $A_s = 1 - p_w$ if both robust and degraded mode are considered as acceptable by management. However, if degraded mode is not considered as acceptable, one could use the more conservative definition of availability as $A_s = p_r$.

We now use some numbers to provide some insight into these formulas summarized in Fig. 11.17 and implemented in the Microsoft Excel `Software-Aging.XLS` workbook that can be found at the book's Web site.

Consider that the software aging rate λ_{ag} is 1/240 per hour, i.e., software will transition from robust to degraded mode every 240 hours on average. The average failure rate from the robust state, λ_{f_1}, is 1/720 per hour and the failure rate from the degraded mode, λ_{f_2} is ten times higher than λ_{f_1}. The

---

Probability (p_d) software in degraded mode:

$$p_d = \left[1 + \frac{\lambda_{f_2} + \lambda_{rej}}{\lambda_{ag}} + \frac{1}{\lambda_{rec}} \left[\lambda_{f_2} + \frac{\lambda_{f_1} (\lambda_{f_2} + \lambda_{rej})}{\lambda_{ag}} \right] \right]^{-1} \qquad (11.8.49)$$

Probability (p_r) software in robust mode:

$$p_r = \frac{\lambda_{f_2} + \lambda_{rej}}{\lambda_{ag}} \times p_d. \qquad (11.8.50)$$

Probability (p_w) software is down:

$$p_w = \frac{1}{\lambda_{rec}} \left[\lambda_{f_2} + \frac{\lambda_{f_1} (\lambda_{f_2} + \lambda_{rej})}{\lambda_{ag}} \right] \times p_d \qquad (11.8.51)$$

Figure 11.17. Software aging and rejuvenation equations.

recovery rate, λ_{rec}, is 2/hour, i.e., it takes on average 1/2 hour to recover. These values are inspired on the values reported in [8].

Figure 11.18 shows how the fraction of time the system is in degraded mode, p_d, varies with the average software rejuvenation interval, i.e., the inverse of the software rejuvenation rate λ_{rej}. According to the figure, if the software is rejuvenated, maybe by a reboot, every 10 hours, it will be in degraded mode 3.5% of the time. On the other hand, if the average rejuvenation interval is 50 hours, the system will be in degraded mode for 10.9% of the time. Site managers can use the equations in this section to determine how often software should be rejuvenated according to their levels of tolerance to degraded performance.

Let us now examine how we can apply the formulas above to a server

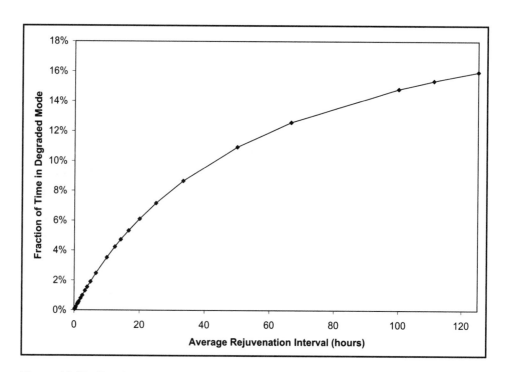

Figure 11.18. Fraction of time in degraded mode vs. average software rejuvenation interval (hours).

cluster used to support a Web site through the following example.

Example 11.7

A high-quality Web site considers that a server is available only when it is delivering its best possible performance, in other words, when it is in robust state. Using the same values for the transition rates $\lambda_{ag}, \lambda_{f_1}, \lambda_{f_2}$, and λ_{rec} used in Fig. 11.18, what is the minimum number of servers needed in the cluster to obtain an overall reliability for the site of 99.999% if the average software rejuvenation interval is 25 hours?

Using the equations derived in this section, we obtain that the reliability of each server, given as p_r, is 0.9271699. Using Eq. (11.5.18) we can compute the minimum number of servers as

$$
\begin{aligned}
n_{min} &= \left\lceil \frac{\ln(1 - 0.99999)}{\ln(1 - p_r)} \right\rceil \\
&= \left\lceil \frac{\ln 0.00001}{\ln(1 - 0.9271699)} \right\rceil \\
&= \left\lceil \frac{-11.51}{\ln 0.0728} \right\rceil = \left\lceil \frac{-11.51}{-2.62} \right\rceil = \lceil 4.39 \rceil = 5 \text{ servers} \quad (11.8.52)
\end{aligned}
$$

If we doubled the software rejuvenation interval to 50 hours, we would need six instead of five servers. ∎

Vaidyanathan et. al. propose and analyze, using Stochastic Reward Nets, two different software rejuvenation policies: time-based, which rejuvenates software at regular intervals regardless of its state, and predictive based policies, in which rejuvenation only takes place when a server transitions into degrade mode, which is what we analyzed [8]. They also discuss an implementation of these policies in the form of Software Rejuvenation Agent (SRA) that monitors consumable resources and estimates the time to exhaustion of these resources. Examples of exhaustible resources for Windows operating systems include memory management counters such as available bytes, committed bytes, non-paged pool, paged pool, handles, threads, semaphores, mutexes, and logical disk utilization. For Linux operating systems, the agent collects equivalent parameters such as memory utilization, swap space, file descriptors, and i-nodes.

11.8.1   Load-Dependent Software Aging Rate

The analysis presented so far assumed that the software aging rate does not depend on the load on the server. In some situations, the higher the load, the faster the aging process is. We could envision using a software aging rate function of the form

$$\lambda_{\text{ag}} = C \times (\overline{n}_s)^a \times \lambda_{\text{ag}}^i \tag{11.8.53}$$

where C and a ($a \geq 0$), are constants, $\overline{n}_s$ is the average number of requests at a server, and λ_{ag}^i is the load-independent software aging rate. Note that when $C = 1$ and $a = 0$ we get the special case of a load-independent aging rate. The solution to this type of situation requires solving a fixed-point equation using the iterative method described in what follows.

- Step 1 (initialization): Set $\lambda_{\text{ag}} = \lambda_{\text{ag}}^i$.

- Step 2: Use the equations in Fig. 11.17 to compute the probabilities p_r, p_d, and p_w.

- Step 3: Set MTTR $= 1/\lambda_{\text{rec}}$ and

$$\text{MTTF} = p_r \times \frac{1}{\lambda_{\text{f}_1}} + p_d \times \frac{1}{\lambda_{\text{f}_2}}. \tag{11.8.54}$$

- Step 4: Use equations in Fig. 11.12 to compute the probability p_k that k servers are down and compute the average arrival rate of requests per server as

$$\overline{\lambda}_s = \sum_{k=0}^{n-1} \frac{\lambda}{n-k} \times p_k. \tag{11.8.55}$$

and use a performance model for the server to compute $\overline{n}_s$ given $\overline{\lambda}_s$.

- Step 5: Compute

$$\lambda_{\text{ag}} = C \times (\overline{n}_s)^a \times \lambda_{\text{ag}}^i \tag{11.8.56}$$

- Step 6 (convergence test): If the relative error in successive values of λ_{ag} is less than a given tolerance stop, otherwise go to Step 2.

Table 11.4 illustrates the iteration process just discussed. The values for λ_{rej}, λ_{f_1}, λ_{f_2}, and λ_{rec} are the same used to generate Fig. 11.18. Other values used in the table are $C = 1$, $a = 1.5$, and $n = 10$. For simplicity in this example, we modeled each server as in infinite population, service rate fixed at 0.8 requests/sec, and infinite queue. At iteration number 4, the percent absolute error in the value of λ_{ag} is negligible, namely 0.000003%.

11.9 Concluding Remarks

In this chapter we saw that availability and reliability are important metrics that define the quality of the service provided by Web and e-commerce sites. The so-called site "brown-outs" may cost millions of dollars to the site depending on the extent of their duration. Performance is also very highly correlated to availability since it is quite usual for things to break when they are stretched. For example, it is not uncommon for software to exhibit degraded performance as traffic increases due to an increase in the use of exhaustible resources such as memory, number of threads, and table entries.

Other metrics of availability for giant-scale services have been proposed.

Table 11.4. Iterations for Load-Dependent Software Aging Rate

It. No.	λ_{ag} (1/hr)	p_r	p_d	MTTF (hrs)	$\overline{\lambda}_s$ (req/sec)	$\overline{n}_s$
0	0.0041667	0.998610	0.000692	719.0488991	1.000778164	4.015612
1	0.0335287	0.993731	0.005540	715.8853469	1.000781628	4.012545
2	0.0334903	0.993738	0.005534	715.8894641	1.000781623	4.015682
3	0.0335295	0.993731	0.005540	715.8852535	1.000781628	4.015682
4	0.0335295	0.993731	0.005540	715.8852533	1.000781628	4.015682

One of them, called *yield*, is defined as the ratio between the number of completed queries and the number of submitted queries [1]. This metric stresses the fact that not all seconds are equal. It is much worse for a system to go down when a large number of queries are being submitted than when traffic is very light. Another metric provided in [1], called *harvest* of a query, is defined as the ratio between the data returned by the query and the total amount of data that would have been returned if all the database nodes of the site were available.

We provided a quantitative analysis of the issues of availability, reliability, performability, and software aging and rejuvenation. We relied in the most part on the state transition diagram techniques presented in Chapter 8 to derive the formulas presented here. These formulas are implemented in the Microsoft Excel workbooks `Availability.XLS`, `Performability.XLS`, and `SoftwareAging.XLS`, which can be found at the book's Web site.

Bibliography

[1] E. A. Brewer, "Lessons from Giant-Scale Services," *IEEE Internet Computing*, July/Aug. 2001, pp. 46–55.

[2] J. Gray, "Dependability in the Internet Era," Presentation at the *High Dependability Computing Consortium* meeting, May 7, 2001, http://research.microsoft.com/~gray/talks

[3] J. Gray, "FT 101," Presentation at University of California at Berkeley, Nov. 11, 2000, http://research.microsoft.com/~gray/talks

[4] Y. Huang, N. Kolettis, and N. D. Fulton, "Software Rejuvenation: Analysis, Module and Applications," *Proc. 25th Symp. Fault Tolerant Computer Systems*, Pasadena, California, June 1995, pp. 381–390.

[5] D. E. Long, A. Muir, and R. Golding, "A Longitudinal Survey of Internet Host Reliability," HP Labs Technical Report HPL-CCD-95-4, Feb. 1995.

[6] D. Patterson, "New Challenges for the Post-PC Era," University of California at Berkeley, April 2001, www.cs.berkeley.edu

[7] K. S. Trivedi, *Probability & Statistics with Reliability, Queuing, and Computer Science Applications*, Prentice Hall, Upper Saddle River, 1982.

[8] K. Vaidyanathan, R. Harper, S. W. Hunter, and K. S. Trivedi, "Analysis and Implementation of Software Rejuvenation in Cluster Systems," *Proc. Joint Intl. Conf. Measurement and Modeling of Computer Syst.*, ACM Sigmetrics and IFIP WG 7.3, Cambridge, Massachusetts, June 16-20, 2001, pp. 62–71.

Chapter 12

Workload Forecasting

12.1 Introduction

Forecasting is the art and science of predicting future events. It has been extensively used in many areas, such as the financial market, climate studies, and production and operations management [10]. For example, one could forecast the number and type of employees, volume and type of production, product demand, volume and destination of products. In the Internet, demand forecasting is essential for guaranteeing quality of service (QoS). It is critical for the operation of Web services. Let us consider the following scenario.

*Unprecedented demand for the newest product slows Web servers
to a crawl. The company servers were overwhelmed on Monday
as a torrent of customers attempted to download the company's
new software product. Web services, in terms of responsiveness
and speed, started degrading as more and more customers tried to
access the service. And it is clear that many frustrated customers
simply stopped trying.*

This undesirable scenario emphasizes the importance of good forecasting
and planning for online environments.

A good forecast is more than just a single number; it is a set of scenarios
and assumptions. Time plays a key role in the forecasting process. The
longer the time horizon, the less accurate the forecast will be. Forecasting
horizons can be grouped into the following classes: short-term (e.g., less than
three months), intermediate-term (e.g., from three months to one year), and
long-term (e.g., more than two years). Demand forecasting in the Web can
be illustrated by typical questions that come up very often during the course
of capacity planning projects. Can we forecast the number of visitors to the
company's Web site in order to plan the adequate capacity to support the
load? What is the expected workload for the credit card authorization service
during the Christmas season? How will the number of messages processed by
the e-mail servers vary over the next year? Implementation of Web services
should rely on a careful planning process, i.e., a planning process that pays
attention to performance and capacity right from the beginning. Planning
the capacity of Web services requires a series of steps to be followed in a
systematic way. One of its key steps is workload forecasting, which predicts
how system workloads will vary over time. The goal of this chapter is to
show how to apply existing forecasting methods and techniques to predict
the future workload for Web services.

12.2   Why Workloads Change?

Before discussing the available forecasting techniques, let us first examine
why the workload changes. Workloads may change in various ways. Let us

take the example of e-mail traffic. It expands along three different dimensions: the number of users, the number of messages per user, and the size of messages. Compounding the problem is the fact that the three dimensions expand at different growth rates. For instance, in company X, management has observed a threefold increase in the number of messages, but the size of the messages went up twenty times in the same period of time, because of attached graphics. Web workloads and traditional workloads change in different ways. Let us see how.

12.2.1   Traditional Workloads

Workloads change; they may grow or shrink, depending on prospective business and technology evolution. Workload growth comes primarily from the following sources: new applications, increase in the volume of transactions and requests processed by existing applications, and enhancements of the application environment. Information technology moves fast. And so do the applications required by companies and users. New database management systems, new security software systems, new multimedia software, and new versions of operating systems are examples of software resources frequently incorporated to old systems. Usually, new software systems demand additional resources from servers, desktops, and networks; they increase the demand on system resources. Workload growth is also correlated with marketing and sales promotions and overall economic factors. In corporate environments, the number of users and other factors that influence the workload are somehow controlled and can be estimated with some degree of accuracy [3].

12.2.2   Web Workloads

It is often said that everything changes so rapidly on the Internet that it is impossible to forecast far into the future [1]. In considering prospects for future workload, one approach is simply looking at the historical data. For example, since the Internet has been growing at about 100% a year for its entire history, one could use this observation to extrapolate the growth rate into the future, and predict that traffic will continue to double each year. But this simple assumption would hardly work for specific Web services. Workload variation on the Web is a complex phenomenon, influenced by factors such as unanticipated publicity and by propagation mechanisms such as word-of-mouth. Due to the nature of propagation on the Web, it is difficult to predict the points in time at which peaks will occur. This problem refers to the *unpredictable demand*, which is a portion of the workload that shows up at random times and takes up all of the system capacity. This situation occurs in many Web services. For example, an unpredictable stock market crash can generate a huge increase in traffic to sites with financial news and analysis. It also spurs traffic spikes in the LANs of companies involved with the stock market. The hundred of millions of host computers and users in the Internet create conditions for unexpected peaks of workloads. For practical purposes, it is valuable to predict the magnitude of possible peak workloads even when its timing cannot be predicted. That helps Web service management prepare for contingencies. Providing high-level QoS during peak periods matters. Companies do not want to lose customers or business that arrive at busy times.

In Web-based environments, workload planning and forecasting play important roles. Businesses must meet customers' expectations in terms of the quality of the service delivered. If the Web site is slow, due to poor capacity or overload, customers may not return. Choices on the Web are numerous and customers can easily switch from one site to another. It is obvious that in online environments, performance problems must be anticipated. And a key step to avoid problems is to forecast the workload and plan the adequate service capacity.

12.3   Forecasting Strategy

In this section, we discuss ways of approaching the workload forecasting problem. Forecasting approaches can be grouped into two categories: quantitative and qualitative. The former relies on the existence of historical data to estimate future values of the workload parameters. The qualitative approach is a subjective process, based on judgments, intuition, expert opinions, historical analogy, commercial knowledge, and any other relevant information. Qualitative forecasting plays an important role in forecasting situations in unstable environments or when little or no historical data is available.

There are methods to handle qualitative forecasting, such as group averaging, group consensus and the Delphi method [10]. Electronic questionnaires, on-line interviews and surveys over the Internet are useful tools for obtaining forecasting information. The Delphi method takes the best judgment estimate from experts concerning some medium-term or long-range events. Then, a process of seeking consensus among the experts is repeated several times to narrow down the initial forecast. As a final result, the Delphi method yields a consensus forecast for future events. Clearly, the difficulty associated with obtaining accurate forecasts from history is the relationship between the future and the past when technological paradigms change at an accelerated pace. For instance, let us take a look at P2P file-sharing systems, such as Gnutella. With Gnutella, file transfer is accomplished via HTTP. Thus, the relation between Gnutella and the Web is simple: Gnutella hosts can be viewed as Web sites, albeit transient ones, and downloading a file from a Gnutella host is technically equivalent to fetching a file from a Web site. This would be equivalent to running a Web server each time you started your browser. P2P applications will effectively turn the traditional consumer PCs into Internet servers which will output large amounts of traffic to other users. The proliferation of this type of users may lead to changes in bandwidth requirements for ISPs and institutions (e.g., universities), especially since the uplink is the one that invariably has the more limited bandwidth [14]. So, it is evident that workload forecasting should take into account qualitative issues, such as technological forecasting. A workload forecasting strategy should combine both quantitative and qualitative approaches, as shown in Fig. 12.1.

The main activities involved in setting up a workload forecasting strategy are:

- *Forecasting Objectives:* Workload forecasting is one of the phases of

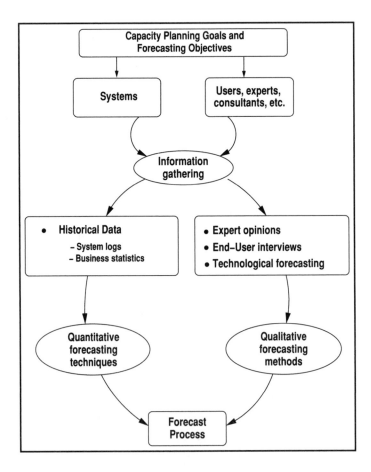

Figure 12.1. Forecasting strategy.

capacity planning. Therefore, the objectives of the forecasting phase are implicitly determined by the goals of the capacity planning project. The purpose of forecasting and decisions taken from it are critical for the definition of the forecasting strategy. What is the desired forecast span, that is, the time horizon for which forecasting is to be performed? How is the forecast to be used? What is the criticality (e.g., cost and expected benefits) of the decisions to be made on top of the forecast workload? These are typical questions that help one establish the objectives of the forecasting phase.

- *Qualitative Forecasting:* Capacity planning projects need medium-range and long-term directions for information technology. Technological forecasting can help predict how the workload will change as a function of future developments of technology.

- *Historical Data:* In selecting the forecasting strategy, one has to look at the several sources of historical data. For example, if the workload is described in business-oriented terms (e.g., number of orders), business statistics should be obtained. On the other hand, if the workload is characterized in terms of resource usage (e.g., processor time), then system logs should be the main source of historical data.

- *Forecasting Process:* Several criteria can be used for selecting forecasting techniques. The first one refers to the forecast span (e.g., short-range, medium-range, and long-term). Other criteria concern the availability of historical data, the data pattern, and the desired accuracy.

- *Forecasting Validation:* Before performing the forecasting, the selected technique should be validated on the available data. This can be done using only part of the historical data to exercise the model. The remaining data, which correspond to actual values, can then be compared to the forecast values to assess the accuracy of the method.

12.4   Forecasting Process

In this step, we discuss how Web workload forecast should be performed. The ultimate goal of a forecasting process is to determine the parameters of the estimated workload for the planning horizon. Characterization parameters can be divided into two groups: component and load intensity. The former describes the service demands required by a component of a class (e.g., request, transaction, command, or job). The second group indicates the load placed on the several platforms of the Web systems (e.g., client desktops, networks, servers, proxies, etc.) by a workload class. Table 12.1 summarizes the modeling parameters that characterize a class of a workload.

Several practical problems are commonly faced by a capacity planner during the forecasting phase. First, it is difficult to obtain reliable information from users when they have to deal with terms they do not quite understand. Workload parameters are too vague for the end-user community. It is also hard to obtain resource usage information of new systems that have not been completely developed yet. Demands for new distributed applications are specially difficult to predict, because each application is unique in terms of its configuration and workload. A framework for obtaining service demands for distributed systems under development is shown in [11]. Forecasting data and information for applications in production come from

Table 12.1. Class Parameters; λ is the Arrival Rate, M is the Number of Customers, and Z the Think Time

Class			Parameter
Type	Component		
Open	Transaction	Demands	λ
Closed	Interaction	Demands	M and Z
Closed	Service	Demands	M

system logs and from the users. Hence, the first step in the workload forecasting process is to consult the business and user community to find out what are the estimates for the workload growth. This process implies in obtaining answers to questions such as:

- What will be the peak number of simultaneous customers next year?

- What will be the arrival rate of trivial transactions of the checking account application?

- What will be the daily number of page views to the company's Web site six months from now?

- What will be the average size of e-mails by the end of next year?

Answers to the above questions should then be converted to the typical workload parameters, shown in Table 12.1. The major problem in contacting users is the nature of the information required by the workload forecasting process. The kind of information shown in Table 12.1 has nothing to do with the user world. Most users do not want to know what is behind the screen of their desktop. One can easily imagine the perplexity of a user trying to answer a question about the amount of bandwidth that his/her Web transactions will demand next year. It is clear that alternative ways should be used to obtain quantitative information on future workloads.

Let us examine an approach that uses business-related information to predict workload growth. In most Web services, some applications or functions account for the majority of the system resource usage. With direct relation to the business of a company, these applications perform functions such as search, browse, and login. The amount of system resources (e.g., Web server, database server, and network) required by these applications can be associated with quantifiable business variables, called key volume indicator (KVI), natural business unit (NBU), or forecasting business units (FBU) [4]. They provide a good indication of the volume of activity of a business or function as illustrated in Table 12.2.

Table 12.2. Natural Business Units

Service	Key Volume Indicator (KVI)
E-mail	Number of accounts
Electronic retailer	Number of concurrent customers
Telemarketing	Number of calls
Portal	Number of concurrent users
Economic news site	Number of registered users
Online traders	Number of shares traded

12.4.1 Workload Forecasting Models

Characterization and forecasting of Web workloads can be accomplished at many levels: business level, user level, application level, protocol level, and resource level. A Web workload can be viewed in a multi-layer hierarchical way, as shown in Fig. 12.2. Relationships can be established among different layers of the hierarchical model. For example, based on business perspectives, one can estimate the number of daily user sessions for six months from now. Using relations such as the average session length and visit ratios to specific functions, the capacity planner analyst can translate sessions into HTTP requests, which can be converted to service demands.

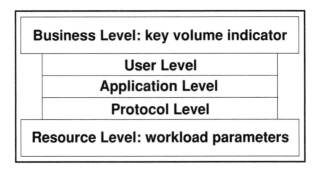

Figure 12.2. Hierarchical forecasting model.

Workload forecasting can be performed at the five layers of the hierarchical model, by either using intra-layer relationships through *causal models* or *trend models* at a given layer. In a model, the predicted variable is called dependent or response variable and the others used to forecast the value are known as independent or predictor variables. In the case of causal models, workload forecast is performed using data from different levels as the dependent variable. The causal model uses business indicators as independent variables and workload parameters as dependent variables. Once the relationship between the independent and the dependent variables is determined, one can try to control the dependent variable. For instance, suppose that a system administrator finds that there is a significant relationship between the number of e-mail accounts and the number of messages sent and received per day. Thus, a regression model can be used to estimate the future number of e-mail messages per day (i.e., the arrival rate) as a function of the number of e-mail accounts. Trend models forecast a single workload variable as a function of time, using historical data and assuming that the past trend will continue into the future. A trend model forecasts a workload descriptor as a function of time, based only on historical data of the descriptor. In the same example, the future message arrival rates could be obtained through a forecasting technique that uses as input data the arrival rates recorded in the e-mail server logs for the recent past.

Let us return to the example of the e-mail message application. As we saw earlier in this chapter, the e-mail workload varies along the following three dimensions: the number of users, the number of messages, and the size of the messages. It has also been noted that the three dimensions expand at different rates of growth. Therefore, if we concentrate our estimate on a single dimension of the problem, important aspects may be missed. Suppose that in addition to the increase in the number of messages, it was observed that the size of the messages increased 10 times in the same period of time because of attached files. As a consequence, two workload parameters will change. The arrival rate changes as a function of the number of messages processed, and the service demand also increases, because larger messages consume more resources to be processed. The important issue here is that the forecasting process should not be restricted to one specific parameter; it should cover all parameters that characterize the different demands of a workload.

12.4.2   A Business-Oriented Methodology

Business-oriented forecasting methodologies assume that the volume of business activity (e.g., KVI) of a Web service may be related to demands for system resources. Management estimate the computing and communication needs in terms of business units, which are then converted to some form of resource requirements (e.g., server processor time, server I/O operations, and bandwidth). The basic steps involved in workload forecasting by using business indicators are [12, 13]:

- Select the Web service demands to be forecast. Look for the business-critical services or the few major services that account for most of the utilization of Web resources. All other applications or services should be lumped together for forecasting purposes.

- Identify the business units associated with the services whose growth will be forecast. For example, the number of orders placed by customers is a good business unit for an order-entry application of an electronic retailer.

- Collect statistics concerning the chosen business units. In the case of an electronic retailer, obtain the rate of orders placed by customers during the periods of interest.

- Summarize the statistics (e.g., resource usage, number of transactions and number of Web requests) of the selected services. In particular, look at periods with heavy demands.

- Translate business units into resource demands. For example, divide the resource usage (e.g., server processor time) in the selected time window by the number of orders processed in the same period. The result is an estimate of the amount of resources (e.g., processor service demand) required by the application server to handle a customer order.

- Forecast the future resource demand as a function of the business units. In the example of an order-entry system, one should use a forecasting technique to estimate the growth in the number of customer orders— the business unit. For example, based on customer behavior model graphs (see Chapter 6), the analyst is able to estimate the number and type of transactions that are associated with a given rate of orders placed by customers. Using some kind of translation technique, the capacity planner should be able to relate the future number of orders to the future workload demand.

12.5   Forecasting Techniques

The literature [5, 6, 10] describes several forecasting techniques. In selecting one, some factors need to be considered. The first one is the availability and reliability of historical data. The degree of accuracy and the planning horizon are also factors that determine the forecasting technique. The pattern found in historical data has a strong influence on the choice of the technique. The nature of historical data may be determined through visual inspection of a plot of the data as a function of time. As displayed in Fig. 12.3, three patterns of historical data can be sharply identified: random, trend, and seasonal. While the trend pattern reflects a workload that tends to increase (or decrease, in some cases), seasonal patterns show the presence of fluctuations. Stationary patterns do not show any sign of systematic increase or decrease. For a stationary series of data, the mean value is a constant and the autocorrelation function is dependent only upon the time displacement. The underlying hypothesis of forecasting techniques is that the information to be forecast is somehow directly related to historical data; this empha-

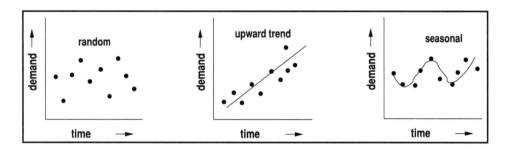

Figure 12.3. Historical data patterns.

sizes the importance of knowing the pattern of historical data. Let us now examine in detail some forecasting methods. There are many commercial packages (e.g., Matlab [9], S-PLUS [2], Microsoft Excel [6]) that perform various methods of forecasting techniques.

12.5.1   Regression Methods

The problem is to predict the value of a random variable Y_t that is generated by an unknown process. For example, suppose that Y_t is the number of simultaneous users at a newspaper site at period of time t. Let $Y_1, Y_2, ..., Y_t$ be the time series that represent the observed values for the number of simultaneous users during periods $1, 2, \cdots, t$. A function $f(\bullet)$ can be developed to describe Y_t:

$$Y_t = f(\bullet) + \epsilon_t$$

where ϵ_t is the error term. The mathematical relationship established between these variables can take many forms. Regression models are used to estimate the value of a variable as a function of several other variables. As we saw earlier, the predicted variable is called dependent variable and the others used to forecast the value are known as independent variables. In the case of causal models, data from sources other than the series being predicted are used. If Y is the event to be forecast and $X_1, X_2, ..., X_n$ are the n variables we believe to be related to Y, then a causal model is represented by the following expression:

$$Y = f(X_1, X_2, ..., X_n).$$

The following sections present ways of computing forecast errors as well as the most commonly used functions to represent relationships between the dependent variable and the independent variables [5].

12.5.1.1   Forecast Error

Error indicators are a way to judge how good a forecast model is. The forecast error for period t is given by $\epsilon_t = Y_t - F_t$, which is the difference between the actual value and the estimated value for period t. The mean error (ME) for n periods of evaluation is given by:

$$ME = \frac{\sum_{t=1}^{n}(Y_t - F_t)}{n} \qquad (12.5.1)$$

The mean of the squared errors (MSE) is given by

$$MSE = \frac{\sum_{t=1}^{n}(Y_t - F_t)^2}{n}. \qquad (12.5.2)$$

The sum of the squared errors, denoted by SSE, is given by:

$$SSE = \sum_{t=1}^{n} \epsilon_t^2 = \sum_{t=1}^{n}(Y_t - F_t)^2$$

12.5.2   Linear Regression

This section presents the simple linear regression analysis used to determine the linear relationship between two variables. The general equation for the regression line is

$$Y = a + b X \qquad (12.5.3)$$

where Y is the dependent variable, X the independent variable, a the y-intercept, and b is the slope of the line that represents the linear relationship between the two variables. The *method of least squares* determines the values of a and b that minimize the sum of the squares of the errors. The regression parameters that minimize

$$\sum_{t=1}^{n}(Y_t - F_t)^2 = \sum_{t=1}^{n}[Y_t - (a + b\,X_t)]^2 \qquad (12.5.4)$$

are

$$b = \frac{n\sum_{t=1}^{n} X_t Y_t - (\sum_{t=1}^{n} X_t)(\sum_{t=1}^{n} Y_t)}{n\sum_{t=1}^{n} X_t^2 - (\sum_{t=1}^{n} X_t)^2} \qquad (12.5.5)$$

$$a = \bar{Y} - b\bar{X} \qquad (12.5.6)$$

where (X_t, Y_t), for $(t = 1, \cdots, n)$, are the coordinates of the n observed data points, $\bar{Y} = (\sum_{t=1}^{n} Y_t)/n$, and $\bar{X} = (\sum_{t=1}^{n} X_t)/n$.

12.5.2.1   The Coefficient of Determination

A particularly useful statistic is the coefficient of determination called R^2. It represents the proportion of variation in the dependent variable that has been explained or accounted for by the regression line. This R^2 indicator ranges in value from 0 to 1 and reveals how closely the estimated y-values correlate to your actual y-values. A coefficient of determination of zero indicates that none of the variation in Y is explained by the regression equation, whereas a coefficient close to 1 indicates that the regression equation is very useful in accurately predicting a Y-value. The coefficient of determination can be computed as

$$R^2 = \frac{\sum_{t=1}^{n}(F_t - \bar{Y})^2}{\sum_{t=1}^{n}(Y_t - \bar{Y})^2}. \qquad (12.5.7)$$

Example 12.1

In many organizations, e-mail is considered a mission-critical application because of its ability to speed up communications. In portal $\mathcal{X}$, e-mail is one of the most heavily used applications. In order to keep the expected level of service, e-mail volume, measured in number of messages, is constantly monitored. In particular, management is concerned about the heaviest periods of e-mail traffic. Table 12.3 displays the e-mail traffic for the peak minute of the past weeks. The goal is to know in advance what will be the number of messages per minute peak for the next few weeks. Let us examine the development of a simple linear regression model to forecast the number of mail messages during the peak minute. The number of messages represents the dependent variable (Y) and the week the independent variable (X). From the data of Table 12.3, we have: $n = 8$, $\sum_{i=1}^{n} x_i y_i = 17{,}080$, $\sum_{i=1}^{n} x_i = 36$, $\sum_{i=1}^{n} y_i = 3{,}663$, $\sum_{i=1}^{n} x_i^2 = 204$, $\left(\sum_{i=1}^{n} x_i\right)^2 = 1{,}296$, $b = 14.20$, and $a = 393.96$. The expression for the linear relationship between the week (X) and the message per minute peak (Y) is $Y = 393.96 + 14.20\,X$, as shown in Fig. 12.4. Thus, we can forecast the number of mail messages during the peak minute for new values of X. For example, the next week is 9, so the forecast number of mail messages per minute is $Y = 393.96 + 14.20 \times 9 = 521.76$. In order to assess how good is the linear regression function, we calculate the coefficient of determination, which is $R^2 = 0.855$.   ∎

Example 12.2

Now, management wants to analyze the growth of the e-mail message system from a different perspective. It has been observed that there is a

Table 12.3. Mail Messages During the Peak Minute

Week	Messages Per Minute Peak
1	420
2	410
3	437
4	467
5	448
6	460
7	507
8	514

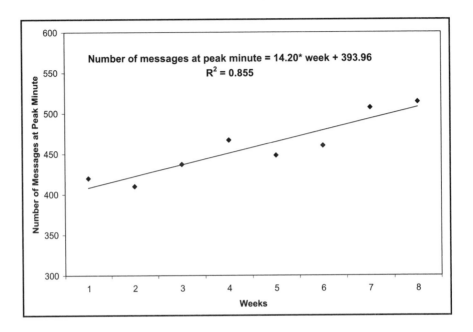

Figure 12.4. Mail messages per peak minute.

relationship between the average hourly number of concurrent logins and the number of e-mail messages sent and received during the hour. The statistics collected during the past eight months are shown in Table 12.4. The objective is to estimate the number of messages sent and received during an hour when the number of concurrent logins reaches 4,000. To answer this question, we use a causal model in which the independent variable is the number of concurrent logins and the dependent variable represents the number of messages sent and received.

$$\text{MessagesSentAndReceived} \; = \; f(\text{ConcurrentLogins})$$

To obtain the function f, we develop a linear regression based on the criterion that minimizes the sum of squared errors, as described in this section. Using the linear regression method, the solution of the causal model is $Y = 9,480.48 + 3.95X$. Thus, for 4,000 concurrent logins (i.e., $X = 4,000$), the estimated number of messages sent and received during the hour (Y) is 25,280 with $R^2 = 0.937$. ∎

Table 12.4. E-mail Statistics

Number of Concurrent Logins	Messages Sent and Received
2,450	19,257
2,765	20,488
2,241	18,152
2,860	21,450
3,011	21,077
2,907	20,639
3,209	22,142

12.5.3   Nonlinear Methods

When a linear function is not able to accurately predict the behavior of a variable, other functions could be used to obtain the forecast curve rather than the straight line of the linear regression method.

An exponential method is useful when it is known that there is, or has been, increasing growth or decline of the workload parameter in past periods. Let us suppose that the workload change is represented by the following:

$$Y_t = a \times b^t \tag{12.5.8}$$

When we take the logarithm of both sides of Eq. (12.5.8), we obtain:

$$\log Y_t = \log a + t \log b$$

By letting $\log Y_t = Y'$, $\log a = a'$ and $\log b = b'$, we can rewrite the above expression as:

$$Y' = a' + b' t$$

The linear regression method can be used to compute a' and b'. Then, the parameters of the exponential model of Eq. (12.5.8) can be obtained [7]. Different models, represented by other functions such as the *Power Function* (i.e., $Y_t = a\ t^b$) and the *Logarithmic Function* (i.e., $Y_t = a + b\ \log\ t$), can be treated in a similar way.

Example 12.3

A financial Web service is growing fast in terms of popularity. Table 12.5 shows the service request traffic for the peak second of the last ten months. Management wants to forecast the future demand in order to upgrade network link and servers to guarantee adequate service level. A characteristic common to many services on the Web is an exponential rate of change. There seems to be common agreement that Web growth is exponential [8]. So, the exponential function $Y_t = a \times e^{bt}$ describes many different phenomena on the Web. The planning analyst wants to fit an exponential function to the set of arrival rates shown in Table 12.5. Taking the natural logarithm of each side of the exponential function, we have:

$$\ln\ Y_t\ =\ \ln\ a + b\ t \tag{12.5.9}$$

Letting $\ln\ Y_t = Y'$ and $\ln\ a = a'$, Eq. (12.5.9) becomes

$$Y' = a' + b\ t \tag{12.5.10}$$

In order to fit an exponential function to the dataset of Table 12.5, we have to obtain the straight line for Eq. (12.5.10).

Using the method of least squares, we obtain $a' = 6.717$ and $b = 0.110$. But $a = e^{a'} = 826.33$. So, the exponential function that describes the peak arrival rate is given by:

$$Y_t = 826.33 \times e^{0.110\ t}.$$

The arrival rate forecast for two months ahead is then $Y_{12} = 826.33 \times e^{0.110 \times 12} = 3093.30$. Figure 12.5 shows the historical data of Table 12.5 along with the exponential fit to the data. ∎

Table 12.5. Number of Requests During the Peak Second

Month (t)	Requests Per Second Peak (Y_t)	ln Y_t
1	1,035	6.942
2	1,100	7.003
3	1,160	7.056
4	1,250	7.130
5	1,350	7.207
6	1,555	7.349
7	1,770	7.478
8	1,950	7.575
9	2,210	7.700
10	2,630	7.874

12.5.4   Moving Average

A simple moving average (SMA) is a forecasting technique that makes the value to be forecast for the next period equal to the average of a number of previous observations. When applied to nearly stationary data, the accuracy achieved by the technique is usually high [4]. A major disadvantage of simple moving averages comes from the fact that only one forecast value into the future can be calculated at a time. This technique is appropriate for short-term forecasting. The forecast value is given by

$$F_{t+1} = \frac{Y_t + Y_{t-1} + \cdots + Y_{t-n+1}}{n} \qquad (12.5.11)$$

where

- F_{t+1}: forecast value for period $t+1$

- Y_t: actual value (observation) at time t

- n: number of observations used to calculate F_{t+1}.

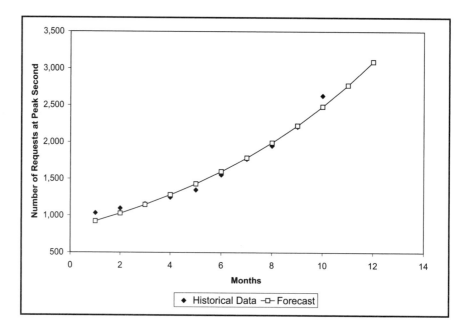

Figure 12.5. Forecasting evolution of peak arrival rate.

As can be noted from Eq. (12.5.11), a forecast value for time $t+2$ cannot be made until the actual value for time $t+1$ becomes known. One problem with this technique is the determination of n, the number of periods included in the averaging. One should try to select a value for n that minimizes the forecasting error, which is defined by the square of the difference between the forecast and actual values. Usually n is typically between 3 and 10 [10].

Example 12.4

In order to keep a high quality of access to the Internet, the IT management of a company keeps track of the network link performance and utilization. The link utilization metric is defined as the amount of data transferred (i.e., bandwidth demand) divided by the available bandwidth. The bandwidth demand is captured during a representative period of time. Peak demand is defined by the busy hour and busy day for the link. The peak bandwidth demand is used for analyzing the available bandwidth and for recommendations regarding re-sizing the link. To anticipate performance problems the network administrator wants to know in advance what will be the bandwidth demand in the next month. Regression methods are used to forecast the bandwidth demand, based on the last eight months as seen in Table 12.6.

When applying the moving averages technique, two values of n were tried (3 and 4) on the existing data. The use of three observations gives the smallest MSE. Thus, the bandwidth demand, in Kbps, for the next month is $F = (1,039 + 1,145 + 1,066)/3 = 1,083.33$. ∎

12.5.5 Exponential Smoothing

Historical trends can be analyzed using the exponential smoothing technique. It uses a weighted average of past observations to forecast the value of the next period. Simple exponential smoothing (SES) is similar to moving average with respect to the way that both techniques calculate the forecast

Table 12.6. Network Link Statistics

Month	Actual Bandwidth Demand (Kbps)	Forecast SMA	Forecast SES ($\alpha = 0.3$)
1	1,100	-	1,100.00
2	1,020	-	1,100.00
3	1,090	-	1,076.00
4	1,255	1,070.00	1,080.20
5	1,195	1,121.67	1,132.64
6	1,039	1,180.00	1,151.35
7	1,145	1,163.00	1,117.64
8	1,066	1,126.33	1,125.85
9	-	1,083.33	1,107.90

value. They both make the average of known observations equal to the forecast value. The difference is that exponential smoothing places more weight on the most recent historical data. The motivation for using different weights stems from the hypothesis that the latest observations give a better indication of the next future. As with moving averages, this technique is appropriate to data that present little variation and for short-term prediction. The forecast value is calculated as

$$F_{t+1} = F_t + \alpha(Y_t - F_t) \tag{12.5.12}$$

where

- F_{t+1}: forecast value for period $t + 1$

- Y_t: actual value (observation) at time t

- $Y_t - F_t$: forecasting error in period t

- α: smoothing weight ($0 \leq \alpha \leq 1$). In practice, $0.05 \leq \alpha \leq 0.30$.

Example 12.5

Let us apply the exponential smoothing technique to the data shown in Table 12.6. The problem is to calculate the estimated bandwidth demand for month number 9, given that we have historical data composed of eight observations. Column three of Table 12.6 shows the forecast values obtained by using the exponential smoothing technique with $\alpha = 0.3$. Note that the forecast value for the first month is set equal to the observed value, since there are no previous observations. The estimated bandwidth for month 9 is $F = 1,125.85 + 0.30 \times (1,066 - 1,125.85) = 1,107.90$. Figure 12.6 depicts the data as well as the results of applying SMA and SES techniques for this and the previous example. ∎

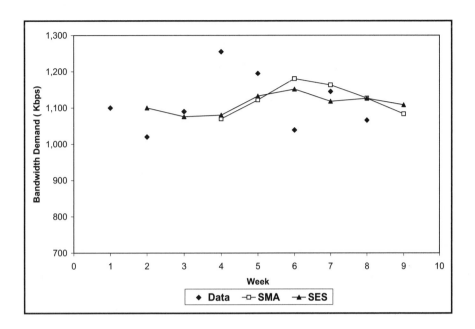

Figure 12.6. Forecasting bandwidth demand.

12.6   Concluding Remarks

Workload forecasting is a key issue in any capacity planning project. In Web environments, performance problems must be anticipated. An efficient way of avoiding problems is to have a good workload forecasting process in place. The basic steps to workload forecasting are

- definition of the forecasting strategy

- selection of the workload to be forecast

- analysis of historical data and estimation of the workload growth

- selection of forecasting techniques

- use of the forecasting techniques on the historical data

- analysis and validation of forecast results

Bibliography

[1] K. Coffman and A. Odlyzko, "Internet Growth: Is There a Moore's Law for Data Traffic?," *Handbook of Massive Data Sets*, J. Abello, P. Pardalos, and M. C. Resende, eds., Kluwer Academic Publishers, 2001.

[2] B. Everitt, *A Handbook of Statistical Analyses Using S-PLUS*, Chapman & Hall, 1994.

[3] S. Lam and K. Chan, *Computer Capacity Planning: Theory and Practice*, Academic Press, London, England, 1987.

[4] H. Letmanyi, *Guide on Workload Forecasting, Special Public. 500-123*, Computer Science and Technology, National Bureau of Standards, 1985.

[5] R. Jain, *The Art of Computer Systems Performance Analysis*, John Wiley and Sons, New York, 1991.

[6] D. Levine, P. Ramsey, and R. Smidt, *Applied Statistics for Engineers and Scientists: Using Microsoft Excel & MINITAB*, Prentice Hall, Upper Saddle River, New Jersey, 2001.

[7] D. Lilja, *Measuring Computer Performance*, Cambridge University Press, Cambridge, England, 2000.

[8] S. Manley and M. Seltzer, "Web Facts and Fantasy," *Proc. 1997 USENIX Symp. Internet Technologies and Systems*, Monterey, California, Dec. 1997.

[9] M. Marcus, *Matrices and Matlab: A Tutorial*, Prentice Hall, Upper Saddle River, New Jersey, 1993.

[10] J. Martinich, *Production and Operations Management : An Applied Modern Approach*, John Wiley and Sons, 1996.

[11] D. A. Menascé and H. Gomaa, "A Method for Design and Performance Modeling of Client/Server Systems," *IEEE Tr. Software Eng.*, vol. 26, no. 11, Nov. 2000, pp. 1066–1085.

[12] J. Mohr and S. Penansky, "A Forecasting Oriented Workload Characterization Methodology," *CMG Trans.*, no. 36, The Computer Measurement Group, June 1982.

[13] D. Sarna, "Forecasting Computer Resource Utilization Using Key Volume Indicators," *AFIPS Conf. Proc.*, vol. 48, 1979.

[14] K. Truelove, "Gnutella and the Transient Web," March 2001, www.openp2p.com

Chapter 13

Measuring
Performance

13.1 Introduction

An ever-growing number of companies rely on the processing capacity of their Web systems. Measuring performance of networked applications, such as on-line transaction processing and Web services, is a key issue in the process of guaranteeing SLAs and preventing problems. It is also an essential step for capacity planning because it collects data for performance analysis and modeling. The input parameters for performance models describe the system configuration, the software environment, and the workload of the system under study. The representativeness of a model depends directly on the quality of input data. Before one starts measuring performance and

479

collecting operational data for a model of an actual system, three questions naturally arise:

- What are the information sources of performance data?

- What are the monitoring tools available for measuring response time and resource usage?

- What techniques are used to calculate model input parameters from typical performance data collected by standard measurement tools?

The main source of information is the set of performance measurements collected from different test points, carefully chosen to observe and monitor the environment under study. Further performance information can also be obtained from product specifications (e.g., hardware, software, and network services) provided by manufacturers and industry standard benchmarks. Usually, typical performance data collected by standard monitoring tools do not match the type of information required as input by queuing network performance models. Raw data collected by performance measurement tools need to be transformed to be useful for modeling. Measurement data, even when collected from well-behaved and stable systems, are likely to exhibit errors. Therefore, any measurement methodology must include a statistical analysis, documentation, and understanding of possible sources of errors in the process [22].

By and large, measurement data has three main uses in performance management: i) detection of operational problems, ii) performance tuning, and iii) capacity planning [3]. To find out what is really happening with computer systems, system and network administrators rely on runtime monitors. These tools continuously collect measurement data from the system and display the status of some key variables that may indicate potential problems, such as high processor or link utilization, excessive paging activity, memory leaks, high error rates, and high peak-to-average ratio of number of concurrent users accessing the site. System administrators need global measurement data to help them obtain a big picture of the system and check if the values of key variables exceed set thresholds.

The second use of measurement data is for performance tuning purposes. Analysts examine performance historical data (e.g., logs and traces) to pinpoint possible causes of performance problems that may harm the system operation. Usually, the first level of tuning occurs at the operating system, based also on system measurements. For example, the file system's layout policy can be altered in a UNIX system with the `tunefs` command to fine-tune its performance [21]. Other forms of tuning or optimization are also possible. Suppose that one measures the performance of a Windows NT server. By examining NT's Performance Monitor results, one concluded that the system was suffering from lack of memory. Before recommending to upgrade the system and add more memory, an optimization could be tried, such as, distributing memory-consuming programs across multiple servers on the network.

The third use of measurement data is for capacity planning purposes. Capacity planning uses measurement data to develop models to predict the performance of future system configurations or to anticipate problems, such as service-level degradation.

In this chapter, the discussion of performance measurement is driven by the need to obtain the input parameters for performance models of Web-based systems. We first present a framework for collecting performance data in network environments. Next, we discuss statistical techniques to assess the meaning of measurements. Because the particulars vary from system to system, we do not focus on any specific product or manufacturer. Instead, we discuss the main issues involved in the process of measuring performance of Web environments. We then present the data needed by performance models and introduce general procedures for transforming typical measurement data into input parameters. These procedures can be thought of as a set of major guidelines for obtaining input parameters for performance models.

13.2   Performance Measurement Framework

Performance management of network-based environments involves monitoring networks, system components, and links to determine response times, resource utilizations, and traffic intensity levels. A performance measurement framework aims at providing a big picture of the quantitative behavior of Web-based systems and the corresponding network infrastructure that supports them. The framework should provide the variety of measurement data required by the three functions of performance management, i.e., detection of operational problems, performance tuning, and capacity planning. In particular, we focus on measurement data for capacity planning purposes. Figure 13.1 shows a measurement architecture for the Web. The triangles represent test points, from which measurement data are usually collected. At a Web site infrastructure, test points specify locations where measurements are conducted. Suppose that one is interested in measuring performance of dynamically generated pages. In this case, we would specify the application server as one of the relevant test points. In the Internet, test points are hosts that either collect performance data or have been configured to respond to measurement queries [22].

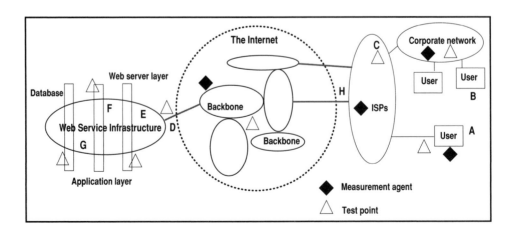

Figure 13.1. Measurement architecture.

The black diamonds in Fig. 13.1 represent measurement agents that run on a host and actually initiate the various measurements. Agents communicate with test points and Web service hosts to perform measurements or collect data. For example, an agent can periodically submit queries to the search engine service of a portal to assess the main components of its response time.

There are two basic approaches to measuring a Web system: active measurement and passive measurement [22]. In the passive mode, a device or an agent watches what the system does but does not add any requests to its workload. This can be done by instrumenting the system or by monitoring it. The passive mode is used to measure traffic flows, count the number of packets, or measure the number of requests that arrive at a Web service. This type of measurement is useful mainly for workload characterization. As an example, one could take passive measurements by looking at the HTTP log of a Web server.

In the active measurement mode, a measurement agent uses the system and analyzes its performance. This type of measurement offer information to performance evaluation and system operation management. In the active measurement arena, commercial companies provide a wide range of services, such as benchmarking end-to-end performance of service providers and tracking the performance of many popular Web sites. Another important characteristic of a measurement approach is measurement location, which includes the locations of both the measurement agents and the test points. Some measurements can be done at a single point. For example, measuring the database server response time. However, end-to-end Web metrics, such as response time and availability, require measurements from many points. In order to characterize a representative part of the Internet user population, the location of measurement agents should be carefully chosen and spread across the globe.

13.2.1   Infrastructure Measurement

A measurement framework should be able to monitor activities in the infrastructure of a Web service. One approach is to measure the resource utilization of the servers and components of the site. In Fig. 13.1, points E and F indicate that performance data is being collected at the Web server layer and the application layer. At point G, it is possible to collect utilization measurements of the LAN segments that make up the site environment. Network sniffers can be installed at point D to inspect network traffic at the links that connect the LAN to a WAN. At point E, operating system tools should be able to measure server performance. At measurement point F, a monitoring API could be embedded directly into the application code to measure response time of the application servers. At points A and B, user-perceived measurements could be collected. These tools provide network managers with global information about traffic load, server response time, and system utilization that can be used to calculate input parameters for performance models. This type of low-level performance data collected at various points of a Web site infrastructure is essential for performance modeling. However, this type of data does not provide the holistic view of performance that is required for capacity planning studies. For example, network delays have to be taken into account when analyzing end-to-end response time.

13.2.2   Application Performance Measurement

While measurements at the resource level are necessary as discussed in the previous section, it is important to realize that the quality of a Web service is measured by the value of high-level application-oriented metrics. Examples include end-to-end response time, availability, and cost per application. These metrics are important to both end users and managers and complement resource-level metrics in any capacity planning study.

13.3   The Meaning of Measurements

Suppose you asked your performance analyst to measure the average response time of search requests to the search engine in your corporate portal. Stated this way, this question is not very precise. The answer of course depends on many factors including the type of queries (e.g., single keyword, complex queries) and the workload at the corporate portal. To make the problem more concrete, let us assume that the question is rephrased as "What is the average response time of single-keyword queries to the corporate portal during the peak hour, i.e., between 10 a.m. and 11 a.m.?"

To answer the question, the performance analyst designed an experiment that consisted of the following steps:

1. Build a set S of single-keyword terms by examining the logs of the past two weeks. For each keyword k in S, compute from the log the frequency f_k of occurrence of keyword k in the log.

2. Write an application that submits a sequence of n requests to the search engine. Each request i $(i = 1, \cdots, n)$ is a query for a randomly selected keyword k from the set S. The selection process follows the frequency of occurrence of the search terms. The application measures and records the response time R_i of each submission.

After running this application for a total of $n = 100$ requests during the peak hour, the analyst computed the average of all response times as

$$\overline{R} = \frac{1}{100} \sum_{i=1}^{100} R_i \qquad (13.3.1)$$

and reported to you an average response time of 0.56 seconds.

How certain can you be of this answer? First of all, if we repeated the experiment we would probably obtain a different value for the average response time. There are two reasons why the answer will not be the same. The first has to do with the fact that the conditions (e.g., current load, buffer state) of the system being measured are not exactly the same every time the experiment is conducted. The second reason for differences in the results may have to do with the experiment itself. For example, since keywords are randomly selected, a pseudo-random number generator has to be used. The sequence of numbers generated by a pseudo-random number generator depends on the value of a *seed* number [13]. If a different seed is used every time the experiment is conducted, we will obtain a different sequence of keywords.

So, what we are trying to do with the experiment is estimate the average value of an underlying random variable $\tilde{R}$ defined in this case as the response time of single-keyword queries during the peak hour. This mean is also called the *population mean* as opposed to the *sample mean*, which is obtained from the n values as

$$\overline{R} = \frac{1}{n} \sum_{i=1}^{n} R_i. \tag{13.3.2}$$

One can also compute the sample variance S_R^2 and the sample standard deviation S_R as

$$S_R^2 = \frac{1}{n-1} \sum_{i=1}^{n} (R_i - \overline{R})^2 \tag{13.3.3}$$

$$S_R = \sqrt{\frac{1}{n-1} \sum_{i=1}^{n} (R_i - \overline{R})^2}. \tag{13.3.4}$$

Suppose now that we run the experiment a total of m times. Each time, we obtain an estimate for the population mean. So, we have m different estimates for the population mean. Can we get a single estimate? Unfortunately we cannot with a finite number of experiments. But, we can make a probabilistic statement of the form

$$Pr\left[c_1 \le E(\tilde{R}) \le c_2\right] = 1 - \alpha \tag{13.3.5}$$

where $E(\tilde{R})$ is the population mean, $(c_1, c2)$ is called the *confidence interval* for the population mean, α is called the *significance level*, $100\,(1 - \alpha)$ the *confidence level*, and $(1 - \alpha)$ the *confidence coefficient* [13]. For example, our analyst might be able to provide an answer of the type

$$Pr\ [0.52 \leq E(\tilde{R}) \leq 0.61] = 0.95. \qquad (13.3.6)$$

This means that the average response time of single-keyword queries at the peak hour is in the interval (0.52 sec, 0.61 sec) with a probability of 0.95, or in other words, with a confidence level of 95%. Another way of interpreting a confidence interval estimate is to say that if all possible samples of size n were taken, then only 95% of them would include the population mean within the confidence interval [15].

We now turn to the problem of finding the lower and upper bounds of the confidence interval given a confidence level. It turns out that, due to the *Central Limit Theorem* [13, 15] it is possible to find these bounds from a single sample. This theorem says that if the observations in a sample are independent and come from the same population that has a mean $E(\tilde{R})$ and standard deviation σ_R, then the sample mean for large samples is approximately normally distributed with mean $E(\tilde{R})$ and standard deviation σ_R/n, where n is the sample size.

If n is large enough, i.e., $n > 30$, a $100\ (1 - \alpha)$ confidence interval for $E(\tilde{R})$ can be computed as

$$(\overline{R} - z_{1-\alpha/2} \times S_R/\sqrt{n}, \overline{R} + z_{1-\alpha/2} \times S_R/\sqrt{n}) \qquad (13.3.7)$$

where $\overline{R}$ is the sample mean, S_R the sample standard deviation, n the sample size, and $z_{1-\alpha/2}$ the $(1 - \alpha/2)$-quantile of a unit normal variate (i.e., a normally distributed random variable with zero mean and standard deviation equal to 1). Fortunately, the values of the quantiles of the unit normal variate are listed in tables of any statistics book [15] and can also be computed with the use of Microsoft Excel's function NORMSINV as

$$z_{1-\alpha/2} = \text{NORMSINV}(1 - \alpha/2). \qquad (13.3.8)$$

Example 13.1

Consider again the analyst of the beginning of this section. She ran the experiment 100 times and obtained a sample average of 0.56 seconds and a sample standard deviation of 0.12 seconds. What are the 95% and 90% confidence intervals for the average response time?

A 95% confidence level means that $\alpha = 0.05$ since $95\% = 100\,(1 - 0.05)$. The value of $z_{1-\alpha/2} = z_{1-0.05/2} = z_{0.975} = \text{NORMSINV}(0.975) = 1.960$. So, using Eq. (13.3.7) we obtain the 95% confidence interval as

$$(0.56 - 1.960 \times 0.12/\sqrt{100}, 0.56 + 1.960 \times 0.12/\sqrt{100}) = (0.537, 0.584)$$

For the 90% confidence interval, $\alpha = 0.1$ and $z_{1-\alpha/2} = z_{1-0.1/2} = z_{0.95} = \text{NORMSINV}(0.95) = 1.645$. So, the 90% confidence interval is

$$(0.56 - 1.645 \times 0.12/\sqrt{100}, 0.56 + 1.645 \times 0.12/\sqrt{100}) = (0.540, 0.580)$$

So, as the example shows, as we reduce the confidence level, the width of the confidence interval is also reduced. For example, for a confidence level of 95%, the width of the interval is 0.047 seconds, while for 90% it is 0.040 seconds. ∎

As we can see from Eq. (13.3.7), the larger the sample size n, the smaller the confidence interval, and therefore, the higher is the confidence on the estimate. So, suppose that our analyst wants to know what the sample size n should be so that a certain confidence level, say 95%, could be obtained so that the estimate on the mean had a precision of 5%. In other words, half the width of the confidence interval should be equal to 5% of the estimated mean. Using the data from the previous example, half the width of the 95% confidence interval is $1.960 \times 0.12/\sqrt{n}$. If we want this to be equal to 5% of the sample mean 0.56 sec, then

$$\frac{5}{100} = \frac{1.960 \times 0.12/\sqrt{n}}{0.56}$$

which implies in

$$n = \left(\frac{100 \times 1.960 \times 0.12}{5 \times 0.56}\right)^2 = 71.$$

So, 71 observations would be enough to provide an estimate on the mean with 5% accuracy at a 95% confidence level. We can generalize this example by saying that the minimum number of observations n to obtain an accuracy of $r\%$ on the estimate of the mean at a $100\,(1 - \alpha)$ confidence level is

$$n = \left\lceil \left(\frac{100 \times z_{1-\alpha/2} \times S_R}{r \times \overline{R}} \right)^2 \right\rceil. \tag{13.3.9}$$

13.4   Measurement Process

What are the most used resources of a given system? Network bandwidth? Server I/O? Client desktop processor time? What is the average end-to-end response time of stock trading transactions? How much CPU time does the e-mail server consume daily? How much bandwidth of the enterprise network is being consumed by Internet traffic? These are examples of typical questions that managers of information technology resources frequently face. To answer quantitative questions about the behavior of computers and networks, one has to measure them. But what does this really mean? System measurement can be viewed as a process that observes the operation of a system over a period of time and records the values of the variables that are relevant for a quantitative understanding of the system [23]. As illustrated in Fig. 13.2, a measurement process involves four major steps:

1. *Specify Measurements:* This is the first step toward measuring Web environments. In this step, one should decide on the performance

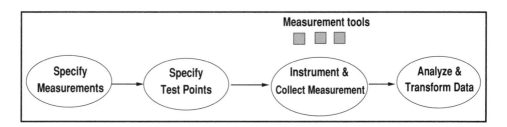

Figure 13.2. A representation of the measurement process.

variables to be measured. For example, consider an Ethernet LAN. Statistics that represent its behavior include measurements such, as packets per second and collisions per second. As another example, suppose we are interested in developing a model for analyzing the behavior of a streaming oriented application. In this case, a metric would be the signal quality, expressed as the proportion of time the service is degraded to the total service time.

2. *Specify Test Points:* One has to specify the points from which performance data will be collected. As an example, one could determine that the starting point is to collect data on the traffic that traverses the LAN where the Web servers are located.

3. *Instrument and Collect Data:* After selecting variables to be observed, one should deploy measurement tools to monitor the system. This involves configuring the tools so that the specified variables are measured during the observation period and the required information is recorded. The Web is a complex system, which exhibits a huge heterogeneity across different sites and at a single site over time. Depending on the measurements defined, one may have to install several measurement tools across different points in the Web, as shown in Fig. 13.1. For instance, if one were interested in obtaining the packet rate on an Ethernet LAN, a LAN analyzer (composed of a network interface, a programmable hardware filter, and a PC), would have to be connected to the Ethernet under observation.

4. *Analyze and Transform Data:* Measurement tools gather very large amounts of raw data, which correspond to a detailed observation of the system operation. Usually, raw data specify time intervals, event counts, and percentages that have to be related to the logical functions of a system. To be useful, these bulky data must be analyzed and transformed into significant information. For instance, logs gener-

ated by software measurement tools typically include a record for each Web request serviced during the monitoring period. These records must be then summarized to yield useful results such as average size of requested files, number of accesses, and file popularity.

In any performance measurement process, the key point is to understand what is being measured and how accurate and reliable are the resulting numbers. Thus, it is essential to know the measurement tools, their capabilities, and their limitations.

13.5   Data Collection Techniques and Tools

Measurement techniques used to collect data can be grouped into several categories: event-driven, sampling, tracing, and indirect [16]. Event-driven monitors generate a record every time an event of one of a set of designated types occurs. Tracing and event-driven are akin. The difference is that tracing records the event that has occurred and some portion of the system state that uniquely identifies the event. For example, instead of simply counting transmission errors, a tracing approach would record the system state with causes of the errors. Sampling techniques periodically inspect the state of a system or component and compute metrics based on these observations. Indirect measurement is used when the metric of interest cannot be directly obtained. For example, one could estimate the average number of simultaneous requests at a Web site by measuring the average site response time and average throughput and then applying Little's Law.

13.5.1   Event-driven

An interrupt that indicates the arrival of a network packet can be viewed as an *event* that changes the state of a system. The state of a system is specified by a set of variables. At the operating system level, the state of the system is usually defined as the number of processes that are in the ready-queue, blocked-queue, and running. Examples of events at this level are: a call to operating system modules, a clock interrupt, and an I/O request. At a higher level, where the number of transactions in memory represents the state of the system, the completion of a transaction can also be considered an event. In the *event mode*, information is collected at the occurrence of specific events. Usually, an event-based measurement tool consists of special codes inserted at specific points of the operating system. Upon detection of an event, the special code calls an appropriate routine that generates a record containing information such as date, time, and type of the event. In addition to that, the record contains some kind of event-related data. In general, measurement tools record the information corresponding to the occurrence of events in buffers, which are later transferred to disk. For example, in UNIX systems, a process record is entered in the accounting log upon process completion.

When the event rate becomes very high, the event handling routines are executed very often, which may introduce a non-negligible overhead in the measurement process. The overhead corresponds to the load placed by the measurement tool on system resources. Depending on the events selected, the event rate, and the amount of data collected, the overhead may reach unbearable levels, such as 30%. Overheads up to 5% are regarded as acceptable for measurement activities [9]. As the event rate cannot be controlled by the software routines, the measurement overhead becomes unpredictable, which constitutes one of the major shortcomings of this class of measurement tools. Overhead in the case of event-based monitoring may not be a problem for network sniffers used in promiscuous mode. In this case, the monitor runs in a dedicated hardware, configured to receive all packets sent between any two stations.

13.5.2   Sampling

In the *sampling mode*, information about the system is collected at predefined instants. Instead of being triggered by the occurrence of an event, the data collection routines of a sampling software tool are activated at predetermined times, specified at the start of the monitoring session. The act of measurement can perturb the system being measured and repeated periodic perturbations can introduce distortions on the measurements. The overhead introduced by a sampling tool depends on two factors: the number of variables measured at each sampling point and the size of the sampling interval. With the ability of specifying both factors, a sampling monitor is also able to control its overhead. On one hand, large sampling intervals result in low overhead. On the other hand, if the intervals are too large, the number of samples decreases and reduces the statistical significance of the variables of interest. The uncertainty of the measured variables depends on the number of samples. As seen earlier in this chapter, statistical methods can be used to assess the confidence in the measured values [13]. Therefore, one has to play with both the size of the sampling and monitoring interval to obtain low overhead and good accuracy . There is a clear tradeoff between overhead and accuracy of measurement results. The higher the accuracy, the higher the overhead. When compared to event trace mode, sampling provides a less-detailed observation of a computer system [11].

13.5.3   Tools

Monitors are tools used for measuring the level of activity of a system, be it a network, a server, or a client computer. The main function of a monitor is to collect data regarding the system's operation. Ideally, a monitor must be an observer of the system under study (e.g., network devices, server, and desktop client), and not in any way a participant. The monitoring activity must be done in such a way as to not affect the operation of the system being measured. This means that the monitoring process should minimally degrade the performance of the monitored system. Two attributes characterize a monitor: mode and type. As we saw in the previous section, monitors perform data collection in three different modes: event, trace, and sampling. There are three types of performance monitors, depending on their implementation approach: hardware, software, and hybrid.

13.5.3.1   Hardware Monitor

A *hardware monitor* is a measurement tool that detects events within a computer system by sensing predefined signals. A hardware monitor examines the state of the computer system under study via electronic probes attached to its circuitry and records the measurements. The electronic probes can sense the state of hardware components of the system, such as registers, memory locations, and I/O channels. There are advantages to hardware monitors. As they are external to the measured system, they do not consume resources from the system. This means that hardware monitors typically do not place any overhead on the monitored system. Another feature is portability. Usually, it is possible to move a hardware monitor to different types of computing environments, since they do not depend on the operating system. There are also potential difficulties associated with the use of hardware monitors for capacity planning. They usually do not access software-related information, such as the identification of a transaction that triggered a given event. Thus, it is difficult to use a hardware monitor to obtain performance measurements that are related to applications or workloads.

13.5.3.2   Software Monitor

A *software monitor* consists of a set of routines embedded in the software of a system with the aim of recording status and events of the system [23]. The routines gather performance data about the execution of one or more programs and about the components of the hardware configuration. They can be activated either by the occurrence of specific events or by timer interrupts, depending on the mode of the monitor. The combination of hardware and software monitors results in a *hybrid monitor*. For instance, many network performance tools are hybrid monitors that combine hardware and software monitoring facilities.

Software monitors basically record any information that is available to programs and operating systems. This feature, along with a great flexibility to select and reduce the amount of performance data, makes software monitors a powerful tool for analyzing computer systems. However, in order to run their routines, software monitors use the same resources they are measuring and may interfere significantly with the system. Depending on the level of overhead introduced, monitoring may yield meaningless results. Some tools, such as the NT Performance Monitor [4], allow users to control the overhead, letting them select the time interval for sampling. Software monitors are generally easy to install and easy to use. The main shortcomings are the overhead and the dependency on the operating system. Measurement data commonly provided by current monitors can be grouped into two categories, according to the information scope.

- *System-level measurements:* show system-wide resource usage statistics. Examples include global CPU and disk utilization, total number of physical I/O operations, page fault rate, and total traffic through a router. This kind of information is usually provided by software monitors that run at the operating system level. As a rule, system-level monitors do not collect statistics by class of application programs.

- *Program-level measurements:* show program-related information. Examples include program identification, elapsed time, CPU time, number of I/O operations per execution, physical memory usage, and application traffic (i.e., packets per second per application). Accounting systems constitute the most common source of program execution information.

There are some classes of tools that may be regarded as software monitors, in the sense that they monitor, via a set of appropriate routines, the behavior of hardware and software systems. However, due to their specific uses, they receive special names: accounting systems, log generators, and program analyzers.

13.5.3.2.1　Accounting Systems　Accounting systems are primarily intended to collect information to be used as a means of apportioning charges to users of a system [5, 9]. These tools are usually an integral part of most multiuser operating systems (e.g., UNIX process accounting log). Although their main purpose is billing, accounting systems can be used as a data source for capacity planning studies. Accounting systems are the easiest way to gather some very important performance information. They allow management to find out what applications users run, how much CPU time is spent with user applications, and how much system time is used by the applications. They should be viewed as the first recourse when one begins a measurement effort. In general, accounting data include three groups of information: identification (e.g., process, user, or application), resource usage indicators (e.g., CPU time, number of I/O operations, and memory usage), and execution times, showing the start and completion times of the processes. Although accounting systems provide a lot of useful data, there are some problems with their use for performance modeling. They do not capture the use of resources by the operating system, i.e., they do not include any unaccountable system overhead.

Another problem refers to the way that accounting systems view some special programs such as database management systems (DBMS) and transaction processing monitors. These programs have transactions and processes that execute within them and therefore are not visible to the accounting system. For example, an Oracle server runs in UNIX as a single process. Because the `sar` command views Oracle as single entities, it does not collect any information about what is being executed inside the Oracle process, such as the transactions processed by the database management system. However, if one wants to model transaction response time, one needs to obtain information about individual transactions. This information is not collected by the accounting system. Hence, special monitors are required to examine the performance of some special programs, such as Oracle.

13.5.3.2.2   Program Analyzers   Instead of monitoring the entire system, *program analyzers* are software tools especially designed to collect information about the execution of individual programs. They can also be used as an optimizer tool, pinpointing those parts of a program that consume significant system resources. For example, most of the workload of large corporations is due to transaction processing, which is usually controlled by single programs known as transaction processing monitors. For performance modeling purposes, the information provided by the accounting logs and operating system facilities is not sufficient. Both types of tools do not look inside the TP environment and only capture global resource usage data. Thus, what is needed is a tool capable of observing and recording events internal to the execution of specific programs. In the case of transaction processing monitors, program analyzers provide information such as transaction count, average transaction response time, mean CPU time per transaction, mean number of I/O operations per transaction, and transaction mix. Examples of program analyzers include monitors for database management systems and transaction processing software.

13.5.3.2.3   Logs   Log files contain information about the services requested from a system, the responses provided, and the origin of the requests. Windows NT Performance Monitor [4] places performance data in a log file that can be exported for further processing and reporting. The analyst can choose the objects to log and specify the monitoring interval and the time interval for sampling.

In the case of the Web, servers keep a log of their activities. Web server logs are text files that contain information about the server activity. Web logs are organized into four separate types: access, referrer, agent, and error. The log used for analyzing performance and behavior of Web servers is the access log, which contains lines with the following types of information:

- *host:* contains the client host name or IP address

- *identification:* shows the identity of the user; no longer used

- *login name or authorization:* contains the authorization user ID used to access protected portions of the site

- *date, time, and zone:* instant at which the request was completed

- *request:* contains the name of the requested file and the operation or method performed (e.g., "GET/HTTP/1.0")

- *status:* specifies the response status from the server; may indicate, for instance, if the request was successful or if the client requested an unauthorized or nonexistent file

- *file size:* indicates the number of bytes transferred in response to a file request

There are many tools, both commercial and public domain, for analyzing Web server logs and measuring Web site activity. They typically provide measures that indicate the degree of exposure and interactivity of a Web site. Some of the metrics used are: number of site accesses per day, number of page accesses per day, average visit duration time, average inter-visit duration time, and average page duration time

Example 13.2

Figure 13.3 displays the access log of a Web site that was collected during a very short time interval. From the log, we want to derive performance measures, such as average arrival rate and average file size of the documents requested from the server. The log entry for a normal request is of the form:

```
hostname - - [dd/mmm/yyyy:hh:mm:ss tz] request status bytes
```

For example, the first line of the log of Fig. 13.3 indicates that the request came from the host perf.xyz.com at 13:41:41 Eastern time on January 24, 2002. The requested document, the index page, and the status code 200

```
perf.xyz.com - - [24/Jan/2002:13:41:41 -0400] "GET i.html HTTP/1.0" 200 3185
perf.xyz.com - - [24/Jan/2002:13:41:41 -0400] "GET 1.gif HTTP/1.0" 200 1210
h0.south.com - - [24/Jan/2002:13:43:13 -0400] "GET i.html HTTP/1.0" 200 3185
h0.south.com - - [24/Jan/2002:13:43:14 -0400] "GET 2.gif HTTP/1.0" 200 2555
h0.south.com - - [24/Jan/2002:13:43:15 -0400] "GET 3.gif HTTP/1.0" 200 36403
h0.south.com - - [24/Jan/2002:13:43:17 -0400] "GET 4.gif HTTP/1.0" 200 441
cs.uni.edu - - [24/Jan/2002:13:46:45 -0400] "GET i.html HTTP/1.0" 200 3185
cs.uni.edu - - [24/Jan/2002:13:46:45 -0400] "GET 2.gif HTTP/1.0" 200 2555
cs.uni.edu - - [24/Jan/2002:13:46:47 -0400] "GET 3.gif HTTP/1.0" 200 36403
cs.uni.edu - - [24/Jan/2002:13:46:50 -0400] "GET 4.gif HTTP/1.0" 200 98995
sys1.world.com - - [24/Jan/2002:13:48:29 -0400] "HEAD index.html" 400 -
```

Figure 13.3. Web access log.

indicates a successful response by the server. The code 400 indicates an
unsuccessful request due to a client error. The size of the file transferred
from the server was 3,185 bytes. Although Web logs can help in workload
characterization, they do not provide all of the information needed by performance models. For instance, there is no information about the elapsed
time required for a document transfer. Also, the log does not show information on the complete set of documents available on the server; it only shows
the documents accessed during the measuring interval.

The measuring interval T is equal to $(13:48:29 - 13:41:41) = 408$ sec.
The number of requests is 11 and the arrival rate is $11/408$ requests/sec. The
average size of the transferred files is $188,117/10 = 18,811.7$ bytes. We also
note that the minimum and maximum file sizes are 441 and 98,995 bytes,
respectively. Once we have a big difference in file sizes it would be useful to
group the documents into classes, to reduce the variability of the measurements, as discussed in Chapter 6. Thus, we could classify the documents
into two types: small and large. The former would have documents up to
4,000 bytes. Thus, this workload would have a class for small documents

with 7 requests and average file size equal to 2,330.9 bytes. The class of large documents has 3 requests and average size of 57,267 bytes.   ■

13.6   Performance Model Parameters

The input parameters for performance models describe the architecture configuration, the software, and the workload of the system under study. This section presents a series of steps for specifying what the parameters are and how to estimate values for the parameters of performance models. These parameters fall into four groups:

- queues or devices

- workload classes

- workload intensity

- service demands

13.6.1   Queues

The first step in obtaining input parameters is to define the queues that make up the model. The scope of the capacity planning project helps to select which queues are relevant to the performance model. Consider the case of a distributed system composed of file servers and workstations connected via a LAN. The capacity planner wants to examine the impact caused on the system by the replacement of the uniprocessor file server by a four-processor server. For example, the system under study could be well represented by an open queuing network model consisting of three queues, which correspond to the file server configuration: one processor and two disks. The workstations are implicitly represented by the arrival rate of read and write requests generated by the workstations. A different performance model, with other queues, would be required if the planner were interested in studying the effect of the LAN utilization on the performance of the distributed system. Therefore, the specific focus of the project may be used to define the components of a performance model.

13.6.2   Workload Classes

To increase the model's representativeness, workloads are partitioned into classes of similar components, as described in Chapter 6. Programs with comparable resource usage may be grouped into the same workload class. Depending on the way a class is seen by a system, it may be classified as *open* or *closed*. The second step in determining the input parameters for a performance model is to define class types. The nature of the real workload is the main factor that influences the choice of class type. A class that represents the set of read and write requests that arrive at a file server may naturally be classified as an open class. Another example of open class is that of a workload generated by Web users. Although the nature of the real workload is important in determining the class type, it is not the only factor to be considered.

Performance modeling considerations are equally important. Consider the case of a Web server in an intranet. All employees of the company request documents, videos, and graphics from the Web server. At first sight, one would classify the workload as closed because of the fixed number of customers (i.e., employees) and due to the nature of the work carried out by the employees (i.e., they submit requests and wait for the responses). However, for capacity planning purposes, it is always recommended to analyze different ways of modeling a workload. In this specific example, the workload could also be viewed as open. The open type is specially suited for representing a load when the number of users of the service is not known in advance or when it is difficult to estimate the think time. Suppose that the company of our example decided to sell online training to other companies. It would be difficult to predict the number of simultaneous users of the service. It would be much easier to estimate the arrival rate of requests based on the correlation between historical arrival rates and the number of employees.

13.6.3   Workload Intensity

Workload intensity parameters give an indication of the number of transactions, requests, processes, or customers that contend for the resources of a network-based computing environment. The arrival rate (λ) indicates the intensity of an open class. Both the number of simultaneous customers (M) and the average think time (Z) specify the intensity of a closed class. Also, the average number of customers in a system is an indication of the load intensity of a closed class.

13.6.4   Service Demands

Queuing network (QN) models represent resources of a computer system. Although QNs may be used to model software resources (e.g., database locks), queuing networks have most frequently been applied to represent hardware resources. However, in modern computer systems, application programs do not see the hardware resources directly. Instead, they view the computer system as a set of services, provided by various layers of software. Clearly, there is a gap between the application program view and the representation provided by a queuing network model. For example, a file server attached to a LAN provides a common service to all other systems on the LAN. The primary service of the file server is to provide the file management capabilities found on time-sharing systems. Thus, when a user program running on a networked workstation executes a command to read a file, it does not need to know where the file is stored. Several pieces of software implement a network file system that provides the service requested by a read command. Then, the following question arises: How are the services provided by software systems represented in a queuing network model? The answer lies in the full understanding of the concept of service demand.

By definition, the service demand of a request at a queue specifies the total amount of service time required by the request during its execution at the queue. It is worth repeating that service demand refers only to the time a request spends actually receiving service. It does not include waiting times. Recall that V_i denotes the average number of visits that a request makes to queue i and S_i represents the mean service time per visit to queue i. The service demand of a request at queue i is given by $D_i = V_i \times S_i$.

Another view for service demand is that derived from measurement data. We know from the Service Demand Law (see Chapter 3) that $D_i = U_i \times T/C_0$, where U_i is the utilization of queue i and C_0 the number of requests completed during the interval T.

Let us examine how the services provided by software layers of a computing environment may be represented by service demand parameters. Looking at the definition of service demand, $D_i = U_i \times T/C_0$, we note that U_i is the only factor amenable to different interpretations, according to the specific environment. The meaning of U_i is key to understanding the concept of service demand in different execution environments. The effects of the various software layers are incorporated into the service demands through the way the utilization is calculated.

Example 13.3

Consider a Web server running on top of a Linux system. The server operation was monitored during a period of $T = 10$ minutes using a built-in trace facility [12] that captures the system activity while the Web server is running. From the trace, a summary report that gives several performance measurements, including processor utilization by the Web server and the Linux kernel, was generated. It was observed that the CPU was 90% busy. It was also noted that 10% of the CPU time was spent on the execution of HTTP code (i.e., %user) and 80% on the operating system kernel (i.e.,%system) [1]. The CPU time spent on the kernel includes the work done by the file system, the network system, and other activities, such as interrupt handling, scheduling, and memory management. The number of HTTP requests counted in the HTTP log was 30,000. We want to calculate the service demand of an HTTP request.

Let $U_{\text{cpu}}^{\text{total}}$ be the total CPU utilization measured by the system monitor. $U_{\text{cpu}}^{\text{HTTP}}$ and $U_{\text{cpu}}^{\text{kernel}}$ denote the CPU utilization by the HTTP processes and OS kernel, respectively. The total CPU utilization is then composed of two parts:

$$U_{\text{cpu}}^{\text{total}} = U_{\text{cpu}}^{\text{kernel}} + U_{\text{cpu}}^{\text{HTTP}}.$$

Thus, the CPU service demand can be computed as

$$D_{\text{cpu}} = U_{\text{cpu}}^{\text{total}} \times T/C_0 = (0.80 + 0.10) \times (10 \times 60)/30{,}000 = 0.018 \text{ sec.}$$

We can note from the above expression that the CPU service demand of an HTTP request includes the services done by the operating system on its behalf.   ■

The resource usage by the operating system is known as *overhead*. Because the overhead of the OS activities represents tasks performed on behalf of application programs (i.e., I/O, network, and security control), a common modeling approach is to distribute the overhead among the various classes of application programs.

13.6.5   Parameter Estimation

Parameter estimation deals with the determination of input parameters from measurement data. Many times, monitors do not provide enough information for calculating the input parameters required by a performance model. Therefore, inferences have to be made to derive the desired parameters. This section discusses general procedures for estimating input parameters.

Once the performance model has been specified and the solution techniques selected, the analyst faces the problem of estimating input parameters for the model. This section outlines the basic steps for obtaining the most common input parameters for performance models. The techniques presented here attempt to use, to the maximum extent possible, the data that are commonly provided by commercially available monitoring tools.

1. *Identify the type of execution environment.* In other words, the analyst has to find out what software layers are underneath the application programs and on top of the hardware. The type of environment determines the way of estimating the workload service demands.

2. *Specify the measurement process.* Once the environment has been typified, the next step involves basic definitions concerning the monitoring tools to be used, the data to be obtained, and the measurement interval (i.e., starting time and duration).

3. *Monitor the system and collect performance data.* The measurement data will be used to estimate the input parameters.

4. *Estimate input parameters.* According to the type of environment and measurement data obtained, calculate input parameters using the appropriate techniques and formulas described in the next sections.

We show now how service demands are computed from measurements obtained from a combination of operating system tools and program analyzers. Consider Fig. 13.4, which illustrates a server process (e.g., file server, database server, or HTTP server) running on top of the operating system. The figure also shows various types of requests, $r_1, \cdots, r_n$, running on top of the server process. In many cases, the operating system is not directly aware of the requests that are running on top of the server and can only provide measurements related to the server as an aggregate viewed as a single process.

Remember that, from the Service Demand Law, the service demand $D_{i,r}$ of a request of class r at a resource i is given by

$$D_{i,r} = U_{i,r}/X_{0,r}.$$

(13.6.10)

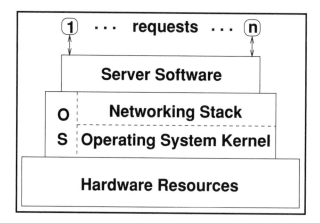

Figure 13.4. Layers for computing service demands.

It turns out that the operating system monitoring tools do not provide, in general, the utilization of several resources on a per-request basis. These tools provide the utilization of the server process. Then, we need to combine information provided by program analyzers with information provided by the OS to derive the utilization for each type of request. We use the information provided by program analyzers or logs to distribute the overall utilization of the server process as measured by the OS to the various types of requests. Consider that we want to obtain the service demands at the CPU for class r requests and that we have the following measurements:

- $U^{\text{os}}_{\text{cpu,server}}$: utilization of the server process at the CPU measured by the operating system

- TotalCPUTime_r: total CPU time for requests of class r measured by a program analyzer at the server level

- $X_{0,r}$: throughput of class r requests measured from a log generated by the server process or from a program analyzer at the server level

Then, the utilization of class r requests at the CPU is

$$U_{\text{cpu},r} = U^{\text{os}}_{\text{cpu,server}} \times \frac{\text{TotalCPUTime}_r}{\sum_{s=1}^{n} \text{TotalCPUTime}_s} \qquad (13.6.11)$$

and the service demand at the CPU for class r requests is

$$D_{\text{cpu},r} = U_{\text{cpu},r}/X_{0,r}. \qquad (13.6.12)$$

Example 13.4

Consider that an HTTP server received 21,600 requests during 1 hour as measured from the HTTP log. An analysis of this log places the requests in three categories according to file sizes: small (up to 20 KB), medium (from 20 KB to 1 MB), and large (larger than 1 MB). Table 13.1 shows the total CPU time for each class of request as obtained from an instrumented HTTP server. It also shows the total number of requests processed in each category. These numbers are obtained from an analysis of the HTTP log. If the overall CPU utilization measured by the OS was 86% and the machine was dedicated to being a Web server, what is the service demand at the CPU for each class of request?

The throughputs per class are

$$X_{\text{small}} = 12,960/3,600 = 3.60 \ \text{requests/sec}$$
$$X_{\text{medium}} = 6,480/3,600 = 1.80 \ \text{requests/sec}$$
$$X_{\text{large}} = 2,160/3,600 = 0.60 \ \text{requests/sec}.$$

The utilizations per class are

$$U_{\text{cpu,small}} = 0.86 \times \frac{1,555}{1,555 + 972 + 389} = 0.46$$

Table 13.1. Measurements for Ex. 13.4

File Size Range	Total CPU Time (sec)	No. of Requests
file size $\leq$ 20 KB	1,555	12,960
20 KB < file size $\leq$ 1 MB	972	6,480
file size > 1 MB	389	2,160

$$U_{\text{cpu,medium}} = 0.86 \times \frac{972}{1,555 + 972 + 389} = 0.29$$

$$U_{\text{cpu,large}} = 0.86 \times \frac{389}{1,555 + 972 + 389} = 0.11.$$

Thus, the service demands per class of HTTP request are

$$D_{\text{cpu,small}} = U_{\text{cpu,small}}/X_{\text{small}} = 0.46/3.60 = 0.13 \ \text{sec}$$

$$D_{\text{cpu,medium}} = U_{\text{cpu,medium}}/X_{\text{medium}} = 0.29/1.80 = 0.16 \ \text{sec}$$

$$D_{\text{cpu,large}} = U_{\text{cpu,large}}/X_{\text{large}} = 0.11/0.60 = 0.18 \ \text{sec.}$$

■

13.7   Obtaining Model Parameters

This section presents a series of examples that illustrate the process of obtaining parameters for performance models of Web systems.

13.7.1   Network

A network management system is a collection of tools for measuring and monitoring the behavior of a network. It provides a big picture of the entire network. The Simple Network Management Protocol (SNMP) provides the basis for collecting performance data from network devices, such as servers, routers, and switches. The SNMP architecture consists of a manager and an agent [2]. The network management application runs on a network management workstation and sends information requests to the managed devices. An agent that runs on the device receives the request, collects the requested measurement, and sends it back to the manager application that keeps the SNMP historical performance database. The information collected by the agents is organized in a tree structure known as Management Information Base (MIB). The performance variables are logically grouped into branches of the tree structure, such as the interface, IP, and TCP. For instance, performance information about routing is found in the IP branch. Most network management products comply with MIB standards.

There are several public tools that perform passive data collection on networks [8]. Examples include: `snoop`, `netramet`, `tcpdump`, `tcptrace`, and `libcoral`. Also, there are freely available active tools for measuring many aspects of network performance, such as `ping`, that measures RTT and `timeit`, which monitors Web server performance by requesting pages from a Web server [6].

Individual LAN segments can be monitored with LAN analyzers, which are a combination of specialized hardware and software or, simply, software. Most monitors consist of a LAN interface, a hardware filter, and a portable PC-based system. These monitors operate in promiscuous mode, examining all frames that pass through the segment. Frames that match given specifications (e.g., destination, source, and port number) are selected and have their information recorded for later analysis. Statistics produced by LAN analyzers for Ethernet networks include metrics such as packets per second, collisions per second, utilization, and CRC errors. Because of the volume of data, LAN analyzers collect only a few minutes of traffic measurements. Packet traces collected by this type of monitor are more useful to operations personnel and network specialists.

When it comes to remote segments, monitor devices gather real-time performance information about a LAN network segment. The Remote Monitoring MIB (RMON) specification provides an industry standard basis to many real-time commercially available network monitors. The RMON specification includes the following goals: offline operation from the central network management system, preemptive monitoring, problem detection and reporting, and value-added data. The RMON probe can also interpret the collected data. RMON devices can respond to multiple network management systems. RMON specifications, though, do not include application-oriented measurement data [3, 14].

Usually, most network performance monitors focus primarily on measurement data needed by operations and performance tuning. Network monitor tools display information such as traffic intensity on various network segments (i.e., LAN and WAN), bandwidth usage, and server utilizations. They do not collect data on application basis. Although sniffers or LAN analyzers provide detailed measurement data, they do not operate continuously, which limits their use in capacity planning. Capacity planning requires higher level information that indicates how the system behaves for longer periods of time. Commercial network monitors can provide part of the measurement data required by analytical models of network-based systems.

Example 13.5

Consider a C/S environment where a database server is accessed by 60 client workstations through a dedicated LAN. The network traffic consists only of the database requests submitted by the clients and the replies sent back by the server. Using a LAN analyzer, the performance analyst monitored the network several times during the peak periods. The average network utilization was 16%. During the same monitoring period, the database performance monitor measured a total transaction rate of 2.0 tps. The analyst wants to know the service demand of a C/S transaction at the LAN. Note that the service demand at the LAN is equal to the average service time for the request plus the average service time for the reply. The average service time per transaction includes all the frames exchanged plus the protocol overheads. From the operational laws (see Chapter 3), we know that

$$D_{\text{network}} = U_{\text{network}}/X_0 = 0.16/2.0 = 0.08 \text{ sec}$$

where D_{network} is the average network service demand of a C/S transaction and X_0 the server throughput.   ■

13.7.2   Server

A server is a combination of hardware platform, operating system, and functional server software, such as HTTP server, DBMS server, file server, and application server. A quantitative description of the server behavior can be obtained through measurements collected at the different layers of the system, as depicted in Fig. 13.5.

A number of system resources need to be monitored to obtain input data for performance models. The resources that have the most impact on server performance are memory, processor, disk, and networking subsystems. In order to develop performance models, different monitor tools are needed to collect data at the different layers of the server. The combination of several tools provides global performance data, as well as application-oriented measurement data. This section discusses some of the standard performance tools that come with the two most popular operating systems for distributed environments: Windows NT and UNIX.

13.7.2.1   Windows NT

Windows NT provides a set of performance tools that can be used to collect and display performance information of any computer in a distributed environment. The main tool to collect data and analyze performance is the NT Performance Monitor [4], which comes with NT. Performance Monitor measures the behavior of computer objects. In the NT environment, an object is a standard mechanism for identifying and using a system resource. The objects represent processes, threads, memory, and physical devices. Objects that always appear in the Performance Monitor include Cache, LogicalDisk,

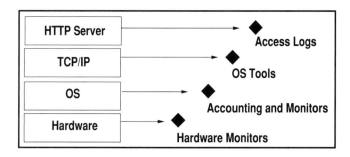

Figure 13.5. Collecting server performance data.

Memory, PagingFile, PhysicalDisk, Process, Processor, System, and Thread. Each object type can have several instances. For example, a system that has multiple processors will have multiple instances of the Processor object type. The Logical Disk object type has two instances if the physical disk has two logical partitions. Some object types (Memory and Server) do not have instances. If an object type has multiple instances, each instance produces the same set of statistics.

The concept of a counter is fundamental to understand NT performance. A counter is an entity for which performance data are available. Counters are organized by object type. A unique set of counters exists for each object, such as processor, memory, logical disk, processes, and other object types that produce statistical information. Performance Monitor collects data on various aspects of software and hardware performance, such as use, demands, rates, and used space. They represent measures such as processor utilization, number of processes waiting for disk, number of network packets transmitted per second, number of visits to a device, and available bytes.

A counter defines the type of data available to a particular counter object. On hardware devices, such as disks, counters count visits to the devices and provides, in many cases, the average device service time. Each object can have multiple counters. There are three types of counters. Instantaneous counters exhibit the most recent measurements. Averaging counters represent a value over a time interval and display the average of the two last measurements. Difference counters show the difference between the last measurement and the previous one. Counters are usually expressed as rates per second or fraction of time a device is used (i.e., utilization expressed in percentage). Table 13.2 displays some counters that indicate system resource usage information.

There are different ways to view the data collected by Performance Monitor, namely: chart, report, alert, and log. A chart displays the value of a counter over time. A report view shows the value of a counter and an alert view triggers an event when the value of a counter reaches a specified thresh-

Table 13.2. NT Performance Monitor Counters

Object	Counter	Description
System	% Processor time	Avg. utilization
System	Processor queue length	No. of requests in queue
Processor	% Processor time	Avg. processor utilization
Processor	% Privileged time	% time in privileged mode
Processor	% User time	% time in user mode
Memory	Pages/sec	Pages read and written/sec
Network interface	Bytes/sec	Network throughput
Physical disk	% Disk time	Avg. disk utilization

old. These three views are more useful for operation problem detection and performance tuning.

Capacity planing uses the log view, which records the counters on disk. Log files can be retrieved by Performance Monitor at a later time for charting and reporting. This tool can be used to gain a better understanding of how efficiently a system is working and what the problems might be if it is performing poorly. Despite its wide applicability, Performance Monitor does not answer capacity planning questions and does not provide basic input data required by analytical models. Another problem is that NT does not have an intrinsic definition of a basic component of a workload, such as transaction, request, interaction, or job. With the standard performance tools available in NT, it is difficult to obtain measurements that would characterize real workloads in terms of interactions or applications. The concept of transaction or interaction is important because it is meaningful from the end-user's viewpoint. It is a key element to define, characterize, and forecast workloads. Thus, if developers want to measure transaction processing times in NT, they must write their code to instrument the applications or base their applications on packages that implement and keep track of transactions or any other unit of work. Another difficulty with the Performance Monitor is that it does not save information about processes [3]. Once a process stops running, its execution information disappears from the system.

Example 13.6

Let us consider a Windows NT Web server running a server (IIS) that provides several Internet services, such as HTTP, FTP, and telnet. The system was monitored during a period of time $T = 900$ seconds. Performance Monitor and IIS collected information about the system performance and resource usage, as shown in Table 13.3. The "GET Request" counter indicates the number of HTTP GET requests received by the Web server during the monitoring period. Let us denote by C_{www} the number of GET requests. Let us also consider that the WWW workload was composed only of GET requests. Thus, our model has two classes. One class represents the WWW service (i.e., HTTP) that handles the GET requests. The second class refers to other services provided by the NT operating system. Based on the values displayed on Table 13.3, we want to calculate the processor service demand for class WWW, made up of GET requests.

The counter "Thread" indicates the processor time used by the threads of the *Inetinf* process that implements the WWW service. We note from Table 13.3 that the processor time attributed to the processes do not add up to the total processor time measured for the system object. It happens that the portion of time captured by monitors varies with both the nature of the workload and the type of operating system. The proportion of total CPU time that is captured by measurement tools is known as *capture ratio*. Although the concept of capture ratio has been defined for CPU time, it also applies to other resource categories. In a more general way, we can define the resource usage capture ratio as the ratio of the resource usage accounted to programs to the resource usage measured by system monitors.

The reason for the difference between total processor time and total process time in this example stems from the fact that the time spent in

Table 13.3. NT Performance Monitor Results

Object	Counter	Value
System	% Total processor time	74.7
System	Processor queue length	2.0
Processor	Interrupts per sec	989.6
User disk	% Disk time	44.8
System disk	% Disk time	10.2
Memory	Page faults per sec	55.3
Thread: WWW	% Processor time	41.21
Process: others	% Processor time	6.55
HTTP service	GET requests	8,120

interrupts is not charged to the processes that were running. However, this time is counted in the overall processor usage. So, to calculate the service demand, we need to distribute the amount of unaccounted time to the two classes. We do that by distributing the total time in proportion to the accounted time displayed in Table 13.3. The CPU utilization of class r is given by

$$U_{\mathrm{cpu},r} = U_{\mathrm{cpu}}^{\mathrm{total}} \times f_{\mathrm{cpu},r}$$

where $U_{\mathrm{cpu}}^{\mathrm{total}}$ is the total CPU utilization and $f_{\mathrm{cpu},r}$ is the fraction of the total CPU utilization that can be attributed to class r (i.e., it is equivalent to the capture ratio) which is given by

$$f_{\mathrm{cpu},r} = \frac{U_{\mathrm{cpu},r}^{\mathrm{os}}}{\displaystyle\sum_{\forall\ \mathrm{class}\ s} U_{\mathrm{cpu},s}^{\mathrm{os}}}$$

where $U_{\mathrm{cpu},r}^{\mathrm{os}}$ is the CPU utilization of class r measured by an accounting system or monitor facility of the OS. So, the service demand, $D_{\mathrm{cpu,www}}$, for class WWW is given by

$$D_{cpu,www} = \frac{U_{cpu,www}}{C_{www}/\mathcal{T}} = \frac{U_{cpu}^{total} \times f_{cpu,www}}{C_{www}/\mathcal{T}}.$$

Plugging the numbers from Table 13.3 into the above expressions, we obtain

$$D_{cpu,www} = 0.747 \times \frac{41.21}{41.21 + 6.55} \times 900/8120 = 0.071 \quad \text{sec}$$

In other words, the execution of a typical GET request demands 0.071 sec of CPU time.   ■

Further considerations on modeling and collecting data for Windows NT are given in [7].

13.7.2.2 UNIX

A UNIX system can be viewed as a combination of several resources: processor, memory, disks, kernel, network, and graphics. There are system tools that measure and yield statistics about the behavior of each class of resource. Performance measurement facilities provide global and per-process results. In this section, we examine some of the standard UNIX measurement facilities. Different UNIX versions (i.e., Linux or versions derived from Berkeley BSD and System V) have different monitoring tools. It is worth mentioning that no single tool provides all the information required by performance models.

A useful tool for workload characterization is System Activity Reporting (`sar`), which is included in many UNIX versions. It is a sampling mode tool that records cumulative and average system activity data, as maintained by the UNIX kernel. `sar` offers several options and reports, as shown in Table 13.4, which displays results of CPU utilization, stratified by system, user, wio, and idle percentage. The results came from the execution of the `sar` command at 3:36 p.m. The meaning of each metric is the following: *sys* corresponds to the percentage of time spent executing code in the system state (i.e., kernel), *usr* refers to the percentage of time spent executing code

Table 13.4. System-Wide sar Statistics

Time	%sys	%usr	%wio	%idle
3:36:00	28	41	25	6
3:41:00	27	48	20	5
3:46:01	26	42	26	6
3:51:00	27	60	12	1
3:56:00	29	59	11	1
4:01:00	28	60	12	1
4:06:01	19	58	12	1
4:11:00	29	55	15	1
4:16:01	29	54	16	1

in the user state, *wio* is the amount of time spent waiting for blocked I/O, and *idle* represents the percentage of time the CPU was idle.

Example 13.7

Consider that a UNIX based Web server was monitored for 40 minutes and that 14,400 HTTP requests were processed during this period as measured from the HTTP log. During the same period, sar was active and provided the measurements given in Table 13.4. If the machine is dedicated to being a Web server, what was the average service demand at the CPU during the measurement period?

The server throughput X was $14,400/(40 \times 60) = 6$ requests/sec. The average CPU utilization can be obtained from Table 13.4 by averaging the values of $(100 - \%\text{idle})$ over the interval. This gives us $U_{\text{cpu}} = 877/9 = 97.4\%$. From the Service Demand Law (see Chapter 3) we get that $D_{\text{cpu}} = U_{\text{cpu}}/X = 0.974/6 = 0.162$ sec.   ∎

There are other commands that provide information on how the system is performing. For instance, ps reports information about processes running on the system. The `vmstat` command (i.e., virtual memory statistics) informs about virtual memory, disk accesses, and CPU utilization. The `iostat` command provides I/O statistics, such as bytes per second, transfers per second, and msec per seek. Information about networking can be obtained with the command `netstat`. It lists the state of all network connections and provides information about the number of packets (e.g., TCP, IP, and UDP) processed by the system.

Different versions of UNIX have accounting systems that differ in a number of respects [5, 17, 21]. The UNIX operating system periodically updates resource usage information for each active process. When a process terminates, the performance information is recorded in the process accounting log file. For UNIX versions derived from System V, the log file is `pacct`. BSD-derived versions have a similar log file, but with a different format. Special commands (e.g., `acctcon` and `sa`) generate several reports from the entries recorded in the accounting log files, as shown in Table 13.5. *Command Name* gives the name of the program. *Number of Commands* indicates the number of times the program was executed during the interval of time covered by the report. The total amount of CPU time accumulated during all executions of the program is given by *Total CPU*. The total amount of elapsed time is denoted by *Total Real*. The average CPU time used to execute the program is *Mean CPU*. *Hog Factor* is the total CPU time divided by the total elapsed time. The unit of time in Table 13.5 is minutes.

Example 13.8

Consider that the results shown in Table 13.5 summarize the log of a 24-hour period of a database server. Suppose that the average CPU utilization reported by the `sar` command for the same period of time is 63.2%. What is the CPU capture ratio for the measurements in Table 13.5? In other words, we want to know how much CPU time was captured by the processes

Table 13.5. Total Command Summary (Times in min)

Command Name	Number of Commands	Total CPU	Total Real	Mean CPU	Hog Factor
oracle	15	421.11	1,880.24	28.07	0.22
mail	150	96.23	319.67	0.64	0.30
grep	300	250.88	1,609.45	2.17	0.16
ls	322	9.09	112.33	0.03	0.08
cd	98	5.75	90.01	0.05	0.06
Total	885	783.06	4,011.70	4.53	0.19

recorded in the accounting log. Recall that the capture ratio was defined as

$$f_{\text{cpu}} = \frac{U_{\text{cpu}}^{\text{acct}}}{U_{\text{cpu}}^{\text{os}}}$$

where $U_{\text{cpu}}^{\text{acct}}$ is the utilization measured by the accounting system and $U_{\text{cpu}}^{\text{os}}$ is the CPU utilization measured by a system-level monitor. Considering that the accounting system shows a "Total CPU" of 783.06 min in a 24-hour (i.e., 1,440-minute) period, the calculated utilization is then $U_{\text{cpu}}^{\text{acct}} = 783.06/1,440 = 54.38\%$. Thus, the capture ratio or the portion of time captured by the accounting system is $f_{\text{cpu}} = 54.38/63.20 = 86\%$. ∎

Once we have obtained the capture ratio, it is easy to estimate the true utilization per class. A detailed analysis of capture ratios and on the method to distribute all unaccounted resource usage among classes of a workload can be found in [20].

13.8 Concluding Remarks

Performance models are useful tools for understanding and predicting the quantitative behavior of Web services. However, the representativeness of a model depends directly on the quality of input parameters. There are two key issues in the process of obtaining input parameters for performance models: performance measurement and parameter estimation. With regard to the measurement process, it is essential to understand what is being measured, how accurate the measurements are, and how reliable the resulting numbers are. This chapter discussed several aspects of the measurement process in a network-based environment and showed techniques and tools used for collecting performance data of a system.

Parameter estimation deals with the determination of input parameters from measurement data. Many times, monitors do not provide enough information for calculating the input parameters required by a performance model. In most cases of real systems, assumptions have to be taken about the behavior of the system and inferences need to be made to derive the desired parameters.

Although this chapter does not focus on any particular product or vendor, it provides a set of general guidelines for transforming typical measurement data into typical input parameters. The guidelines can be applied to real problems in a straightforward manner. Because of the uncertainties associated with the process of estimating parameters, it is necessary to validate the model. An in-depth discussion of validation and calibration techniques is found in [20]. The main thrust of this chapter was on how to obtain parameters for existing Web and C/S systems. However, if C/S systems are under development, one needs to estimate service demands using different techniques. A framework for doing this is given in [19].

Bibliography

[1] J. M. Almeida, V. Almeida, and D. Yates, "Measuring the Behavior of a World-Wide Web Server," *Proc. Seventh Conf. High Perform. Networking (HPN)*, IFIP, April 1997, pp. 57–72.

[2] J. Blommers, *Practical Planning for Network Growth*, Prentice Hall, Upper Saddle River, New Jersey, 1996.

[3] J. P. Buzen and A. N. Shum, "Beyond Bandwidth: Mainframe Style Capacity Planning for Networks and Windows NT," *Proc. 1996 Comput. Measurement Group (CMG) Conf.*, Orlando, Florida, Dec. 8–13, 1996, pp. 479–485.

[4] R. Blake, *Optimizing Windows NT*, Microsoft Press, Seattle, Washington, 1993.

[5] J. Bouhana, "UNIX Workload Characterization Using Process Accounting," *Proc. 1996 Comput. Measurement Group Conf.*, San Diego, California, Dec. 8–13, 1996, pp. 379–390.

[6] N. Brownlee and C. Loosley, "Fundamentals of Internet Measurement," *CMG Journal of Computer Resource Management*, Issue 102, Spring 2001.

[7] J. P. Buzen and A. N. Shum, "Considerations for Modeling Windows NT," *Proc. 1997 Comput. Measurement Group Conf.*, Orlando, Florida, Dec. 9–12, 1997, pp. 219–230.

[8] Cooperative Association for Internet Data Analysis, www.caida.org

[9] J. Cady and B. Howarth, *Computer System Performance Management and Capacity Planning*, Prentice Hall, Upper Saddle River, New Jersey, 1990.

[10] Y. Ding, "Performance Modeling with Application Response Measurement (ARM): Pros and Cons," *Proc. 1997 Comput. Measurement Group Conf.*, Orlando, Florida, Dec. 9–12, 1997, pp. 34–45.

[11] P. Heidelberger and S. Lavenberg, "Computer Performance Methodology", *IEEE Trans. Comput.*, vol. C-33, no. 12, Dec. 1984.

[12] D. Helly, *AIX/6000 Internals and Architecture*, McGraw-Hill, New York, 1996.

[13] R. Jain, *The Art of Computer Systems Performance Analysis*, John Wiley and Sons, New York, 1991.

[14] A. Leinwand and K. Conroy, *Network Management: A Practical Perspective*, Addison Wesley, Reading, Massachusetts, 1996.

[15] D. Levine, P. Ramsey, and R. Smidt, *Applied Statistics for Engineers and Scientists: Using Microsoft Excel & MINITAB*, Prentice Hall, Upper Saddle River, New Jersey, 2001.

[16] D. Lilja, *Measuring Computer Performance: a Practitioner's Guide*, Cambridge University Press, Cambridge, United Kingdom, 2000.

[17] M. Loukides, *System Performance Tuning, A Nutshell Handbook*, O'Reilly & Assoc., 1991.

[18] D. A. Menascé, K. Nguyen, and D. Nguyen, "Performance Modeling of a UNIX Communications Server," *Proc. 1997 Comput. Measurement Group Conf.*, Orlando, Florida, Dec. 9–12, 1997, pp. 211-218.

[19] D. A. Menascé and H. Gomaa, "A Method for Design and Performance Modeling of Client/Server Systems," *IEEE Tr. Software Eng.*, vol. 26, no. 11, Nov. 2000, pp. 1066–1085.

[20] D. A. Menascé, V. A. F. Almeida, and L. W. Dowdy, *Capacity Planning and Performance Modeling: From Mainframes to Client-Server Systems*, Prentice Hall, Upper Saddle River, New Jersey, 1994.

[21] E. Nemeth, G. Snyder, S. Seebass, and T. R. Hein, *UNIX System Administration Handbook*, 3rd ed., Prentice Hall, Upper Saddle River, New Jersey, 2000.

[22] V. Paxson, G. Almes, J. Mahdavi, and M. Mathis, "Framework for IP Performance Metrics," Network Working Group, The Internet Society RFC 2330, May 1998.

[23] C. Rose, "A Measurement Procedure for Queueing Network Models of Computer Systems," *Computing Surveys*, vol. 10, no. 3, Sept. 1978.

Chapter 14

Wrapping Up

14.1   Introduction

Computing and communications systems are becoming more distributed and more integrated into the fabric of daily life [15]. Businesses and individuals are increasingly depending on Web services for day-to-day operations. Web services connect departments within organizations, multiple organizations, companies, and the general population. Web services are dynamic and their functionality is in constant evolution. The demand for Web services are unpredictable and exhibit fast growth. Streaming media traffic and the demand generated by portable and embedded devices are also increasing. This is the reality of online services on the Web. It gives rise to problems in designing, building, and operating these services. Planners, designers, and providers of Web services face challenges to meet what society and users expected from information technology systems: availability, trustworthiness, and reliability [17, 15].

In recent years, the number of news stories focusing on outages of e-commerce and Web service providers has grown steadily [4]. Many high-profile companies that provide service on the Web have experienced operational failures. Examples abound. Problems with unscheduled maintenance took e-retailers offline. Human errors blocked access to a major Web site for nearly 24 hours. Financial Web services experienced intermittent outages as the volume of visitors to their Web sites increased. Users and investors could not access real-time quotes during those outages. A report [10] showed that online brokerage firms were concerned with system outages and with the inability to accommodate growing numbers of online investors. Such operational problems have resulted, in many cases, in extremely degraded performance, unsatisfied users, and heavy financial losses.

Web services rely on large-scale systems, that consist of thousands of computers, software components, and users. At this point, a question arises: How can organizations cope with the increasing complexity of applications based on large-scale systems? It is evident that quantitative methods are needed to understand, analyze, design, and operate such large-scale systems. Quantitative models that help designers and managers assess many different usage scenarios, exploring the design and operational space of large-scale systems. Trends point toward ever-increasing demands on Web services. Thus, capacity problems will continue to exist in the future and will likely become more prevalent as new Web services are planned and deployed and more and more users gain access to the Internet. Capacity planning techniques are needed to avoid the pitfalls of inadequate capacity and to meet users' expectations in a cost-effective manner. This book gives the reader the foundations required to carry out capacity planning and quantitative studies of the behavior of Web services.

14.2   Characteristics of Large-Scale Systems

Web services are a good example of large-scale systems. Some of the defining characteristics of such systems are discussed below. Large-scale systems rely on large and distributed structures: the Internet and the Web. They exhibit complex and highly variable behavior [15]. Demands and patterns show high variability. Web services have in common the following characteristics:

- Largeness of Scale and Complexity

  The Web is a *complex system* comprised of many interacting elements connected by various network media whose behavior is governed by network and application protocols [9]. Components share information in many ways, with numerous feedback loops, producing complex behaviors. New links and routers are added continually, spurring the uncontrolled and decentralized growth of the system. Two characteristics of the Web pose new challenges to the effective design, analysis, and control of the Internet: rapid explosion of scale and demand for quality of service (QoS). As a consequence, predicting Web performance and availability is difficult and requires proper tools and methods [2].

- Heterogeneity

  The Web is a large and heterogeneous system. It relies on networks made of components and subsystems drawn from many vendors, including commercial off-the-shelf (COTS) technology and customized technologies. This process results in a high level of heterogeneity within systems. This heterogeneity makes difficult and costly the process of designing, building, and maintaining online services.

- Distributed Operation and Management

  In the environemnt of Web services, the distribution of their operations and administration span across many different organizational units. For example, an online service usually makes use of third-party services, such as credit authorization, banner ads, etc. Also, the physical infrastructure is composed of hundreds or thousands of devices (e.g., servers, routers, firewalls, modems, etc.) Replacing or upgrading software and hardware components [8] is a challenge. In the Web, online companies have to be able to replace and upgrade components of their infrastructure without disrupting customer services. Imagine deploying a new version of the cache control software to tens of thousands of cache servers of a large CDN. In demanding environments, such as Web services, the cost of maintenance and administration is very high and is approximately 10 times as high as the purchase cost of the hardware [16]. New tools and automated operational support methodologies are needed to improve the operation and administration of Web services.

In any service provider site, whether financial services, merchants or government services, it is necessary to guarantee the quality of service, represented by key issues such as trustworthiness and security, performance, and availability. These are properties that should be pursued in the design and implementation of large-scale information systems.

- Trustworthiness and Security

  Large-scale information systems support mission-critical applications in industry, government, and society. These systems must be extremely trustworthy. The requirements are broader and deeper than security alone. The trustworthiness of systems and applications should cover various issues such as correctness, reliability, availability, robustness, and security [15].

- Scalability

  The infrastructure of Web service should be designed so that quality of service scales with demand. For instance, it may be very difficult to access a major newspaper or TV site after some very important breaking news due to site overload. And, as noted in [8], "those are the most important times to be able to get the service." Therefore, scalability is a critical issue. A Web service infrastructure is said to be scalable when it provides adequate service levels even when the workload increases above expected levels.

- Availability and Reliability

  As information services based on the Web become ubiquitous, with everyone using these systems, the requirements for availability and reliability will increase dramatically. Availability should focus mainly on the services provided rather than on system components. New approaches to analyze and model availability and reliability have appeared recently. Patterson [3] takes a new perspective on availability. Web services can exist in a large number of degraded, but operational, states between *down* and *up*. Availability metrics must capture the spectrum of degraded states, measuring not only whether a system is up or down. For example, metrics should combine QoS and performance to represent availability.

This books extends the scope of capacity planning. Instead of focusing only on performance, the book presents a model-based approach to cover performance, availability, and cost. In other words, the focus of capacity planning shifts from performance to the quality of service provided by Web systems.

14.3   Model-Based Approach

A key aspect of this book is the use of a quantitative approach to analyzing Web services. The main techniques are based on three types of models: workload, performance, and availability models. The first model results from understanding and characterizing the workload and the second from a quantitative description of the system behavior. There is a significant body of work on workload characterization of Web workloads. Some of the characteristics considered deal with file size distributions, file popularity distribution, self-similarity in Web traffic, reference locality, and user request patterns. A number of studies of different Web sites found file sizes to exhibit heavy-tailed distributions and object popularity to be Zipf-like.

Instead of relying on intuition, ad hoc procedures, and ROTs to understand and analyze the behavior of Web services, we provide in this book a uniform and formal way of dealing with performance and availability problems. The models discussed here are based on the theory of queuing networks, operational analysis, and probability. Delays in networked environments consist of two parts: service times and waiting times. The former are defined as the time spent using resources such as processors, routers, disks, communication links, and network segments. Waiting times arise when several requests contend for the use of a finite-capacity resource. Performance models are used to compute waiting times from service times and from load intensity parameters. This book focuses on explaining how to compute service times and on how to use them to build and solve performance models that calculate waiting times. Other performance metrics of interest are also derived from the solution of these models. These metrics include throughput, utilization, response time, and average queue lengths.

The methods used to compute service times for the various types of network, processing, and storage elements are derived from abstractions of the behavior of these elements and from intrinsic performance and functional characteristics. The book shows how to compute service times for single disks, disk arrays, routers, Local and Wide Area Networks. The procedures used for these cases can be easily generalized to deal with cases not specifically covered here. As an example, the performance impact of using cryptography for message transmission can be assessed by properly adjusting network and processing service times to reflect the change in message size due to the cryptographic transformations and the processing time needed to encrypt and decrypt messages [14]. Other security techniques, such as the use of network authentication protocols and firewalls can be treated similarly [6, 7].

Waiting time computations are based on the solution of queuing models. Two broad categories of models were considered in this book: system- and component-level models. System-level models treat a subsystem as a black box. Only the input, represented by the arrival rate of requests, and the output behavior, represented by the throughput, are considered at this level. System-level models are represented by the set of possible states a system can be found in, along with the possible transitions between states and the rates at which they occur. For example, a system-level model of a Web server looks only at the arriving HTTP requests and the corresponding HTTP responses. On the other hand, to examine the impact of the Web server components (e.g., disks, processors, and network links) and its architecture on its throughput, one needs to explicitly represent the components and architecture. This can be accomplished by a component-level model based on single and multiclass queuing networks, in which components are represented by queues. Connections between queues reflect the system architecture and the flow of requests between the components. The component-level models presented here capture the essential behavior of the main elements of network-based environments and represent the effect of contention for shared resources. Models of other network components can be integrated with queuing network models through the use of load-dependent servers as discussed in [13].

This book shows how queuing network models can be used to account for Web-specific workload characteristics. In particular, the burstiness of the Web traffic can be incorporated into the models by properly inflating the service demands by a burstiness factor computed from measured operational data. Heavy-tailed distributions of document sizes are modeled through the use of multiple classes in a queuing network model. Class attributes can be used to differentiate the access frequency for different types of objets. Simple examples of models for tiered architectures of Web services are also shown. System- and component-level models can be further classified into open and closed models, depending on the size of the population. Open models have an unknown and potentially infinite population. This is the case of a public Web site on the Internet. On the contrary, a closed model is characterized by a known and finite population. For example, the intranet Web site of a company is only available to its employees. Therefore, the population of users of this server is known and finite.

Performance and availability models can be used to answer typical what-if questions frequently faced by managers of Web services. Examples of the application of models are discussed throughout the book. Some questions that can be answered by these models are, "Are the the resources of the service adequate to handle load spikes?" "Is the corporate network able to sustain the traffic?" "How do I assess the impact of streaming media applications on the infrastructure of the Web service?" What is the required number of Web servers to obtain an overall reliability for the service of 99.99%?", "What is the workload model to be used in a load testing of the future Web service?" and "What should be the bandwidth of the link that connects the company to the Internet so that acceptable service levels are provided to visitors of our services?"

14.4   Concluding Remarks

Performance has been a concern in the design of many important systems for the past 30 years. Recent research has focused on using the queuing models described in this book as a component of a dynamic controller that continuously checks the site performance against desired SLAs and determines the best possible configuration for the current workload [11, 12].

The past and future of system performance evaluation have been discussed in several meetings and forums [5, 18]. In today's world, the problems of availability, maintainability, and scalability have become at least as important as performance [3, 8]. These problems tend to get worse as systems grow. Computing is headed towards an era in which the focus is shifted away from single isolated boxes towards complex evolving networks, such as the Web and the Internet. Millions of small embedded and portable devices and large-scale service providers are typical components of the future scenario. This will also magnify the complexity of future Web services. Four critical areas were identified in the area of performance evaluation and analysis of computer and networked systems [5]:

1. the increasing complexity of today's and future systems,

2. the need to bridge the gap between theoretical and practical work,

3. the need to better educate engineers and analysts on performance issues, and

4. the need for industry to accept and integrate performance evaluation techniques as a standard practice in system design and implementation.

This book is an attempt to address these challenging issues.

Bibliography

[1] D. Bertsekas and R. Gallager, *Data Networks*, 2nd ed., Prentice Hall, Upper Saddle River, New Jersey, 1992.

[2] E. A. Brewer, "Lessons from Giant-Scale Services," *IEEE Internet Computing*, July/Aug. 2001, pp. 46–55.

[3] A. Brown and D. Patterson, "Towards Availability Benchmarks: A Case Study of Software RAID Systems," *Proc. of the Usenix Annual 2000 Technical Conference*, San Diego, California, 2000.

[4] F. Douglis and M. F. Kaashoek, "Scalable Internet Services," *IEEE Internet Computing*, July/Aug., 2001, pp. 36–37.

[5] G. Haring, C. Lindemann, and M. Reiser, eds., "Performance Evaluation of Computer Systems and Communication Networks," *Dagstuhl-Seminar-Report; 189, 15.05.-19.09.97 (9738)*, Schloss Dagstuhl, Germany, Sept. 1997.

[6] A. Harbitter and D. A. Menascé, "The Performance of Public Key Enabled Kerberos Authentication in Mobile Computing Applications," *Proc. Eighth ACM Conference on Computer and Communications Security (CCS-8)*, Philadelphia, Pennsylvania, Nov. 5-8, 2001.

[7] A. Harbitter and D. A. Menascé, "Performance of Public Key-Enabled Kerberos Authentication in Large Networks," *Proc. 2001 IEEE Symposium on Security and Privacy*, Oakland, California, May 13-16, 2001.

[8] J. Hennessy, "The Future of Systems Research," *Computer*, IEEE, Aug. 1999.

[9] B. Huberman, P. Pirolli, J. E. Pitkow, and R. Lukose, "Strong Regularities in World Wide Web Surfing," *Science*, April 3, 1997.

[10] M. Meehan, "Update: System Outages Top Online Brokerage Exec's Concerns," *Computerworld*, April 4, 2000.

[11] D. A. Menascé, D. Barbará, and R. Dodge, "Preserving QoS of E-commerce Sites Through Self-Tuning: A Performance Model Approach," *Proc. 2001 ACM Conference on E-commerce*, Tampa, Florida, Oct. 14-17, 2001.

[12] D. A. Menascé "Using Performance Models to Dynamically Control E-Business Performance," *Proc. 11th GI/ITG Conference on Measuring, Modelling and Evaluation of Computer and Communication Systems*, Aachen, Germany, Sept. 11-14, 2001.

[13] D. A. Menascé, V. A. F. Almeida, and L. W. Dowdy, *Capacity Planning and Performance Modeling: From Mainframes to Client-Server Systems*, Prentice Hall, Upper Saddle River, New Jersey, 1994.

[14] D. A. Menascé and V. A. F. Almeida, *Scaling for E-Business: Technologies, Models, Performance, and Capacity Planning*, Prentice Hall, Upper Saddle River, New Jersey, 2000.

[15] National Academy of Sciences, *Making IT Better: Expanding Information Technology Research to Meet Society's Needs*, National Academy Press, Washington, D.C., 2000.

[16] D. Patterson, "New Challenges for the Post-PC Era," University of California at Berkeley, www.cs.berkeley.edu

[17] F. Schneider, ed., "Trust in Cyberspace," Computer Science and Telecommunications Board (CSTB), National Research Council, National Academy Press, Washington, D.C. 1999.

[18] Sigmetrics, *Proc. 1997 ACM Sigmetrics Int. Conf. Measurement Modeling of Comput. Syst.*, Seattle, Washington, June 15–18, 1997.

Appendix A

Glossary of Terms

ACID The basic transaction properties of atomicity, consistency, isolation, and durability.

Accounting Systems Tools intended primarily as means of apportioning charges to users of a system.

ADSL See *Asymmetric Digital Subscriber Line.*

Analytic Model Set of formulas and/or algorithms used to generate performance metrics from model parameters.

Arrival Theorem The number of customers seen by an arriving customer to a system is equal to the mean number of customers found in steady-state if the arriving customer were removed from the system.

Artificial Models Models that do not make use of any basic component of the real workload. Instead, these models are constructed out of special-purpose programs and descriptive parameters.

ARPA See *Defense Advanced Research Projects Agency.*

Asymmetric Digital Subscriber Line A variation of Digital Subscriber Line, designed for an upstream data flow (client-to-server), which is a fraction of the downstream data flow (server-to-client).

Asynchronous Transfer Mode A method for dynamic allocation of bandwidth using a fixed-size packet, called cell.

Availability Metric used to represent the percentage of time a system is operational.

Average Degree of Multiprogramming Average number of transactions or customers that are concurrently in execution in a system.

ATM See *Asynchronous Transfer Mode.*

Bandwidth Specifies the amount of data that can be transmitted over a communications link or network per unit of time, usually measured in bits per second.

Baseline Model Performance model of a computer system in its current situation (i.e., before any modifications on the parameters are investigated). The baseline model must be calibrated and validated using measurements of performance metrics from the actual system.

Basic Component Generic unit of work that arrives at a system from a external source.

Batch Class of programs executed in batch mode, which can be described by its multiprogramming level. For modeling purposes, we call this type of processing as *continuous processing.*

Benchmarking Running a set of standard programs on a machine to compare its performance with that of others.

Bottleneck Resource that saturates first as the workload intensity increases. It is the resource with the highest service demand.

Bridge A device that forwards traffic between network segments based on data link layer information.

Browser A program that allows a person to read hypertext.

Burstiness A characteristic of the WWW traffic that refers to the fact that data are transmitted randomly, with peak rates exceeding the average rates by factors of 8 to 10.

Cache A small fast memory holding recently-accessed data, designed to speed up subsequent accesses to the same data. Although caching techniques have been most often applied to processor-memory access, they also have been used for a local copy of data accessible over a network.

Calibration Technique used to alter the input or output parameters of a baseline model of an actual system so that the output parameters of the calibrated model match the performance of the actual system being modeled.

Capacity Planning Process of predicting when future load levels will saturate the system and of determining the most cost-effective way of delaying system saturation as much as possible.

Capture Ratio Process of managing and predicting the capacity of a system in order to continuously meet the quality of service requirements.

Carrier Sense with Multiple Access/Collision Detection The access method used by local area networking technology, such as Ethernet.

CDN See *Content Delivery Network*.

CGI See *Common Gateway Interface*.

Class Concept used in a performance model to abstract the parameters of a workload that are relevant to performance.

Class Population Maximum number of customers of a class.

Client Process that interacts with the user and is responsible for (1) implementing the user interface, (2) generating one or more requests to the server from the user queries or transactions, (3) transmitting the requests to the server via a suitable interprocess communication mechanism, and (4) receiving the results from the server and presenting them to the user.

Client/Server (C/S) The client/server computing model is predicated on the notion of splitting the work to be performed by an application between two types of processes—the client and the server. The server accepts requests for data from a client and returns the results to the client.

Client Think Time Average time elapsed between the receipt of a reply from the server and the generation of a new request.

Closed Model Queuing model of a system with a fixed number of customers. Customers circulate among the system resources. The number of customers in the system at all times is fixed and the number of possible system states is finite.

Clustering Analysis Process by which a large number of components are grouped into clusters of similar components.

Command Unit of user-submitted work in an interactive system.

Common Gateway Interface A protocol for processing user-supplied information through Web server scripts.

Conservation of Total Probability Equation Equation that specifies that the sum of the steady-state probabilities is 1. That is, the system must always be in one of the known system states.

Content Delivery Network A set of coordinated caching systems implemented through proprietary networks and data centers. Used to meet the demand of Web content by serving it from the cache closest to the requesting browser.

Convolution Algorithm An iterative technique for efficiently finding the solution of closed queuing networks.

Cryptography The study of techniques for encrypting and decrypting data, i.e., encoding data so that they can only be decoded by specific individuals.

C/S See *Client/Server.*

CSMA/CD See *Carrier Sense with Multiple Access/Collision Detection.*

Customer Entities that flow through a system receiving service from its various queues.

DARPA See *Defense Advanced Research Projects Agency.*

Database Management System Collection of programs that enable users to create and maintain a database.

DBMS See *Database Management System.*

Defense Advanced Research Projects Agency An agency of the U.S. Department of Defense responsible for the development of new technologies for use by the military.

Delay Queue Queue in which no queuing is allowed.

Disk Controller Device that decodes the device-specific I/O commands (e.g., seek and transfer) into control signals for the associated disks.

Dhrystone A synthetic benchmark program intended to be representative for system programming, with emphasis on integer and string operations.

Disk Array A storage system that consists of two or more disk drives designed to improve performance and/or reliability.

DNS See *Domain Name Server.*

Domain Name Server The DNS is a distributed, replicated, data query service that provides host IP address based on host names.

FDDI See *Fiber Distributed Data Interconnect*

Fiber Distributed Data Interconnect A high-speed (100 Mbps) LAN standard, whose underlying medium is fiber optic.

Effective Capacity Largest system throughput at which response time remains within the service levels.

Elapsed Time Total time spent by a job from its submission until its completion. This corresponds to the response time concept, except that it is generally used for batch workloads.

Event-Based Monitor Monitor that collects information at the occurrence of specific events.

Flow Equilibrium Assumption Principle that equates the customer's rate of flow into a system state to the customer's rate of flow out of that state.

File Transfer Protocol A service to transfer files to and from one host to another over a network.

Firewall Mechanism used to protect data and computers from activities of untrusted users.

FTP See *File Transfer Protocol.*

Functional Characterization Description of the programs or applications that make up the workload.

Global Workload Set of transactions submitted to a computer system.

Heavy-tailed Distribution A random variable X follows a heavy-tailed distribution if $P[X > x] \sim x^{-\alpha}$, as $x \to \infty$ for $0 < \alpha < 2$.

Homogeneous Workload Assumption All requests that make up the workload are assumed to be statistically identical.

HTML See *Hypertext Markup Language.*

HTTP See *Hypertext Transfer Protocol.*

Hypertext Markup Language A language that allows authors to specify the appearance and format of multimedia documents, in particular Web documents.

Hypertext Transfer Protocol The protocol used by the World Wide Web, that defines how client browsers and Web servers communicate with each other over a TCP/IP connection.

Integrated Services Digital Network A technology that combines voice and digital network services in a single medium, making it possible to offer this combination of services through a single wire.

Interactive Class On-line processing class with components generated by a given number of PCs or workstations with a given think time.

Internet The global set of interconnected networks that uses TCP/IP.

Internet Protocol The protocol that defines the format of packets used on the TCP/IP Protocol Suite and the mechanism for routing a packet to its destination.

Internet Service Provider A company that provides other companies or individuals with access to, or presence on, the Internet.

Intranet A private Internet deployed by an organization for its internal use and not necessarily connected to the Internet. Intranets are based on TCP/IP networks and Web technologies.

IP See *Internet Protocol.*

ISAPI Microsoft's programming interface between applications and their Internet Server.

ISDN See *Integrated Services Digital Network.*

ISP See *Internet Service Provider.*

IT Information Technology.

I/O path Physical connection between memory and an I/O device.

Java An object-oriented, distributed, interpreted, architecture-neutral, portable, multithreaded, dynamic, programming language developed by Sun Microsystems.

LAN See *Local Area Network*.

Little's Result Fundamental and general result that states that the number of customers in a system is equal to the product of the arrival rate of customers to the system and the mean time that each customer stays in the system (i.e., the customer's mean response time).

Linpack A benchmark that measures the performance of two routines of a collection of routines that solve various systems of simultaneous linear algebraic equations.

Load-Dependent Queue Queue whose rate of service delivery is not constant but rather is a function of the number of customers in the queue.

Local Area Network A network intended to serve a small geographic area.

Management Information Base The set of named items an SNMP management station can query or set in the SNMP agent of a device. To monitor a remote device, such as a router, a manager fetches values from MIB variables.

Maximum Degree of Multiprogramming Maximum number of transactions or customers of a class that can be in execution at a given time.

Maximum Transmission Unit The largest amount of data that can be sent across a given network using a single packet.

Mean Time Between Failures Average time between consecutive failures of a system.

Mean Time to Failure Average time it takes a system to fail.

Mean Time to Recover Average time it takes a system to recover from a failure.

Mean Value Analysis Elegant iterative technique for solving closed queuing networks. It iterates over the number of customers.

MIB See *Management Information Base.*

Mission-Critical Applications Those applications that are fundamental to running the business.

Model Validation Process of verifying if a model captures accurately key aspects of a system. As a rule of thumb, if a model can accurately predict various changes to the system, the model is termed "validated."

Model Calibration Process of modifying a model so that it can be validated.

Modification Analysis Analysis of the variation of the performance behavior of a system as a function of the variation of its workload, hardware, and software parameters.

Monitors Tools used for measuring the level of activity of a computer system.

MTBF See *Mean Time Between Failures.*

MTTF See *Mean Time to Failure.*

MTTR See *Mean Time to Recover.*

MTU See *Maximum Transmission Unit*

Multiclass Models Models where customers may be partitioned into different classes. Each class has unique device service demands and routing behavior.

MVA See *Mean Value Analysis.*

Natural Business Unit A quantifiable business variable that gives an indication of the volume of activity of a business.

NBU See *Natural Business Unit.*

Network File System A protocol developed by Sun Microsystems, which lets a computer access files over a network as if they were on its local disks.

Network Interface Card An adapter circuit board installed in a computer to provide a physical connection to a network.

NFS See *Network File System.*

NIC See *Network Interface Card.*

NSAPI Netscape's programming interface between applications and their Web Server.

Open Model Queuing model of a system with an infinite customer population. Customers arrive from the outside world, receive service, and exit. The number of customers in the system at any one time is variable. Usually, infinite buffer sizes are assumed and the number of possible system states is infinite.

Operational Analysis Assumes that the input parameters of the system model are all based on measured quantities.

Overhead System resources (e.g., processor time and memory space) consumed by activities that are incidental to, but necessary to, the main tasks. Examples include the operating system overhead involved in user program execution or the Web server overhead needed to process HTTP requests.

P2P See *Peer-to-Peer*.

Packet Switching A communication paradigm in which data units of a maximum size, packets, are individually routed between hosts, with no previously established communication path.

PDU See *Protocol Data Unit*.

Peer-to-Peer A collaborative and distributed approach used to support many different applications such as compressed music file sharing, disk space sharing, file sharing, or even computing cycle sharing.

Performance Model A system's representation used for predicting the values of performance measures of the system.

Physical I/O Operations Operations that correspond to actions performed by an I/O subsystem to exchange blocks of data with peripherals.

Prediction Model Model that, once calibrated, is used to answer "what if" performance prediction questions.

Program Analyzers Software tools intended to collect information about the execution of individual programs.

Protocol A set of formal rules describing how computers interact, especially across a network.

Protocol Data Unit An international standard denomination for packet.

Proxy Server A special type of World Wide Web server that acts as an agent, representing the server to the client and the client to the server. Usually, a proxy is used as a cache of items available on other servers that are presumably slower or more expensive to access.

Queue Set composed of a resource and its associated waiting queue.

Queue Length Number of customers in the system, including both customers in service as well as enqueued customers.

Queuing Network Set of interconnected queues.

RAID See *Redundant Arrays of Inexpensive Disks.*

Real Workloads All original programs, transactions, and commands processed during a given period of time.

Redundant Arrays of Inexpensive Disks A storage system that provides improved availability and/or performance.

Resource Saturation State that occurs when the utilization of a resource reaches 100%.

Reliability Measures the probability that a system is functioning properly and constantly over a fixed time period.

Remote Procedure Call A paradigm for implementing the C/S model. In general, a program invokes service across a network by making modified procedure calls.

Residence Time Total time spent by a request, transaction, or program at a resource.

Resource-Oriented Characterization Description of the consumption of the system resources by the workload.

Response Time Interval of time from when a customer arrives to a system until the customer completes service and exits the system.

ROT See *Rules of Thumb.*

Round Trip Time A measure of the current delay on a network, found by timing a packet bounced off some remote host.

Router A device that forwards traffic between networks, based on network layer information and routing tables.

RPC See *Remote Procedure Call.*

RTT See *Round Trip Time.*

Rules of Thumb A method or procedure based on experience and common sense.

Sampling-Based Monitor Monitor that collects information about the system at predefined instants of time.

Scheduling Policies Policies responsible for assigning customers to be executed by a server over time in order to reach system objectives, such as minimizing average response time or maximizing throughput.

Server Process Process, or set of processes, that collectively provide services to clients in a manner that shields the client from the details of the architecture of the server's hardware/software environment. A server does not initiate any dialogue with a client; it only responds to requests. Servers control access to shared resources.

Service Demand Sum of the service times at a resource (e.g., CPU, disks) over all visits to that resource during the execution of a transaction or request.

Service Level Agreements A contract between the service provider (e.g., IT department or ISP) and the end user or business unit. It sets specific goals for response time, throughput, overall uptime, and cost.

Service Time Time spent at a resource (e.g., CPU, disks) receiving service from it each time a transaction or request visits that resource.

Shortest Positioning Time First A disk scheduling policy in which the request chosen to be serviced is the one that yields the shortest positioning time (i.e., seek + rotational time).

Shortest Seek Time First A disk scheduling policy in which the request chosen to be serviced is the one that yields the shortest seek time.

Simple Network Management Protocol The Internet standard protocol developed to manage nodes on an IP network.

Simple Object Access Protocol A World Wide Web Consortium draft note describing a way to use XML and HTTP to create information delivery and remote procedure mechanisms.

Simulation Model A computer program that mimics the behavior of a system and provides statistics on the performance metrics of the system under study.

Single-Class Models Models where all customers are indistinguishable with respect to their device service demands and routing behavior.

SLA See *Service-Level Agreements*.

SMDS See *Switched Multimegabit Data Service*.

Software Performance Engineering Process of constructing software systems that meet performance objectives.

SNMP See *Simple Network Management Protocol*.

SOAP See *Simple Object Access Protocol*.

SPEC See *Standard Performance Evaluation Corporation*.

SPECmark The term used to collectively refer to the CPU ratio speed metrics.

SPECrate A throughput metric based on the SPEC CPU benchmark, that measures the capacity of a system for processing specific tasks in a given time interval. It is also used to evaluate how much work one or more processors can accomplish.

SPECratio Measures how fast a given system might be. It is obtained by dividing the elapsed time that was measured for a system to complete a specified job by the reference time. The reference time is the amount of time that a particular benchmark requires to run on a given reference platform.

SPECweb A standardized benchmark developed by SPEC to measure a system's ability to act as a Web server.

SPTF See *Shortest Positioning Time First*.

SQL See *Structured Query Language*.

SSTF See *Shortest Seek Time First*.

Standard Performance Evaluation Corporation SPEC is an organization of computer industry vendors dedicated to developing standardized benchmarks and publish reviewed results.

Steady State Long-term average behavior after any initial transient effects have dissipated.

Structured Query Language The standard language for defining and accessing relational databases.

Switched Multimegabit Data Service An emerging high-speed, datagram-based public data network service developed by Bellcore.

Synthetic Models Workload models constructed using basic components of the real workload as building blocks.

System Monitors Monitoring tools (hardware or software) that collect global performance statistics (i.e., do not attempt to distinguish among workload classes).

T1 A term for a digital carrier facility that transmits at 1.544 Mbps.

T3 A term for a digital carrier facility that transmits at 44.736 Mbps.

TCP See *Transmission Control Protocol*.

TCP/IP The protocol suite used in the Internet.

Telnet The Internet standard protocol for remote login service, that runs on top of TCP/IP.

Theoretical Capacity Maximum rate at which a computing system can perform work.

Think Time Interval of time that elapses since the user receives the prompt until he/she submits a new transaction.

Throughput Rate at which customers depart from the system measured in number of departures per unit time.

Time Windows Intervals of time during which the system, the workload, and the performance indexes are observed.

Token Ring A type of LAN with ring topology that uses token passing for access control.

TPC See *Transaction Processing Performance Council.*

TPC-C An on-line transaction processing (OLTP) benchmark suite. Order-entry provides a conceptual model for the benchmark.

TPC-H A benchmark suite to assess the cost/performance of a particular system processing decision support applications. TPC-H models a decision support environment in which complex and adhoc business-oriented queries are submitted against a large database.

TPC-W A transactional Web benchmark that simulates the activities of an online bookstore.

Transaction On-line processing class that groups components that arrive at a computer system with a given arrival rate.

Utilization of a Device Fraction of time that the device is busy, or equivalently, the percentage of time that at least one customer is in the system receiving service.

Transaction Processing Performance Council A nonprofit corporation founded to define transaction processing and database benchmarks.

Transmission Control Protocol The most common transport layer protocol used on the Internet as well as on LANs.

UDP See *User Datagram Protocol.*

URL See *Uniform Resource Locator.*

Uniform Resource Locator A syntactic form used for identifying documents on the Web.

User Datagram Protocol A connectionless protocol that uses IP to deliver datagrams.

Validation Desirable characteristic of a model, seldom achieved in practice. A validated model of a system accurately mimics the actual behavior of the system in all aspects and can be used to predict the performance of the system under system or workload changes. The only truly validated model of a system is the system itself.

XML Extensible Markup Language. Markup language that allows users to define their own tags.

WAN See *Wide Area Network.*

WAP See *Wireless Application Protocol.*

Web A common short name for the World Wide Web.

Web server A combination of a hardware platform, operating system, server software and contents.

Web Service Description Language An XML format for describing network services as a set of endpoints operating on messages containing either document-oriented or procedure-oriented information.

Webstone A configurable C/S benchmark for HTTP servers.

Whetstone A small benchmark program for measuring floating point calculations.

Wide Area Network A network that covers a large geographical region.

Wireless Application Protocol Set of protocols to allow all sorts of wireless devices, such as Web-enabled phones, PDAs, and pagers, to access Web services at regular Web sites.

Workload Characterization Process of partitioning the global workload of a computer system into smaller sets or workload components composed of transactions or requests having similar characteristics, and assigning numbers that represent their typical resource demand and intensity.

Workload Model Representation that mimics the real workload under study.

Workload Saturation State that is said to have been reached for a given workload when the service level for that workload is violated.

Workstation Response Time Time interval elapsed between the instant a transaction or command is submitted until the answer to it begins to appear at the user's workstation.

World Wide Web A C/S architecture that integrates various types of information on the global Internet and on IP networks.

WSDL See *Web Service Description Language.*

WWW See *World Wide Web.*

Zipf's Law States that if one ranks the popularity of words (denoted by ρ) in a given text by their frequency of use (denoted by f), then $f \sim 1/\rho$.

Appendix B

Downloads

The book's Web site contains several Microsoft Excel workbooks that implement the various formulas and algorithms described in the book as well as some of the examples presented in the book. To download them, go to www.cs.gmu.edu/~menasce/ webservices/ and click on "Downloads." The book's Web site also contains a sample of an HTTP log and a program to compute the burstiness factor of an HTTP log.

B.1 The Microsoft Excel Workbooks

The Microsoft Excel workbooks are organized by chapter. Most have Visual Basic^{R} modules associated with them. A Help worksheet is available in some of the workbooks to provide details about their operation. All worksheets have cells that contain input parameters and cells that contain computed values from the input parameters. Different colors are used to distinguish between the two types of cells. Also, the workbook structure and computed cells are password-protected to prevent the workbook from being unintentionally damaged. We recommend that you always work on a copy of the workbook and never on the original. If you want to modify the copy, you can use the password "2001" to unprotect the workbook.

The example workbooks are not listed here but can be seen on the Web site. The other workbooks are:

Chapter 2: `TCPModel.XLS` contains formulas to compute the throughput of a TCP connection as a function of several parameters.

Chapter 3: `ServTime.XLS` contains the formulas needed to compute service times on single disks, disk arrays, networks, as well as the operational laws.

Chapter 3: `PageDownloadTime.XLS` contains the formulas used to compute the download time of a Web object and of a Web page composed of multiple objects.

Chapter 5: `Cost.XLS` contains a template for computing startup and operational costs of Web-based systems.

Chapter 8: `SysMod.XLS` implements various system-level models including

- infinite population, fixed service rate, and unlimited queue size
- infinite population, fixed service rate, limited queue size
- infinite population, variable service rate, and unlimited queue size
- infinite population, variable service rate, and limited queue size
- finite population, fixed service rate, unlimited queue,
- finite population, fixed service rate, limited queue
- finite population and variable service rate

Chapter 9: `OpenQN.XLS` implements the algorithm to solve multiclass open queuing networks and provides utilizations, queue lengths, residence times, and response times.

Chapter 9: `ClosedQN.XLS` implements the algorithm to solve multiclass closed queuing networks and provides utilizations, queue lengths, residence times, response times, and throughputs.

Chapter 10: `WebModels.XLS` contains worksheets to compute service demands for performance models for the Web. In particular, this workbook contains worksheets for computing service demands for the client side with and without a proxy cache and for the Web server side. Once the service demands are computed, they can be copied and pasted into the proper location of the `ClosedQN.XLS` (for the client side) and `OpenQN.XLS` (for the server side) workbooks for model solving.

Chapter 11: `Availability.XLS` contains formulas for the computation of the availability of single systems and that of systems in series and in parallel.

Chapter 11: `Performability.XLS` contains formulas for the computation of system performability.

Chapter 11: `SoftwareAging.XLS` contains formulas for the computation of system availability under software aging situations.

Chapter 12: `Forecast.XLS` implements some Web workload forecasting methods.

B.2   HTTP Log Sample and Program

The file `httplog.txt` under the Chapter 10 link is a sample of an HTTP log with 20,000 lines. Host ids were eliminated from the log to preserve the privacy of the clients of that particular site. The file `burst.c` under the same link is a C program that computes the burstiness parameters a and b described in Chap. 10. This program has three parameters:

- `-f` <name>: name of the file containing an HTTP log

- `-e` <number>: number of epochs, i.e., the number of equal subintervals of the interval during which the log was obtained

- `-r` <number>: number of requests to be processed in the log. If this parameter is not specified, it is assumed to be equal 10,000, the value of the variable "maxreq" in the program `burst.c`

For example, to compute the burstiness parameters for the log in file `httplog.txt` for 50 epochs, type

```
burst -f httplog.txt -e 50 -r 20000
```

Index